Decolonial Psychology

This cutting-edge book re-imagines what a truly decolonial psychology could look like. It explores questions of what counts as psychological knowledge and whose knowledge is valid, and who controls the production of knowledge in psychology. This book builds on the expanding knowledge base in decolonial psychology to meaningfully address the varied social and psychological trajectories of decolonization and liberation.

Featuring a wide range of international contributors, this book is grounded in an ethic of inclusion and includes contributions from researchers as well as contributions from those who engage in decolonial work outside of academia. It considers how the discipline of psychology could be transformed and how it can embrace a decolonial resistance with ideas about justice, freedom, and liberation. Drawing together a variety of expertise and ways of knowing that centers psychological research from the Global South, this book explores how we can decolonize the field and curriculum of psychology, imagining new future possibilities for the discipline.

Accessibly and compellingly written, this will be essential reading for students and researchers interested in decolonizing psychology. It will be especially relevant for upper-level undergraduate and postgraduate students of cultural psychology, social psychology, and community psychology, as well as researchers, psychologists, and activists working with marginalized communities looking for ways to produce socially just knowledge.

Sunil Bhatia is Professor of Human Development at Connecticut College, USA.

Jesica Siham Fernández is an Assistant Professor in the Department of Ethnic Studies at Santa Clara University, USA.

Christopher C. Sonn is Professor of Psychology at Victoria University, Australia.

Decolonial Psychology

Academic and Activist Perspectives

Edited by
Sunil Bhatia, Jesica Siham Fernández and Christopher C. Sonn

Routledge
Taylor & Francis Group
NEW YORK AND LONDON

Designed cover image: © Mary Goslett (artist)

First published 2026
by Routledge
605 Third Avenue, New York, NY 10158

and by Routledge
4 Park Square, Milton Park, Abingdon, Oxon, OX14 4RN

Routledge is an imprint of the Taylor & Francis Group, an informa business

ISBN: 9781032794693 (hbk)
ISBN: 9781032790220 (pbk)
ISBN: 9781003492214 (ebk)

DOI: 10.4324/9781003492214

Typeset in Times New Roman
by codeMantra

Contents

Contributors

Sandra Patricia Acosta Salazar is a PhD candidate in the postgraduate program in social psychology at the Federal University of Ceará (UFC).

Joanna Alexi has Cypriot heritage, was born in Larrakia Country, and is now living on Whadjuk Noongar Boodja. She is a research fellow in the Transforming Indigenous Mental Health and Wellbeing project at the University of Western Australia, where her work focuses on decolonizing psychology education and mental health-care systems.

Shaun Awatere (Ngati Porou) supports Māori in sustainably managing collective assets and prepares iwi and hapū for climate change planning. He collaborates with Nga Pae o Te Māramatanga researchers to summarize the impacts of climate change on whānau, hapū, iwi, and businesses in Aotearoa, New Zealand, focusing on risks, uncertainties, and adaptation strategies.

Brendon R. Barnes is Professor of Psychology at the University of Johannesburg. He writes in psychology, environmental health, and justice. His work focuses on "behavior" in environmental studies, critical methodologies, and youth climate activism. He is Chairperson and Co-Founder of the Climate, Environment and Psychology Division of the Psychological Society of South Africa. He has won teaching, academic citizenship, mentoring, and research awards.

Kendon Bell (Ngāti Maru, Ngāti Porou ki Harataunga) is a Senior Research Manager and Economist at Scarlatti (NZ), specializing in environmental and agricultural economics, statistical modeling, and climate change adaptation, including work with an equity focus.

Nuria Ciofalo is a Professor and Co-Founder of the Community, Liberation, Indigenous, and Eco-Psychologies specialization at Pacifica Graduate Institute. She has co-authored the books *Indigenous Psychologies in an Era of Decolonization* (2019) and *Weaving Pathways Towards Decoloniality through Indigenous Community-Based Research and Cosmopraxes* (2014) with Maya, Mazatec, and Zapotec community leaders from Chiapas and Oaxaca, Mexico.

Tinyiko Chauke is a senior researcher at the Chief Albert Luthuli Research Chair at the University of South Africa and holds a Doctorate in Psychology. Through Afro-centric and decolonial methodologies, she crafts narratives that challenge the status quo, aiming to reshape identities and joining a chorus of many scholars who seek to foster a just future for African communities.

William (Bill) Cochrane is a Senior Lecturer in the School of Psychological and Social Science at the University of Waikato. His primary research interests center on inequality and labor markets, especially the spatial dimensions of these issues. He is a descendant of the Te Rarawa iwi.

Lillian Comas-Díaz is a Clinical Professor in the Department of Psychiatry and Behavioral Sciences at the George Washington University. Her work centers on liberation-decolonial psychology, feminism of color, multiculturalism, and psychotherapy. Lillian maintains a private practice in Washington, DC.

P.J. DiPietro is a scholar/activist and Associate Professor of Women's and Gender Studies at Syracuse University. They specialize in decolonial transfeminism and Afro-Latinx political thought. P.J. is the author of *Sideways Selves* (2025) and co-editor of *Trans Philosophy* (2024) and *Speaking Face to Face* (2019). They co-chair the Association of Jotería Arts, Activism, and Scholarship.

Pat Dudgeon is a Bardi woman from the Kimberley. She is a psychologist and fellow of the Australian Psychological Society, and a Professor at the University of Western Australia's School of Indigenous Studies. Her areas of research include Indigenous social and emotional well-being and suicide prevention.

Jenny Escobar studies the healing and justice initiatives of survivors of state violence, centering their agency and knowledge as the foundation for building a decolonial praxis of local and transnational healing through memory practices, restorative and transformative justice, and the inclusion of non-human relatives.

Mary Goslett is a Yuin woman living on the lands of the Eora Nation. Mary is an artist, weaver, clinical psychologist, and Board Member of the Australian Indigenous Psychologists Association (AIPA) and an associate fellow of the University of Western Australia.

Albertus Harimurti teaches Psychology at the Universitas Sanata Dharma, Indonesia, focusing on critical perspectives and theories. He founded Nalarasa.com, a platform for alternative psychological thought. Currently, he is archiving the development of psychology in Indonesia, contributing to a deeper understanding of its historical and theoretical foundations.

Shelly P. Harrell, a Professor at Pepperdine University's Graduate School of Education and Psychology, studies cultural and sociopolitical dimensions of suffering and healing. Her current work is developing Sankofa Theory and Practice, a comprehensive, African-centered theory that centers reconnection and interconnection as core processes for healing the many harms of disconnection emanating from oppression and coloniality.

Tanja Hirvonen is Jaru and Bunuba from the East Kimberley, Western Australia, and Wakaya from the Barkly, Northern Territory. She is a Clinical Psychologist working as a Director of Wellbeing, managing a team of well-being practitioners who provide therapeutic supports to the Aboriginal and Torres Strait Islander workforce. She is also a mid-career researcher with the Centre of Best Practice in Aboriginal and Torres Strait Islander Suicide Prevention and a Senior Lecturer at the University of Sydney in the School of Psychology.

Darelle Howard is a senior tutor in the School of Psychological and Social Science at the University of Waikato. Her research interests are unified within a decolonial perspective and along the intersection of inequity and policy in a capitalist-colonial state.

Susan James is Chair of the Community, Liberation, Indigenous, & Eco-Psychologies MA/PhD specialization at Pacifica Graduate Institute. Her work focuses on the theory and application of coloniality/decoloniality frameworks to current social and environmental conditions. She also explores the role of African diasporic Indigenous spiritualities in resistance and fugitivity.

Karen Jarratt-Snider is Professor of Applied Indigenous Studies at Northern Arizona University. Her areas of research and teaching interests are Indigenous environmental justice, social justice issues affecting Indigenous Peoples, and US federal Indian policy. She is Co-Editor of the *Indigenous Justice* book series (University of Arizona Press).

Juliana Alves Jenipapo Kanindé is the cacique of the Jenipapo Kaninde Indigenous people in Ceara, northeast Brazil. She is also the first secretary for Indigenous Peoples of the Ceara State Government and holds a Master's degree in Anthropology from the University of the International Integration of Afro-Brazilian Lusophony.

B. Andi Lee is a postdoctoral psychological associate working in private practice in Los Angeles, California, and a visiting scholar at the Institute for the Study of Race and Culture at Boston College. Her work centers Global Majority liberation with a focus on disability justice, resistance, healing, and belonging.

Monica E. Madyaningrum is an Associate Professor at Sanata Dharma University, Yogyakarta. She specializes in community psychology, participatory research, and disability studies. Her work explores disability activism and critical approaches to psychological teaching and learning.

Nick Malherbe is a researcher at the Institute for Social and Health Sciences, University of South Africa, the Violence, Injury and Social Asymmetries Research Unit, University of South Africa, and South African Medical Research Council. His research concerns violence, visual methods, and discourse. He has written on these topics using several different frameworks and approaches. He works with social movements, cultural workers, and young people. Ideas of community cohesion, solidarity, and reflexivity feature throughout his work.

Irum Maqbool is based at the University of Cambridge researching narratives of everyday lived experiences of young people growing up in Lahore, Pakistan. She is interested in exploring navigation of material and social spheres of life world: school, family, and friends as these cosmopolitanize. Her work contributes to a decolonial understanding of lived realities of young people, which addresses social stratification, spatiotemporal, and relational dimensions of individual meaning making.

Bridgette Masters-Awatere (Te Rarawa, Ngāi te Rangi, Tūwharetoa ki Kawerau) is also an Associate Dean Māori at the University of Waikato. Her research interests focus on whānau well-being, which has her working in solutions-focused transdisciplinary teams. She works with the intention of producing resources and publications that can help deepen understanding of Māori Psychologies.

Hana R. Masud is a Chicago-based researcher and Lecturer committed to dismantling Western hegemonic narratives. Her work critiques the colonial logic that marginalizes oppressed peoples, challenging binary thinking through bold, decolonial scholarship. Her writing unapologetically reclaims cultural narratives and amplifies resistance, centering liberation and justice at the heart of her academic praxis.

Zenobia Morrill, PhD, is an Assistant Professor in the Clinical Psychology Department at William James College. Her research areas include psychotherapy process, critical and liberation psychologies, and qualitative inquiry. Previously, she served as a Research Officer to the United Nations' Special Rapporteur on the Right to Health, and in 2023, she was the recipient of the Division 24 of the American Psychological Association's Sigmund Koch Award for early career contributions to psychology. She is also a licensed practicing psychologist and the senior research associate of the Center for Psychological Humanities and Ethics at Boston College. She is an Editorial Board Member of the Psychology and the Other Book Series and an executive member on several American Psychological Association (APA) division boards.

James Ferreira Moura Jr. is a Professor in the postgraduate program in psychology at the Federal University of Ceara and the Institute of Humanities at the University of the International Integration of Afro-Brazilian Lusophony. He is a community psychologist who has worked with quilombola and Indigenous communities in processes of counter-colonial resistance in the Global South in the Amazon and Northeast regions of Brazil.

Juliana Murta de Lima is a PhD candidate in the postgraduate program in social psychology at the Federal University of Ceará (UFC). He has a Master's degree in Psychology (UFC).

Marina Pereira Passos Campos is a PhD candidate in the postgraduate program in social psychology at the Federal University of Ceará (UFC) and at the University Federico II of Naples.

Larissa Niemann Pellicer is a Master's degree candidate in the postgraduate program in social psychology at the Federal University of Ceará (UFC).

Rosa Pitaguary is the leader of the Pitaguary Indigenous people of the Monguba village in the state of Ceara, northeast Brazil. She studies anthropology at the University of the International Integration of Afro-Brazilian Lusophony.

Chela Sandoval teaches Liberation Philosophy at the University of California, Santa Barbara. Her Doctorate is in the History of Consciousness. Her books include *Methodology of the Oppressed*, *Performing the Latina/o/x Borderlands*, *The Chicano Studies Reader*, and *Metodología de la Emancipación.* Her SWAPA essays elucidate the structures of consciousness and becoming that provide entry to the "house of difference," a *nepantla*-world space defined by Audre Lorde and Gloria Anzaldúa.

Mercedes Santana is a visionary trauma psychologist, dedicated to healing the deep wounds of oppression and colonialism. With a focus on culture, identity, and community, her work embraces decolonial and liberation-based practices, shaping a more compassionate, inclusive approach to education, training, and clinical care in psychology.

Mohamed Seedat's present research is focused on the social anatomy of public protests, grassroots cultures of violence and peace, and the psychologies underlying ongoing and renewed global struggles for a decolonized, caring society. He has supported community-engaged research, the capacitation of next generation, socially engaged researchers and academic leaders, and the transformation of writing cultures in the academy.

Puleng Segalo is a Fulbright scholar and a Full Professor of Psychology and is currently holding the position of Chief Albert Luthuli Research Chair at the University of South Africa. Her areas of specialization include Africa-centered psychology, gender and trauma, and decolonial feminism in psychology. Her research focuses on historical trauma, visual methodologies, and gendered suffering.

Belle Selkirk is a Noongar woman living on Wadandi Boodja. She is a clinical psychologist and research fellow in the Transforming Indigenous Mental Health and Wellbeing project at the University of Western Australia, focusing on Indigenous psychology, cultural safety, and decolonizing psychology education and practice.

Chetan Sinha is a Psychology Professor at OP Jindal Global University, India. He authored *The Power Dynamics of Education: Shaping the Structure of School Education in India* (2023). He writes on the psychology of power applied to different psychological domains, emphasizing social representations, social identity, and critical pedagogy.

Janan Akram Shouhayib is a researcher whose work focuses on Lebanese women's relationships to land, culture, and colonial histories. She received her doctorate in Critical Social/Personality Psychology from The Graduate Center (CUNY) in 2024 and currently works at the Middle East Studies Association.

Antonio Ailton de Sousa Lima is a PhD candidate in Psychology at the Federal University of Ceará (UFC) and Bachelor's degree in Sociology at the University of International Integration of Afro-Brazilian Lusophony (UNILAB).

Shahnaaz Suffla is a Professor at the Institute for Social and Health Sciences, University of South Africa; the Violence, Injury and Social Asymmetries Research Unit, University of South Africa; and South African Medical Research Council. Her research interests draw from the intersections of critical and decolonial community, African and peace psychologies, and are located within liberatory philosophies and epistemologies. Her work includes a focus on health, safety, and peace promotion interventions in the context of structural violence, participatory engagement as a site of activism, resistance and social change, and Africa(n)-centered knowledge creation.

Socorro Taynara Araújo Carvalho is a psychologist (CRP-11/18903) with a Master's degree in Psychology from the Federal University of Ceará (UFC). She works as a psychologist at the Psychological Support Center (NAPSI) of the Faculdade 05 de Julho (F5) and is also a University Lecturer on the Psychology course at the Faculdade de Educação da Ibiapaba (FAEDI) and on lato sensu postgraduate courses.

Britton Williams, PhD, LCAT, RDT-BCT, is an artist, activist, drama therapist, and storyteller. She is a multitude of hyphens, contradictions, and ands. She is an educator and student – a thinker and dreamer. She is deeply and urgently concerned with the possibilities that live with/in radical (re)imagining and the inextricable connectedness of healing and liberation.

Foreword

I vividly recall first meeting my grandmother, Bertha (Gone) Snow. A rising senior in college, I resided with my auntie Roxanne on our reservation in north-central Montana during the summer of 1991. Reared elsewhere in Montana by an adoptive mother, I had ventured “home” to Fort Belknap just three months earlier at age 24, and I still welcomed the ongoing introductions to my extensive reservation kin. One day, Roxy arranged a visit with her aunt Bertha (my maternal grandfather’s oldest sister, or my grandmother in the Indian way, who was then aged 73). We drove the 20 miles to Grandma Bertha’s rural HUD home in the Three Buttes district of the reservation, hoping she would regale us with sagacious stories. Grandma welcomed us, received our gifts of elk steaks and cigarettes, and settled in for a visit. At one point during the next five hours, we relocated to the kitchen table, where Grandma recounted the devastating impacts of the Roman Catholic Mission’s historical Indian boarding school on our Aaniiih people. Funded by the US government to “civilize” Indigenous people, these boarding schools operated under the slogan, Kill the Indian, Save the Man.

“My father told me what things were like when the Catholic priests first arrived here with their boarding school down at the Mission,” Grandma said with a sigh.

> I call the Old Timers who were used to the nomadic buffalo-hunting way of life the Defeated Nation, because when the Whites came, all they could do was hope for death. Everything they had ever known was gone and they had no reason to live. The young people at that time, though, I call the Lost Nation. They were taken from their families and locked away in this boarding school where the White people beat them with hoses for speaking their own language. They had a choice: either learn English real quick, or don’t say anything. Their Indianness was stamped out. Dad said that the priests sometimes went too far and killed some of those children. They’re buried down there between the Mission and the cemetery. But even if a kid died of natural causes, no one informed his parents. Sometimes parents died while kids were locked away, but it didn’t matter. The kids were lucky if they found out before they left school. The priests didn’t want those children to be influenced by anything Indian during their long years at boarding school.

Consequently, according to Grandma, “It didn’t take long for us to lose our traditional ways. The Whites outlawed our religious ceremonies, and we were confined to the reservation like cattle.” As Aaniiih people, we had long been responsible for the ritual care of two sacred Pipes, the Flat Pipe – a gift to us from Supreme Being at our inception as a people – and the Feathered Pipe – a gift to us from the Thunder Being in more recent centuries. Eminent Aaniiih men were intermittently selected as priests for these Pipes, occasioning transfer of esoteric ceremonial knowledge and protocols for conducting seasonal ceremonies that conveyed health, help, and long life for our people. But decades of reservation captivity, religious repression, and involuntary assimilation of our young people interrupted this intergenerational transfer of sacred Pipe knowledge and practice. By the end of World War II, old The Boy was the last Aaniiih leader to retain the relevant knowledge to ritually open our sacred Flat Pipe bundle at community gatherings. He did so on a few brief occasions prior to his death a decade after the war's end.

Grandma Bertha was present at one of these gatherings. As she recounted,

> I was there once after the war when old The Boy, who was keeping that Flat Pipe, decided to open its sacred wrappings to show it to some White people. He laid it out just so for those goddamned White people to look at, while I stood there watching them.

Grandma paused for what seemed like ten seconds, fighting the tears, and struggling to speak. When she resumed, her voice was a different pitch, her words wobbly:

> And then, I don't know what happened to me, because I've never felt like that before. I ran up to the Pipe, and dropped to my knees in front of it, and bent over, and kissed it. I looked like a damn fool in front of all those White people, but I didn't have a choice in the matter. Maybe I was kissing it goodbye.

Grandma allowed herself to weep freely for a short while, as my auntie and I joined her. Soon, she regained her composure. "But it's no use crying over spilled milk. The milk is spilt. There's nothing we can do about it. The other way leads to crippling bitterness, and what use is that? We have to move on."

Grandma, like her parents before her, was a devout Roman Catholic. But a younger generation of Aaniiihs began to embrace and reclaim Indigenous traditional ceremonies and practices – though not Flat or Feathered Pipe rituals – during the Red Power movement of the 1970s. Her youngest brother, my Grandpa Fred V. Gone, was a pioneer in this respect, leading to occasional religious tensions between them:

> My brother Fred visited me the other day, and he saw my Catholic shrine on top of the television and began to attack my beliefs. I asked him what right he thought he had to criticize my beliefs, seeing that I had never uttered a word against his attempts to revive Indian spirituality. I told him to get the hell out of my house! I won't allow that. We have to adapt to the world around us. God brings in the old to replace the new.

But in the ensuing years, as our relationship deepened through many more visits, our Aaniiih Pipes featured prominently in her stories, often with tears, always with angst. "My way is Catholic, now," she had averred. "Somehow, God must have wanted it this way." But her tenor, her tone, and her tears contravened her conviction.

A short while later, inspired by the words of my Grandma Bertha, I committed to my very first independent research project as a graduate student in psychology to explore Aaniiih cultural identity on Aaniiih terms (Gone, 1996, 1999; Gone et al., 1999). The immediate challenge was methodological: how best to appreciate the sophistication, nuance, and dynamics of paradoxical claims by modern – yet still culturally distinctive – Aaniiih people that "there are no Aaniiihs today" or "Aaniiih ways are gone." Given the prevailing methodological preference for variable-analysis within the "two disciplines of scientific psychology" (Cronbach, 1957) – experimental and correlational studies, respectively – what were the prospects for psychological inquiry into a particular group identity that was forged through colonial subjugation and consequently crafted from its own overt disavowal? That these dynamics entailed important and interesting psychological processes seemed indisputable (e.g., Gone, 2006, 2017, 2024; Gone & Alcántara, 2010), so the challenge became one of identifying and adopting promising theoretical frames and innovative analytic methods that might afford accurate insight into questions surrounding love, loss, belonging, healing, narrative, culture, power, and indigeneity. In the memorable instance of first meeting my own grandmother (as recounted above), numerous opportunities for pursuing alter-Native knowledge production in psychology suggest themselves.

We need sophisticated psychological accounts not just of individual differences but also of shared community consciousness, such as longstanding Aaniiih reverence for our sacred Pipes and more recent implications of their decline (or even demise). We need sophisticated psychological account not just of personal rights, choices, and pursuit of happiness but also of kinship roles, duties, and pursuit of belonging, such as the obligation of an Aaniiih elder to instruct younger relatives about the history and significance of a family's place within a broader ethnos or peoplehood. We need sophisticated psychological accounts not just of shared social norms but also of individual efforts to appropriate tradition in novel ways, such as a young Aaniiih woman who, for seemingly inexplicable reasons, is moved in a public ceremonial gathering to creatively apply familiar funerary practices in kissing the Pipe goodbye. We need sophisticated psychological accounts not just of telling what one knows, knowing what one is talking about, and keeping one's answers short (Shweder, 1996). Rather, we also require accounts of the ineffable and inexpressible admixture of confusion, grief, rage, and loss that accompany forbidding existential predicaments, such as one Aaniiih elder's efforts to live and love and heal in the midst of poverty and pain not of her own making: "Somehow, God must have wanted it this way."

For the study of psychology within American Indian and other Indigenous communities, these questions oblige consideration of the conditions of coloniality. Moreover, such inquiry envisions emancipation and pursues practical impact in the urgent undoing of these conditions. Thus, Indigenous America registers as one complex global site in dire need of Decolonial Psychology, an endeavor dedicated to "building knowledge from below" that might "uplift [Indigenous and other colonized] voices, create space for affirmation and a reclamation of their stories, and support their movements for hope, healing and transformation that will lead us toward the possibility of decolonial liberation" (Bhatia et al., this volume). In this respect, we are deeply fortunate to benefit from plentiful exemplars of envisioning and enacting decolonial psychology within this handbook, including proposed and demonstrated interventions in psychology that reflect "new decolonial ways of thinking, being, doing, and relating" (Bhatia et al., this volume), whether through education, application, or methodology. I am deeply honored to commend this important and impactful work to you.

Joseph P. Gone, PhD
Aaniiih-Gros Ventre
Harvard University

Preface and Acknowledgments

All books have many births and rebirths from their conception to publication. The first birth of this book took place when Eleanor Taylor, the senior editor for Social Psychology at Routledge, invited Sunil Bhatia in May 2022 to explore the idea of creating an edited volume on the current scholarship in decolonial psychology. Eleanor and Sunil met several times in early June 2022 over Zoom to discuss what such a book could contribute to the growing field of decolonial psychology. What emerged from those conversations was that Eleanor placed no constraints on this book's vision and gave Sunil considerable freedom in envisioning the substance and content of the handbook.

Over the pandemic times in 2021, Sunil was already in a deep and rich conversation with two brilliant, generous, and creative decolonial scholars, Christopher Sonn and Jesica Siham Fernández, about the future of decolonial psychology and what it needed to do to dismantle and decolonize the university. The three of us had already felt that the current decolonial turn in psychology required expanding its geographies by including artists, activists, First nations, and Indigenous peoples, those in the zones of exclusion, in the struggle with global and local forms of colonialism re-existing/resisting through art, land rights, Indigenous revitalization, and cultural reclamation projects.

The second birth of this book took place when, as an organic next step, Chris, Jesica, and Sunil took up the mantle of editing and organizing the framework for this book. In the early fall of 2022, Chris, Jesica, and Sunil met multiple times to discuss the substance of the volume, and we kept centering the following question: *To whom are we accountable in our research, for what purposes, and how do we present our knowledge*?

Our starting point for such a book proposal began with acknowledging that, since colonization has existed, people from the colonized worlds have found ways to resist it through acts of collective love, solidarity, and mobilizing freedom struggles. For some groups, resisting decolonization has meant resisting the annihilation of their Indigenous people and population – a resistance that has led to accumulated historical trauma and prolonged collective suffering. For others, struggles of decolonization have meant decolonizing the nation states from modern European colonial powers and establishing a new way of doing, being, living, and thinking. It involves engaging in what Fanon (1963) described as political, psychological, and cultural decolonization for the majority of humanity, often seen as *The Wretched of the Earth*.

We acknowledge that our collective work in this volume on decolonizing psychology has been built on the shoulders of our ancestors and predecessors who had to take far greater risks and face enormous personal and collective suffering on their path to decolonial resistance. Our volume would represent a small contribution to the decolonizing psychology movement paved for us by many freedom fighters, dreamers, warriors, resisters, and activists from various lands, languages, and living conditions.

Our initial discussions highlighted that the concept of love and collective healing, as embodied and enacted, should challenge institutionalized practices of scientism because love and healing cannot be scientifically operationalized and contained by the standards of Euro-American psychology. Indeed, our discussions affirmed the need to re-imagine the pluriversal possibilities for psychology. Through extended discussion, we refined our proposal and converged on organizing the contributions around three sections and overriding themes:

1 Decolonizing the Curriculum of Psychology: Concepts, Stories, Lives, and Possibilities
2 Indigenous Retrieval and Community Building Across Self, Body, Place: Psychology of Healing Resistance and Relationality
3 Disrupting Methods: Going Beyond the University

A harvest is another form of birth and is made possible by the collective work of those who seed, till, water, fertilize, care for, and nourish the soil – it is a shared process and responsibility of care and integrity to generate such a bounty. We view *Decolonial Psychology: Academic and Activist Perspectives* as representing the blossoms and blooms of collaborative efforts; it is our offering in times of precarity, uncertainty, and polycrisis. Yet amidst these conditions, we are strengthened and affirmed by the connections among many scholars, practitioners, artists, activists, educators, and healers. The handbook was made possible by you, by us, and how we have come together to reflect on the decolonial turn wherever we are, and wherever we look, feel, and breathe.

We thank the contributing authors and their collaborators for generously sharing their research projects, learning experiences, and the challenges they encountered, along with their hopes and dreams. We also thank the reviewers who offered insightful commentary on each contributing chapter; their reflections enhanced each chapter and broadened our perspective as editors on organizing each chapter within its corresponding section. Writing is a process that requires consistency, commitment, and curiosity, all of which the contributing authors demonstrated in their delivery of drafts, revisions, and final versions.

We are grateful for their care, receptiveness to feedback, and openness during this journey toward creating the handbook. Lastly, we are profoundly thankful to Dr. Joe Gone for writing the beautiful foreword to this book. His beautifully written and intensely personal foreword conveys the harmful effects of colonialism and its continuities in the present. Sunil's sabbatical at Harvard University's Anthropology Department allowed him to devote considerable time to this volume. The invitation to Harvard was due to the efforts made by Indigenous scholar Joe Gone, who secured a visiting scholar's appointment for Sunil and found a beautiful office space overlooking the majestic Harvard Divinity School. He is profoundly grateful to Joe Gone for his generosity and sincere collegiality. We are thankful to the senior editors at Routledge, Eleanor Taylor and Emilie Coin, who deftly guided us throughout the preparation of the final manuscript. Without their steadfast support, this volume would not have come to fruition. We are grateful to Helena Parkinson for her assistance in finalizing the manuscripts. We sincerely appreciate the collegiality of Angela Paredes Castro, who provided editorial support in preparing the final manuscripts.

An edited volume of this magnitude, which took years to create, resulted from all three authors' solidarity and intellectual efforts. However, we want to highlight the enormous contributions of our colleague Christopher Sonn, whose labor, generosity, and love during the final phase of editing this volume helped us reach the finish line. As editors, we recognize one another's decolonial spirit, collective thinking, and enduring friendship.

Sunil Bhatia, Jesica Siham Fernández, and Christopher C. Sonn

1 Introduction

Expanding Geographies of Decolonial Psychology

Sunil Bhatia, Jesica Siham Fernández and Christopher C. Sonn

Expanding Geographies of Decolonial Psychology

In the preface to the fourth edition of *The Bridge Called My Back*, Gloria E. Anzaldúa (2015) writes that those who are marginalized have an intimate understanding of their oppression. Anzaldúa claims that the feeling of subjugation:

> ...brewed in our beds, tables, and streets; screaming out in anger is a necessary state in our evolution into freedom. But do we have to dwell forever on that piece of terrain, forever stuck in the middle of that bridge? This land of thorns is not habitable. We carry this bridge inside us, the struggle, the movement toward liberation. ... to wait for that glimmer of recognition to pass between us, to let the force of our being penetrate the other with gentleness. Touching is the act of making love, and if political touching is not made with love, no connections, no linkings happens.
>
> (xxiii–xxiv)

In a raw and radical manner, Anzaldúa presents a conceptualization of liberation rooted in love, connection, and healing with others. She further argues that by believing in hope and recognizing the rocks and thorns of our past, we sow seeds of possibility and (r)evolution, focusing on the "rain, sunlight, and spiderwebs glistening on both" (p. xxvii).

Similarly, in the *Methodology of the Oppressed*, Chela Sandoval (2000) asserts that it is "love that can access and guide our theoretical and political 'movidas' (moves, movements)—revolutionary maneuvers toward decolonized beings" (p. 158). The concept of love and collective healing as embodied, enacted, and affective subjectivities poses a challenge to institutionalized practices of positivism and scientism because love and healing cannot be scientifically operationalized to meet the standards of Euro-American psychology. Yet, these humanizing conditions and ways of being can serve as powerful ethical principles for fundamentally decolonizing psychology. Indeed, they can offer a foundation for a more humane and humanizing psychology that honors our interdependence and the pluriversalities of our life experiences. We are guided by the intention to understand how the decolonial turn—decoloniality, decolonizing, and anti-colonial praxes—engage, interrupt, shift, and open up or strive to transform psychology.

Euro-American psychological science remains the dominant framework for developing core theories of self, identity, cognition, and emotions, primarily based on individuals living in the United States and Europe. By exporting such perspectives, these theories are often presented as

DOI: 10.4324/9781003492214-1

universal, scientific, and relevant to most of humanity, thus reinforcing colonial logic. Thalmayer et al. (2021) highlighted the assumed universality of these theories in stating:

> …it may be fair to conclude that 11% of the world's population is now being represented in psychology's most prominent journals, but that 89% of the world remains neglected in this database. The improved inclusion of this 89% remains an ethical, intellectual, and professional imperative for psychological science.
>
> (p. 128)

The colonial imposition of Euro-American psychology must be acknowledged and named, especially given that it fails to include the experiences of people from the Global South—who are indeed the Majority World—and underrepresented groups from the so-called Global North. The partitioning of the Global North and the Global South represents another dichotomous binary, which is reinscribed in psychological discourse.

Euro-American psychology, which actively exports psychological knowledge worldwide, is considered a "hegemonic psychology." Euro-American psychology, with its focus on individualism, stems from modernity's conception of the Western self as universal and distinct from social relations and history. Since its inception, psychology has been plagued by its fixation on linear notions of "development" and "progress." Indeed, it has sought to reform itself, only to revert to its former state; a wolf in sheep's clothing remains a wolf. Adopting an imperial guise, contemporary Euro-American psychology embodies a neocolonial shift in the developing world through new instruments, discourses, and forms of knowledge production, misaligned with the principles of love and collective healing that form the foundation of psychology wellness. As Henrich et al. (2010) research demonstrates, an American undergraduate student is 4,000 times more likely to be randomly selected as a subject for research than a random non-Western individual. How can love and collective healing be realized when psychological research overlooks the diversity of lived experiences, as well as the voices and desires of non-Western peoples?

The January 2023 Trends Report issued by the *Monitor on Psychology* and published by the *American Psychological Association* stated: "Psychology has a long history of being led primarily by White men and including mainly White study participants" (Santoro, 2023, p. 50). Santoro further notes, "An analysis of 26,000 empirical articles on cognitive, developmental, and social psychology published from 1974 to 2018 found that questions of race tend to be largely forgotten and most journal publishers are White" (p. 51). "Additionally, the studies that do take race into consideration are usually written by White scientists and employ few participants of color" (Roberts et al., 2020 cited in Santoro, 2023, p. 51).

Echoing longstanding insights from decolonial scholars, the report affirms that scholarship in psychology is plagued by racial and cultural bias.

As a recommendation, the report encourages scholars and practitioners in the field to prioritize foregrounding experiences of historically marginalized groups. To this, we add that it is not sufficient to just document such experiences, nor it is just and liberatory to focus on stories of trauma, pain, and challenges; rather, we must uplift their voices, create space for affirmation and a reclamation of their stories, and support their movements for hope, healing, and transformation that will lead us toward the possibility of decolonial liberation.

The Decolonial Turn in Psychology

An emerging perspective from the discipline of critical race and ethnic studies that has developed within psychology is referred to as the *decolonial turn*. We identify this perspective and its transdisciplinary lineage because the *decolonial turn* is a movement—an ongoing and iterative relational process. In psychology, the *decolonial turn* has illuminated how contemporary psychological science and theories are inextricably connected to the legacy of colonialism—coloniality and settler colonialism—perpetuated through the Eurocentric linkage of power and knowledge (Adams et al., 2015; Bhatia et al., 2024; Fernández, et al., 2021; Kessi, 2017; Ratele, 2019; Sonn & Stevens, 2021). One aspect of the *decolonial turn* is that it recenters and validates the experiences, knowledge, and narratives of people who live in the Majority World (Adams, et al., 2015; Maldonado-Torres, 2017), those positioned below the line of the human (Fanon, 1982). Decolonization is an important unfinished undertaking that requires dismantling the structures that created and sustained 500 years of colonialism while also aiming for transformation, creativity, and the re-making of relationships, knowledge, and worlds anew—apart from colonial logics (Fernández et al., 2021; Mignolo & Walsh, 2018; Smith, 2012). While the concept of the *decolonial turn* is emerging, decolonial thinking and resistance are not new phenomena. As long as colonization has existed, people from the colonized worlds have expressed decoloniality—theoretical and political "movidas" (Sandoval, 2000), as well as love and connection as forms of bridging (Anzaldúa, 2015) toward freedom in diverse ways. This has occurred in various geopolitical contexts since modern forms of colonization began in the early 16th century (Mignolo, 2007).

The *decolonial turn* highlights how "coloniality" continues to reflect the current asymmetrical power relations between the West and the Majority World, or the Global North and South (Bhatia, 2018). To offer an example, we note how superficial practices of demanding diversity, equity, and inclusion statements have done little to alter the structures of colonial power. As seemingly performative expressions, including diversity as merely demographic categories or a cultural variable in the psychological canon does not challenge the hegemonic paradigms of knowledge construction, the dominant culture, or the social practices that define what is considered canonical knowledge. Rather, such statements provide a comforting myth that functions to help gloss over the brutal and enduring legacies of colonization and slavery. Incorporating diverse bodies and voices into a colonized system only creates the illusion of embracing diversity, allowing it to be perceived as open-minded while failing to alter the structures that perpetuate coloniality and dominance initially.

Broadly speaking, calls for "decolonization" have political and methodological coordinates and referents. Most importantly, it serves as a way to orient and think about the world:

> which takes colonialism, empire and racisms as its empirical and discursive object of study; it resituates these phenomena as key shaping forces of the contemporary world. … it offers alternative ways of thinking about the world and alternative forms of political praxis.
>
> (Bhambra, et al., 2018, p. 2)

While colonialism as a formal administrative process has ended in many former colonies, decolonial scholars argue that coloniality persists long after colonialism has concluded (Quijano, 2000). Global inequalities and ecological inequities rooted in colonialism and "global coloniality" disproportionately impact people from previously colonized countries, as well as environments devastated by European exploitation, genocide, theft, and extraction (Ndlovu-Gathsheni, 2020). Different forms of coloniality and the ways it is enacted and experienced are maintained:

> alive in books, in the criteria for academic performance, in cultural patterns, in common sense, in the self-image of peoples, in aspirations of self, and so many other aspects of our modern experience. In a way, as modern subjects we breathe coloniality all the time and every day.
>
> (Maldonado-Torres, 2007, p. 243)

The legacy of colonialism and coloniality has shaped the core foundations of Euro-American psychology. Thus, decolonizing psychology entails a commitment to envisioning new decolonial ways of thinking, being, doing, and relating. Our disciplinary transformation—a reimagining—has been articulated by researchers, scholars, practitioners, and activists from various parts of the world, in different modalities and publications across diverse areas of psychology and beyond (e.g. Adams, et al., 2015; Bhatia, 2018; Bhatia & Priya, 2021; Ciofalo, 2021; Comas-Díaz, et al., 2024; Dudgeon & Walker, 2015; Dutta, et al., 2022; Fernández, et al., 2021; Gone; 2021; Kessi, et al., 2022; Kiguwa & Segalo, 2018; Malherbe & Ratele, 2022; Neville et al., 2024; Pickren & Pickren, 2021; Ratele, 2019; Sonn et al., 2024; Smith, 2012; Suffla et al., 2015; Teo, 2015; Tuck & Yang, 2012; Watkins, 2019).

The vision of a decolonial psychology has been primarily shaped by psychologists who are Black, Indigenous, people of color, those with marginalized genders, and immigrants. While the experience of colonization has been central to the lived experiences of psychologists from historically underrepresented groups, they have additionally encountered multiple intersections of exclusion and oppression. The concepts of decolonization and decoloniality, as theories and modes of inquiry, have been particularly significant for populations in formerly colonized countries. These groups still bear the burdens of colonialism, and their lands have been stolen. For many, colonization continues to be a painful experience marked by trauma, dispossession, and racism colonialism.

We believe that another psychology is possible, and we offer the *Handbook on Decolonial Psychology* as a resource—a movement and a bridge—to assist psychology and psychologists in envisioning the contours of a decolonial "counter-psychology" as practice. A psychology with a pedagogy, method, and praxis that prioritizes love and healing, and wellbeing of "Black, Indigenous, and colonized people in struggles for decolonization and decoloniality" over professional rewards, academic mobility, and individual achievement (Maldonado-Torres, 2021, p. xiv). To this end, Maldonado-Torres (2021) issued a call to transform decolonial psychology by elevating and centering the voices of "poets, essayists, visual artists, playwrights, movement leaders, community organizers, and performers who reveal catastrophic dimensions of our world" (Maldonado-Torres, xiii). Our handbook answers that call and brings together a collection of authors who break the boundaries between research/activism, theory/praxis, classroom/community, and pedagogy/research. These binaries are themselves constructions that have emerged from the colonial history of the academies. While the *decolonial turn* in psychology has provided us with critical knowledge in connecting questions of race, empire, and colonialism to knowledge production and power structures, there is a pressing need for more historically and geographically specific, granular, and situated accounts of decolonization around the globe.

Reimagining a psychology distinct from the dominant Eurocentric model requires engaging in practices of cultural reclamation, Indigenous retrieval, and crafting new counterstories of decolonial psychology. Our book—because it is yours, to be shared, and circulated—is rooted in the idea that to decolonize is to transform the discipline and to imagine "possibilities differently" (Escobar, 2020, p. x), and as Ciofalo (2021, p. 2) proposes "making the road caminando de otra manera" (walking in a different/other way). To imagine a new transformative decolonial psychology, we have to challenge what "our world" means and what "possibilities" mean, and who we are accountable to in the field of psychology. A decolonial psychology and pedagogy must address the tensions and ruptures that arise. These tensions, when embraced, can foster new ideas and actions toward decolonial resistance projects, which have been articulated by various scholars and activists across a range of disciplines, localities, and geographies, and with radically different perspectives on justice, freedom, and liberation. Although psychology has remained far from the liberatory path, we do not waver in our pursuit of actualizing a psychology for liberation, freedom, and transformative justice.

Tilling the Roots and Routes of Decolonial Psychology

Decolonization, according to Tuck and Yang (2018), means refusing to collaborate on social justice projects that "rely on the benevolence of the state or of the dominant in the society" or "justice projects that require us to prove humanity or worth … or justice projects which require us to appeal to the people who abuse us" (Tuck & Yang, 2018, p. 8). Significant epistemological differences exist in decolonial, postcolonial, and decolonization approaches, each offering radical possibilities to challenge and dismantle the coloniality of psychological sciences (Bhatia, 2020; Bhatia & Priya, 2018; Macleod et al., 2020). Recognizing the pluriversality and diverse approaches to decolonization is essential. For instance, for some groups, decolonization involves reclaiming land and sovereignty. For others, it means detaching from the Euro-American power-knowledge nexus. Additionally, some recognize that the devastating legacy of colonial encounters cannot be reversed; hence, there is an urgent need to build a decolonized world for the vast majority of individuals suffering from poverty, casteism, hunger, unemployment, inadequate housing, lack of education and sanitation, and the crises of climate change.

The handbook builds on the expanding knowledge base in decolonial psychology to meaningfully address these varied social and psychological trajectories of decolonization and liberation. Rooted in a commitment to inclusion, we aim to highlight the work of scholars and activists who challenge the dichotomies between community and university. Their locations and positionalities illustrate that liminal space of possibility, tension, and radical hope—what Anzaldúa (1987) calls *Nepantla* and Hill Collins (1986) refers to as the "outsider within". Bringing a range of perspectives together, the handbook critically examines recent calls to decolonize psychology by recentering and retrieving silenced, ignored, and omitted pieces of knowledge and practices. The collective work we showcase aims to normalize the invisible plural histories of psychology emerging from various places, spaces, and *movidas* (movements).

One of the central questions that guide the handbook is the following: What does "building knowledge from below" look like? What does psychology from below look like—and, relatedly, what does it do—when we center relationality, care, love, community, and healing embedded in pluriversal epistemologies and ontologies? In the subsequent pages, we invite you to consider these as you reflect and engage with the articulated, situated, and complex accounts of decolonial projects and liberation struggles that are brewing—like seeds sprouting from tilled soil—in multiple geographies and in various sites beyond North America and Euro-American research practice.

Speaking to the hegemonic centers of the Global North has often resulted in erasure, leading to emotional exhaustion for subaltern and underrepresented scholars. Therefore, the handbook is not to be conceived of as a pedagogical tool that "speaks to" or "dialogues" with hegemonic psychology. Historically, scholars from marginalized positions have had to carry the *emotional labor* burdens of educating, explaining, translating, and being the floor mat to appease the dominant knowledge systems (e.g. Canham, 2024). Speaking from anti-colonial and antiracist perspectives often leads to exclusion from the canon, experiencing gaslighting, being reshaped into an "exotic" researcher, or being assimilated into whiteness, thus becoming co-opted into mainstream thought.

A critical aspect of decolonization is epistemological decolonizing (Quijano, 2000; Richards, 2014; Smith, 2012). We understand this as an active, iterative, and continuous process of critical reflexivity and praxis that involves delinking from Euro-American knowledge systems, theories, ideas, and practices rooted in colonialism and coloniality (Mignolo, 2007). We recognize psychology as having multiple platforms of enactment: self/community, classroom, research, activism, and popular culture, including the arts, theater, poetry, and mythology. The project of decolonization is vibrant and bold—it requires all of us—and it necessitates a distinct approach at each phase of the process. In the handbook, we argue that epistemologically decolonizing psychology from within involves addressing questions of how we can *dismantle* the colonial structure of academia, including the university and beyond, as we strive to be creative and innovate. Epistemic decolonization highlights the cultural values, hidden curricula, and assumptions inherent in Euro-American colonial knowledge systems (Smith, 2012). In this pursuit, we pose an overarching question and critically and urgently ask the following complementary questions:

- What does it mean to teach/research/organize/develop policy/engage in healing practices with a decolonizing praxis that involves struggle?
    - What constitutes psychological knowledge, and whose psychological knowledge is considered valid?
    - To whom are we accountable in our research, for what purposes, and how do we present our knowledge?

The Seeds, Buds, and Blossoms: Sections and Contributing Chapters

Section I. Decolonizing the Curriculum of Psychology: Concepts, Stories, Lives, and Possibilities

We have collected contributions from critical scholars based in various countries, both in the majority and minority worlds. These contributions add to the growing body of work that illustrates the roots and routes of the decolonial turn in psychology, highlighting the possibilities for alternate psychologies. We have organized the book into three parts: the first section focuses on efforts aimed at decolonizing the curriculum of psychology; the second discusses ways Indigenous and subaltern knowledges contribute to healing, resistance, and relationality, and the third section emphasizes methods and applications beyond the university.

Chapter 2 suggests that psychology has been complicit with the colonial project in Australia. However, the discipline has a role in supporting Aboriginal and Torres Strait Islander wellbeing by embedding notions and practices of cultural safety and anchoring pedagogy and practices in First Nations worldviews, standpoints, and experiences. The work illustrates a national empowerment and transformation project that centers on Aboriginal and Torres Strait conceptions of Social Emotional Wellbeing. Chapter 3 shares the efforts to create a decolonizing curriculum in Indonesia, a context increasingly challenged by the neoliberalization of the university. The authors demonstrate that the rearticulation of local education philosophies, which view education as "a humanizing pathway toward compassion-based solidarity and dignified humanity," can counter the "ego-centric self" and the decontextualized curriculum characterizing psychology education in Indonesia. Chapters 4 and 5 follow the tradition of testimonios to offer multi-voiced stories of creating curricula across localities while remaining rooted in place. As concluded by Ciofalo et al., they highlight various decolonial orientations in:

> Co-constructing a transdisciplinary curriculum with a substantial focus on epistemologies of the Global South and its diasporas within the academy requires ongoing navigation of institutionally embedded modernism/coloniality, and a hopeful gaze toward decolonial futurities. In this chapter, we intended to make a radical intervention in the coloniality of psychology to generate through anti-, post-, and de-colonial perform-antics an uncharted praxis that needs a new name. (p. 59)

Chapter 5 presents dialogues centered on love and care within decolonial journeys and liberatory practices. The authors refer to their praxis as decolonial alchemy, which is described as "a fundamentally relational and communal process of what emerges when we share our stories with one another, when our lived experiences intersect. Alchemical transformations begin when truth is articulated within a community." The authors generously share their testimonios and pose questions for consideration as we explore the processes of self, relational, and collective transformation in decolonial alchemy. Chapter 6 critically analyzes the impact of colonialism on formal education in India and its role in sustaining various oppressive hierarchies. This chapter also presents an approach grounded in the perspectives of historically marginalized individuals to reimagine schooling as a venue for activism and social change.

Section II. Indigenous Retrieval and Community Building across Self, Body, and Place: Psychology of Healing Resistance and Relationality

In the second section of the book, there is a focus on the retrieval, reclamation, and centering of subaltern knowledges, practices, and experiences. Chapter 7 echoes the Indigenizing projects introduced in Chapter 2 and mobilizes participatory action research and counter-storytelling methods in solidarity with the Pitaguary and Jenipapo-Kanindé peoples in Brazil to elevate traditional healing practices. Chapter 8 examines methods for restorative and transformative justice as vehicles for spiritual solidarity. The chapter also outlines the practice of circles and its foundations of deep listening as key elements for memory practices and nurturing the spiritual solidarity.

Chapter 9 is an innovative project based on lifting what Dillard (2000) referred to as endarkened epistemologies. The author challenges, disrupts, and, in dialogue with archives and community, creates and curates knowledge otherwise, histories of the aesthetics of healing. The chapter calls for the inclusion of "Black aesthetics and onto-epistemologies in mental health care practice and education." Chapter 10 draws on mother gatherings as a methodology embodied in the Arabic saying "al-umm bitlim". In alignment with several other chapters that focus on lived and embodied knowledge, relationality, and spirituality, this chapter weaves together stories of loss and grief along with processes of re-existence. The author states that "… mothering—of ourselves, of others, of the land—born of grief and nurtured by the land, is a testament to the enduring power of love, even in the face of despair".

Chapters 11 and 12 highlight the possibilities for decolonial theory and practice in clinical contexts. Chapter 11 draws on a rich archive of critical and decolonial thought that challenges binaries and invokes in-between and border spaces as liminal areas that offer alternative onto-epistemologies for clinical and therapeutic practice. This chapter suggests that "Through an interstitial sensibility, plurality is held, opening up possibilities for the creation of a decolonial dynamic of thinking, doing, and relating between client and therapist." Efforts to envision decolonial practice in Chapter 12 reimagine the dominant foundations of psychological practice through the baskets of knowledge, *wangii wadhan biyay*, as a basis for culturally safe practice in the Australian context.

Section III. Disrupting Methods: Going beyond the University

In the third section, the six chapters advance alternative theories, methods, and tactics for decolonial work. Chapter 13 shows how Kuapapa Maori methodology and epistemology can be mobilized to critique dominant science on climate change and advance alternative needed understandings. Chapter 14 asks the question about land, which is at the forefront of many decolonial struggles around the world. The chapter uses South Africa as a case study to raise questions about the psychopolitical question of land and its centrality in decolonial struggles. Chapters 15 and 16 provide strong examples of archiving as a decolonial practice. Both chapters center on her stories and emphasize the need for archival retrieval as essential to addressing gendered and racialized absences in official records. In many ways, the chapters argue for and illustrate how official narratives, dominant falsehoods, and silences can be contested while frameworks for memory and re-membering can be expanded. Chapters 17 and 18 address the realities and capabilities of young people in building meaningful lives within the contexts of cosmopolitanization in India and the involvement of youth in climate justice activism, respectively.

In this volume, we observe the expanding efforts of many scholars, activists, researchers, and other contributors to reimagine a psychology that can facilitate the creation of Fanon's decolonized world. These efforts involve examining the sites of coloniality within the discipline, as well as the creative attempts to develop modalities for decolonial enactments in borderlands and various in-between spaces, traversing disciplinary boundaries to foster new possibilities for pluriversal psychologies with loving perception (Lugones, 2016).

References

Adams, G., Dobles, I., Gómez, L. H., Kurtiş, T., & Molina, L. E. (2015). Decolonizing psychological science: Introduction to the special thematic section. *Journal of Social and Political Psychology, 3*(1), 213–238. https://doi.org/10.5964/jspp.v3i1.564

Anzaldúa, G. (1987). *Borderlands/La frontera: The new mestiza.* Aunt Lute Books.

Anzaldúa, G. (2015). Foreword, 2001. In C. Moraga & G. Anzaldúa (Eds.), *This bridge called my back: Writings by radical women of color* (4th ed, pp. xxxiv–xl). SUNY Press.

Bhambra, K. G., Gebrial, D., & Nişancıoğlu, K. (2018). *Decolonizing the university.* Pluto Press.

Bhatia, S. (2018). *Decolonizing psychology: Globalization, social justice, and Indian youth identities.* Oxford University Press.

Bhatia, S. (2020). Decolonization and coloniality in human development: Neoliberalism, globalization and narratives of Indian youth. *Human Development, 64*(4–6), 207–221. https://psycnet.apa.org/doi/10.1159/000513084

Bhatia, S., & Priya, K. R. (2018). Decolonizing culture: Euro-American psychology and the shaping of neoliberal selves in India. *Theory & Psychology, 28*(5), 645–668. https://doi.org/10.1177/0959354318791315.

Bhatia, S., & Priya, K. R. (2021). Coloniality and psychology: From silencing to recentering marginalized voices in postcolonial times. *Review of General Psychology, 25*(4), 422–436. https://doi.org/10.1177/10892680211046507

Bhatia, S., Long, W., Pickren, W., & Rutherford, A. (2024). Engaging with decoloniality, decolonization, and histories of psychology otherwise. In L. Comas-Díaz, H. Y. Adames, & N. Y. Chavez-Dueñas (Eds.), *Decolonial psychology: Toward anticolonial theories, research, training, and practice* (pp. 61–85). American Psychological Association. https://doi.org/10.1037/0000376-004

Canham, H. K. (2024). The black failure of psychology – an errant walking away. *Annual Review of Critical Psychology, 18*, 1298–1311.

Ciofalo, N. (2021). Making the road caminando de otra manera: Co-constructing decolonial community psychologies from the Global South. *American Journal of Community Psychology*, *69*, 426–435. https://doi.org/10.1002/ajcp.12562

Collins, P. H. (1986). Learning from the outsider within: The sociological significance of black feminist thought. *Social Problems*, *33*(6), 14–32. https://doi.org/10.2307/800672

Comas-Díaz, L., Adames, H. Y., & Chavez-Dueñas, N. Y. (Eds.). (2024). *Decolonial psychology: Toward anticolonial theories, research, training, and practice.* American Psychological Association.

Dillard, C. B. (2000). The substance of things hoped for, the evidence of things not seen: Examining an endarkened feminist epistemology in educational research and leadership. *International Journal of Qualitative Studies in Education, 13*(6), 661–681. https://doi.org/10.1080/09518390050211565

Dudgeon, P., & Walker, R. (2015). Decolonising Australian psychology: Discourses, strategies, and practice. *Journal of Social and Political Psychology, 3*(1), 276–297. https://doi.org/10.5964/jspp.v3i1.126

Dutta, U., Azad, A. K., & Hussain, S. M. (2022). Counterstorytelling as epistemic justice: Decolonial community-based praxis from the global south. *American Journal of Community Psychology*, *69*(1–2), 59–70. https://doi.org/10.1002/ajcp.12545

Escobar, A. (2020). *Pluriversal politics: The real and the possible.* Duke University Press. https://doi.org/10.1215/9781478012108

Fanon, F. (1982). *Black skin, white masks* (1st Evergreen ed.). Grove Press.

Fernández, J. S., Sonn, C. C., Carolissen, R., & Stevens, G. (2021). Roots and routes toward decoloniality within and outside psychology praxis. *Review of General Psychology, 25*(4), 354–368. https://doi.org/10.1177/10892680211002437

Gone, J. P. (2021). Decolonization as methodological innovation in counseling psychology: Method, power, and process in reclaiming American Indian therapeutic traditions. *Journal of Counseling Psychology, 68*(3), 259–270. https://doi.org/10.1037/cou0000500

Henrich, J., Heine, S. J., & Norenzayan, A. (2010). Most people are not WEIRD. *Nature*, *466*(7302), 29–29. https://doi.org/10.1038/466029a

Kessi, S. (2017). Community social psychologies for decoloniality: An African perspective on epistemic justice in higher education. *South African Journal of Psychology*, *47*(4), 506–516. https://doi.org/10.1177/0081246317737917

Kessi, S., Suffla, S., & Seedat, M. (2022). Towards a decolonial community psychology: Derivatives, disruptions and disobediences. In S. Kessi, S. Suffla, & M. Seedat (Eds.), *Decolonial enactments in community psychology* (pp. 3–12). Springer International Publishing. https://doi.org/10.1007/978-3-030-75201-9_1

Kiguwa, P., & Segalo, P. (2018). Decolonising psychology in residential and open distance e-learning institutions: Critical reflections. *South African Journal of Psychology, 48*(3), 310–318. https://doi.org/10.1177/0081246318786605

Lugones, M. (2016). The Coloniality of Gender. In W. Harcourt (Ed.), *The Palgrave handbook of gender and development* (pp. 13–33). Palgrave Macmillan. https://doi.org/10.1007/978-1-137-38273-3_2

Macleod, C. I., Bhatia, S., & Liu, W. (2020). Feminisms and decolonising psychology: Possibilities and challenges. *Feminism & Psychology*, *30*(3), 287–305. https://doi.org/10.1177/0959353520932810

Maldonado-Torres, N. (2007). On the coloniality of being: Contributions to the development of a concept. *Cultural Studies*, *21*(2–3), 240–270. https://doi.org/10.1080/09502380601162548

Maldonado-Torres, N. (2017). Frantz Fanon and the decolonial turn in psychology: From modern/colonial methods to the decolonial attitude. *South African Journal of Psychology*, *47*(4), 432–441. https://doi.org/10.1177/0081246317737918

Maldonado-Torres, N. (2021). Decolonial psychology as a counter-catastrophic science. In G. Stevens, & C. C. Sonn (Eds.), *Decoloniality and epistemic justice in contemporary community psychology* (pp. vii–xv). Springer.

Malherbe, N., & Ratele, K. (2022). What and for whom is a decolonising African psychology? *Theory & Psychology, 32*(1), 116–130. https://doi.org/10.1177/09593543211027231

Mignolo, W. D. (2007). Introduction: Coloniality of power and de-colonial thinking. *Cultural Studies*, *21*(2–3), 155–167. https://doi.org/10.1080/09502380601162498

Mignolo, W., & Walsh, C. E. (2018). *On decoloniality: Concepts, analytics, praxis*. Duke University Press.

Ndlovu-Gatsheni, S. (2020). The Dynamics of epistemological decolonisation in the 21st century: Towards epistemic freedom. *Strategic Review for Southern Africa, 40*(1), 16–48.

Neville, H. A., Lee, B. A., & Maghsoodi, A. H. (2024). Decolonizing and building liberatory psychological sciences. In L. Comas-Díaz, H. Y. Adames, & N. Y. Chavez-Dueñas (Eds.), *Decolonial psychology: Toward anticolonial theories, research, training, and practice* (pp. 89–118). American Psychological Association. https://doi.org/10.1037/0000376-005

Pickren, G. W., & Pickren, W. E. (2021). Signposts to decolonial futures in understanding and addressing our present crises. *Journal of the History of the Behavioral Sciences, 57*(4), 315–318. https://doi.org/10.1002/jhbs.22147

Quijano, A. (2000). Coloniality of power, eurocentrism, and Latin America. *Nepantla: Views From South, 1*(3), 533–580.

Ratele, K. (2019). *The world looks like this from here: Thoughts on African psychology*. WITS University Press.

Richards. (2014). Decolonizing globalization studies. *The Global South, 8*(2), 139. https://doi.org/10.2979/globalsouth.8.2.139

Roberts, S. O., Bareket-Shavit, C., Dollins, F. A., Goldie, P. D., Mortenson, E. (2020). Racial Inequality in Psychological Research: Trends of the Past and Recommendations for the Future. *Perspectives on Psychological Science, 15*(6), 1295–1309. doi: 10.1177/1745691620927709.

Sandoval, C. (2000). *Methodology of the oppressed.* University of Minnesota Press.

Santoro, H. (2023). *Psychological research is changing, Emerging trends in psychology*. American Psychological Association. https://www.apa.org/monitor/2023/2023-01-monitor.pdf

Smith, L. T. (2012). *Decolonizing methodologies: Research and Indigenous peoples* (2nd ed.). Zed Books.

Sonn, C. C., & Stevens, G. (2021). Tracking the decolonial turn in contemporary community psychology: Expanding socially just knowledge archives, ways of being and modes of praxis. In G. Stevens & C. C. Sonn (Eds.), *Decoloniality and epistemic justice in contemporary community psychology* (pp. 1–19). Springer International Publishing. https://doi.org/10.1007/978-3-030-72220-3_1

Sonn, C. C., Fernández, J. S., Moura, J. F., Madyaningrum, M. E., & Malherbe, N. (2024). Decolonisation in and beyond community psychologies: A transnational plurilogue. In C. C. Sonn, J. S. Fernández, J. F. Moura Jr., M. E. Madyaningrum, & N. Malherbe (Eds.), *Handbook of decolonial community psychology* (pp. 1–22). Springer Nature Switzerland. https://doi.org/10.1007/978-3-031-67035-0_1

Suffla, S., Seedat, M., & Bawa, U. (2015). Reflexivity as enactment of critical community psychologies: Dilemmas of voice and positionality in a multi-country photovoice study. *Journal of Community Psychology, 43*(1), 9–21. https://doi.org/10.1002/jcop.21691

Teo, T. (2015). Critical psychology: A geography of intellectual engagement and resistance. *American Psychologist, 70*(3), 243–254. https://doi.org/10.1037/a0038727

Thalmayer, A. G., Toscanelli, C., & Arnett, J. J. (2021). The neglected 95% revisited: Is American psychology becoming less American? *American Psychologist*, *76*(1), 116–129. https://doi.org/10.1037/amp0000622

Tuck, E., & Yang, K. W. (2012). Decolonization is not a metaphor. *Decolonization: Indigeneity, Education & Society, 1*(1), 1–40.

Tuck, E., & Yang, K. W. (2018). Introduction: Born under the rising sign of social justice. In E. Tuck, & K. W. Yang (Eds.), *Toward what justice? Describing diverse dreams of justice in education* (pp. 1–18). Routledge.

Watkins, M. (2019). *Mutual accompaniment and the creation of the commons*. Yale University Press.

Part 1

Decolonizing the Curriculum of Psychology

Concepts, Stories, Lives, and Possibilities

2 Embracing Social and Emotional Wellbeing Can Create Transformational Change in Psychology

Belle Selkirk, Joanna Alexi, Tanja Hirvonen and Pat Dudgeon

Introduction

Aboriginal and Torres Strait Islander peoples[1] are one of the oldest continuous living cultures known in the world, having thrived on the lands now referred to as Australia for more than 60,000 years. Aboriginal and Torres Strait Islander peoples comprised of up to 260 diverse nations, each with its own way of knowing, being, and doing (Indigenous knowledges) that promote harmonious and sustainable ways of life that prioritise equitable relationships between cultural groups, kinship networks, and the environment (Dudgeon et al., 2014c).

Colonisation is not a single historical event; it remains an ongoing process characterised by deliberate policies, harmful practices, and actions that have impacted Aboriginal and Torres Strait Islander peoples over decades. This enduring colonial legacy is woven throughout Australian society, embedded in the structures and systems of the workforce, education, legal and policing institutions, social support, healthcare, politics, and government. The persistent and systematic imposition of Western ideologies within Australian society perpetuates a colonial advantage that sustains the benefits of settler-colonial society while simultaneously oppressing and marginalising Aboriginal and Torres Strait Islander peoples (Moreton-Robinson, 2015; Watego et al., 2021). For over 230 years, colonial influences have continuously disrupted Aboriginal and Torres Strait Islander sophisticated and intricate knowledge systems, adversely impacting Aboriginal and Torres Strait Islander peoples' health, wellbeing, and capacity for self-determinism (Dudgeon & Bray, 2023; Dudgeon et al., 2014b). The forceful removal of Aboriginal and Torres Strait Islander children, along with the deliberate separation of families from kinship and cultural foundations, was a strategic colonial initiative aimed at disempowering Aboriginal and Torres Strait Islander peoples and communities. Consequently, Stolen Generation survivors and their descendants continue to experience poor health and wellbeing outcomes compared to other Aboriginal and Torres Strait Islander peoples (Healing Foundation, 2021). Despite extensive documentation of these ongoing negative impacts, "there has still been no systematic government response to the needs and rights of Stolen Generations survivors and their descendants" (Healing Foundation, 2021, p. 4), nor has there been adequate implementation and resourcing of Indigenous-led solutions (Healing Foundation, 2025).

The discipline of psychology is deeply rooted in Western ideologies that perpetuate colonial violence and the oppression of Aboriginal and Torres Strait Islander peoples and knowledges (Clark & Hirvonen, 2022; Dudgeon & Bray, 2023; Selkirk et al., in press). Psychological policy, practice, theory, research, and education have historically denied and undermined Indigenous knowledges (Fish et al., 2023) while positioning Western knowledges as the highest degree of evidence base (Dudgeon & Bray, 2023; Dudgeon et al., 2017, 2020). The unequal power differential of Western ideologies in psychology promotes the belief of a universal psychology superior to all other

DOI: 10.4324/9781003492214-3

knowledges and cultures. The result of this is the imposition of Western psychological frameworks and the denial of Indigenous psychologies, wisdoms, rights, and lived experiences (Bhatia & Priya, 2021; Fish & Gone, 2024; Readsura Decolonial Editorial Collective et al., 2022). Furthermore, the ongoing epistemic violence of Western psychology maintains settler-colonial hierarchies of power in the discipline of psychology while simultaneously exacerbating poorer health outcomes and equity for Aboriginal and Torres Strait Islander peoples (Clark & Hirvonen, 2022; Dudgeon et al., 2014b; Fish & Gone, 2024; Selkirk et al., in press).

This is, in contrast to psychology's ethos, to promote and support wellbeing. Psychology has been harmful to Aboriginal and Torres Strait Islander peoples (Carey et al., 2017; Dudgeon et al., 2014b). This has been recognised by the Australia Psychological Society (APS) who issued a formal apology in 2016, acknowledging the discipline's role in the oppression of Aboriginal and Torres Strait Islander peoples through the imposition of Western psychology frameworks, diagnostic systems, assessments, and interventions (Australian Psychological Society, 2016; Carey et al., 2017). The Apology also noted APS' silence in policy matters that directly impacted the health and wellbeing of Aboriginal and Torres Strait Islander peoples. The APS Apology came about after decades of Indigenous leadership and advocacy, highlighting the necessity for a redistribution of power and epistemic justice within the discipline (Carey et al., 2017). This Apology signifies a commitment to systemic change and decolonising practice, aiming to create a future where Aboriginal and Torres Strait peoples determine the healthcare agenda and foster more authentic collaboration and respect. The critical need for Indigenous knowledges in psychology as a matter of epistemological justice and self-determination is evident. One example of Indigenous knowledges in psychology is social and emotional wellbeing (SEWB) (SEWB; Gee et al., 2014), which this chapter will describe in detail. First, we discuss the decolonising psychology movement in Australia and the formidable roles of Indigenous-led initiatives in psychology.

Decolonising Psychology

For psychology to truly support Aboriginal and Torres Strait healing and flourishing, the discipline must advocate for embedding Indigenous knowledges, while also engaging in authentic and consistent decolonising systemic transformation. Decolonising psychology requires challenging power differentials by privileging and valuing Indigenous leadership and knowledges, thus decentring Western epistemologies and settler-colonial dominance in psychology. It involves redistributing power and responsibilities, acknowledging Indigenous sovereignty, and fostering genuine partnerships between Indigenous and non-Indigenous psychologists. This transformative process, though uncomfortable and complex, is vital for achieving epistemic justice and human rights within the discipline of psychology in Australia (Dudgeon et al., 2021; Dudgeon & Walker, 2015; Selkirk et al., in press).

Indigenous knowledges, including Indigenous psychologies, offer holistic and relational ontologies and epistemologies integral to the wellbeing of Aboriginal and Torres Strait Islander peoples. Through the rise of Indigenous psychology in Australia and acts of Indigenous self-determination, Aboriginal and Torres Strait Islander peoples are collectively asserting sovereignty by shaping theories, discourses, and practices in psychology. Indigenous psychology as a discipline and practice is considered a form of cultural reclamation that actively works towards decolonising psychology and achieving epistemic justice (Dudgeon, 2021).

In Australia, Indigenous psychology is a central component of the decolonising psychology movement, both as a matter of epistemic justice and in providing culturally safe[2] solutions to support the wellbeing of Aboriginal and Torres Strait Islander peoples. The decolonising movement in Australia has a long history of advocacy by Aboriginal and Torres Strait Islander leaders, scholars, health practitioners, and communities who have worked tirelessly to disrupt and reshape the power distribution and relationship between settler-colonial discourses in psychology and Indigenous psychologies (Selkirk et al., in press).

Some of the early movements and efforts in decolonising psychology in Australia can be traced to the 1980s, when a small but determined group of psychologists gathered in Sydney for the 24th International Congress of Psychology. The psychologists began a journey of bringing awareness to the negative impacts of oppressive policies within psychology and the minimal efforts to address Aboriginal and Torres Strait Islander wellbeing (Clark & Hirvonen, 2022). In 1991, the APS facilitated the establishment of the APS Aboriginal and Torres Strait Islander Peoples and Psychology Interest Group. The focus of this group has been in the promotion of Indigenous psychology and advocacy of issues related to Aboriginal and Torres Strait Islander peoples (Australian Psychological Society, 2024).

Another momentous step in the movement was the formation of the Australian Indigenous Psychologists Association (AIPA) in 2008 under the auspices of the APS. In 2019, AIPA became incorporated and now functions as an autonomous peak community-controlled organisation representing Aboriginal and Torres Strait Islander psychologists across the nation (Australian Indigenous Psychologists Association, 2021). Despite funding limitations, AIPA have achieved a number of important milestones in psychology policy, practice, and education reform. For example, through the advocacy of AIPA, the APS developed a Reconciliation Action Plan in 2012 (Australian Psychological Society et al., 2012) and formally apologised to Aboriginal and Torres Strait Islander peoples for their role in mistreatment and impact on wellbeing (Australian Psychological Society, 2016). AIPA supported decolonising movements in psychology education and practice (Dudgeon et al., 2016a, 2016b, 2016c) and actively worked with the Psychology Board of Australia (PsyBA) on a number of initiatives to support culturally safe practice.

In addition, the transformative programme known as the Australian Indigenous Psychology Education Project (AIPEP) has further led the way in decolonising psychology. This project is led by Bardi psychologist and Professor Pat Dudgeon AM and supported by AIPA, who provide Indigenous governance and collaboration on a number of projects within AIPEP. The first iteration of AIPEP occurred from 2013 to 2016 and was recently re-vitalised in 2020. At its core, AIPEP provides leadership in decolonising efforts within the domains of psychology, higher education, Aboriginal and Torres Strait Islander student support, and workforce capacity building in psychology practice. For a comprehensive overview of AIPEP, including its impact in systemic change, see Selkirk et al. (in press).

As a result of AIPEP, AIPA, and the ongoing advocacy of Aboriginal and Torres Strait Islander psychologists, positive and optimistic outcomes in decolonising the psychology discipline can already be seen. For example, in 2019, the Australian Psychology Accreditation Council (APAC) made a policy change requiring higher education providers (HEPs) to embed cultural responsiveness, including with Aboriginal and Torres Strait Islander peoples, in their curricula (Australian Psychology Accreditation Council, 2019). Since then, 80% of HEPs have joined a community of practice led by AIPEP to actively decolonise their curricula and student support (Selkirk et al., in press). Furthermore, important systemic and policy shifts are underway across organisations and peak bodies of psychology practice, particularly the PsyBA, who in 2023 proposed changes to their general registration competencies of psychologists and the introduction of a new psychology code of conduct to align with cultural safety amendments to National Law (Australian Health Practitioner Regulation Agency, 2022; Psychology Board of Australia, 2024a, 2024b).

Practically, efforts to decolonise education, practice, and policy are necessary for Indigenous knowledges and paradigms of wellbeing to be equally heard and prioritised in supporting Aboriginal and Torres Strait Islander health and wellbeing. Evidence suggests that culturally grounded interventions provide a promising and successful approach to improving mental health and wellbeing outcomes with Aboriginal and Torres Strait Islander peoples (for example, see: Dudgeon, et al., 2025; Dudgeon et al., 2024a, 2022; Mia et al., 2017; Smith et al., 2017; Summerton & Blunden, 2022). Recognition of this in the policy, practice, and education of psychology remain central to decolonising efforts and improving systems of care. The multidimensional paradigm of **SEWB** (Dudgeon, et al., 2025; Gee et al., 2014; SEWB) is one example of the ontological and epistemological innovations that Indigenous knowledges in psychology offers, which can rebuild and strengthen Aboriginal and Torres Strait Islander peoples' health and wellbeing. The paradigm of SEWB, including its components and importance to supporting harmony in wellbeing is discussed in the next section.

Social and Emotional Wellbeing

SEWB describes a holistic whole-of-life worldview of health and wellbeing as articulated by Aboriginal and Torres Strait Islander peoples. In their seminal chapter, Gee et al. (2014) detail a model of SEWB in which Aboriginal and Torres Strait Islander health and wellbeing is influenced by connections with, and between, domains of body, mind, family and kinship, community, culture, Country, and spirituality. As described by Dudgeon et al. (2025); "SEWB model centres culture and describes a whole-of-life, collective worldview and a sense of self that is grounded in family and inseparable from the cultural wellbeing of the whole community" (p. 8). A core feature of the model is that it considers the diverse expressions and experiences of individuals and communities across the lifespan and time and place-based contexts (Dudgeon et al., 2025). It does so by embedding the importance of historical, political, cultural, and social determinants of health as core to the model. Consequently, the SEWB model encourages health and wellbeing to be framed and understood within the intricate ecosystem in which we exist, live, and thrive (Dudgeon et al., 2025).

The articulation of the SEWB model as we know it today was developed in 2012 by members of the AIPA and validated through consultation with Aboriginal and Torres Strait Islander communities across Australia (Dudgeon et al., 2025; Gee et al., 2014). What was available in the mental health sector was culturally ineffective in its ability to support Aboriginal and Torres Strait Islander peoples. It is recognised that holistic conceptions of SEWB have a long and rich history in the context of Aboriginal and Torres Strait Islander health and wellbeing. The use of the term "SEWB" as a reflection of holistic health and wellbeing can be traced to the early advocacy of Aboriginal Community-Controlled Health Organisations (ACCHOs) in the 1970s. In 1979, the then National Aboriginal and Islander Health Organisation (now known as the National Aboriginal Community-Controlled Health Organisation) embraced the following definition of health and wellbeing:

> Aboriginal health does not mean the physical wellbeing of an individual, but refers to the social, emotional, and cultural wellbeing of the whole community. For Aboriginal people this is seen in terms of the whole-life-view. Health care services should strive to achieve the state where every individual is able to achieve their full potential as human beings, and must bring about the total wellbeing of their communities.
>
> (Gee et al., 2014, p. 56)

It was this definition that was used in the first National Aboriginal Health Strategy and later in the landmark *Ways Forward National Consultancy Report on Aboriginal and Torres Strait Islander Mental Health* (Swan & Raphael, 1995), which further stipulated nine guiding principles that underpinned SEWB. Following years of advocacy by Aboriginal and Torres Strait Islander health experts, practitioners, scholars, peoples, and communities, a national action plan was developed,

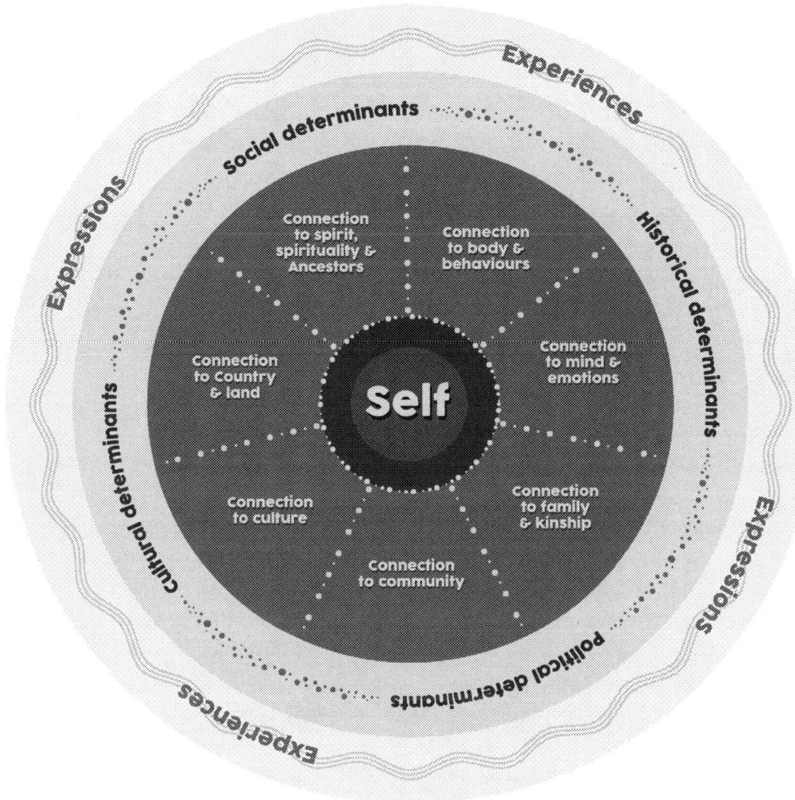

Figure 2.1 Model of SEWB (adapted by Gee et al., 2014)

known as the National Strategic Framework for Aboriginal and Torres Straits Islander People's Mental Health and Social and Emotional Well Being 2004–2009 and subsequently 2017–2023 (hereafter referred to as the 2004 and 2017 SEWB Framework, respectively; Commonwealth of Australia Department of Prime Minister and Cabinet, 2017; Social Health Reference Group, 2004).

The SEWB model articulated in 2012 and published in the seminal book chapter by Gee et al. (2014) built upon these earlier definitions and expressions of SEWB and incorporated feedback from comprehensive consultations held with Aboriginal and Torres Strait Islander communities across Australia. The final SEWB model was validated by over 300 community members (Dudgeon et al., 2025; Gee et al., 2014). Since the seminal work of Gee et al. (2014), the SEWB model has been widely researched and implemented across both placed-based and national levels throughout Australia (Dudgeon et al., 2025). Dudgeon et al. (2025) explain that the SEWB model exists alongside complementary health and wellbeing models across diverse communities in Australia and globally. Figure 2.1 illustrates the resulting SEWB model that was developed, adapted from the original Gee et al. (2014) depiction.

Domains of SEWB

Dudgeon and colleagues (2025) eloquently explain that while the domains of SEWB are presented theoretically separate, they are interrelated and interdepending, interacting with each other in dynamic ways contextual to the individual and collective experiences, expression, histories, and contexts.

> The interrelation and harmony of these connections are impacted by the diverse ways in which individuals and families experiences and express aspects of the SEWB domains according to their different needs or in response to external circumstances and determinants of health.
>
> (Dudgeon et al., 2025, p. 15)

We discuss each domain below, prefacing the importance of understanding the interconnectedness of all facets in this whole-of-life model.

Body and Behaviour

Connection to this domain refers to the physical health of a person, and the biological markers that contribute to the physical wellbeing of people, such as nutrition, illness, and disability (Dudgeon et al., 2025; Gee et al., 2014). Associated with feelings of "strong and healthy," this domain is closely linked to the physical environment and Country (including waterways, seas, skies, plants, and animals). Access to clean water, clean air, good nutrition, and physical movement within thriving eco-environments are essential. Both Indigenous knowledges, supported by contemporary research, have shown the physical health benefits of both being and caring for Country (Dudgeon et al., 2025; Taylor-Bragge et al., 2021).

Mind and Emotions

This domain is indicative of the diverse spectrum of cognitive, emotional, and psychological human experiences and basic psychological needs such as physical and cultural safety, secure and safe relationships, a sense of control and agency, connection and belongingness, emotion regulation and resilience, self-esteem and self-worth, meaning and purpose. Positive connections in mind and emotions are interlinked with other domains, such as spirituality, Country, and cultural identity. For example, engaging in cultural learning, through methods such as storytelling and yarning, fosters a positive sense of emotional wellbeing, identity formation, belongingness, and building knowledge of ways to cope, problem solve, and behave (Dudgeon et al., 2025; Gee et al., 2014).

Family and Kinship

This important domain recognises that relationships to family and kinship systems play an important role in the wellbeing and functioning of Aboriginal and Torres Strait Islander peoples' lives. Aboriginal and Torres Strait Islander peoples have multiple networks and connections surpassing time and distance. Here, family and kinship refer to building and maintaining interconnection via cultural ties, family networks, and reciprocal relationships. Harmonious kinship connections foster essential social and cultural experiences linked to a strong sense of cultural identity, belongingness, and a cultural framework for relational caregiving, roles and responsibilities within families, communities and Country. Within these intricate structures are protocols of behaviour and obligations, maintenance of lore and ceremony, and knowledge transmission (Dudgeon et al., 2025, 2022; Gee et al., 2014).

Community

Community connections are supportive of holistic Aboriginal and Torres Strait Islander wellbeing. Community is representative of collective spaces where family and kinship networks and building identity occur, and where personal connections and sociocultural ways of being develop, grow, or are maintained. Notions of community are commonly connected to place/Country, kinship, cultural and ancestral connections. However, the contemporary experience of community has evolved with the growing diversity of Aboriginal and Torres Strait Islander identities. Even within this diversity, values of relationship, reciprocity, and respect remain a common strength-based philosophy of many Aboriginal and Torres Strait Islander communities (Dudgeon et al., 2025; Gee et al., 2014).

Culture

Connecting to culture refers to Aboriginal and Torres Strait Islander peoples' opportunity and capacity to create, sustain, or re-connect with a secure and strong relationship with one's Aboriginal and/or Torres Strait Islander cultural heritage, as well as everyday cultural practices and belief systems. This is inclusive of the related knowledge systems, ways of doing, and laws that encompass that culture (Gee et al., 2014). Cultural wellbeing may include spending time on Country, establishing/maintaining relational connections, learning/maintaining language, engaging in ceremony and storytelling, day-to-day cultural practices and expressions, self-determination and leadership (Dudgeon et al., 2025). It is important to note that defining and articulating culture can be complex, and conceptualisations of culture may differ across diverse peoples and contexts.

Country and Land

Connection to Country (including land, waterways, seas, skies, plants, and animals) describes the deep relationship to an area that Aboriginal and Torres Strait Islander peoples have a spiritual, ancestral, cultural, or kinship association with. There is a deep belief that a connection to land—or place—extends far beyond physical geography. It embraces all the plants, animals, and other beings that live and grow upon it. Traditional practices boasted true sustainability for the generations to come. Food, medicine, and places for ceremonies and everyday life provided by and shared with the land were critical for survival. For many, developing and maintaining a connection with land and Country is intricately connected with spirituality, kinship, and cultural responsibilities (Gee et al., 2014). Being on Country and caring for Country is associated with positive experiences of wellbeing and identity and has been found to mitigate stressors in SEWB domains. Specific activities may include learning about/from Country, ceremonial practices, stewardship and conservation practices, activities related to traditional foods and medicines, and visiting places of importance and special meaning (Dudgeon et al., 2025).

Spirituality and Ancestors

Aboriginal and Torres Strait Islander worldviews are linked with connections to ancestors and spirituality. "Spirituality is often described as the interconnectedness between all things" (Dudgeon et al., 2025, p. 29) and encompasses all SEWB domains including the "inner being" (Smith et al., 2023) and conceptualisations of the self that is both relational and autonomous (Dudgeon et al. 2025). Spirituality includes cultural groups' knowledges passed on by ancestors which include rituals, ceremonies, stories, and other cultural practices that interconnect a person with land and place (Dudgeon et al., 2025). Everyday cultural practices shape moral practices that guide behaviour and influence personal and familial obligations, roles, and responsibilities (Gee et al., 2014). Spirituality is experienced and expressed in a diversity of ways and across a range of contexts, including contemporary Aboriginal and/or Torres Strait Islander healing practice settings, alongside or in combination with other religions, as a holistic philosophy of care ethos, and in other varied forms that peoples and communities shape (Gee et al., 2014).

Determinants of Health

Central to understanding SEWB is the broader understanding that holistic health and wellbeing are influenced by determinants of health that exist in connection to Aboriginal and Torres Strait Islander peoples and influence everyday lives. Determinants of health are referred to as the non-medical factors that influence health and wellbeing. They are the conditions in which people are born into, grow, live, work, and age, and they are the wider range of forces that continue to shape the daily life of people and communities (World Health Organisation, 2024). "Truth-telling, consciousness raising, and reconciling historical, political, social, and cultural determinants are necessary to healing and promoting SEWB" (Dudgeon et al., 2025, p. 34). These forces include historical, political, cultural, and social determinants of health, which are represented in the outer circle of the SEWB diagram (Figure 2.1), which are described in turn, below.

Historical Determinants of Health

This is referred to as the historical context of colonisation and its ongoing legacy negatively impacting the health and wellbeing of Aboriginal and Torres Strait Islander peoples. This determinant of health includes the continuing impact of historical government policies, and the impact of cultural displacement and land dispossession enforced upon Aboriginal and Torres Strait Islander peoples, families, and communities (Gee et al., 2014). The historic Bringing Them Home report (Human Rights and Equal Opportunity Commission, 1997) was the inaugural government investigation that recorded the experiences of Stolen Generations survivors and the effects of their enforced separations. According to the survivors, one of the most significant outcomes was the emphasis on truth-telling. Disappointingly, a recent report has estimated that only 6% of the 83 recommendations made in the Bringing Them Home report have been implemented by the Australian government, highlighting 28 years of "unfinished business" (Gerard & Bates-McKay, 2024)

Political Determinants of Health

In the powerfully titled report "Are you waiting for us to die," the Healing Foundation (2025) calls to light the ongoing injustice and political failings of the Australian movement to address the historical, political, and social determinants of health impacting on Aboriginal and Torres Strait Islander wellbeing. What is now considered a historical determinant of health was once a current political determinant of health, and as we can see from the Healing Foundation (2025) report, failings to address historical determinants are therefore inextricably linked to political determinants of the present. That is, political determinants of health are considered current government policies and systems, political parties in government, and other formalised political practices that impact on health and wellbeing, in both helpful and unhelpful ways. Central to political determinants of health are self-determination, Indigenous-led decision-making, access to resources, and sovereignty. A recent example in Australia's history was the Voice to Parliament referendum held on the 14th of October 2023, an opportunity to recognise Aboriginal and Torres Strait Islander peoples in the Constitution by establishing an Aboriginal and Torres Strait Islander Voice. This political determinant of health had the potential to positively impact and give voice to Aboriginal and Torres Strait Islander peoples and communities on matters affecting Aboriginal and Torres Strait Islander lives. This Referendum is now another historical determinant of health, which in the wake of the prevailing "No" vote profoundly and negatively impacted on the health and wellbeing of Aboriginal and Torres Strait Islander peoples. Denial of constitutional recognition and what this means going forward continues to impact wellbeing profoundly (Chamberlain et al., 2024).

Cultural Determinants of Health

Cultural determinants of health are strength-based determinants that position Aboriginal and Torres Strait Islander ways of knowing, being, and doing and self-determination as integral to wellness. There is significant overlap between cultural determinants of health and domains of SEWB in that the sociocultural landscape in which an individual and their family are situated can have a positive or negative influence on wellbeing. Determinants of health related to culture include the protective influences of connecting with culture, transmission of knowledge, maintenance and revival of languages, and relationship with land and Country (Bourke et al., 2018; Milroy et al., 2017; Zubrick et al., 2014). However, it also relates to Aboriginal and Torres Strait Islander leadership, self-determination, and sovereignty at local and national levels (Lowitja Institute, 2020; Salmon et al., 2019). Research has shown that cultural determinants of health are protective against psychological stress and can interrupt the transmission of transgenerational traumas across generations (Chandler & Dunlop, 2015; Chandler & Lalonde, 1998, 2008; Mia et al., 2017). Therefore, a community's capacity and empowerment "to embody and transmit cultural values, principals, practices, and traditions" (Dudgeon et al., 2025, p. 16) are imperative to wellbeing.

Social Determinants of Health

Social determinants of health refer to socioeconomic and psychosocial factors that can enable flourishing or inequities in communities in turn impacting on health and wellbeing outcomes. They include factors such as the environment that families and communities live in. This includes safe and sustainable housing, stable income and resourcing, employment and educational opportunities, access to community resources and facilitates, clean ecosystems and environments, degree of exposure to psychosocial stressors (e.g. gender equity, racism, trauma, violence, climate change), and demographic facets including gender identity, cultural background, and age (Zubrick et al., 2014). Social determinants of health are therefore closely linked to political determinants of health including decision-making and leadership in the matters that directly and indirectly impact Aboriginal and Torres Strait Islander peoples (Dudgeon et al., 2025).

Taken together, the model of SEWB articulates a culturally grounded whole-of-life perspective of health and wellbeing. This holistic perspective considers the complex local and national context in which Aboriginal and Torres Strait Islander peoples live and the many domains influencing health and wellbeing. Importantly, it is the harmony and balance of these domains, together with strength-based determinants of health that are considered to strengthen SEWB.

The SEWB model contrasts the Western biomedical view of wellbeing, the dominant discourse from which psychology is predominantly understood and practiced (Deacon, 2013; Gee et al., 2014). Biomedical models of wellbeing view health and wellbeing from a disease-deficit perspective, where mental health conditions are reduced to biological and/or psychological abnormalities that exist within a person, and wellbeing is considered the absence of illness (Goslett & Selkirk, 2023). Not only is this the antithesis of Aboriginal and Torres Strait Islander conceptualisations of wellness, but the domination of biomedical models silences the knowledges that has maintained wellness and flourishing for thousands of years (Dudgeon et al., 2023a, 2025). Furthermore, despite the intensified focus of treatment from a biomedical perspective in mental health systems, the rate of mental health or behavioural conditions has increased in the general population in recent times (Australian Bureau of Statistics, 2018). Sadly, rates of mental health conditions are even higher among Aboriginal and Torres Strait Islander peoples, and from 2013 to 2018, the rates of suicide remained two times the rate for non-Indigenous peoples (Productivity Commission for the Steering Committee for the Review of Government Service Provision, 2020). In fact, for Aboriginal

Table 2.1 Example of CSEWB Programme Schedule

Self: Introduction and storytelling Self: CSEWB framework and colonial history • Self: Individual wellbeing and developing confidence • Self & Family: Stress management and interpersonal skills • Self & Family: Importance of family and elders • Self & Family: Communication and building relationships • Parenting: Strengths of family 1—intergenerational trauma • Parenting: Strengths of family 2—child development • Community: Local and national histories and cultures • Community: Our future and self-determination • Community: Leadership and reciprocity • Review & Celebration

Note. Table adapted from Transforming Indigenous Mental Health and Wellbeing (2021)

and Torres Strait Islander peoples, the Closing the Gap target 14—aimed at moving towards zero suicides—remains unmet (Australian Institute of Health and Welfare, 2025). Aboriginal and Torres Strait Islander leaders, advocates, and health professionals have called for changes to psychology systems to recognise culturally grounded models of wellbeing, and an adequately skilled workforce, to better meet the needs of Aboriginal and Torres Strait Islander peoples (Dudgeon et al., 2017; Dudgeon & Walker, 2015; Edwige et al., 2022).

The SEWB model is a sophisticated and comprehensive framework, and when understood and utilised appropriately in policy, workforce, and practice has strong efficacy in promoting overall health and wellbeing (Dudgeon et al., 2023b, 2022; Pearson et al., 2020). Dudgeon et al. (2025) highlight in their recent narrative review "SEWB model represents a paradigm for holistic health and wellbeing, which has transformed policy and practice" (p. 7). SEWB is being implemented and embedded widely from health policy, to curricula, and to local programmes (Dudgeon et al., 2025). However, the SEWB model can be misunderstood and misused if not understood and implemented correctly. Flawed judgements and decisions can arise if practitioners do not have a comprehensive understanding of the model, its principles, and approaches. This can lead to potential ineffective interventions, policies, and outcomes. Ongoing systemic approaches to education is key to supporting the decolonisation of psychology. Decolonising psychology seeks to embed holistic, culturally grounded models of wellbeing, such as SEWB, into psychology systems, services, policy, and education. In so doing, the psychology workforce that supports service provision can better meet the needs of Aboriginal and Torres Strait Islander peoples in culturally responsive and safe ways (Dudgeon & Burgess, 2021).

Finally, there are many examples of the application and operationalising of SEWB throughout Australia. Dudgeon and colleagues (2025) provide a helpful overview that readers can explore for further learning. In the preceding and final section, we discuss one example of SEWB in practice, the *National Empowerment Project (NEP)* and the *Cultural, Social, Emotional Wellbeing Program*, to elucidate how this can happen in the systems and services that psychologists and health professionals currently work within.

Example: Embracing Indigenous Psychology and SEWB in Psychological Practice to Facilitate Cultural Safety

The NEP is an exemplary initiative of both SEWB and decolonising praxis that upholds Aboriginal and Torres Strait Islander self-determination, sovereignty, and knowledges. Spearheaded by Indigenous psychologist Professor Pat Dudgeon AM, the first NEP sets out to explore strategies for addressing the underlying causes of psychological distress and suicide risk through amplifying cultural, social, and emotional wellbeing (CSEWB) and resilience among Aboriginal and Torres Strait Islander individuals, families, and communities. Through an Aboriginal Participatory Action Research (APAR) (APAR; Dudgeon et al., 2020), the NEP engaged in extensive consultations with 11 Aboriginal communities nationwide representing a total of 457 community members and leaders (Dudgeon et al., 2014a). Community members and leaders articulated that successful approaches need strong Indigenous governance, be community-owned and led, flexible to local contexts and resources, be strength-based, culturally responsive, and encompassing of holistic wellness (Transforming Indigenous Mental Health and Wellbeing, 2021). The success of the community consultation resulted in the development of an innovative national Indigenous-led and culturally grounded programme that bolsters Aboriginal and Torres Strait Islander SEWB while simultaneously mitigating psychological distress (Dudgeon et al., 2022).

The centrality of Aboriginal and Torres Strait Islander culture and knowledges was a major recommendation of the NEP community consultations, leading to a reconceptualisation of the foundational SEWB model (Dudgeon et al., 2022; Gee et al., 2014) and proposal of the CSEWB programme (Transforming Indigenous Mental Health and Wellbeing Project, 2021). Continuing the vision of NEP, the CSEWB programme empowers Aboriginal and Torres Strait Islander communities, strengthening family and community bonds, and fostering positive cultural identity. Transformational growth is facilitated through SEWB education, nurturing robust relational and community networks, and capacity building in crucial life skills such as problem-solving, conflict resolution, effective communication, and goal setting. "Truth-telling, and connections to Country, spirituality and cultural identity are built into every aspect of the program" (Transforming Indigenous Mental Health and Wellbeing, 2021). Delivered across 12 sessions, CSEWB programme incorporates different elements of SEWB (such as connection to culture, family, community, and spirit), as well as emphasising the restoration and strengthening of the relational self, family, and community. Utilising Aboriginal and Torres Strait Islander methodologies, such as storytelling and yarning, the CSEWB programme delves into important topics such as Aboriginal and Torres Strait Islander family structures, positive parenting and bonding, and Aboriginal and Torres Strait Islander histories and stories (Dudgeon et al., 2022). See Table 2.1 for programme example. Importantly, each CSEWB programme is designed and facilitated by community researchers and leaders, ensuring it flexibly aligns with local contexts, needs, and relationships. Community empowerment, self-determination, and relationship building are key to CSEWB programme success (Mia et al., 2017; Transforming Indigenous Mental Health and Wellbeing, 2021).

The CSEWB programme has since been successfully implemented within three urban Western Australian communities (Dudgeon et al., 2022), two rural Queensland communities (Mia et al., 2017), and a women's prison pre-release centre in Western Australia (Dudgeon et al., 2024a, 2024b). The impact CSEWB programmes delivered in the urban and rural communities were measured via semi-structured interviews and culturally adapted Stores of Most Significant Change (Dudgeon et al., 2022; Mia et al., 2017). These methodologies were chosen due to the alignment with Aboriginal and Torres Strait Islander pedagogies, including APAR approach. Thematic analyses showed participants experienced greater individual and collective healing and holistic wellbeing, empowerment and resilience, family connection, cultural identity, and positive sense of selfhood (Dudgeon et al., 2022; Mia et al., 2017). The CSEWB programme delivered in the women's pre-release centre measured impact through interviews, Stores of Most Significant Change, and pre/post Kessler Psychological Distress Scale—K5 (a brief five-item measure of general psychological distress). Results indicated that while there was no significant change evidence via qualitative measures, quantitatively participants reported enhanced SEWB including overall personal growth, greater sense of self and cultural pride, greater connections with culture and kinship, greater understanding colonial history and the influence it had on their family and community, improved knowledge and skills in parenting, and increased motivation and commitment to being role models in their community (Dudgeon et al., 2024a, 2024b).

Taken together, the collective evidence of the CSEWB programme delivered in these diverse communities and contexts affirms that culturally grounded programmes based in the SEWB model and Indigenous self-determination is effective in improving wellbeing and reducing psychological distress. While the impact of the CSEWB programme is evident through individual participant experiences, it is important to also recognise its interconnectedness with the wellness of Aboriginal and Torres Strait Islander families and communities. The positive impact of the CSEWB programme is far-reaching (Dudgeon et al., 2024a, 2024b, 2022; Mia et al., 2017). This is why a core feature of the CSEWB programme is that it must be community-owned and led (consistent with APAR approach). "Community engagement and endorsement is maintained at all stages of the program" (Transforming Indigenous Mental Health and Wellbeing, 2021, p. 2). The central learning here is that the CSEWB programme is holistic and community-centred, consistent with the SEWB model outlined by Gee et al. (2014). It is not a manualised treatment programme that separates the SEWB domains, a common misconception of the model. Working collaboratively with Aboriginal and Torres Strait Islander communities in determining place-based needs, governance, engagement, and readiness is key (Transforming Indigenous Mental Health and Wellbeing, 2021).

The CSEWB programme is decolonising theory in practice that facilitates psychological wellness, empowerment, cultural reclamation, and healing for Aboriginal and Torres Strait Islander peoples. Furthermore, the foundational principles of SEWB promote experiences of cultural safety for Aboriginal and Torres Strait Islander peoples, specifically; culturally grounded and holistic, community-led and self-determined, flexible and strength-based, and informed by human rights and determinants of health. As articulated by Dudgeon and colleagues (2022), "The SEWB framework that underpins the CSEWB reclaims an Aboriginal discourse, acknowledging the role of colonisation in disrupting the mental health and wellbeing of Aboriginal and Torres Strait Islander peoples" (p. 1). The CSEWB programme demonstrates the value and innovation that Aboriginal and Torres Strait Islander ways of knowing, being, and doing bring to culturally safe psychological practice. Embracing Indigenous knowledges and SEWB in psychology can facilitate transformational change and empowerment for Aboriginal and Torres Strait Islander peoples while also disrupting the cycles of colonialism.

Conclusion

Aboriginal and Torres Strait Islander knowledges are tens of thousands of years old and hold great wisdom, strength, and connectedness to supporting holistic health and wellbeing. Yet the ongoing forces of colonialism continue to suppress and deny these vital knowledges in Australian systems and structures. These attacks maintain power differentials, racism, and settler-colonial domination that continue to cause insurmountable devastation to Aboriginal and Torres Strait Islander health and wellbeing. There are now over four decades of Indigenous-led research, policy, and advocacy articulating the imperative need to transform systems and structures to align with and privilege Aboriginal and Torres Strait Islander ontologies and epistemologies. Psychology, as the study of human behaviour, is uniquely positioned to lead this transformative challenge. By decentring Western epistemologies and embracing Indigenous knowledges—such as SEWB, which promotes Aboriginal and Torres Strait Islander wellness and cultural safety—we can forge more culturally effective pathways towards healing. As stated in the APS Apology (2016), the discipline of psychology must continue to listen more, talk less; follow more, steer less; advocate more, comply less; include more, ignore less; collaborate more, command less. The CSEWB programme described in this chapter is one example of the innovations Indigenous knowledges bring to psychology. Embracing SEWB in psychology supports cultural safety and decolonising efforts, disrupts epistemic violence in the discipline of psychology, and empowers Aboriginal and Torres Strait Islander health, wellbeing, and flourishing.

Acknowledgements

We acknowledge the sovereign custodians, Elders, and ancestors of the lands upon which chapter was written—the Noongar peoples (B.S., J.A., P.D.) and Yagara/Yugara (T.H.) peoples. We honour the strength and resilience of all Aboriginal and Torres Strait Islander peoples, and Indigenous peoples across the world. We are a collective of Indigenous academics and psychologists (B.S., Noongar; T.H., Bunuba and Jaru; P.D., Bardi), and an academic committed to the practice of allyship (J.A., Greek-Cypriot) working in the space of social and emotional wellbeing, Indigenous psychology, and decolonising practices. The authorship order of this chapter was driven by the decision-making and governance of the Indigenous authors.

Notes

1 Note on Terminology. The term Indigenous in this chapter respectfully refers to Indigenous peoples in a global or international context, unless referenced otherwise, such as when referencing Indigenous knowledges or Indigenous psychology. When referencing Indigenous peoples in an Australian context, the chapter respectfully refers to Aboriginal and Torres Strait Islander peoples. Further glossary terms can be found in Selkirk et al. (2024).

2 As defined by Australian Health Practitioner Regulation Agency (AHPRA), cultural safety is "determined by Aboriginal and Torres Strait Islander individuals, families and communities. Culturally safe practise is the ongoing critical reflection of health practitioner knowledge, skills, attitudes, practising behaviours and power differentials in delivering safe, accessible and responsive healthcare free of racism" (Australian Health Practitioner Regulation Agency 2020).

References

Australian Bureau of Statistics. (2018). *Mental health, 2017–2018 financial year*. Australian Bureau of Statistics. https://www.abs.gov.au/statistics/health/mental-health/mental-health/latest-release

Australian Health Practitioner Regulation Agency. (2020). *The national scheme's Aboriginal and Torres Strait Islander health and cultural safety strategy 2020–2025*. Australian Health Practitioner Regulation Agency. https://www.ahpra.gov.au/About-Ahpra/Aboriginal-and-Torres-Strait-Islander-Health-Strategy/health-and-cultural-safety-strategy.aspx

Australian Health Practitioner Regulation Agency. (2022). *Joint statement: Aboriginal and torres strait islander health and cultural safety at heart of national law changes* https://www.ahpra.gov.au/about-ahpra/ministerial-directives-and-communiques/national-law-amendments/joint-statement.aspx#:~:text=Cultural%20safety%20is%20determined%20by%20Aboriginal%20and%20Torres,safe%2C%20accessible%20and%20responsive%20healthcare%20free%20of%20racism.

Australian Indigenous Psychologists Association. (2021). *Background / history*. Australian Indigenous Psychologists Association. https://indigenouspsychology.com.au/about-us/#history

Australian Institute of Health and Welfare. (2025). Closing the gap targets: Key findings and implications, catalogue number IHW 294, AIHW, Australian Government. https://www.aihw.gov.au/reports/indigenous-australians/closing-the-gap-targets-key-findings-implications/contents/about

Australian Psychological Society, Reconciliation Australia, & Australian Indigenous Psychologists Association. (2012). *The Australian psychological society reconciliation action plan 2011–2014*. Australian Psychological Society. https://psychology.org.au/getmedia/7d79e559-e5ab-4d5a-b5a1-3986a433ec62/rap-booklet_final_web.pdf

Australian Psychological Society. (2016). *The APS Apology to Aboriginal and Torres Strait Islander People*. Retrieved February 15, 2021, from https://www.psychology.org.au/About-Us/who-we-are/reconciliation-and-the-APS/APS-apology

Australian Psychological Society. (2024). Aboriginal and Torres Strait Islander peoples and psychology. Australian Psychological Society. https://groups.psychology.org.au/atsipp/

Australian Psychology Accreditation Council. (2019). *Accreditation standards for psychology programs*. Australian Psychology Accreditation Council. https://apac.au/wp-content/uploads/2021/09/APAC-Accreditation-Standards_v1.2_rebranded.pdf

Bhatia, S., & Priya, K. R. (2021). Coloniality and psychology: From silencing to re-centering marginalized voices in postcolonial times. *Review of General Psychology*, *25*(4), 422–436. https://doi.org/10.1177/10892680211046507

Bourke, S., Wright, A., Guthrie, J., Russell, L., Dunbar, T., & Lovett, R. (2018). Evidence review of Indigenous culture for health and wellbeing. *International Journal of Health, Wellness & Society*, *8*(4). https://doi.org/10.18848/2156-8960/CGP/v08i04/11-27

Carey, T., Dudgeon, P., Hammond, S., Hirvonen, T., Kyrios, M., Roufeil, L., & Smith, P. (2017). The Australian Psychological Society's Apology to Aboriginal and Torres Strait Islander People. *Australian Psychologist*, *52*, 261–267. https://doi.org/10.1111/ap.12300

Chamberlain, C., Anderson, I., Fredericks, B., Calma, T., & Eades, S. (2024). Indigenous peoples' health after Australia's No vote. *British Medical Journal*, 384. https://doi.org/10.1136/bmj.q24

Chandler, M. J., & Dunlop, W. L. (2015). Cultural wounds demand cultural medicines. In M. Greenwood, S. De Leeuw, & N. M. Lindsay (Eds.), *Determinants of indigenous peoples' health: Beyond the social* (pp. 78–89). Canadian Scholars' Press.

Chandler, M. J., & Lalonde, C. (1998). Cultural continuity as a hedge against suicide in Canada's First Nations. *Transcultural Psychiatry*, *35*(2), 191–219. https://doi.org/10.1177/136346159803500202

Chandler, M. J., & Lalonde, C. E. (2008). Cultural continuity as a protective factor against suicide in First Nations youth. *Horizons*, *10*(1), 68–72.

Clark, Y., & Hirvonen, T. (2022). Decolonising Australian psychology: The influences of Aboriginal psychologists. In S. Kessi, S. Suffla, & M. Seedat (Eds.), *Decolonial enactments in community psychology* (pp. 213–233). Springer. https://doi.org/10.1007/978-3-030-75201-9_11

Commonwealth of Australia Department of Prime Minister and Cabinet. (2017). *National strategic framework for Aboriginal and Torres Strait Islander peoples' mental health and social and emotional wellbeing* 2017–2023. Commonwealth of Australia. https://www.niaa.gov.au/sites/default/files/publications/mhsewb-framework_0.pdf

Deacon, B. J. (2013). The biomedical model of mental disorder: A critical analysis of its validity, utility, and effects on psychotherapy research. *Clinical Psychology Review*, *33*(7), 846–861. https://doi.org/10.1016/j.cpr.2012.09.007

Dudgeon, P., & Bray, A. (2023). The Indigenous turn: Epistemic justice, Indigenous knowledge systems, and social and emotional well-being. In J. Ravulo, K. Olcoń, T. Dune, A. Workman, & P. Liamputtong (Eds.), *Handbook of critical whiteness* (pp. 1–19). Springer. https://doi.org/10.1007/978-981-19-1612-0_31-1

Dudgeon, P., & Burgess, Z. (2021). Healing among Indigenous people is more crucial now than ever. Here's a way forward. *The Guardian*. https://www.theguardian.com/commentisfree/2021/jul/06/healing-among-indigenous-people-is-more-crucial-now-than-ever-heres-a-way-forward

Dudgeon, P., & Walker, R. (2015). Decolonising Australian psychology: Discourses, strategies, and practice. *Journal of Social and Political Psychology*, *3*(1), 276–297. https://doi.org/10.5964/jspp.v3i1.126

Dudgeon, P., Bray, A., D'Costa, B., & Walker, R. (2017). Decolonising psychology: Validating social and emotional wellbeing. *Australian Psychologist*, *52*(4), 316–325. https://doi.org/10.1111/ap.12294

Dudgeon, P., Bray, A., Darlaston-Jones, D., & Walker, R. (2020). *Aboriginal participatory action research: An Indigenous research methodology strengthening decolonisation and social and emotional wellbeing*. Lowitja Institute. https://www.lowitja.org.au/page/services/resources/Cultural-and-social-determinants/mental-health/aboriginal-participatory-action-research-an-indigenous-research-methodology-strengthening-decolonisation-and-social-and-emotional-wellbeing

Dudgeon, P., Bray, A., & Walker, R. (2023a). Embracing the emerging Indigenous psychology of flourishing. *Nature Reviews Psychology*, *2*, 259–260. https://doi.org/10.1038/s44159-023-00176-x

Dudgeon, P., Carlin, E., & Agung-Igusti, R. (2023b). *Evaluation of the Aboriginal health council of Western Australia's ACCHS social and emotional wellbeing service model: Summary - Interim evaluation report 2023.* https://research-repository.uwa.edu.au/files/356522954/3._Summary_SEWB_Service_Model_Evaluation_Interim_Report_FINALv2.3.pdf

Dudgeon, P., Chang, E. P., Chan, J., Mascall, C., King, G., Collova, J. R., & Ryder, A. (2024a). Evaluation of the cultural, social and emotional wellbeing program with Aboriginal women in the Boronia pre-release centre for women: A mixed methods study. *Medical Journal of Australia*, *221*(1), 55–60. https://doi.org/10.5694/mja2.52354

Dudgeon, P., Cox, A., Walker, R., Scrine, C., Kelly, K., Blurton, D., Bolardaras, J., Bracknell, C., Brennan, T., Butorac, A., Charles, A., Collard, L., Duffin, W., Grogan, G., Hams, K., Hansen, C., Holland, C., Ingram, D., Mascall, C.,… Taylor, N. (2014a). *Voices of the people : The national empowerment project: National summary report 2014: Promoting cultural, social and emotional wellbeing to strengthen Aboriginal and Torres Strait Islander communities*. Commonwealth of Australia. https://healthinfonet.ecu.edu.au/key-resources/publications/28606/?title=Voices+of+the+Peoples++the+National+Empowerment+Project++national+summary+report+2014++promoting+cultural++social+and+emotional+wellbeing+to+strengthen+Aboriginal+and+Torres+Strait+Islander+communities&contenttypeid=1&contentid=28606_1

Dudgeon, P., Darlaston-Jones, D., & Alexi, J. (2021). Decolonising psychology: Why voice matters. In A. Hay (Ed.), *Griffith Review: States of Mind* (72nd ed., pp. 159–166). Griffith University. https://doi.org/10.25904/1912/4126

Dudgeon, P., Darlaston-Jones, D., Phillips, G., Newnham, K., Brideson, T., Cranney, J., Hammond, S., Harris, J., Herbert, J., Homewood, J., & Page, S. (2016a). *Australian Indigenous Psychology Education Project curriculum framework*. https://indigenouspsyched.org.au/wp-content/uploads/2021/07/Curriculum-Framework.pdf

Dudgeon, P., Darlaston-Jones, D., Phillips, G., Newnham, K., Brideson, T., Cranney, J., Hammond, S., Harris, J., Herbert, J., Homewood, J., & Page, S. (2016b). *Australian Indigenous Psychology Education Project guidelines for increasing the recruitment, Retention and Graduation of Aboriginal and Torres Strait Islander Psychology Students*. University of Western Australia. https://indigenouspsyched.org.au/wp-content/uploads/2021/07/RRG-Guidelines.pdf

Dudgeon, P., Derry, K. L., Mascall, C., & Ryder, A. (2022). Understanding Aboriginal models of selfhood: The national empowerment project's cultural, social, and emotional wellbeing program in Western Australia. *International Journal of Environmental Research and Public Health*, *19*(7), 4078. https://www.mdpi.com/1660-4601/19/7/4078

Dudgeon, P., Gibson, C., Walker, R., Bray, A., Agung-Igusti, R., Derry, K., Gray, P., McPhee, R., Sutherland, S., & Gee, G. (2025). *Social and emotional wellbeing: A review*. Lowitja Institute. https://www.lowitja.org.au/wp-content/uploads/2025/02/SocialandEmotionalWellbeing_aReview.pdf

Dudgeon, P., Harris, J., Newnham, K., Brideson, T., Cranney, J., Darlaston-Jones, D., Hammond, S., Herbert, J., Homewood, J., Page, S., & Phillips, G. (2016c). *Australian Indigenous Psychology Education Project workforce capabilities framework*. University of Western Australia. https://indigenouspsyched.org.au/wp-content/uploads/2021/07/Workforce-Framework.pdf

Dudgeon, P., King, G., Millson, C., Collova, J., Mascall, C., & Chan, J. (2024b). *I will no longer starve my spirit or my soul: A mixed methods evaluation of the long-term benefits of the culture, social, and emotional wellbeing program in a pre-release centre in Western Australia.* University of Western Australia. https://cbpatsisp.com.au/wp-content/uploads/2024/12/I-Will-No-Longer-Starve-My-Spirit-Or-My-Soul.pdf

Dudgeon, P., Rickwood, D., Garvey, D., & Gridley, H. (2014b). A history of Indigenous Psychology. In P. Dudgeon, H. Milroy, & R. Walker (Eds.), *Working together: Aboriginal and Torres Strait Islander mental health and wellbeing principles and practice* (pp. 39–54). Commonwealth of Australia.

Dudgeon, P., Wright, M., Paradies, Y., Garvey, D., & Walker, I. (2014c). Aboriginal social, cultural and historical contexts. In P. Dudgeon, H. Milroy, & R. Walker (Eds.), *Working together: Aboriginal and Torres Strait Islander mental health and wellbeing principles and practice* (pp. 3–24). Commonwealth of Australia.

Dudgeon, P. (2021). Decolonising psychology: Self-determination and social and emotional wellbeing. In B. Hokowhitu, A. Moreton-Robinson, L. Tuhiwai-Smith, C. Andersen, & S. Larkin (Eds.), *The Routledge handbook of critical Indigenous studies* (1st ed., pp. 100–113). Routledge.

Edwige, V., Alexi, J., Selkirk, B., & Dudgeon, P. (2022). Australia needs to decolonise its mental health system and empower more Indigenous psychologists. *The Guardian*. https://www.theguardian.com/commentisfree/2022/jun/02/australia-needs-to-decolonise-its-mental-health-system-and-empower-more-indigenous-psychologists

Fish, J., Ansloos, J., O'Keefe, V. M., & Gone, J. (2023). Truth and reconciliation for whom? Transitional justice for Indigenous peoples in psychology. *American Psychologist, 79*(4), 618–630. https://doi.org/10.1037/amp0001234

Fish, J., & Gone, J. P. (2024). Beyond decolonization: Anticolonial methodologies for Indigenous futurity in psychological research. In L. Comas-Díaz, H. Y. Adames, & N. Y. Chavez-Dueñas (Eds.), *Decolonial psychology: Toward anticolonial theories, research, training, and practice* (pp. 119–141). American Psychological Association. https://doi.org/10.1037/0000376-006

Gee, G., Dudgeon, P., Schultz, C., Hart, A., & Kelly, K. (2014). Aboriginal and Torres Strait Islander Social and Emotional Wellbeing. In P. Dudgeon, H. Milroy, & R. Walker (Eds.), *Working together: Aboriginal and Torres Strait Islander mental health and wellbeing principles and practice* (pp. 55–68). Commonwealth of Australia.

Gerard, A., & Bates-McKay, M. (2024). *Discussion paper on the unfinished business of the Bringing them home report* Healing Foundation. https://cdn.healingfoundation.org.au/app/uploads/2025/02/11122618/THF_BTH_Discussion_Paper.pdf

Goslett, M., & Selkirk, B. (2023, September 11–15). *Wangi wadhan biyay (Baskets of Listening and Respect)* [Conference Presentation]. Healing Our Spirits Worldwide Conference, Vancouver, British Columbia, Canada.

Healing Foundation. (2021). *Make healing happen: It's time to act.* Healing Foundation. https://apo.org.au/sites/default/files/resource-files/2021-06/apo-nid312583.pdf

Healing Foundation. (2025). *'Are you waiting for us to die?' The unfinished business of bringing them home.* Healing Foundation. https://cdn.healingfoundation.org.au/app/uploads/2025/02/11171935/BTH_Report_Are-you-waiting-for-us-to-Die-Final-2025-1.pdf

Human Rights and Equal Opportunity Commission. (1997). B*ringing them home: Report of the national Inquiry into the separation of aboriginal and torres strait islander children.* Human Rights and Equal Opportunity Commission. https://humanrights.gov.au/our-work/bringing-them-home-report-1997

Lowitja Institute (2020). *Culture is key: Towards cultural determinants-driven health policy – Final Report.* https://www.lowitja.org.au/wp-content/uploads/2023/06/Lowitja_CultDetReport_210421_D14_WEB.pdf

Mia, T., Dudgeon, P., Mascall, C., Grogan, G., Murray, B., & Walker, R. (2017). An evaluation of the national empowerment project cultural, social, and emotional wellbeing program. *Journal of Indigenous Wellbeing*, *2*(2), 33–48. https://journalindigenouswellbeing.co.nz/media/2024/05/An-Evaluation-of-the-National-Empowerment-Project-Cultural-Social-and-Emotional-Wellbeing-Program.pdf

Milroy, J., Dudgeon, P., Cox, A., Georgatos, G., Bray, A., & Luxford, Y. (2017). What the people said: Findings from the regional roundtables of the Aboriginal and Torres Strait Islander suicide prevention evaluation project. *Journal of Indigenous Wellbeing*, *2*(1), 16–32. https://journalindigenouswellbeing.co.nz/media/2024/05/What-the-people-said-Findings-from-the-regional-Roundtables-of-the-Aboriginal-and-Torres-Strait-Islander-Suicide-Prevention-Evaluation-Project.pdf

Moreton-Robinson, A. (2015). *The white possessive: Property, power, and Indigenous sovereignty.* University of Minnesota Press.

Pearson, O., Schwartzkopff, K., Dawson, A., Hagger, C., Karagi, A., Davy, C., Brown, A., & Braunack-Mayer, A. (2020). Aboriginal community controlled health organisations address health equity through action on the social determinants of health of Aboriginal and Torres Strait Islander peoples in Australia. *BMC Public Health*, *20*(1), 1859–1859. https://doi.org/10.1186/s12889-020-09943-4

Productivity Commission for the Steering Committee for the Review of Government Service Provision. (2020). *Overcoming Indigenous disadvantage key indicators 2020 overview.* Commonwealth of Australia. https://apo.org.au/sites/default/files/resource-files/2020-12/apo-nid309865.pdf

Psychology Board of Australia. (2024a). *Professional competencies for psychologists.* Australian Health Practitioner Regulation Agency. https://www.psychologyboard.gov.au/Standards-and-Guidelines/Professional-practice-standards/Professional-competencies-for-psychology.aspx

Psychology Board of Australia. (2024b). *Code of conduct. Australian health practitioner regulation agency.* Psychology Board, AHPRA. https://www.psychologyboard.gov.au/Standards-and-Guidelines/Professional-practice-standards/Code-of-conduct.aspx#

Readsura Decolonial Editorial Collective, Ratele, K., Reddy, G., Adams, G., & Suffla, S. (2022). Decoloniality as a social issue for psychological study. Journal of Social Issues, *78*, 7–26. https://doi.org/10.1111/josi.12502

Salmon, M., Doery, K., Dance, P., Chapman, J., Gilbert, R., Williams, R., & Lovett, R. (2019). *Defining the indefinable: Descriptors of Aboriginal and Torres Strait Islander peoples' cultures and their links to health and wellbeing.* Lowitja Institute and Mayi Kuwayu Study. https://www.lowitja.org.au/wp-content/uploads/2023/05/Defining_Indefinable_report_FINAL_WEB.pdf

Selkirk, B., Alexi, J., Hirvonen, T., Goslett, M., Ohan, J., & Edwige, V. (2024). *Listening more: Embedding cultural safety in supervision. A guide for psychology supervisors.* The University of Western Australia. https://doi.org/10.26182/6kc9-em03

Selkirk, B., Gibson, C., Dudgeon, P., & Alexi, J. (in press). Decolonising psychology education in Australia through the Australian Indigenous Psychology education project. *American Psychologist.* https://doi.org/10.1037/amp000149

Smith, S., O'Grady, L., Cubillo, C., & Cavanagh, S. (2017). Using culturally appropriate approaches to the development of KidsMatter resources to support the social and emotional wellbeing of Aboriginal children. *Australian Psychologist*, *52*(4), 299–305. https://doi.org/10.1111/ap.12284

Smith, P. (Kamilaroi), Rice, K., Schutte, N., & Usher, K. (2023). Healing through meaning as an aspect of spirituality for Indigenous Australians: A qualitative study. *AlterNative: An International Journal of Indigenous Peoples*, *198*(3), 626–634. https://doi.org/10.1177/11771801231193169

Social Health Reference Group. (2004). *National strategic framework for aboriginal and Torres Strait Islander peoples' mental health and social and emotional wellbeing* 2004–2009. Australian Department of Health and Ageing. https://healthinfonet.ecu.edu.au/key-resources/policies-and-strategies/2940/?title=Social+and+emotional+well+being+framework++a+national+strategic+framework+for+Aboriginal+and+Torres+Strait+Islander+mental+health+and+social+and+emotional+well+being+2004+2009&contenttypeid=1&contentid=2940_1

Summerton, J., & Blunden, S. (2022). Cultural interventions that target mental health and wellbeing for First Nations Australians: A systematic review. *Australian Psychologist*, *57*(6), 315–331. https://doi.org/10.1080/00050067.2022.2130026

Swan, P., & Raphael, B. (1995). *Ways forward: National consultancy report on aboriginal and torres strait islander mental health.* Commonwealth of Australia. https://library.bsl.org.au/jspui/bitstream/123456789/353/1/Ways%20forward_vol.1%20&%202%20_1995.pdf

Taylor-Bragge, R. L., Whyman, T., & Jobson, L. (2021). 'People needs country: The symbiotic effects of landcare and wellbeing for Aboriginal peoples and their countries'. *Australian Psychologist*, 56(6), 458–471. https://doi.org/10.1080/00050067.2021.1983756

Transforming Indigenous Mental Health and Wellbeing Project. (2021). *The national empowerment project (NEP): Cultural, social and emotional wellbeing (CSEWB) program.* University of Western Australia. https://doi.org./10.5281/zenodo.10042911

Watego, C., Singh, D., & Macoun, A. (2021). *Partnership for justice in health: Scoping paper on race, racism and the Australian health system.* Lowitja Institute. https://www.lowitja.org.au/wp-content/uploads/2023/05/Lowitja_PJH_170521_D10-1.pdf

World Health Organisation. (2024). *Social determinants of health.* World Health Organisation. https://www.who.int/health-topics/social-determinants-of-health#tab=tab_1

Zubrick, S., Shepherd, C., Dudgeon, P., Gee, G., Paradies, Y., Scrine, C., & Walker, R. (2014). Social determinants of social and emotional wellbeing. In P. Dudgeon, H. Milroy, & R. Walker (Eds.), *Working together: Aboriginal and Torres Strait Islander mental health and wellbeing principles and practice* (pp. 93–107). Commonwealth of Australia.

3 Decolonizing Psychology Education in the Indonesian Context

Toward a Socio-Historically Engaged Pedagogy

Monica E. Madyaningrum and Albertus Harimurti

Introduction

In this chapter, we aim to discuss our experiences as educators at a university in Indonesia, which increasingly feel socio-historically alienating and mechanistically standardized under the dominant neoliberal orientation. Specifically, we will reflect on our experiences through a decolonial lens, situating the current state of Indonesian universities in relation to the ongoing reproduction of colonial logics that shape the approach to higher education in the country.

We argue that the diminishing role of universities in Indonesia as a foundation for critical voices and solidarity results from a historical disconnection that has marginalized the thoughts of Indonesian educational philosophers. Historically, these thinkers played a crucial role in developing educational models that fostered solidarity and resistance against injustices and oppressions, especially during the colonial era. By drawing insights from these philosophers, we contend that decoloniality in the context of higher education in Indonesia involves intentional endeavours to resist alienating education—education that disconnects universities from their societies, reinforces existing social hierarchies, marginalizes the underprivileged, and discourages learners from questioning and engaging with societal issues.

In doing so, we will engage in an archival retrieval of the works of notable Indonesian philosophers, educators, and social activists—such as Driyarkara (1913–1967) and Mangunwijaya (1929–1999)—who are recognized for their contributions to education, knowledge sovereignty, and humanity. Both figures were instrumental in the history of Indonesian education and developed their philosophies within the broader context of the anti-colonial movement. Their key ideas emphasize education as a humanizing pathway toward compassion-based solidarity and dignified humanity, reflected in Indonesian concepts such as *belarasa* and *kesetiakawanan*. Additionally, we will describe how we have put our commitment to resisting alienating education into practice through our newly established postgraduate programme in critical psychology.

A Brief Description of Indonesian Higher Education under Neoliberal Climate

To provide context for our chapter, we will begin by briefly describing the current climate of higher education in Indonesia, which frames our daily experience as educators. Specifically, we will outline the prevailing trends in and critiques to higher education under a neoliberal framework, a situation not unique to Indonesia, as similar patterns are observed globally (e.g., Bottrell & Manathunga, 2018; Manathunga & Bottrell, 2018; Shin, 2018). In this section, we will illustrate how these global trends have been transformed into national policies and practices within the Indonesian higher education context.

Critiques of the neoliberalization of higher education in Indonesia have become a focal point for several scholars (e.g., Mulya, 2016; Rosser, 2015; Sakhiyya & Mulya, 2023; Sunendar & Andriany,

DOI: 10.4324/9781003492214-4

2023). Grounded in a general understanding of neoliberalism as an economic and political ideology emphasizing free markets, privatization, and minimal government intervention, these scholars view the neoliberalization of higher education in Indonesia as a trend toward operating universities as market-driven businesses, with various consequences. These consequences include the commodification of higher education, where the value of academic activities is determined primarily by their market worth (Sunendar & Andriany, 2023); a shift toward vocationalizing education, with universities positioned mainly as professional training centres to meet labour market demands (Subkhan, 2023); and increased demands for self-sustaining funding sources due to reductions in public funding, often resulting in higher tuition fees at many institutions. As a result, higher education increasingly becomes an elitist space that normalizes injustices, further disconnected from the concerns of ordinary people, especially those disadvantaged by the market-driven economy and politics (Rakhmani & Sakhiyya, 2024).

Over the past five years, criticisms regarding the neoliberalization of higher education in Indonesia have intensified through the implementation of the *Merdeka Belajar—Kampus Merdeka* (Independent Learning—Independent Campus) policy, or popularly abbreviated as MBKM (see for example, Rakhmani, 2024). Launched by the Indonesian Ministry of Education, Culture, Research, and Technology in early 2020, MBKM serves as a national framework for educational governance from primary to higher education. As its name suggests, this policy is grounded in the ideal of independent learning, emphasizing students' autonomy and their right to pursue learning experiences that align with their interests and potential, whether acquired through on or off-campus learning experiences (Direktorat Jenderal Pendidikan Tinggi, 2020).

This policy is implemented through various regulations, including those that give students the flexibility to design their learning pathways, such as provisions for undertaking cross-programme study, inter-university learning, and off-campus working experiences that can be converted into academic credits. This flexibility is seen as a significant breakthrough of the MBKM policy, as it is believed to break down barriers between disciplines, institutions, and even between campus and the broader society. Such a learning model is thought to produce graduates with a broad mindset, unconfined by narrow disciplinary boundaries, enabling them to address societal issues that are often multidimensional and cannot be approached from a single academic perspective. Through this educational model, it is hoped that learning on campus will become increasingly well-connected to real-world issues, preventing universities from becoming ivory towers disconnected from their societies (Direktorat Jenderal Pendidikan Tinggi, 2020).

While envisioned as an innovative policy to make higher education in Indonesia more responsive to societal needs and challenges, the implementation of MBKM poses a risk of further alienating the higher education sector from the community, particularly marginalized groups in the Indonesian society. Such risks are heightened because this educational framework primarily emphasizes building connections between universities and *Dunia Usaha—Dunia Industri* (the business and industrial sectors). This orientation toward industry and the business world is institutionalized through several programmes including annual competitive research funding schemes offered by the ministry for projects involving collaboration between universities and industry. Additionally, student allowances are provided for those participating in internships within the business sector. Furthermore, the number of collaborations between universities and industry has been formalized as a key indicator for assessing the quality of performance of higher education institutions (Direktorat Jenderal Pendidikan Tinggi, 2020).

In such a climate, the idea of universities as places for fostering a culture of knowledge that supports the marginalized and oppressed in society is increasingly sidelined. Underpinning the MBKM framework is a developmentalist perspective that assumes the quality of life for all, including the most disadvantaged groups, will improve as a nation's economy becomes stronger and more competitive on a global scale through business and industrial innovations. Consequently, from the MBKM viewpoint, discussions about disadvantaged groups tend to focus on how universities can assist these groups in acquiring knowledge and skills to enhance their economic competitiveness. In other words, the role of universities is to help the disadvantaged adjust better to the existing system, despite the fact that this system is the very cause of their disadvantages due to its unjust and exploitative nature.

As a result, the understanding of universities' ethical responsibility to stand in solidarity with the disadvantaged—challenging and striving to change the unjust economic and political systems—remains largely unexplored in higher education. On the other hand, the history of the birth of Indonesia as an independent nation highlights the significant role played by indigenous thinkers and educational philosophers on the ethical responsibilities of education institutions toward its nation. Their ideas on education, particularly higher education, emphasized the importance of educational institutions as spaces where national solidarity is built to resist colonial injustices through solidarity with the oppressed and marginalized. However, these philosophies have increasingly faded from the landscape of higher education in Indonesia. This irony serves as the starting point of our chapter, in which we argue that one consequence of neoliberalism in higher education in Indonesia is the disconnection between contemporary educational practices and the teachings of indigenous educational philosophers, who emphasized the critical role of education in fostering solidarity and resistance against social injustices. With this argument, therefore, we view the relevance of situating our argument within a broader discussion of decoloniality.

The Role of Education in Fostering Solidarity and Resistance against Social Injustices: Learning from Indonesian Educational Philosophers

The birth of Indonesia as a nation capable of liberating itself from centuries of colonization cannot be separated from the significant contributions of indigenous educational thinkers and philosophers, whose ideas have shaped the spirit of resistance against colonialism. One of their most important contributions is their role in creating liberating educational approaches that are rooted in and responsive to local historical and cultural contexts, while also emphasizing the ethical responsibilities of education toward the marginalized and oppressed in society. Given the limited space available, this chapter will specifically examine the thoughts of two figures, Driyarkara (1913–1967) and Mangunwijaya (1929–1999), as both were key figures in the history and development of the university where the authors currently work.

Driyarkara: Hominisasi, Humanisasi, and Belarasa

Prof. Dr. N. Driyarkara, S. J., was born on June 13, 1913, during the early period of anti-colonial movements in the Dutch East Indies. His birth era coincided with the implementation of the Ethical Policy by the Dutch Colonial Government, a policy enacted as a moral responsibility toward the colonized society. Like many educated individuals of his time, Djentoe—Driyarkara's birth name—began his education at Sekolah Rakjat (colonial public school) in 1919, later continuing to the Hollandsch Inlandsche School (HIS) on December 22, 1925. After graduating from HIS, Driyarkara moved to Malang, East Java, Indonesia where his encounter with Jesuit priests inspired him to join the Society of Jesus.

Driyarkara subsequently moved to Yogyakarta to attend a middle-level seminary equivalent to junior high school. A few years later, on September 7, 1935, he officially became a member of the Society of Jesus and pursued further studies at Girisonta, Semarang, Central Java, Indonesia. After completing his theological and philosophical education, Driyarkara was ordained as a Jesuit priest on January 6, 1947, by Bishop Albertus Soegijapranata, S. J., at St. Joseph's Church, Gedangan, Semarang, Central Java, Indonesia. A few months later, amid the turmoil of Indonesia's independence and the *Operation Kraai* (1947–1949), Driyarkara was assigned to continue his theological studies in Maastricht, the Netherlands.

Driyarkara returned to Indonesia in 1952. In 1955, the Society of Jesus appointed him as the head of a teachers' college known as *Perguruan Tinggi Pendidikan Guru* Sanata Dharma, which later became *Institut Keguruan Ilmu Pendidikan* Sanata Dharma (IKIP Sanata Dharma; Institute of Teacher Training and Education). These years also marked the establishment of psychology faculties in Indonesian universities. At the time, Slamet Iman Santoso, recognized as the Father of Indonesian Psychology, initiated the founding of the Faculty of Psychology at the University of Indonesia in Jakarta (Dahlan et al., 2007). Concurrently, Kurt Danziger was assisting in establishing a psychology programme at the Faculty of Pedagogy at Gadjah Mada University in Yogyakarta (Danziger, 2009). In 1960, Driyarkara was awarded the title of professor by the Faculty of Psychology at the University of Indonesia. During the 1960s, alongside Slamet Iman Santoso and Fuad Hassan, other prominent figures in Indonesian psychology, Driyarkara conceptualized a higher education institution for philosophy, which was inaugurated in 1969—two years after his death—under the name Sekolah Tinggi Filsafat Driyarkara (Driyarkara School of Philosophy), located in Jakarta.

There is no doubt that Driyarkara's contributions to education and pedagogy, philosophy, theology, and psychology had a significant impact on Indonesia. One of the key concepts that emerged from the ecosystem cultivated by Driyarkara—rooted in Jesuit values—was *belarasa*. This term is derived from one of the four principles of Jesuit education: *kompeten* (competence), *berhatinurani* (conscience), *belarasa* (compassion), and *komitmen* (commitment). Of these, the translation most imbued with Indonesian-Javanese thinking is *belarasa*, which is the Indonesian adaptation of the word "compassion." In Indonesian, *belarasa* is a neologism formed from *bela* (which in English means "to care for" or "to nurture") and *rasa* (which can be translated as "sense," "thought," "feeling," "sensation," or "intuition"). In Javanese terminology—the mother tongue of Driyarkara—the concept of *rasa* carries mystical complexity. The Javanese often refer to *rasa* as a form of intuitive logic or a kind of inner feeling (a communication of the heart). Meanwhile, in Indonesian, *rasa* can encompass both physical and emotional senses. In Javanese mystical logic, *rasa* serves as a tool for grasping the truth of the inner world (Stange, 2007).

Driyarkara's years of study in Europe coincided with the rising prominence of existential philosophy. This tradition of existentialist thought was later developed by Driyarkara in formulating his philosophy of education, which became the foundation for both IKIP Sanata Dharma and the Driyarkara School of Philosophy. Driyarkara (1961/2006) viewed education as an existential problem—a mode of human existence in the world. He often cited Heidegger and Merleau-Ponty in his educational writings. According to Driyarkara, education is a process of enculturation or a means of cultural development through living together. Thus, the aspect of collective life becomes a relevant context for Indonesian culture. For Driyarkara, the notion of the "I" is only meaningful within the context of the "We." He asserted that:

> If humans must humanize themselves, and this means becoming cultured, then by necessity they must also cultivate together because our mode of existence is inseparable from co-existence. Thus, culture cannot be something for oneself alone. Therefore, culture is socio-culture.
>
> (Driyarkara, 1961/2006, p. 279)

Since education is a socio-cultural process, the element of social concern or solidarity becomes crucial. Driyarkara, the ecosystem he established, and his successors emphasized this element in the concept of *belarasa*. Sunarko (2020) highlights that in the term compassion is the word "passion," which refers to "suffering." This indicates that compassion is closely related to those who suffer. However, as Sunarko explains:

> Compassion or *belarasa* is not merely a feeling of pity towards someone who is suffering. A person with *belarasa* does not turn a blind eye to the reality of suffering experienced by others around them. They allow their life to be intervened by the suffering of others. More than just pity, the word *belarasa* carries an active movement, a duty to be open, to perceive others' suffering, to express it (when necessary), to show tangible solidarity, and to take concrete actions to alleviate the suffering.
>
> (Sunarko, 2020, p. 47)

Referring to the above, for Driyarkara, education is not merely about developing competence but also about humanizing individuals, which he termed *hominisasi* (the process of becoming human) and *humanisasi* (the higher development of humanity). According to Driyarkara, humans are not merely biological beings but also persons, subjects who are capable of understanding themselves, positioning themselves within their circumstances, making decisions, and determining their own course. However, this personal growth does not occur in isolation; through education, individuals "must also grow as members of society. They must grow within and from the circumstances they experience" (Driyarkara, 1961/2006, p. 433). This sense of responsibility and role as members of society necessitates that individuals continually learn about *belarasa*. Only through the encounter between the learner and their community can the questions about what attitudes and actions are needed truly emerge.

Mangunwijaya: Pemerdekaan and Kesetiakawanan

Y. B. Mangunwijaya, Pr., commonly known as Romo Mangun, was born on May 6, 1929, in Ambarawa, Central Java, Indonesia. In addition to being a Catholic priest, Mangunwijaya was renowned as an architect, lecturer, activist, writer, literary figure, and cultural thinker—though he personally refused to be called a cultural figure, which was ascribed to him by others. Around 1993, Mangunwijaya established the Mangunan Experimental Elementary School in Mangunan, Kalitirto, Berbah, Sleman, Yogyakarta, as an embodiment of his commitment to the poor. According to Mangunwijaya, emancipation for the poor at that time needed to focus on primary education.

Throughout his life, particularly in his reflections, Mangunwijaya (2020) observed the contrasts between his youth and the era he faced in the 1990s. He critically noted that the education system of the time, particularly at the primary level, suppressed children's exploration and creativity. He argued that teachers had transformed into instructors, bureaucratic administrators, commanders, or handlers, reducing students to "little political cadres." Mangunwijaya emphasized that the true purpose of education should be to

> guide and assist students in recognizing and developing their potential so that they can become independent, mature, and whole individuals;... free human beings who are also concerned with and in solidarity with others, striving to achieve an increasingly genuine humanity, with an increasingly whole, harmonious, and integrated self-identity and self-image.

Mangunwijaya documented his ideas on primary education—including his vision, comprehensive understanding, teaching methods, pedagogy, and more—through his daily journals, which were later compiled into a book by his colleagues and students. His colleagues noted that Mangunwijaya had a strong oral tradition, and thus, many aspects of the indigenization he practiced were transmitted through everyday interactions.

In several of his writings, Mangunwijaya emphasized solidarity with the poor. However, according to his close colleagues, the term he often used in speech was "setia kawan" (Mulyatno, 2020; C. B. Mulyatno, personal communication, October 7, 2024). The use of this phrase was not trivial; it was an effort to indigenize the term to make it more accessible to the social class he aimed to uplift. Mangunwijaya used "setia kawan" in the context of Indonesia's diversity. He preferred terms that resonated with the Indonesian people. In the tradition of Liberation Theology and activism, the term "solidarity" is commonly used. Meanwhile, the literal translation of "setia kawan" into English is "loyalty to friends." The term "kawan" (friend) reflects his attempt to localize the spirit of solidarity within the framework of social concern.

Another term he employed was "pemerdekaan" (liberation). Unlike Liberation Theology, which uses the term "liberation," Mangunwijaya preferred "pemerdekaan," which he felt was more grounded in Indonesian thought. According to Mangunwijaya (1996/1999), "the term liberation often carries liberal connotations or, worse, suggests a *semau gue* (self-serving attitude)." Thus, he opted for "pemerdekaan," which referred to liberating humanity from all forms of bondage, whether it be ignorance, injustice, falsehood, physical limitations, disease, natural dangers, colonialism, or human exploitation.

Although Mangunwijaya's ideas and movements may seem to convey Marxist overtones, he was cautious in explicitly referencing Karl Marx. One could be anti-capitalist, anti-colonialist, and anti-imperialist without being Marxist. This stance was understandable in Indonesia, where Marxist teachings and ideas were banned after the genocide of the suspected communist in 1965 (Herlambang, 2013; Wahid, 2018; Wieringa & Katjasungkana, 2019). Mangunwijaya (2020) wrote that he deliberately changed the name of his foundation from "Gerakan Edukasi Dasar" (Elementary Education Movement) to "Dinamika Edukasi Dasar" (DED) (Dynamic Elementary Education). He explained that "the term 'movement' was uncomfortable for many people…" Mangunwijaya believed that the term "dynamic" was more appropriate, even though DED was indeed intended as "a movement, a collaboration within a network of communication and mutual support among many individuals, experts, institutions, and schools that shared the same goals and ideals. In other words: a dialogue." Despite this, Mangunwijaya continued to use Marxist-influenced terminology, particularly from Liberation Theology, such as conscientization.

Decolonizing Higher Education: Lessons from Driyarkara and Mangunwijaya on Social Responsibility

Analysing the brief biographies of Driyarkara and Mangunwijaya reveals that both thinkers addressed general educational philosophy rather than specifically focusing on higher education. However, as part of his Jesuit mission, Driyarkara was later tasked with initiating a higher education institute. Despite this, their ideas on education remain highly relevant for examining contemporary issues in higher education, particularly concerning models of education that: (1) disconnect learners from the socio-historical contexts in which they live, (2) perpetuate social inequality and injustice, and (3) discourage learners from engaging with societal issues.

From the wealth of ideas articulated by Driyarkara and the educational ecosystem he helped develop, alongside Mangunwijaya's contributions, we highlight the concepts of *belarasa* (compassion) and *kesetiakawanan* (solidarity) as essential to addressing current challenges in higher education. These concepts foreground the social responsibility of education—what Driyarkara termed "social ethics"—as an antithesis to the neoliberal ethos characterizing the current "Merdeka Belajar" era. While neoliberal ethics prioritize the "self-governed nuclearized personhood" (i.e., the mentality of an individual who perceives themselves as solely responsible for their own success and failure), social ethics emphasize the "political agency" of learners, encapsulated in the oft-repeated notion of youth as agents of social change.

Engaging with Driyarkara's and Mangunwijaya's ideas does not imply an uncritical acceptance of their philosophies, particularly within the framework of decoloniality. Acknowledging their roles as Catholic priests—a position tied to the historical processes of colonization, including the marginalization of local belief systems through Christianization—requires grappling with a "contradictio in terminis." Furthermore, their intellectual trajectories emerged from an educational system that positioned Eurocentric ethics and epistemologies as superior to precolonial traditions in the archipelago.

Nevertheless, despite the problematic origins of their intellectual frameworks from a decolonial perspective, Indonesian history records their significant contributions as public intellectuals whose ideas inspired intellectual, social, and political movements opposing the very injustices targeted by decolonial movements: social inequities, imposed hierarchies of being, oppression, victim-blaming ideologies, and historical and political alienation.

This irony resonates with our own daily experiences as educators in Indonesian higher education today. Living the spirit of decolonization requires navigating and negotiating multiple tensions and contradictions, often with imperfect outcomes. We acknowledge that we are sometimes complicit in paradoxes and inconsistencies. Learning from Driyarkara and Mangunwijaya, however, these contradictions do not necessarily preclude advocacy for change and social movements. For instance, while Driyarkara and Mangunwijaya represented a hegemonic institution—the Catholic Church—they used religious values to advocate for solidarity and resistance against injustice. A notable example is Mangunwijaya's activism as a leader of a hunger strike alongside displaced farmers whose land was expropriated by the government for dam construction. This reflects Indonesia's commonalities with social resistance movements elsewhere, such as the transformative role of religion in liberation theology in Latin America.

Grounded in Driyarkara's and Mangunwijaya's reflections on the social responsibility of education, as embodied in the principles of *belarasa* and *kesetiakawanan*, the following discussion will focus on their relevance to psychology education in Indonesia. Specifically, we will examine aspects of psychology education in Indonesia that have, directly or indirectly, contributed to the marginalization of the idea of social responsibility in higher education.

Psychology, Orientation toward Egocentric Self, and the Fading of Social Justice as an Ethical Orientation

The literature on decolonial psychology has extensively examined how psychology, both as a discipline and as a practice, contributes to the reproduction of colonialism. One prominent way this occurs is through the imposition of assumptions regarding the universal applicability of Western psychological theories, including their conceptualization of the self. Key markers of personhood in Western societies, such as individualism, personal autonomy, and achievement, are often positioned as universally relevant, regardless of cultural contexts (Adams et al., 2018; Pickren, 2020).

In the context of psychology education in Indonesia, this tendency is manifested in the canonization of Western theories of personhood within the curriculum. This process not only marginalizes local conceptualizations of personhood—an issue that has recently been challenged by the development of indigenous psychology in Indonesia—but also mainstreams the construction of selfhood according to Western paradigms. These paradigms are typically characterized by an egocentric understanding of the self, which stands in contrast to the relational and communal perspectives more prevalent in many non-Western societies.

We draw on the term egocentric self from Kirmayer (2007) to describe the tendency within psychology to position individualism as a central marker of how personhood is defined and experienced. This tendency has been disseminated through the imposition of Western psychological theories and psychotherapeutic practices as the primary standards to emulate. With its orientation toward the egocentric self, psychology often frames individuals as isolated and independent entities, primarily defined by their personal histories and achievements. Discussions of individuals tend to emphasize personal attributes—such as traits, behaviours, and internal processes—as the primary determinants of their experiences, while overlooking the significant influence of relational, communal, and cultural contexts.

Reflecting on our own experiences as psychology students and later as educators, we contend that this tendency contributes to psychology students' lack of sensitivity to the historical, social, cultural, and political structures that profoundly shape how individuals construct their identities and experience the world. Furthermore, psychology students often lose their critical capacity to recognize that the theories they learn in academia are products of specific historical and cultural contexts. As a result, these theories may not always be relevant for understanding and explaining how individuals conceptualize and experience personhood within their own societies.

For example, through developmental theories conceptualized by scholars from Western societies, psychology students in Indonesia have become highly familiar with the concept of adolescence as an in-between phase from childhood to adulthood. In this transitional stage, individuals in their teenage years or early twenties are often depicted as "in the making," preoccupied primarily with themselves and their narrow social worlds (e.g., peers). Consequently, they are generally seen as lacking the capacity to assume broader social roles and responsibilities.

In contrast, studies from history, anthropology, and oral traditions in Indonesian society (see, for example, Anderson, 2006) suggest that the conceptualization of adolescence as an in-between phase—characterized predominantly by immaturity—is not historically rooted in the way human development has been constructed in Indonesia. The history of Indonesia's emergence as an independent nation highlights the category of "pemuda" (youth) as signifying individuals who were courageous and capable of assuming substantial social and political responsibilities, despite being in the same biological age range typically classified as adolescence in Western developmental psychology. Founding figures of Indonesia, such as Driyarkara and Mangunwijaya, began taking on significant political roles in their late teens or early twenties.

Recognizing this historical context reveals the irony in how discussions of individuals in this age group within developmental psychology classrooms often focus on micro and self-centred issues, such as identity crises, hormonal changes, and romantic relationships. While these topics are undoubtedly relevant to understanding individuals from biopsychological perspectives, when such perspectives dominate the study of youth, psychology education in Indonesia misses an opportunity to explore questions that are more contextualized within the nation's history and development. For instance, a more context-sensitive approach could examine the socio-cultural constructs and practices that enabled young people during Indonesia's formative years as an independent nation to prioritize political agency and social responsibility as central pillars of their sense of personhood.

The emphasis on egocentric views of the self in psychology education is reinforced by the neoliberal climate that characterizes contemporary higher education. Neoliberalism, as a socio-cultural orientation, tends to promote a conception of human beings as independent, self-contained entities responsible for their own success, well-being, and behaviour (McGuigan, 2014; Teo, 2018). This perspective is reproduced in psychology education through its focus on individual problems and personal responsibility, often sidelining the impact of structural and systemic factors—such as poverty, discrimination, or political oppression—on mental health and behaviour. Consequently, students may develop a narrow understanding of mental health, with limited awareness of how social injustices and structural inequalities shape individuals' well-being.

By centring on an egocentric view of the self, psychology education under neoliberal influence often prioritizes the development of marketable skills aimed at diagnosing and treating individual behaviours. As a result, students may be less inclined to engage with the social or ethical dimensions of psychological knowledge and practice, including the role their work in addressing or perpetuating social inequalities (Keast, 2020; Mulya, 2016). In such an educational context, ethical concerns are frequently reduced to "procedural ethics," focusing primarily on compliance with professional standards and legal regulations (Guillemin & Gillam, 2004, p. 261).

For us, this context underscores the importance of revisiting the ideas of Indonesian educational philosophers such as Driyarkara and Mangunwijaya, who emphasized social justice as an ethical orientation in education, as reflected in their concepts of *belarasa* (compassion) and *kesetiakawanan* (solidarity). Drawing on this foundation, we interpret decolonizing psychology education in Indonesia as a pedagogical practice that shifts away from egocentric views of the self toward a more justice-oriented understanding of humanity. In the following section, we share our endeavour in enacting this vision of decoloniality within the newly established Master's Programme in Critical Psychology at our university.

Decolonizing Psychology Education in Indonesia: The Emergence of Critical Psychology at Universitas Sanata Dharma

Both Driyarkara and Mangunwijaya made significant contributions to the development of education in Indonesia. As the founder of Universitas Sanata Dharma, Driyarkara introduced the ethos of educational humanism grounded in social ethics, emphasizing that "humans are companions to one another" (*homo homini socius*). He opposed this model of sociality to one characterized by predation and exploitation among individuals. Meanwhile, Mangunwijaya actively sided with marginalized communities. He provided extensive accompaniment to urban poor populations, advocating for emancipatory ways of life and thought. Beyond shaping human mentalities, Mangunwijaya was also known as an architect who designed sustainable riverside community layouts in Yogyakarta. The philosophies and commitments of these two figures have profoundly influenced the development of [masked name] Faculty of Psychology in 1996.

Our Faculty initially focused on mainstream psychology following North American traditions. From its inception, the Faculty adopted "communication" as its tagline, emphasizing its importance in shaping the curriculum. However, between 2008 and 2012, the focus began to shift toward "communication and culture," interpreted through various psychological frameworks: Culture Psychology, Cross-Cultural Psychology, Indigenous Psychology, and Cultural Psychology. While the first three perspectives gained traction within Indonesian psychological traditions, Cultural Psychology, as developed at the Faculty, evolved most robustly.

Unlike other perspectives, the Faculty's interpretation of Cultural Psychology acknowledges that social contexts do not merely influence but also fundamentally determine human psychology (see Ratner, 2012). This perspective aligns with Critical Psychology's assertion that human subjectivity is embedded within the societal realm. This alignment reflects the socio-humanistic roots of the university's founding, drawing upon disciplines like Philosophy, History, Sociology, Anthropology, Literature, and Political Science—fields older than psychology—that have influenced the faculty's scholarly development.

By 2023, in response to the evolution of psychological science from positivist to constructivist paradigms, the Faculty launched the Master's Programme in Psychology (Programme Studi Psikologi Programme Magister), popularly known as the Master's in Critical Psychology.

The programme's name emerged after internal debates, reflecting its commitment to amplify the ethos of Critical Psychology. Three naming options were considered. The first is Master of Psychology, a conventional name used by many programmes in Indonesia, offering broader appeal to prospective students but lacking in explicitly articulating the Faculty's critical stance. The second is Cultural-turn Psychology that proposed by Supratiknya (2021, 2023, 2024), a founding member of the Faculty, this name draws from encounters with Cultural Studies, Thomas Teo's psychological humanities (Teo, 2017), and Svend Brinkmann's cultural psychology (Brinkmann, 2016). It represents a paradigm shift akin to the linguistic or interpretative turn in socio-humanistic sciences. The third framework is Critical Psychology, as articulated by Ian Parker (2007) and Thomas Teo (2015). These works emphasize that Critical Psychology is fundamentally concerned with the societal embeddedness of subjectivity, the dynamics of power and resistance, emancipatory practices, and the critique of social injustices. This name highlights the programme's solidarity with global movements addressing exclusion and injustice. Despite regional variations, Critical Psychology universally confronts hegemonic ideologies and structural inequalities, adapting to local socio-political contexts. The decision to adopt "Critical Psychology" as the programme's name reflects a commitment to aligning with global epistemic communities and advocating for social justice.

Globally, Critical Psychology has flourished as both a scholarly discipline and a social movement, shaped by distinct regional histories. In Europe, particularly in Britain, Critical Psychology originated from concerns surrounding the psy-complex in everyday life, along with critiques from academics and professionals regarding the superficiality of psychological theories and practices, which were seen as indistinguishable from common sense. This development was also intertwined with the social movements of the 1960s and 1970s (Parker, 2006). In Latin America, particularly in Venezuela, Montero and Montenegro (2006) argue that Critical Psychology carries an explicit political motivation, rooted in the empowerment of citizens and the reclamation of public spaces. This perspective rejects the notion of academic and professional neutrality. Furthermore, in Latin America, the tradition of Liberation Theology has shaped the mission of academics and professionals to contribute to liberation from authoritarian regimes.

In Africa, Critical Psychology emerges from a long-standing anti-colonial ethos cultivated over centuries of resistance by African communities. Specifically, Painter et al. (2006) note that in South Africa, Critical Psychology developed as a dual response to mainstream psychology. First, mainstream psychology was criticized as a product and supporter of inequitable political systems, particularly the racist and capitalist apartheid regime. Second, Critical Psychology sought to reframe psychology as a socially relevant, progressive, and even revolutionary practice, grounded in new epistemological, theoretical, and methodological foundations. In the context of its emergence in Asia, particularly in Japan, Igarashi (2006) observes that Critical Psychology did not arise primarily in response to the needs of Japanese society but rather as a consequence of the inadequacy of mainstream psychology in addressing those needs. Since the 1950s, psychological research in Japan has been dominated by the replication of studies originating from North America, rendering it largely irrelevant to the lived experiences and subjectivities of the Japanese people.

While there are shared goals of challenging the knowledge production of mainstream psychology, each region manifests distinct motives and approaches. In other words, the models of Critical Psychology that develop in various parts of the world reflect local hegemonic ideologies and injustices. Consequently, each context gives rise to its own unique form of Critical Psychology.

Regionally, Southeast Asia's colonial history and Global South identity present unique economic and political challenges. Economically, the region is characterized by labour exploitation for global consumption, while local populations face economic vulnerability. Politically, military-backed regimes often perpetuate authoritarianism and align with elites over the public interest (Anderson, 1998).

In Indonesia, national issues such as economic inequality, social conflict, oligarchy, agrarian disputes, and the complexities of a multi-ethnic, multi-religious society present further challenges. Locally, in the Special Region of Yogyakarta, rapid socio-cultural transformations manifest in diminishing green spaces, increasing population density, and horizontal conflicts as structural symptoms of broader inequalities.

Acknowledging these global, regional, national, and local dynamics, the faculty has developed a curriculum that integrates diverse Critical Psychology approaches (Fakultas Psikologi USD, 2023). Drawing from postcolonial conditions and power disparities, the programme emphasizes Community Psychology and Psychology of Well-being. While acknowledging the dominance of positivist ideologies rooted in American and European traditions, we have also incorporated theoretical perspectives grounded in Marxism, Semiotics, and Psychoanalysis. To foster academic publications and debates within Critical Psychology, the methodologies we offer emphasize the unfolding of psychological phenomena within their societal embeddedness. Examples include emancipatory action research and psychosocial approaches. Ultimately, our goal is to develop a form of Psychology from an Indonesian perspective. While this vision remains in its formative stages, the faculty is committed to addressing Indonesia's unique societal challenges, gradually shaping a psychology that resonates with the nation's socio-cultural identity.

In the learning process, the Master of Psychology Programme at Sanata Dharma University offers three types of courses: Core Courses, Expanded Courses, and Enrichment Courses. Core Courses refer to a set of courses recommended by the *Asosiasi Penyelenggara Pendidikan Tinggi Psikologi Indonesia* (Indonesian Association of Psychology Higher Education Institutions, abbreviated as AP2TPI). These Core Courses are divided into six groups: (1) mastery of basic psychological concepts, (2) research methods, (3) basic assessment skills, (4) basic intervention skills, (5) communication skills, and (6) ethical understanding and self-development. Expanded Courses are mandatory courses that reflect the distinctiveness of the Faculty, particularly in the tradition of Critical Psychology. Meanwhile, Enrichment Courses provide students with opportunities to broaden their knowledge within the framework of Critical Psychology. Each student is required to complete a minimum of 54 credit units, encompassing these three types of courses, within four semesters.

The curriculum structure, consisting of the aforementioned three types of courses, is translated into various subjects, taking into account the learning outcomes of each. The credit weight of each course is determined based on the depth of the learning outcomes and the breadth of the subject matter. For example, the course "Foundations of Critical Psychology" (3 credits), which falls under Core Courses, aims to provide an analytical foundation for understanding psychological phenomena as context-bound, negotiated, fluid, and emancipatory. Similarly, the course "Emancipatory Community Psychology" (4 credits) develops an understanding of community psychology from an emancipatory perspective, emphasizing social change and community empowerment. Additionally, students are required to choose Enrichment Courses such as "Reflective Pedagogy," a term frequently used by Driyarkara, and "Work Psychology and Alienation." These latter two courses are designed in response to our concerns, as members of contemporary Indonesian society, regarding issues pertaining to academic subjects within academic spheres and labour subjects within the framework of citizenship.

Currently, we have 25 students enrolled in our programme, representing diverse undergraduate backgrounds. The majority of our students come from psychology, while others are from education and theology. Among these students, several are actively engaged in social movements and art activism. Their connections with local communities continuously challenge them to examine the relevance of their ideas within the framework of Critical Psychology. These students also routinely facilitate public discussions involving diverse audiences, such as disability activism, political movements, and other social movements. Importantly, these discussions do not overlook the dominance of mainstream psychology within Indonesia. Instead, the dialectical interaction between mainstream and critical psychology creates opportunities for transformative shifts in thought.

In Indonesia, there are approximately 45 Master's programmes in psychology, divided into academic (science-focused) and professional (practice-oriented) tracks. In 2023, the Indonesian government introduced a ministerial regulation on professional psychology education, setting standards and procedures for the field (Kementerian Pendidikan, Kebudayaan, Riset, dan Teknologi, 2023). This regulation shifted professional psychologist training from the master's level to being accessible to graduates of bachelor's programmes in psychology. The Master's Programme in Critical Psychology falls within the academic (science-focused) category, with a curriculum load of 54 credits. While the development of Critical Psychology has emerged sporadically within individual master's programmes, it has only recently gained institutional and organizational focus, with [masked name] being a primary advocate.

The curriculum and student profile of the Master's Programme in Critical Psychology at [masked name] emphasize four key learning outcomes aligned with the principles of decoloniality. First, the programme aims to cultivate knowledge that fosters critical awareness of psychology as a cultural product shaped by specific historical and political contexts. Second, the curriculum acknowledges the limitations of psychology's atomistic view of humanity. Third, it seeks to build sensitivity to how this atomistic perspective can reproduce or normalize social injustices. Lastly, supported by the interdisciplinary backgrounds of faculty and students, the programme explores alternative psychological approaches that promote social justice. This interdisciplinary focus is deeply rooted in the university's historical tradition of liberal arts education.

It may still be too early to fully assess the impact of these four key learning outcomes on students and the broader context. Nevertheless, a collection of student reflections compiled in a book chapter (Madyaningrum et al., 2024) offers an initial glimpse into how our students have experienced their learning journey in the Master's Programme in Critical Psychology at [masked name]. Below are excerpts from three of our students' reflections:

> Studying Critical Psychology has encouraged me to see humans and their behaviors as more complex and nuanced, preventing a reliance on a 'single story.' Critical Psychology urges us to contextualize human behavior within broader frameworks, rather than examining it solely in isolation. Understanding humans in a more complex and contextualized manner would be impossible if we relied only on theoretical tools offered by mainstream psychology.
>
> (Masked name)

> [As a teacher] Learning Critical Psychology has helped me recognize that the root of a student's problem is not always the student themselves. It might lie within their family, school, or the surrounding community as a social system. This insight has driven me to understand that psychology must also strive for interventions that are systemic in nature.
>
> (Masked name)

> [T]his master's programme has helped me place the social activism I have been engaged in within a broader horizon. [...] History shows that street demonstrations have often been catalysts for significant change. However, this does not diminish the value of resistance carried out by educators who campaign anti-mainstream models of primary or secondary education, or by those advocating for local food sovereignty by rejecting instant noodles. These efforts are crucial components of the long-term struggle against injustice.
>
> (Masked name)

These reflections emphasize how studying Critical Psychology enables students to appreciate the contextual complexity of human behaviour, paving the way for systemic interventions. Moreover, it demonstrates the potential of applying Critical Psychology within the realm of social activism, enriching transformative practices with a more nuanced understanding of strategies for change.

Observing the transformative experiences and shifts in worldview among the students, it is not an overstatement to be optimistic about a gradual epistemological shift in the understanding of human psychology. This transformation represents a movement from neoliberal ethics to social ethics, as envisioned by Driyarkara and Mangunwijaya. Such a shift highlights the emerging potential for psychology to become more relevant and significant in addressing everyday life within society.

While the aforementioned four goals guide our daily practices, we recognize that their implementation is not without imperfections. Navigating tensions and ironies is an inherent part of our daily journey. One clear example is the tensions between equipping students with the conceptual and methodological skills needed to critique—or even deconstruct—sociopolitical systems, while simultaneously recognizing that such competencies may not be necessarily competitive in the job markets. This is particularly true in a society dominated by market-driven labour structures that emphasize graduate employability.

Graduates with skills that align with existing systems are more likely to be favoured over those who seek to question, let alone challenge, those very systems. The knowledge and skills developed in our programme provide a strong foundation for careers in academia or research. However, we are fully aware that opportunities in these fields are extremely limited in our context, as research and higher education are not priorities for policymakers. Pursuing such a path often means choosing precarity over security and stability.

To navigate this tension, we strive to incorporate methodological training into students' learning experiences—methods that may still be applicable should they find themselves working within hegemonic systems. For example, we introduce photovoice and transect analysis as tools for data collection and analysis, ensuring that students acquire skills that retain relevance even in constrained professional settings.

Conclusion

This chapter contends that psychology education in Indonesia requires decolonization to more effectively address the nation's distinctive social and historical contexts. The decolonization process is essential given the dominance of Western paradigms in Indonesian psychology education, which remains heavily influenced by Western theories and practices that are largely individualistic (egocentric) in nature. Such an orientation neglects relational and communal conceptions of the self, which are more aligned with Indonesian cultural values. Furthermore, neoliberalism exacerbates the egocentric focus in psychology education by emphasizing the development of marketable skills while disregarding structural and systemic factors that influence mental health. Consequently, students often lack sensitivity to issues of social justice and structural inequality.

In this context, the educational philosophies of Driyarkara and Mangunwijaya are particularly relevant for fostering a social ethic amidst the prevailing neoliberal ethos that undermines the academic community's social responsibility toward human lived experiences. Both figures emphasize the importance of social responsibility in education. The concept of *belarasa* and *kesetiakawanan* provide a foundational framework for developing psychology education oriented toward social justice.

As a concrete step toward decolonizing psychology education, [masked name] has initiated a Critical Psychology Master's Programme. This programme aims to enhance students' critical awareness of psychology as a cultural product, acknowledge the limitations of atomistic perspectives within psychology, build sensitivity to the social justice implications of such views, and explore alternative psychological approaches that align with social justice values. Although the programme is still in its early stages, [masked name]'s commitment to developing a "Psychology from an Indonesian Perspective" is expected to serve as a model for decolonizing psychology education in Indonesia.

References

Adams, G., Estrada-Villalta, S., & Ordóñez, L. H. G. (2018). The modernity/coloniality of being: Hegemonic psychology as intercultural relations. *International Journal of Intercultural Relations*, *62*, 13–22. https://psycnet.apa.org/doi/10.1016/j.ijintrel.2017.06.006

Anderson, B. R. O. G. (1998). *The spectre of comparisons: Nationalism, Southeast Asia, and the world*. Verso.

Anderson, B. R. O. G. (2006). *Java in a time of revolution: Occupation and resistance, 1944–1946*. Equinox Publishing.

Bottrell, D., & Manathunga, C. (Eds.). (2018). *Resisting neoliberalism in higher education volume I: Seeing through the cracks*. Springer. https://doi.org/10.1007/978-3-319-95942-9

Brinkmann, S. (2016). *Diagnostic cultures: A cultural approach to the pathologization of modern life*. Routledge. https://doi.org/10.4324/9781315576930.

Dahlan, W., Harbunangin, B., Rumeser, J. A. A., & Sriamin, L. S. (2007). *Dialog psikologi Indonesia: Doeloe, kini dan esok (Indonesian's psychology dialog: Past, present and tomorrow)*. Penerbit Himpsi Jaya.

Danziger, K. (2009). Confession of a marginal psychologist. In L. P. Mos (Eds.), *History of psychology in autobiography* (pp. 89–130). Springer. https://doi.org/10.1007/978-0-387-88499-8_3

Direktorat Jenderal Pendidikan Tinggi. (2020). *Buku panduan Merdeka Belajar Kampus Merdeka* [Handbook of Independent Learning – Independent Campus]. Kementerian Pendidikan dan Kebudayaan. https://dikti.kemdikbud.go.id/wp-content/uploads/2020/05/Buku-Panduan-Merdeka-Belajar-Kampus-Merdeka-2020-1.pdf

Driyarkara, N. (1961/2006). *Karya lengkap Driyarkara: Esai-esai filsafat pemikir yang terlibat penuh dalam perjuangan bangsanya*. Gramedia, Kompas, Kanisius & Ordo Serikat Jesus Provinsi Indonesia.

Fakultas Psikologi USD. (2023). *Buku pedoman akademik 2023 Program Magister Psikologi Fakultas Psikologi Universitas Sanata Dharma*. https://www.usd.ac.id/f113/agenda/[1FEB]%20Magister%20Psikologi%20USD%20-%20Buku%20Pedoman%20Akademik%202023.pdf

Guillemin, M., & Gillam, L. (2004). Ethics, reflexivity, and "ethically important moments" in research. *Qualitative Inquiry*, *10*(2), 261–280. https://doi.org/10.1177/1077800403262360

Herlambang, W. (2013). *Kekerasan budaya pasca 1965: Bagaimana Orde Baru melegitimasi anti-komunisme melalui sastra dan film*. Marjin Kiri.

Igarashi, Y. (2006). Role of critical psychology in Japan: Protest against positivistic psychology and search for new knowledge of the mind. *Annual Review of Critical Psychology*, *5*, 156–166. www.discourseunit.com/arcp/5

Keast, S. (2020). Psychology education and the neoliberal episteme in Australia. *Theory & Psychology*, *30*(4), 507–527. https://doi.org/10.1177/0959354320926574

Kementerian Pendidikan, Kebudayaan, Riset, dan Teknologi. (2023). Peraturan Menteri Pendidikan, Kebudayaan, Riset, dan Teknologi Nomor 43 Tahun 2023 tentang Pendidikan Profesi Psikologi. https://peraturan.bpk.go.id/Details/289737/permendikbudriset-no-43-tahun-2023

Kirmayer, L. J. (2007). Psychotherapy and the cultural concept of the person. *Transcultural psychiatry*, *44*(2), 232–257. https://doi.org/10.1177/1363461506070794

Madyaningrum, M. E., Risakotta, T. T., Murtyoastuti, A., Mahendra, P. A. R. P & Nugroho, G. W. (2024). Bukan unifikasi melainkan kontekstualisasi: 15 tahun kemudian. In A. Harimurti (Ed.), *Psikologi berhampiran budaya* (pp. 197–211). Sanata Dharma University Press.

Manathunga, C., & Bottrell, D. (Eds.). (2018). *Resisting neoliberalism in higher education volume II: Prising open the cracks*. Springer. https://doi.org/10.1007/978-3-319-95834-7

Mangunwijaya, Y. B. (1999). Teologi pemerdekaan. *Manusia pascamodern, semesta, dan tuhan*. Kanisius.

Mangunwijaya, Y. B. (2020). *Sekolah merdeka: Pendidikan pemerdekaan*. Kompas.

McGuigan, J. (2014). The neoliberal self. *Culture Unbound*, *6*(1), 223–240. https://doi.org/10.3384/cu.2000.1525.146223

Montero, M., & Montenegro, M. (2006). Critical psychology in Venezuela. *Annual Review of Critical Psychology*, *5*, 257–268. www.discourseunit.com/arcp/5

Mulya, T. W. (2016). Neoliberalism within psychology higher education in Indonesia: A critical analysis. *ANIMA Indonesian Psychological Journal*, *32*(1), 1–11. https://doi.org/10.24123/aipj.v32i1.579

Mulyatno, C. B. (2020). Pengantar: Kembalikan pendidikan pada anak. In Y. B. Mangunwijaya (Ed.), *Sekolah merdeka: Pendidikan pemerdekaan* (pp. ix–xvii). Kompas.

Painter, D., Blanche, M. T., & Henderson, J. (2006). Critical psychology in South Africa: Histories, themes and prospects. *Annual Review of Critical Psychology*, *5*, 212–235. www.discourseunit.com/arcp/5

Parker, I. (2006). Critical psychology and critical practice in Britain. *Annual Review of Critical Psychology*, *5*, 89–100. www.discourseunit.com/arcp/5

Parker, I. (2007). Critical psychology: What it is and what it is not. *Social and Personality Psychology Compass, 1*(1), 1–15. https://doi.org/10.1111/j.1751-9004.2007.00008.x

Pickren, W. E. (2020). Coloniality of being and knowledge in the history of psychology. In V, Balz & L., Malich (Eds.), *Psychologie und Kritik* (pp. 329–343). Springer. https://doi.org/10.1007/978-3-658-29486-1_15

Rakhmani, I., & Sakhiyya, Z. (2024). Inequalities and social sciences in neoliberal Indonesia. *International Social Science Journal*, *74*(251), 9–23. https://doi.org/10.1111/issj.12429

Rakhmani, I. (2024). "Merdeka Belajar": A cultural political economy of Indonesia's Neoliberalising nationalist university. *Masyarakat: Jurnal Sosiologi*, *29*(1), 1–25. https://scholarhub.ui.ac.id/mjs/vol29/iss1/6

Ratner, C. (2012). *Macro cultural psychology: A political philosophy of mind.* Oxford University Press.

Rosser, A. (2015). Neo-liberalism and the politics of higher education policy in Indonesia. *Comparative Education*, *52*(2), 109–135. https://doi.org/10.1080/03050068.2015.1112566

Sakhiyya, Z., & Mulya, T. W. (Eds.). (2023). *Education in Indonesia: Critical perspectives on equity and social justice*. Springer. https://doi.org/10.1007/978-981-99-1878-2

Shin, J. C. (Ed.). (2018). *Higher education governance in East Asia: Transformations under neoliberalism.* Springer. https://doi.org/10.1007/978-981-13-2469-7

Stange, P. (2007). *Politik perhatian: Rasa dalam kebudayaan Jawa.* LKiS.

Subkhan, E. (2023). Vocationalizing education: The dangers of link-and-match paradigm for the students' future. In S. Zulfa & W. M. Teguh (Eds.), *Education in Indonesia: Critical perspectives on equity and social justice* (pp. 77–97). Springer. https://doi.org/10.1007/978-981-99-1878-2_5

Sunarko, A. (2020). Teologi belarasa dan harapan akan perdamaian (Refleksi teologis). In F. Purwanto & A. T. E Purwanto (Eds.), *Membangun gereja sebagai gerakan yang cerdas dan solider: Apresiasi terhadap kegembalaan Ignatius Kardinal Suharyo* (pp. 47–62). Sanata Dharma University Press.

Sunendar, D., & Adriany, V. (2023). 'It's all about the product': Doing research in neoliberal times in Indonesian higher education. *Globalisation, Societies and Education*, 1–11. https://doi.org/10.1080/14767724.2023.2212438

Supratiknya, A. (2021). Penelitian kualitatif dan membaca simtomatik dalam psikologi. In V. D. S. Hartoko & A. Harimurti (Eds.), *Refleksi, diskresi, dan narasi: Sejarah perjumpaan dengan psikologi* (pp. 16–43). Sanata Dharma University Press.

Supratiknya, A. (2023). Dari psikologi kritis dan psikologi kultural-historis ke psikologi berhampiran budaya. *Retorik, 11*(1), 75–107.

Supratiknya, A. (2024). Produksi pengetahuan dalam psikologi berhampiran budaya. *Suksma: Jurnal Psikologi Universitas Sanata Dharma*, *15*(2), 147–170.

Teo, T. (2015). Critical psychology: A geography of intellectual engagement and resistance. *American Psychologist, 70*(3), 243–254. https://doi.org/10.1037/a0038727

Teo, T. (2017). From psychological science to the psychological humanities: Building a general theory of subjectivity. *Review of General Psychology, 21*(4), 281–291. https://doi.org/10.1037/gpr0000132

Teo, T. (2018). Homo neoliberalus: From personality to forms of subjectivity. *Theory & Psychology*, *28*(5), 581–599. https://doi.org/10.1177/0959354318794899

Wahid, A. (2018). Campus on fire: Indonesian universities during the political turmoil of 1950s–1960s. *Archipel* [Online], *95*. https://doi.org/10.4000/archipel.612

Wieringa, S. E., & Katjasungkana, N. (2019). *Propaganda and the genocide in Indonesia: Imagined evil.* Routledge. https://doi.org/10.4324/9780429440243

4 Co-Creating Transdisciplinary Decolonial Curricula

Nuria Ciofalo, Chela Sandoval, P.J. DiPietro, Susan James, Karen Jarratt-Snider and Jenny Escobar

Introducing Concepts

Western academic education emerged from geopolitical zones—those of hegemonic Europe—during the era labeled as an "Age of Reason and Enlightenment" (1685–1815). The Western educational system developed in tandem with formally categorized definitions of what it means to know, to feel, to understand, to be[1]; to be "human," "civilized," "able," and "beautiful." Their discoveries and definitions were taken up as an obligation, as moral imperatives to bring enlightenment to the "darkness" of the planet.

Colonization has been [il]logically justified by Enlightenment thoughts. Western university systems became disciplinary silos where knowledge is compartmentalized, specialized, and commodified for capitalist reproduction. Today, the ecological, economic, political, and psycho-social effects of the Western academy reinforce a world broken into hierarchically organized geopolitical locations that function according to neoliberal values, patriarchal heterosexism (imposed only two legitimate genders), racism (superior and inferior racialization), ableism (only abled individuals are valued by capitalism), extractivism (extracting knowledge, workforce, and natural resources), and environmental destruction.

This chapter advances examples of decolonial thoughts, interventions, and processes that our collective, a council of six scholar-activists, has developed as alternative curricula. Our aim is to challenge the siloed, reductionist nature of academic disciplines and their imbrication in modernist/colonial institutions, and to bring relief to the commodified human beings and relationships supported by westernizing university models. Our writing collective is bound by our shared commitment to co-create alternative de-, anti-, and postcolonial-futurist visions, to co-construct what knowledge, being, becoming, peace, and freedom are and can be.

Guide to Understanding What Follows

The following six meditations provide five different approaches to teaching and learning, yet each contribution contains elements that link with the others. Our collective work aims toward replacing the previous Enlightenment and Anthropocene eras that center "man," with a set of principles that herald a new era that centers the Earth and all beings, one we might identify as "the Ecocene." Each of the members of our collective has worked to engineer the Ecocene, understood as *de*colonizing and *post*colonial in function. We believe that this coming Ecocene era can undo previous supremacies and replace them with a focus on the wellbeing of the Earth (Bolom Pale, 2020; Escobar, 2016; Gudynas, 2014; Karera, 2019; Wynter, 2014). These authors, like ourselves, work toward this era wherein ecological deterioration is no longer possible and where, instead, all beings, including the planet, are cared for in relationality. Our collective work organizes around

DOI: 10.4324/9781003492214-5

the magnification of radical healing and of what Sandoval calls "the social physics of peace" (Sandoval, 2000). These can connect human, non-human kin, ancestors, nature, and the cosmos.

The praxes and pedagogical explorations that follow have brought about shifts in curricula, teaching and learning, research, community praxes, and especially in the possibilities for consciousness, psyche, and embodiment. We ask that teachers and students worldwide join us in preparing the transdisciplinary processes, tactics, strategies, and creative possibilities in multi-localities we propose here. We offer five pedagogical approaches for constructing anti-, post-, and decolonial transdisciplinary curricula. We begin with (1) Indigenous cosmovisions (Jarratt-Snider and Ciofalo) because these have been denied and made invisible in the Western academy, yet they contain the hopeful and provocative articulations that are also embedded within and energizing the following five contributions. Next (2) Sandoval argues for a structured approach to storytelling and witnessing that, once enacted, becomes a pedagogy of emancipation. Escobar builds upon this in her (3) description of the power of restorative justice (RJ) in classroom settings, while (4) DiPietro insists that "anti-violence" and "harm reduction" are processes that generate "onto-epistemic transformations" in the classroom. Lastly, (5) James offers examples of the enactment of all these pedagogical approaches in a transdisciplinary graduate program called Community, Liberation, Indigenous, and Eco-Psychologies (CLIE). Readers will recognize six distinct authorial voices rising below as each person offers their strongest approaches that best allow them to bring the Ecocene into the classroom.

The Collective's Shared Project

The six authors of this document are members of a transcontinental collective of scholar-activists who have worked for many decades to create decolonizing university curricula. We have gathered to collect our thinking from many locations, from the Four Sacred Mountains of the United States (US) Southwest; from Argentina's Andeans mountains and Haudenosaunee territory in the Central New York area; from Puebla, Nahuatl territory of Mexico; from Colombia, Latin America; from the Genizaro pueblos of Abiquiu and Canones, and San Jose, California, and from the African diaspora, Harlem, New York. Our combined interest and ethical commitment are to reassemble the structures of human knowledge, praxis, and understanding, to shift these away from Enlightenment's routinized locations, and to experiment with the many other possibilities. Though we join from many geopolitical and ideological genealogies and locations, we identify similarly as people of a kindred psychic domain, that which philosopher Gloria Anzaldua (1987) described as the domain of "los atravesados," that is, those "who cross over, pass over, or go through the confines of the normal" to repair, call up what matters, experiment with possibilities, and discover the new (p. 25).

Los atravesadxs, including authors Aimé Cesaire, Gerald Vizenor, Franz Fanon, Bea Medicine, Shirly Lew, Azizah al Hibri, and Audre Lorde have created, in recent centuries, interventions in colonial curricula. Our group interweaves a collective praxis identifying the contours of living transdisciplinary curricula. Each of us links differently to the ecologies of knowledge that exist in the Global South and its diasporas. Each of us has tested our approaches with graduate and undergraduate students and from within and against our diverse disciplines. This document interweaves our learning and unlearning. Our work links transcontinentally with those who dare to "cross over the confines of the normal," those who have survived the differential conditions of fugitivity, the creatives whose works emerge from "the colonial wound" (Lugones, 2010, p. 750), elders and youth who generate acts of imagination, recovery, of the meta-ideology that requires re-imagining, and the politics of refusal, resistance, delinking, and accommodation for dignified lives dancing, singing, chanting, and celebrating. Our experimentation is with curricular approaches that counter coloniality/modernity.

We are conscious that, by actively confronting the coloniality of power (Quijano, 2000), we face paradoxical and contradictory challenges, obstacles, and struggles. Critical to this work is perform-antics, which broadly conceived entail cultural interventions such as tactics, strategies, and pedagogies that affirm egalitarian individual and collective liberation (Sandoval, 2012, p. 7). Our creation of "decolonial perform-antics" and of making present the futurism of decolonial studies remain incomplete projects that will always require relationships of exchange and support among global populations. Our chapter thus addresses a plurality of perform-antics and voices from collaborative pedagogies that rise from diverse geopolitical settings and loci of enunciation (Mignolo, 2009). We invite our readers to join our ongoing plurilogue (instead of mono or dialogue) toward decolonizing pedagogical enactments. Let us work toward building transformative solidarity among us and those with whom we work, while developing our commitments to transdisciplinary curricula.

Five Pedagogical Techniques

Ciofalo and Jarratt-Snider Call Up: "Indigenous Onto-Epistemologies and Praxes as Decolonial Pedagogies"

Scientific knowledge emerged in the West as an only-one-world paradigm of universality (Silvia Rivera Cusicansqui, 2018, Aymara–Bolivia; Vilma Almendra, 2021, Nasa and Misak–Colombia; Vine Deloria, Jr. 1997–Dakota; Yásnaya Aguilar Gil, 2020, Mixe–Oaxaca). This paradigm supported colonization and imperialistic exploitation of Indigenous lands and Peoples, causing epistemicide (the erasure of knowledges), ecocide (environmental destruction), linguicide (the erasure of languages), and genocide. Well-known Latin American decolonial scholars in North American universities argue that science has maintained modernity and ongoing coloniality (Maldonado-Torres, 2016; Mignolo & Walsh, 2018; Quijano,2000). Scientific psychology is a product of Western regimes of knowledge and practice that were imposed on Indigenous cultures globally (Bahtia, 2019; Cajete, 2002; Dutta, 2016; Ndlovou-Gatsheni, 2021; Sonn & Stevens., 2021). Despite this, Indigenous movements worldwide continue to fortify their cultures and cosmovisions, developing and expanding their systems of knowledge and praxes.

These movements from the Global South and its diasporas in the North have sustained lineages of holistic and interdependent cosmovisions. They delink from Western paradigms and the Anthropocene. As Tuck (2009) states, we must "… recognize the need to document the effects of oppression on our communities but also to consider the long-term repercussions of thinking of ourselves as broken" (p. 409). Operating within a brokenness complex, Eurocentrism relies on damage-based narratives propagated by the hegemonic academic archive, Indigenous psychologies instead center on desire-based narratives. As scholar-activists we need to be aware of our ethical responsibility to the communities with which we partner, recognizing their agentic capacities and creative contributions to address the social pathologies we face due to neoliberal violent structures still anchored in coloniality.

We need to emphasize three aspects of Indigenous cosmovisions. (1) Community, social, and cultural wellbeing includes the rights of the Earth (Bolom Pale, 2020, 2016; Gudynas, 2014). (2) Knowledge creation includes ceremony (Wilson, 2008). (3) Praxis is relational, promoting an affective conviviality for interdependence (Ciofalo, 2019). Indigenous cosmovisions inform pedagogies that promote cultural health and wellbeing entangled within onto-epistemologies (systems of knowledge based on the nature of being as informed by cosmovisions) and praxeologies (systems of actions guided by the former) that contribute to the emergence of the Ecocene. In the following pages, we will review several examples of these cosmovisions that promote collaborative pedagogies to co-create pluriversality toward decoloniality in *comunalidad*, a Mesoamerican construct defined below. We focused on contributions from Turtle Island and Abya Yala.[2] Yet, we are deeply aware that there are many more worldwide.

Jarratt-Snider Calls Up: "Native American Contributions"

Most Indigenous Peoples consider all in the world "around us" as relations. Our non-human relatives—the animals, plants, places, and the elements—all form part of our existence (Cajete, 2002). As relatives, they demand respect and help Indigenous Peoples understand our place in the larger world. Non-Indigenous Western ontologies, in contrast, often place humans at the center of the world, and value those needs and experiences above all else, creating a hierarchy that predisposes humans with the "right" to treat the Earth, the natural world, the non-human Indigenous relatives as disposable commodities (Jarratt-Snider, 2020). Those commodities are intended to serve the wants and comforts of human beings. It is unsurprising, then, that the US history has built dogma around the "American experience" steeped in Westward expansion and "American exceptionalism," wrapped in the challenge and pride of conquering the land and Indigenous Peoples (Deloria, Jr. 1997; Wheelock, 2006). This dogma was, of course, steeped in colonialism that spread as a weapon as swift, intense, and deadly as a mega wildfire whose flames were fanned against Indigenous Peoples in Canada, Australia, and New Zealand with near template—like similarities, and in various forms throughout other parts of the world. In contrast, by viewing the world around us as replete with non-human relatives, thus understanding the world in a *relational* sense, humans are but a part of, not apart from nature and the natural world.

These knowledge banks became systems of Traditional Indigenous Knowledges (TIKs), or Traditional Ecological Knowledges (TEKs)—knowledge accumulated through observation and experience over time (Cajete, 2002; Deloria, Jr., 1997). Indigenous epistemologies, in turn, build upon Indigenous ontologies by observing the natural world, our non-human relatives, and our own interactions with that natural world (Cajete, 2002; Deloria Jr., 1997; Ermine, 1995; Gegeo & Watson-Gegeo, 2001). Observations over long periods of time are a foundational element to science, and thus we could refer to TEKs as Traditional Indigenous Science (TIS). Western epistemologies, however, built upon ontologies that placed the production of knowledge into a hierarchy designed to ensure the place of Caucasians at the top, with other "races" as inferior (see, for example, Deloria, Jr., 1997; Grande, 2018; Puwar, 2004). It followed, then, that knowledge produced by these inferior "races," including TEKs/TIS, would be inferior to knowledge produced (Western Science) by the superior race.

Vine Deloria, Jr. (1997) traces the subjugation of TEKs/TIS as "myth" and "superstition" in comparison to Western Science and debunks many scientific "truths" long established and accepted by scholars. In doing so, Deloria, Jr., upends what scholars think they know about such truths, for example, the Bering Strait theory. Deloria, Jr. also reminds us of a stark difference between Western Science and TIK. While both are based on observations over time, as noted above, Western Science, he contends, is devoted to discovering and sharing knowledge widely, while practitioners of Indigenous science know that with knowledge comes responsibility (Cajete, 2002; Deloria, Jr., 1997). Among many Indigenous Peoples, furthermore, knowledge that can be trusted is knowledge passed on by an individual who is known to the community, rather than one with scholarly credentials with no connection to the community (Deloria, 1997; Gegeo & Watson-Gegeo, 2001).

Indigenous ontologies of relationality, in turn, create identity based on place. Sacred places hold positions in the sphere of relationality to tell us who we are as Indigenous persons. *Sa chata ohoyo*—I, Karen, am a Choctaw woman—which I know because, in part, of a particular sacred place. For the Diné, there are four sacred mountains in the Southwestern US. Deloria, Jr. (1973)

reminds us of Indigenous spirituality and "religions," to use a Western term, that are land-based, rather than building or text-based, as are major Western religions. Whereas Christianity was used as a weapon of colonization against Indigenous Peoples in the dispossession of and ongoing occupation, destruction, pollution, poisoning, and desecration of Indigenous lands, Indigenous Peoples see places that tell us who we are, non-human relations that are to be honored, and places that must be respected. Both Indigenous ontologies and epistemologies exist in contrast to coloniality, naturally informing and contributing richly to transdisciplinary, decolonial curricula. Earth justice, through Indigenous lenses, is simply a natural concept of one's place in the natural world of non-human relatives, and the resulting relationship of respect that comes with an understanding of the inherent relationality of humans and non-humans within the ecological systems of our planet (Deloria, Jr. 1973, 1997; Gone, 2016; Wildcat, 2009).

Ciofalo Calls Up: Mesoamerican Contributions

Coloniality imposes separations and racial hierarchies where the white race is superior, and others are inferior. Gender that is viewed as patriarchal and masculine is considered superior to the feminine and matriarchal, as well as other transgender and gender-variant configurations. Separations cause impacts that rise exponentially considering intersectionality and other factors. For example, geopolitical zones separate the Global North labeled as superior from the Global South labeled as inferior. However, these geopolitical zones coexist in both regions. Sylvia Marcos (2014) stated that in Mesoamerican onto-epistemologies the body is not separate from the mind and territory. It is not defined as only physical and material and does not set a limit or border between an exterior and interior existence. Marcos[3] added that the body of the Indigenous women, referring particularly to Maya women, is intimately linked to the land, spirituality, and the ancestors. This cosmovision constitutes a relational onto-epistemology that is "mujerista" (nourished by the agency of activist women from the Global South) and a *Pedagogía Comunitaria Decolonial* delinked from philosophies of life that separate the rational from the irrational and emphasize affection and intuition (Fernández, 2022; Marcos, 2006; Trujillo, 2019).

In "Eso que le llaman comunalidad/That what is called communality," Zapotec scholar-activist from Oaxaca, Jaime Martínez Luna (2015) explained that *comunalidad* offers the creation of a future that is not only close to their cosmovisions and cosmopraxes but also to one that is necessary for the planet. This conception of comunalidad is based on a social justice that centers on we (nostrxs). For this reason, it is a *Justicia Nóstrica* (We-Justice) for a dignified life that includes the agency of all living systems coexisting on the planet. These cosmogonies nóstricas (we-cosmovisions) are not individualized, fragmented, or anthropocentric, generating embodied decolonial pedagogies that coexist in pluriversality centering the Earth, spirituality, sacred rites, the body-territory (*cuerpoterritorio*), feelings and affection, ceremonies recreating ontological relationalities, mujerista epistemologies and pedagogies (Nava Morales, 2020), and *Lekil kuxlejal,* a Tzotzil construct from the Highlands of Chiapas that means holistic wellbeing, spirituality, and sustainability (Bolom Pale, 2020). Nava Morales (2020) stated that the defense for a dignified life recognizes struggles and marks in the individual and collective bodies due to colonial, patriarchal, and capitalist violence expressed in the claim made by Indigenous women: "My body as my primal defense territory/mi cuerpo como primer territorio de defensa" (p. 288). Through solidarity and comunalidad, these women protectors of territory web healing strategies "as a cosmic and political road/como camino cósmico político" (p. 293).

The Zapatista movement is an example of a pedagogy that guides the formulation of community-based theories that promote embodied praxes based on their own cosmovisions as cosmopraxes that generate self-determination (Shirzad, 2021). The Zapatistas have resisted governmental and global neoliberal violence by applying organizational tactics and strategies generated autonomously by their own healing, educational, and reciprocal political and economic systems. Their movement manifests the decolonial turn (Shirzad, 2021). An impressive example is "La Escuelita," which fosters "intergalactic dialogue," as they call it, engaging critical academics, scholar-activists, practitioners, and communities around the world to envision promising alternatives outside of neoliberalism. An indispensable element to generate pedagogies otherwise is the centering of Indigenous onto-epistemologies and praxes of resistance, refusal, fugitivity, and creativity through the preservation of their languages that keep their ancestral knowledges and philosophies alive and give words deep meanings informed by their rich cosmovisions (Aguilar, 2020). The educational autonomy allows for the preservation of cultures and languages through the transmission of traditional knowledges and praxes (*saberes y haceres tradicionales*). This autonomy based on collective territory constitutes what Martínez Luna (2015) called a sacred space of reciprocal relationships between humans and nature.

Sandoval Calls Up: "StoryTelling-WitHnessing as Wor(l)d Art Performance Activism"

The great social activist Gloria Anzaldua (1987) disclosed a method for creating solidarity across the differences of war. Anzaldua activates this method through a practice of storytelling that can "transform the storyteller *and* the listener into something, or someone else," she writes, something other than the present, already conditioned and structured individual self we are encouraged to become in all its cultural and social glory; something else beyond that socially produced, seemingly unique nexus of body/mind/emotions. Yes, and more, Anzaldua agrees with Franz Fanon that this method can *re*create our malleable "souls," so that the dynamic matrix that we are can be granted new life. This method that relies upon the "ability of story to transform the storyteller *and* the listener" can be comprehended as an artform wherein "storytelling and witnessing" are understood as irrevocably linked: storytelling *is* witnessing, witnessing *is* storytelling. Since both storytelling and witnessing are always in relation, always in response, always with each other, always in transformation (Sandoval, 2000), when I witness I am "with" you, I am witHnessisng-storytelling-wit(H)nessing. Thus, I introduce one of the SWAPA techniques (Storytelling-WitHnessing Wor(l)dArt Performance as Activism) that are central to the mode of activism I am addressing here.

The Storytelling and radical witHnessing I introduce here can be seen as "de-colonial perform-antics" which were developed out of the 1970s–80s US social movement today recognized as third-world feminism. This social movement was based on underground gatherings where trans-continental exchanges of music, drumming, speaking, moving, acting, and loving materialized as SWAPA (Sandoval, 2000). How else could these social activists find alliances across their profound differences of language, color, culture, caste, sexuality, gender, nation and being? Storytelling-WitHnessing became a US third-world feminist artivist ritual.

Anzaldua (1987) described these meetings by saying that storytellers and active witHnesses can be understood as tricksters and "shape-changers;" she says that if the word 'shaman' and the Nahuat word *nagual* signify 'shapeshifting,' then self-aware practitioners of SWAPA must become 'naguala,' self-aware 'agents of transformation,' artivists who use storytelling-witHnessing processes 'to modify and shape' themselves and the world. Over years, the method of SWAPA was enacted and refined within what was first referred to as a "shaman-witness" ceremony then later as a "naguala-wit(h)ness-naguala" ceremony (Sandoval, 2012). SWAPA became a decolonial perform-antic that asks practitioners to speak their "truths" in-and-through formalized trades and substitutions of meaning. Exchanges are not structured as "spoken word" performances, nor as competitive art events for "slam-ing" meanings apart, though there are some similarities (Alvarez, 2015).

A SWAPA decolonial perform-antic, however, as a highly structured exchange of meaning occurs in the form of a gift-giving-receiving-giving, a type of call-and-response or potlatch-like ceremonialized event. The SWAPA method contains a toolkit for delinking and becoming anew, it represents the event of "gathering-us-in-ness" as described by Toni Cade Bambara, and it is an experience out of which emerges visionary platforms for action. SWAPA trading shifts practitioners away from the social physics of war and toward a social physics of peace. SWAPA exchanges release their practitioners from the vigorous network of informatics that activate the social physics of war; SWAPA techniques allow entrance to the "house" Audre Lorde (1984) described as difference, a pluriversal space explained Arturo Escobar (2021), where we can begin to generate the social physics of peace.

Pedagogical Participation, Procedures, and Goals

Twenty-person SWAPA sessions look like this: every participant shares the same set of readings, signs or presentations, then they collectively discuss its meanings. At the next session, each participant individually stands-and-delivers by reading out loud one idea/quote or concept that most provoked, moved, challenged, or inspired them during the previous session. They also give a prepared two-paragraph explanation of what stimulated their particular choice of sign(s). Every standing/delivering "Giver/naguala" is "witHnessed," one witness at a time around the entire circle. WitHnessing is highly structured as "compassionate listening" and is the most hard learned SWAPA technique. The process involves self-consciously engaging in aesthesis, in listening, hearing, and selecting a giver's quote, idea, word, phrase, or concept that most moves the witness through their self-conscious attention to their own aesthesis. Then the witHness gives their selection back to the Giver/naguala as a gift reproduced as concretely as possible.

SWAPA "witHnessing" is a brief, one-minute, highly structured, bio-semiotic event modeled according to principles of "nonviolence" created by thinker/activists Marshall Rosenberg, Thich Nhat Hahn, Martin Luther King, Roland Barthes, and Gloria Anzaldua. An example of a formal witHness exchange structure and process is depicted sequentially in Table 4.1. Remembering that the applied techniques of SWAPA and the naguala-witHness-naguala ceremony are always experimentally done in "Labs"—Co-laboratories—where modes of investigation, experimentation, and creativity take place. Participants test what it means to see, read, and perceive differently; to think, write, speak, witHness, and meta-witness, differently. The experimentation is with what Anzaldua calls "making soul," on one side and on the other, with what making-kinship means, across all external and internal differences.

In more traditional academic terms, SWAPA pedagogies translate knowing into five different academically recognized areas, which I teach in my courses as described in Table 4.2. The SWAPA process teaches us to witness and self-reflexively describe our own perceptions, to share these through creative expression, and to publicly perform them in the safety of a ritualized storytelling-witHnessing process summarized here as the naguala-witHtness-naguala ceremony.

We began undoing the current social physics of war, imbued with competition, divisiveness, and agonistic hierarchies and instead identify, create, and develop techniques for elevating and fortifying the social physics of love. These are the approaches, pedagogies, techniques, methods, and theories necessary to break the artifactual social, cultural, and colonial divisions hurting our planet.

What are the pedagogical goals and objectives of SWAPA and the naguala-witHness-naguala ceremony? To awaken curiosity, hope, and new ways of perceiving and knowing. To strengthen our meta-witnessing abilities; generate new kinships between and across differences, and to inspire social activists and enliven us with the courage to act on behalf of egalitarianism. I came to the academy inspired by the possibilities of integrating the knowledges of my countrypeople into

Table 4.1 Structure of Formal witHness Exchange

WitHness	*Giver/naguala*
Each witHness offering is unique and creatively different. Say: "When I hear (see, perceive) you say (move, shake, give) xxx, I feel xxx."	The Giver/naguala actively listens to each witHness but does not respond. Continue standing, silently listen, and receive each witness without agreement or negation, before sitting down to become only another witHness in a circle of witnesses—and the process begins again.
witHness and Giver/naguala	
As each witHness in the circle gives back what they individually and differently heard and experienced, one-by-one (while the still standing naguala-performer begins to understand the scope of their own powers as a meaning-maker). The words, concepts, and meanings witHnesses take in, and give back, are recognized by all as aesthesis/perceptions that are being-translated-live through the matrices of the surprisingly different bodies/minds/emotions and the psychic, social, and cultural worlds of each listener, whose witHnessing sometimes gets it right, sometimes wrong, or who gets something altogether different from the Giver/naguala's own intentions.	
witHness and Giver/naguala group exit formal ceremonial structure	
This portion of the ceremony completed, the group exits the ceremonial structure and enters an open circle to discuss the sign-reading and meanings produced during the ceremony. Like the first, this second circle also is designed to strengthen the muscles of self-reflexive perception—that is, to strengthen participant abilities to "meta-witness" how and what they have produced as a Giver/naguala, as a witHness, or as community member.	

Table 4.2 SWAPA Pedagogies & Academically Recognized Areas

	SWAPA pedagogy, how to...	*Academically recognized areas*
A	..."read" signs	Using Barthesian, Peircean, Anzalduan, and bio-semiotic models of bio-semiotics and aesthesis, i.e. the Signifier/Signified/Sign, la facultad and the signifyin' monkey
B	...deconstruct signs	Using Lugonian and Derridean anti-binarism and Saussurean language models
C	... build upon signs to create new, more complex-level meanings and ideologies, and/or deconstruct them	Using Fanonian, Thich Naht Hahnian, Sandovalian, and Althusserian models
D	... recognize and develop in oneself a differential perceptual ability that is mobile and kinetic as well as firm and focused	This is the "differential" skill necessary for living in and producing "a world where many worlds exist," Escobaran, Zapatista, Jungian and Anzalduan versions of nepantla
E	All four of the technologies above, once learned, are guided by another technology, that of "democratics"	This term names a focus on ethics—of self-reflexive aesthesic, psychic, collective, and collaborative analysis and action wherein power is engaged and "read" on behalf of egalitarianism (Derrida, Lugones, Anzaldua)

academic forms of knowing, understanding, and envisioning. I am pleased to see my students, over the years, carry these skills, understandings, passions, perceptions, and knowledges forward with the aim of decolonizing and releasing our planet from the social physics of war.

Escobar Calls Up: "Restorative Justice as Transformative Solidarity in Classrooms and Communities"

One of the ways to build a decolonial praxis within educational settings is using RJ. RJ is a set of values and practices that aim to rehumanize those often treated as disposable, unseen, and unheard in educational spaces. It has been implemented in various educational settings. The use of talking circles, games, collective accountability processes, and educational-wide policies that embody the social justice principles of RJ have been implemented to combat the continued effects of punitive rules embedded in the school-to-prison to-deportation pipeline (Davis, 2019; González & Epstein, 2022). Notably, suspension and expulsion are mainly enforced upon students of color and LGBTQI students and leads to an increased likelihood of these students being system-impacted, and for those undocumented leading to their deportation. From a decolonial lens, RJ provides a framework in which institutions and communities can intentionally implement (re)humanizing and healing/reparations efforts at a collective level, understanding colonization as part of the first harm that continues to permeate every aspect of our current state, and in need of repair through accountability and justice (Valandra & Wapȟáha Hokšíla, 2020).

As one of the core faculty at the CLIE program and as a restorative practitioner before returning to academia, I, Jenny, have implemented restorative practices in my courses while simultaneously assessing ways to create a more heart-centered approach within the program as a whole. In the classroom, I create opportunities for students and myself to engage in community-building activities that emphasize somatic, creative, and whole-being approaches to reconnecting with ourselves and each other. I often start courses by leading different activities that connect us to our bodies, spirit, the land around us, and each other by modeling to students what vulnerability can look like in academic spaces that often perceive these practices as not part of the "official" academic learning objectives. I then invite students to lead us into their imaginations of activities which often supersede my offerings and show the hunger and collective need for connection that students crave. These interruptions that aim to disrupt the way we default into learning (always sitting down, lecturing, talking, power points, etc.), create ways of being that embody learning instead, and are at the heart of building pedagogies toward decoloniality.

Inevitably with these practices, generational harms and unmet collective needs for justice and repair surface, showing that with the urge to be human also comes the desire for accountability. At CLIE, students and their communities of belonging embody different positionalities and lived experiences across the spectrum on the coloniality of being, with a clear divide between those that come from lineages of generational wealth and racial privilege, and those that do not. In this context, RJ cannot stay at the community-building level only instead its values and practices that lead toward accountability have to be integrated. One of the ways I have witnessed students do this has been through the deepening of relationships of accountability and engaging with a curriculum that shows them the history and present-day ongoing impacts of coloniality, providing them with the language, theories, and concrete examples of what decoloniality praxes requires and looks like (Escobar, 2022).

Accountability, individual and collective, can only truly emerge from relationships we care about and value. Individuals are more ready to change and admit where they went wrong, with those they care about because they have a shared sense of responsibility to love each other. How do we translate this love ethos at a collective and institutional level? We build cultures of authentic relationships while simultaneously engaging in the heart work of making space for conflict, discomfort, and even fallouts between community members to arise. This work can start in educational institutions but cannot stay there. The work has to live outside of existing systems to truly build decolonial futures without constraints.

To build a pedagogy toward decoloniality outside of existing institutions and systems, we need to implement a transformative justice (TJ) approach. While RJ strategies can help us start the process of disrupting the conventional ways of teaching, learning, mentoring, and all the other extraneous productivity work that is expected of students and professors alike, TJ seeks to build collective and community-based systems of care and justice. TJ, as a political and social justice movement with a liberatory orientation, can lead the way to creating something outside of what exists (Dixon & Piepzna-Samarasinha, 2020). This will require divorcing from the collective assumptions we hold of what constitutes legitimate ways of learning and starting from the beginning again. What if higher education was run by community members such as elders and youth? What if we taught with the land and non-human kin in mind and to whom we were accountable? What if instead of hierarchical degrees, education was truly seen as a human right and learning centers were based on themes and interests for all to access? What if one of the main tasks of higher education is to account for "undoing the first harm" of settler colonialism, as proposed by Valandra & Wapȟáha Hokšíla (2020)? These ideas are not new and have been implemented by many social justice movements such as the Black Panther's community schools, political education workshops facilitated by a vast number of organizations, and the teachings of spiritual communities to name a few examples. The roadmap, with its many roads and turns, has been laid out already, it is a matter of collectively working toward making this a reality as we choose repeatedly to continue paving the way toward a decolonial pedagogy.

DiPietro Calls Up: "Harm Reduction as Onto-Epistemic Justice"

At CLIE, I, PJ, engage in two unique yet complementary learning environments. I lead two courses: "Practicing Decoloniality and Anti-Racism" and "Psychology of Violence and its Prevention." Within the decolonial framework we've established, I view these settings as transformational spaces. My pedagogy aims to cultivate a collective approach to the learning process, encouraging accountability among co-learners. This collective mode of learning requires strategies, tactics, and perform-antics imbued by non-Western cognitive dispositions, such as uncertainty, complexity, and open-ended understanding (Lugones & Price, 1995).

In "Practicing Decoloniality and Anti-Racism," we explore the collective statement of the Harm-Free Zone (HFZS), which originated in the Bronx, New York, as a community-centered vision to eliminate racist harms (SpiritHouse-nc.org/harm-free-zone). My intent is to create "situations" that evoke uncertainty and open-ended understanding. I invite the CLIE cohort to reflect on instances where we've encountered radical practices. These practices have become part of a shared repository, and practitioners often return to them because they affirm alternatives to harm and injustice. The situations I create encourage participants to engage with this repository, even if we have a distant connection to it. The HFZS helps participants gain insight into deep grassroots work within a two-block radius of the Bronx. This collective addresses the prison industrial complex by examining its roots, particularly the connection between capitalism's brutal accumulation through dispossession and the twinned pathologization of underground economies. The statement also aims to undo epistemic injustice in three ways: (a) by offering a community-of-color critique of racializing capitalism; (b) by denouncing the ideological operations that reduce communities of color to individuals who view their circumstances as personal failures rather than as byproducts of structural inequalities; and (c) by confronting the contradictions of police brutality, recognizing that interpersonal harm—prompting state police intervention—distorts the nature of structural violence.

Co-learners cultivate more than just an ideological corrective to the epistemic harms outlined above. Given our distance from the community that originated the HFZS, we discuss what this distance means and how it shapes our approach. Does the university's model of ornamental inclusion, which relativizes contrasting experiences, hinder a genuine collective examination of the HFZS? Does the statement encourage the classroom to acknowledge the communal aspects of our learning environment and the university itself? Many students feel comfortable applying the HFZS framework to their professional contexts, where they serve minoritized populations. However, I gingerly encourage them to adopt a broadening practical disposition that, informed by an understanding of epistemic injustice, allows for an affective navigation of our realities. This means confronting our own limitations in recognizing that, despite the perceived distance between us and jails, our freedom often depends on the incarceration of populations deemed fungible.

The second phase focuses on redefining accountability. While we are not directly accountable to the collective that authored the HFZS, we embrace the statement's sense of communal accountability and its rejection of moral claims. Such claims assume that individuals are agents of choice and action. We instruct each other on the implications of a carceral paradigm in our lives. We arrive at a more communal approach to accountability, addressing the material and epistemic damage interwoven with carceral logics and their connections to depersonalization and white supremacy. This learning situation facilitates a decolonial turn, an immersion into localized pluriverses, exploration of uncharted emotional responses to carceral logics, and the possibility of co-authoring accountability. I believe this curricular process benefits from emphasizing pluriversal perform-antics. The classroom collectively mobilizes an intersubjective response to affective, epistemic, and political injustices. This response is not solely about understanding; it is about praxis.

In the second learning environment, "Psychology of Violence and its Prevention," I present another opportunity to enhance our affective responses to epistemic and political violence. The curriculum for this class is rooted in decolonial feminism, focusing on interrogating the metaphysical, epistemological, and political imposition of gender as a category of the human (Lugones, 2008; Wynter, 2003). By examining the (in)visibility of negatively racialized populations as gendered subjects (Carastathis, 2019; Hammonds, 1994), we explore, recover, and recalibrate bodily projects that extend beyond gender as an onto-epistemology (DiPietro, 2019, 2025). Third-world women and women of color feminisms study bodily projects often denied recognition by Western curricula and paradigms. By exploring gender as a colonizing imposition, we engage with carnal and bodily politics that transcend traditional notions of gender. This exploration prompts us to reconsider whether gender, typically presented as a tool for feminist liberation, might perpetuate epistemic violence. I invite my classroom co-learners to confront the complex realities of ungendering and non-gender within anti-racist, postcolonial, and decolonial narratives and socio-cultural interpretations. Gloria Wekker's *The Politics of Passion* (2005) serves as a key text for understanding ungendering and non-gender within this curriculum.

The situations I describe carry different ethical implications. In the context of the HFZS, we may lack firsthand experience with incarceration, whereas the ubiquity of gender as a heuristic lens is pervasive. Wekker's work highlights how traditional gender constructs often obscure, distort, and erase non-Western embodiments. She focuses on *mati work* (mati wroko), an Afro-diasporic institution of intimate belonging that contests monogamous heterosexuality among working-class Afro-Surinamese *women*. Wekker's subversion of ethnography captures the non-Western ways of living and being with others, illustrating how erotic, impassionate, selfhood is produced through activity. It is crucial for our decolonial praxis to collectively establish an affective disposition toward *mati work*. We connect this shift in perspective to the remote sense of accountability gained through our engagement with the HFZS. While we may not practice *mati work* ourselves, we develop a shared understanding of the harms gender inflicts not only on Afro-Surinamese working-class women but also on ourselves. The HFZS invites us to adopt a deeper, less individualistic approach to selfhood, nurturing a collective response to the idea of a "harm-free zone" as a resource within a justice-oriented framework. Our learning environment seeks to create space for the epistemic and ontological relevance of *mati work* in our lives.

Wekker exemplifies this shift. Initially, she relied on traditional ethnographic rapport and assumed her Afro-diasporic status would facilitate smooth communication with her subjects. Ultimately, her engagement with Winti religion and its West African grammatical principles fostered a dynamic and felt dexterity of mind, body, and spirit. For instance, Wekker recounts a moment with Mis' Juliette, an eighty-four-year-old partaker in *mati work*. Attempting to anchor the mati work to a Western model of sexual identity, Wekker asked Mis' Juliette if she *was a mati* ("Juliette na wan matisma, no?"). Juliette annoyingly replied, "But since I'm sleeping with women, *then I mati*" (p. 13). For Afro-Surinamese Creole women, a decolonizing turn entails Winti religion and its underwriting of communal rather than individualizing sexual identities.

Teaching "Psychology of Violence and its Prevention" challenges both modernist and postmodern interpretations of sexual identities. The rationality that characterizes Western psychology has widened to include performative critiques of sexuality (Butler, 2004). While students may have familiarity with these critiques, the CLIE cohort seeks to move beyond them. They foreground multiplicity in ways that transcend the individualistic frameworks often found in Western thought. They engage in affective fashion the subject-object divide, transforming it from within through a humble invocation of non-secular perspectives. Recognizing the Eurocentric roots of Butler's and other posthumanist accounts of gender allows this cohort to broaden epistemic and political pathways. Together, we collectivize the task of identifying these accounts as instances of onto-epistemic injustice. Inspired by Wekker, who provincializes lesbian identity and experience, the CLIE cohort embraces terms like ungendering and non-gender. Our learning experiences encourage us to demarginalize *mati work*, acknowledging that through these situations, we can begin the process of affective, theoretical, and political reparation to our lived experiences.

James Calls Up: "Transdisciplinarity and Decoloniality in CLIE: Toward an Emergent Curriculum and Praxis"

Faculty and students of the CLIE at Pacifica Graduate Institute have been engaged in co-constructing curriculum that delinks from Eurocentric regimes of knowledge. CLIE faculty and students share our tentative understandings, collaborative research, and strategies to ensure space for decoloniality in our classrooms. We understand that decoloniality can emerge when epistemologies, which are unknown, or have been silenced by and excluded from the Western canon, are centered (Bhambra et al., 2018). As a graduate specialization within an institution of Depth Psychology historically implanted in Eurocentrism as an organizational and curricular foundation, we are uniquely positioned to wedge a widening crack in the structure to forge a divergent curriculum within its confines. The necessary shift involves expanding the scope of philosophies of the unconscious already at the margins of mainstream theory to extend them globally, introducing locally situated cultural epistemologies. An initial step was to disrupt modernist ontological assumptions that separate humans with agency from passive "matter" in the environment, available for ownership and resource extraction. This is a difficult task for psychologists who rely on assumed capacities to observe, assess, interpret, and control their personal imprint in any environment through self-reflection. In addition, the modernist lens is embedded with codes of coloniality, linked with histories of genocide, chattel slavery, racial and gender hierarchies, fixed positionalities, and inherent individualism. The aspiration was to consider these logics alongside decoloniality that imagines the world as a pluriverse where alternative regional worlds of knowing and living have yielded diverse possibilities for healthy, creative, and sustainable lives.

Rethinking curriculum involves the incorporation of the many ecologies of knowledge associated with world-making practices and different outcomes for environments and human communities (James & Lorenz, 2021). Reaching such goals requires transdisciplinary thought about the conditions of all beings, including cosmologies that impart agential relationships across spiritual realms (De la Cadena, 2015). These systems of knowledge involve relationality among all beings, living and non-living, ancestral veneration, and regular ritual practice that informs daily communication, and decision-making in many communities (Abímbọlá, 2021; Alexander,

2005; Kimmerer, 2013; Martin & Mirraboopa, 2003; Olupona, 2011; Simpson, 2018; Zauditu-Selassie, 2018).

As exemplified in Bantu-Kongolese philosophies by the DiKenga dia Kongo cosmogram (Fu-kiau, 2001), where the perpetual life cycle is divided into quadrants marked by birth, maturity, death, beginnings, and return to birth. Situated horizontally across the center of the circle is the Kalunga balancing plane, a porous interface between living and ancestral worlds that allows for communications and active engagement across the line, requiring integrated ethics. The transcendent relationality transmitted in this context crosses the rational lines demarcated within coloniality, and it is less likely to be accepted as part of the "decolonial turn" in the academic world. It appears to exceed what is tolerable among scholars and is often relegated to belief systems and myths rather than what is considered real (Escobar, 2021). Related scholarship typically can be found in anthropological work, African diaspora religious studies, and some Indigenous studies curricula. In CLIE, these concepts are integrated with various courses throughout the curriculum, mainly in Depth and Indigenous psychologies and methodologies courses. As exemplars, the scholarship and pedagogies outlined above contribute to the CLIE curricula via their roles as faculty and invited adjunct/guest faculty.

Another area where we have reinterpreted theorizations is in ecopsychologies, which, in its origins as a discipline, espouses conceptualizations of individuals' relationships with a separate "nature." It asserts the psychological and medicinal benefits of humans becoming more closely connected with the natural world. In addition, theories of reciprocity are promoted about people healing themselves in nature while tending to it. In CLIE, we have subsumed ecopsychologies with Indigenous environmental sciences and relational ontologies that experience the natural environment and all beings within it as kin, to be cared for, revered, and cultivated. These frameworks de-escalate the power and role of humans and assert that we are a part of the natural world. Students are introduced in introductory coursework to text such as Arturo Escobar (2016), *Thinking and Feeling with the Earth*; Vandana Shiva (2013), *Everything I Know I Learned in the Forest*; Natasha Myers (2016), *Photosynthetic Mattering*; Malcolm Ferdinand (2022), *Decolonial Ecology: Thinking from the Caribbean World*; and Juan López Intzín (2021), *Sp'ijilal O'tan: Knowledges and Epistemologies of the Heart.* This scholarship begins the process of reorientation to concepts of ecological wellbeing while introducing relationality. It also initiates rehistorization as a restorative practice to provide genealogies of ideas, events, and lifeways that have been altered over time to reinforce hegemonic principles.

Early curricular experiences of unlearning and relearning challenge students who have all been educated in standard hierarchical undergraduate and, for some, graduate learning models. Thus, the educational implications involve labor beyond teaching and learning, but a willingness to engage in a reorienting to text and research approaches. Some students arrive with community experiences that map more closely to the types of communal examples presented in coursework. For others, it is a long road away from prescribed individualism. In general, students can enter and remain in a liminal space in the first and, at times, the second year of the program until they find grounding in their areas of interest. The related community practitioner environment also appears to be at a turning point, where there is some realization that many of the intervention strategies, imposed and initiated within communities of color, have yielded few of the long-term desired goals. As a result, alternative modes of community engagement that increasingly involve collective research projects from conceptualization through analyses and dissemination are becoming more prevalent. Applying decolonial solidarity among communities and universities to co-construct alternatives to modernity and coloniality, we can pursue the promotion of creative and transformative praxes.

Scholars and students engaged in this work face the ongoing challenge to recognize and resist what Sylvia Wynter (2014) referred to as re-channeling, or the consumption of acts of resistance by the hegemonic system for consumption back into coloniality. Given this particular sociopolitical moment, it feels worthwhile to pause and observe the mass of decolonial theory pouring through publication circuits in the social sciences. Originating mainly from scholars representing Cultural Studies, Literature, African American Studies, Philosophy, Third-World Feminisms, and Gender Studies, it is interesting to witness psychological application. While this feels like an opening to new possibilities, questions remain about how much re-channeling is happening. Might modernist trappings be embedded in politics of recognition and static identity reinforcements typically foundational in decolonial projects? In reviewing the revolutionary work of Indigenous cosmovisions and pedagogies, racial and gender justice, RJ, harm reduction, rights, and equality over the past 60 years in the US, we can learn from the experiences, successes, and failures of those missions, including the recent Black Lives Matter protests and abolitionist demands of 2020. What is clearly in plain sight is the construction of an unanticipated response built into the system that is prepared to "enlist our best efforts to defeat them as part of its arsenal" (Akómoláfé, 2021, n.p.).

Conclusion: Co-Creating Possibilities beyond Disciplinary Silos

Psychology has been historically legitimized within Western scientific paradigms imposed as universal truths taught in universities used to maintain and perpetuate colonization, oppression, exclusion, and erasure of other epistemologies and praxes. Because psychology has been a disciplinary architect that supports the invention and perpetuation of deficit theories applied to people in and of the Global South regions, we are also tasked with immediate critical analysis of guiding work within the academic canon. Moreover, it is inside the modernist paradigm where we find ourselves as raw material for psychology's consumption through endless theories of marginalization, trauma, and damage narratives (Rivera Cusicanqui, 2018; Tuck, 2009). Linda Tuhiwai Smith (2012) asserted that knowledge has been organized and compartmentalized into disciplines as an embodied way of disciplining bodies, which Foucault has argued was the main principle that generated the academic disciplines in the eighteenth century. In our educational endeavors we seek to overcome compartmentalization and disciplinary silos by integrating various perspectives from the social sciences based on non-Western epistemologies and praxes.

Our collective has developed diverse "decolonial pedagogies" that address the contemporary pathologies of coloniality including racism, violence, heteropatriarchy, ableism, and the desecration of the environment (ecocide). Racial aggressions and entrenched Eurocentrism in curricula have always been pointed to by students and faculty of color within insider spaces, still such aggressions remain normalized within classroom contexts. Confrontations to this situation are ongoing and full of contestation. The authors of this chapter have found that integrating ontologies, epistemologies, and survivance (Vizenor coined this term as surviving and resistance strategies) that support decoloniality in the curriculum are hopeful alternatives to damaged-based narratives and pathology-modeled, missionary/savior investments, and assimilationist-oriented theories often connected and applied to communities of color. Whenever possible, we thus encourage all scholar-teachers to attempt reflexivity when developing curricula and praxes and while acknowledging the realities and implications of equivocation and misinterpretation within cultural contexts where professionals enter as outsiders to avoid "intellectual imperialism" (Readsura Decolonial Collective, 2022, p. 260) and uncritical reflection on positionalities as James and Lorenz (2021) emphasized could reproduce essentialist and "...fix[ed] identities in terms of the racist and violent metrics of coloniality –1/4 this and ½ that—as slave math" (cited in Decolonial Editorial Collective, 2021, p. 2). At the same time, we recognize that similar discernment categories for understanding and acting among professionals may, or may not, exist.

As demonstrated in this chapter's authorship, we have been graced with formidable scholar colleagues engaged in similar, longstanding struggles in the academic world who are willing to join us in solidarity. It is through these relationships that we have become equipped to open and expand curricular pathways. Students benefit enormously from the range of leading scholars they study with. Scholars join as invited faculty in this collective from departments of Indigenous Studies, Chicano/Chicana Studies, Community and Liberation Psychology, Philosophy, Women and Gender Studies, Asian Studies, Performance Studies, Environmental Studies, African American Studies, Religious Studies, Jungian Psychology, Conflict Resolution, and Evaluation. This weaving of disciplinary trajectories and genealogies converges around liberatory action, decoloniality, and fugitivity and encourages the emergence of psychologies otherwise.

To co-construct a decolonial pedagogy building transformative solidarity and imagining innovative pluriversities (instead of universities), we need to embrace alternatives to the pervasive market education, caused by our current political system, that maintains coloniality, hetero-patriarchal oppression, marginalization, and exclusion. Co-constructing a transdisciplinary curriculum with a substantial focus on epistemologies of the Global South and its diasporas within the academy requires ongoing navigation of institutionally embedded modernism/coloniality, and a hopeful gaze toward decolonial futurities. In this chapter, we intended to make a radical intervention in the coloniality of psychology to generate through anti-, post-, and decolonial perform-antics an uncharted praxis that needs a new name.

Notes

1 The influential French philosopher and mathematician Renee Descartes in 1637 laid out the "first" principle for understanding how to educate a human being. Individuals must come to self-consciously realize that "I think, therefore I am" and that "I think"—and therefore—"I exist" (*Discourse on Method*, 1637). Descartes' second book *Meditations on First Philosophy* (1641) gives us the image of naturalized binary oppositions as coupled meanings that naturally privilege one side over the other, such as mind over body or thinking over feeling. In that same work, Descartes also provides the philosophical foundations by which science has been instituted inside the institutionalization of western educational systems, thus the ferocious compartmentalization and legitimization of the academic and intellectual divide between the human, social, and natural sciences. These DesCartian premises such as these remain foundational to the organization of contemporary educational institutions. They represent particular situated and European versions of reality, thus the types of "knowledges" passed on to coming generations remain siloed and limited by the coloniality of power.

2 Both denominations, Abya Yala and Turtle Island, are political in nature and signal an ongoing cross-border resistance. Abya Yala is an Indigenous term borrowed from the Kuna language and that can be glossed as "land of full maturity." They seek to decenter the settler-colonial state throughout the continent. See Bergman et al. (2020).

3 Sylvia Marcos studies this principle of dual complementarity in Mesoamerica and its secret revelations about the nature of everything that exists. Marcos's approach owes much to the labor of curanderas, graniceras, shamans, and midwives of Morelos state in Mexico. Doña María is one of the healers with whom Marcos worked (2006).

References

Abímbọlá, K. (2021). *Ifá: An expository of Ifá literary corpus, Ìbàdàn.* Oxford University Press.

Aguilar Gil, Y. E (Yásnaya) (2020). *Manifiestos sobre la diversidad lingustica.* Almadía Ediciones.

Akómoláfé, B. (2021, September 24). *Making sanctuary with Bayo Akomolafe* [Video]. Youtube. https://www.youtube.com/watch?v=Jg_MAj1tF8I&t=1045s

Alexander, J. (2005). *Pedagogies of crossing: Meditations on feminism, sexual politics, memory, and the sacred.* Duke University Press.

Almendra, V. (2016). Palabrandando: Entre el despojo y la dignidad. In C. Walsh (Ed.), *Pedagogías decoloniales Tomo II: Prácticas insurgentes de resistir* (pp. 209–244). Editorial Universitaria Abya-Yala.
Alvarez, E. F. (2015). Jotería pedagogy, SWAPA, and Sandovalian approaches to liberation. *Aztlán: A Journal of Chicano Studies, 39*(1), 215–227. https://doi.org/10.1525/azt.2014.39.1.215
Anzaldua, G. (1987). *Borderlands la frontera: The new mestiza.* Aunt Lute.
Bahtia, S. (2019). Searching for justice in an unequal world: Reframing Indigenous psychology as a cultural and political project. *Journal of Theoretical and Philosophical Psychology, 39*(2), 107–114. https://doi.org/10.1037/teo0000109
Bhambra, G. K., Gebrial, D., & Nisancioglu, K. (2018). *Decolonising the university.* Pluto Press.
Bolom Pale, M. (2016). Didáctica de la resistencia desde el lekil kuxlejal del pueblo originario y la educación intercultural en contextos educativos pluriculturales. In C. Y. Quintero Reyes & F. Reyes Escutia (Eds.), *Trazos del tiempo: Hacia una escuela sustentable e intercultural* (pp. 99–125). Biblioteca de la Nueva Escuela.
Bolom Pale, M. (2020). *Lekil kuxlejal, un concepto tsotsil que implica una forma de vida sustentable.* Universidad Autónoma de México (UNAM) Global. https://unamglobal.unam.mx/global_revista/lekil-kuxlejal-un-concepto-tsotsil-que-implica-una-forma-de-vida-sustentable/
Butler, J. (2004). *Undoing gender.* Routledge.
Cajete, G. (2002). *Native science and sustaining Indigenous communities.* Cambridge University Press.
Carastathis, A. (2019). *Intersectionality, origins, contestations, horizons.* University of Nebraska Press. https://doi.org/10.2307/j.ctt1fzhfz8
Ciofalo, N. (Ed.). (2019). *Indigenous psychologies in an era of decolonization.* Springer.
Davis, F. (2019). *The little book of race and restorative justice: Black lives, healing, and US social transformation.* Good Books.
De la Cadena, M. (2015). *Earth beings: Ecologies of practice across Andean worlds.* Duke University Press.
Deloria, V. Jr. (1973). *God is red: A native view of religion.* Putnam Publishing.
Deloria, V. Jr. (1997). *Red earth, white lies: Native American and the myth of scientific facts.* Fulcrum.
DiPietro, P. J. (2019). Beyond benevolent violence: Trans* of color, ornamental multiculturalism, and the decolonization of affect. In P. J. DiPietro, J. McWeeny, & S. Roshanravan (Eds.), *Speaking face to face: The visionary philosophy of María Lugones* (pp. 197–216). State University of New York Press.
DiPietro, P. J (2025). *Sideways selves, Travesti and jotería struggles across the Américas.* University of Texas Press.
Dixon, E., & Piepzna-Samarasinha, L. L. (2020). *Beyond survival: Strategies and stories from the transformative justice movement.* AK Press.
Dutta, U. (2016). Prioritizing the local in an era of globalization: A proposal for decentering community psychology. *American Journal of Community Psychology, 58*, 329–338. https://doi.org/10.1002/ajcp.12047
Ermine, W. (1995). Aboriginal epistemology. In M. Battiste, & J. Barrman (Eds.), *First-Nations education in Canada: The circle unfolds* (pp. 101–112). UBC Press.
Escobar, A. (2016). Thinking-feeling with the Earth: Territorial struggles and the ontological dimension of the epistemologies of the south. *Revista de Antropología Iberoamericana, 11*(1), 11–32. https://doi.org/10.11156/aibr.110102e
Escobar, A. (2021). Reframing civilization: From critique to transitions. *Globalizations*, 1–18. https://doi.org/10.1080/14747731.2021.2002673
Escobar, J. (2022). The role of memory practices in building spiritual solidarity for survivors of state violence. *American Journal of Community Psychology, 69*, 403–414. https://doi.org/10.1002/ajcp.12570
Ferdinand, M. (2022). *Decolonial ecology: Thinking from the Caribbean world.* Polity Press.
Fernández, J. S. (2022). A mujerista liberation psychology perspective on testimonio to cultivate decolonial healing. *Women & Therapy, 45*(1), 1–26 https://doi.org/10.1080/02703149.2022.2095101
Fu-kiau, K. K. B. (2001). *African cosmology of the bantu-Kongo: Tying the spiritual knowt, principles of life and living.* Athelia Henrietta Press.
Gegeo, D., & Watson-Gegeo, K. (2001). "How we know": Kwara'ae rural villagers doing indigenous epistemology. *The Contemporary Pacific, 13*(1), pp. 55–88. https://doi.org/10.1353/cp.2001.0004

Gone, J. P. (2016). Alternative knowledges and the future of community psychology: Provocations from an American Indian healing traditions. *American Journal in Community Psychology, 58*, 314–321. https://doi.org/10.1002/ajcp.12046

González, T., & Epstein, R. (2022). Critical race feminism, health, and restorative practices in schools: Centering the experiences of Black and Latina girls. *Michigan Journal of Gender & Law, 29*(2), 490. https://doi.org/10.36641/mjgl.29.2.critical

Grande, S. (2018). Refusing the university. In E. Tuck, & K. Wayne Yang (Eds.), *Toward what is justice? Describing diverse dreams of justice in education* (pp. 47–65). Routledge.

Gudynas, E. (2014.) Programa Democracia y Transformación Global (PDTG); Red Peruana por una Globalización con Equidad (redGE); CooperAcción, and Centro Latino Americano de Ecología Social (CLAES).

Hammonds, E. (1994). Black holes and the geometry of Back female sexuality. *A Journal of Feminist Cultral Studies, 6* (2-3): 126–145.

James, S., & Lorenz, H. (2021). Back to the source: Moving upstream in the curricular rivers of coloniality. *Review of General Psychology, 25*(4), 385–404. https://doi.org/10.1177/10892680211046509

Jarratt-Snider, K. (2020). Environmental injustice, land, and American Indian religious freedom. In K. Jarratt-Snider, & M. O. Nielsen (Eds.), *Indigenous environmental justice* (pp. 36–58). Tucson: University of Arizona Press.

Karera, A. (2019). Blackness and the pitfalls of Anthropocene ethics. *Critical Philosophy of Race, 7*(1), 32–56. https://doi.org/10.5325/critphilrace.7.1.0032

Kimmerer, M. (2013). *Braiding sweetgrass*. Milkweed Editions.

López Intzin, J. L. (2015). *Sp'ijilal O'tan: Knowledges or epistemologies of the heart*. Hemi Press. https://resistantstrategies.hemi.press/735-2/

Lorde, A. (1984). *Sister outsider: Essays and speeches*. Crossing Press.

Lugones, M., & Price, J. (1995). Dominant culture: El deseo por un alma pobre (The desire for an Impoverished soul). In D. A. Harris (Ed.), Multiculturalism *from the margins* (pp. 103–127). Bergin & Garvey.

Lugones, M. (2008). The coloniality of gender. *Worlds & Knowledges Otherwise, 2*(2), 1–17. https://globalstudies.trinity.duke.edu/projects/wko-gender

Lugones, M. (2010). Toward a decolonial feminism. *Hypatia, 25*(4), 742–759.

Maldonado-Torres, N. (2016). *Outline of ten theses in coloniality and decoloniality*. https://fondation-frantzfanon.com/outline-of-ten-theses-on-coloniality-and-decoloniality/

Marcos, S. (2006). *Taken from the lips: Gender and eros in Mesoamerican religions*. Brill.

Marcos, S. (2014). Feminismos ayer y hoy. *Poiésis, 8*(13), 8–29. https://doi.org/10.19177/prppge.v8e1320148-29

Martin, K., & Mirraboopa, B. (2003). Ways of knowing, ways of being and ways of doing: A theoretical framework and methods for Indigenous research and Indigenist research. *Journal of Australian Studies, 27*(76), 203–214. https://doi.org/10.1080/14443050309387838

Martinez Luna, J. (2015). Conocimiento y comunalidad. *Bajo el Volcán, 15*(23), 99–112. https://www.redalyc.org/pdf/286/28643473006.pdf

Mignolo, W. (2009). Epistemic disobedience, independent thought and decolonial freedom. *Theory, Culture & Society, 26*(7–8), 1–23. https://doi.org/10.1177/0263276409349275

Mignolo, W., & Walsh, C. (2018). *On decoloniality: Concepts, analytics, and praxis*. Duke University Press.

Mingus, M. (2016). *Pods and pods making worksheet*. Bay Area Transformative Justice Collective. https://batjc.wordpress.com/resources/pods-and-pod-mapping-worksheet/

Myers, N. (2016). Photosynthetic mattering: Rooting into the plantoprocene. EASST/4S Meeting in Barcelona, Presentation on Elements Thinking Panel.

Nava Morales, E. (2020). Ecos de la comunalidad en Oaxaca a inicios del siglo XXI. *IdeAs[enLigne], 16*. https://journals.openedition.org/ideas/9121

Ndlovou-Gatsheni, S. (2021). The cognitive empire, politics of knowledge and African intellectual productions: Reflections on struggles for epistemic freedom and resurgence of decolonisation in the twenty-first century. *Third World Quarterly, 42*(5), 882–901. https://doi.org/10.1080/01436597.2020.1775487

Olupona, J. (2011). *City of 201 gods. Ilé-Ifé in time, space, and the imagination*. University of California Press.

Puwar, N. (2004). *Space invaders: Race, gender, and bodies out of place*. Berg Publishers.

Quijano, A. (2000). Coloniality of power and Eurocentrism in Latin America. *International Sociology, 15*(2), 215–232. https://doi.org/10.1177/0268580900015002005

Readsura Decolonial Editorial Collective. (2022). Psychology as a site of decolonial analysis. *Journal of Social Issues, 78*(2), 255–277. https://doi.org/10.1111/josi.12524

Rivera Cusicanqui, S. (2018). *Un mundo ch'ixi es possible: Ensayos desde un presente en crisis*. Tinta Limón, Colección Nociones Comunes.

Sandoval, C. (2000). *Methodologies of the oppressed*. University of Minnesota Press.

Sandoval, C. (2012). Introduction: Toward a decolonial performatics of Latina and Latino borderlands. In A. J. Aldama, C. Sandoval, & P. J. Garcia (Eds.), *Performing the Latino and Latina US borderlands* (pp. 1–30). Indiana University Press. https://www.jstor.org/stable/j.ctt16gzjdt

Shirzad, Y. (2021). Zapatismo and the decolonial turn: Liberation and autonomy in Mexico and across the globe. *International Studies Undergraduate Honors Theses*, *23*. https://scholarworks.seattleu.edu/intl-std-theses/23

Shiva, V. (2013.). Everything I know I learned in the forest. *Yes Magazine*. https://www.yesmagazine.org/issues/what-would-nature-do/vandana-shiva-everything-i-need-to-know-i-learned-in-the-forest

Simpson, L. B. (2018). *As we have always done*. University of Minnesota Press.

Smith, L. T. (2012). *Decolonizing methodologies: Research and Indigenous peoples*. Zen Books.

Sonn, C. C., & Stevens, G. (2021). Tracking the decolonial turn in contemporary community psychology: Expanding socially just knowledge archives, ways of being and modes of praxis. In G. Stevens, & C. C. Sonn (Eds.), *Decoloniality and epistemic justice in contemporary community psychology* (pp. 1–19). Springer Nature Switzerland AG. https://doi.org/10.1007/978-3-030-72220-3_1

Trujillo, C. C. (2019). Colonialidad del poder y colonialidad del género. Sentipensar las luchas de las mujeres indígenas en Abya Yala desde los mundos en relación. *Revista de Sociología Lima, Perú, 28*, 27–48. https://doi.org/10.15381/rsoc.v0i28.16894

Tuck, E. (2009). Suspending damage: A letter to communities. *Harvard Educational Review, 79*(3), 409–427. https://doi.org/10.17763/haer.79.3.n0016675661t3n15

Valandra, E. C., & Wapȟáha Hokšíla, W. (2020). Undoing the first harm: Settlers in restorative justice. In E. C. Valandra, & W. W. Hokšíla (Eds.), *Colorizing restorative justice: Voicing our realities* (1st ed., pp. 325–370). Living Justice Press.

Wekker, G. (2005). *The politics of passion*. Columbia University Press.

Wheelock, R. M. (2006). The American story: The impact of myth on American Indian policy. In S. Pavlik, & D. R. Wildcat (Eds.), *Destroying dogma: Vine Deloria, Jr. and his influence on American society*. 105-130. Fulcrum Publishing.

Wildcat, D. R. (2009). *Red alert: Saving the planet with Indigenous knowledge*. Fulcrum Publishing.

Wilson, S. (2008). *Research is ceremony: Indigenous research methods*. Fernwood Publishing.

Wynter, S. (2003). Unsettling the coloniality of being/power/truth/freedom: Toward the human, after man, its overrepresentation—An argument. *CR: The New Centennial Review*, *3*(3), 257–337. https://doi.org/10.1353/ncr.2004.0015

Wynter, S. (2014). *On being human*. Duke University Press.

Zauditu-Selassie, K. (2018). Dancing between two realms: Sacred resistance and remembrance in African American culture. *The Journal of Interreligious Studies*, *23*, 46–64.

5 Decolonial Alchemy

From Oppression to Liberation

B. Andi Lee, Mercedes Santana, Shelly P. Harrell and Lillian Comas-Díaz

> Dialogue cannot exist, however, in the absence of a profound love for the world and for people. The naming of the world, which is an act of creation and re-creation, is not possible if it is not infused with love. Love is at the same time the foundation of dialogue and dialogue itself... If I do not love the world – if I do not love life – if I do not love people – I cannot enter into dialogue.
>
> Paulo Freire, Pedagogy of the Oppressed, pp. 89–90

Introduction

This chapter is an invitation to dialogue in the service of illuminating decolonial transformations. In writing it, we have been in dialogue with each other, with those in our professional and cultural lineages who have come before us, and those who will come after us. It is also an invitation to you, the reader. Grounded in love, we risk sharing our experiences and transformative journeys toward decolonial and liberatory practice. We invite you to actively engage with our stories, ask questions, connect to your own journeys, and potentially be with discomfort. We ask you to embody whatever arrives in your mind, body, and soul while interacting with our narratives. Decolonizing means to fight, undo, and overcome colonial ways that have shaped our economic, political, and social structures, our knowledge practices, interpersonal relationships, and the self (Ratele et al., 2018). Decolonizing is fundamentally both relational and transformational. It is to enter a relationship of loving and humanizing ourselves and others, with a committed intentionality to transform oppressive colonialities. We center an ethic of love and care in our decolonial practice. We understand love as more than the absence of hate and oppression. Since decolonization is ultimately a liberatory process such that decoloniality entails liberation (Torres Rivera & Torres Fernandez, 2024), decolonial love is the necessary ingredient in the alchemy within which our collective and interconnected liberation will emerge.

Decolonial alchemy is offered here as the interactive, creative, transformative process of healing from the wounds and harms of colonialism/coloniality. Dictionary definitions of alchemy describe it as a powerful and magical process of transmutation or change where something of high value is created from base ingredients (Merriam-Webster, n.d.). Alchemy has been suggested as a metaphor for psychological process of transformation (Breitbart, 2017) and is a central concept within Jungian theory (Robertson, 2017). Ancient alchemy sought to transmute lead into gold through combining various elements. As we bring together the base elements of our ancestral and lived experience, we are igniting an alchemizing process to co-create and extract "the gold" of our transformations from coloniality and oppression, toward decoloniality and liberation. Ancient alchemy also involved the process of extraction, of identifying and illuminating the most active and core ingredients. Thus, the healing of decolonial alchemy deconstructs before it reconstructs and creates. There is inquiry, investigation, and extraction. These processes allow any unnecessary

DOI: 10.4324/9781003492214-6

or dangerous compounds to be identified. Harrell (2023) suggests that healing includes the release and removal of that which is toxic and does not serve wellness. In decolonial alchemy, toxins are released when we defy and disrupt silencing and erasure that functions to maintain white supremacy colonial culture. Definitions of alchemy also consistently refer to a magical, mysterious, or miraculous process. The dual nature of alchemy refers to the presence of matter and spirit, both material and mystical processes, both physical and transpersonal activities (Robertson, 2017). A synergy can happen in contexts of communal sharing that cannot be predicted, that is uniquely co-created through combining the ingredients of our stories, our lives, our beings. These unanticipated miracles occur when we embrace the radical hope and imagination of possibilities beyond current conditions. These possibilities of radical hope emerge from a co-activation of collective memory, agentic action, and faith in possibilities of liberation (Mosley et al., 2020). This zone of possible miracles is an important aspect of what sustains engagement through the intensity of experience when transformative changes are in motion.

The alchemical process is interactive. Similarly, our decolonial alchemy is a fundamentally relational and communal process of what emerges when we share our stories with each other, when our lived experiences make contact. Alchemical transformations are initiated when truth is spoken aloud in community. It is in this dialogic process that the potential for making gold happens. The decolonial nature of our testimony breaks the isolation where colonialism thrives and transmits. A collective braid of testimony is a profound act of reclamation and liberation as embodiment of our truth sheds the complex layers of conditioning, allowing us closer to our essence. The deep wisdom in the African principle of Ubuntu teaches "I am because we are." It is an affirmation that any individual entity has roots and interdependencies with a larger collective across time and place. As ancient alchemy sought to transform what was impure and damaged into something of high value, we seek to transform the damage of oppression into expressions of healing and flourishing. In alchemy, there is a rebirthing process. The alchemizing of the ingredients of our *testimonios* (e.g., ancestral reclamations and reconnections, stories of suffering and redemption, recognition of global/collective solidarity, cultivation of critical consciousness, spiritual practices) produces something bigger than our individual stories that is decolonizing and liberatory.

Elements of Alchemy: How We Came Together

We four sisters found ourselves working in harmony within a larger group of decolonial and liberation-based scholars and practitioners. During her APA presidential term, Dr. Thema Bryant invited each of us individually to serve on a task force focusing on transforming the field of psychology toward decolonial and liberation-based practices. We are a sisterhood of intersectional feminist warriors who promote love, justice, joy, and reclamation in psychology. We came together with a spiritual sense to answer the call to share ourselves with the collective. We hope to change the oppression narrative, validate, disrupt, and inspire the generations of readers. Our voices woven together represented a beautiful tapestry of *testimonio* as members of the Global Majority in psychology. Our *testimonios* carry our lineages and are imbued with sacredness. Each generation of our tapestry has experienced otherness for rejecting the colonizing status quo and moving into a felt sense alignment with our higher calling. Our work as disruptors, solidarity seekers, weavers, and healers was inherited from our lineages, as we continue to confront coloniality inside and outside of psychology. True to decolonization, we accepted the invitation to move a symposium at the American Psychological Association's 2023 annual convention to action by delivering this chapter. We are holding the tears of pain, reception, validation, and inspiration of our audience forward. It is our prayer that this chapter will continue to inspire, validate, heal, and transform our readers further into their process of liberation and decolonizing. As stated by Ignacio Martín-Baró (1994), we confirm and are rooted in the notion, "Liberation is the horizon of psychology."

We channel our stories through the decolonial/liberation paradigm of *testimonio*, rooting ourselves in a decolonial position to disrupt Western psychology's prominent narratives and incomplete truths. Using a decolonial paradigm of sharing our lived experiences, continues to call back our power from being manipulated or edited in ways that align with the status quo. *Testimonio* is sacred in its ability to highlight the impact of systemic oppression in the context of an individual's lived experience (Comas-Diaz, 2020). In that fashion, it extends autoethnography (and or, testimonio) and encompasses the possibility of inciting social change via enhancing the loudening the silenced narratives within psychology (Silva et al., 2021).

Testimonio within a liberation psychology framework allows individuals to reclaim their authentic experiences in the socio-political context, thus freeing one's ancestral, lived, and collective truths from colonial shame applied by Western psychology (Carmona & Luciano, 2014). *Testimonios* are the building blocks of relational resiliency and vital for the validation of survival of each (Cervantes, 2020; Comas-Díaz, 2006; Delgado Bernal et al., 2012; Latina Feminist Group, 2001). Our methodology of *testimonio* is grounded in liberation psychology's commitment to collective wellness with preference to those most harmed by oppression (Martin-Baró, 1994), the Indigenous Latin American concept *buen vivir* (Walsh, 2010), and feminisms of color (Bryant-Davis & Comas-Diaz, 2016). The theme of interconnectedness and the centering of love are central to each of these foundations of our orientation to *testimonio*. The concept of *buen vivir* entails the right to live a full life through harmonious relationships between people, nature, environment, and cosmos (Walsh, 2010). As self-described Black queer womanist Angelique Nixon reminds us, everything is connected – justice, healing, freedom, joy, rebellion – hence change begins with each one of us being honest about our truth to enact sustainable change for the collective (Nixon, 2020). Her BRACE model identifies five processes in the movement toward decolonial healing justice: burn, resist, act, care, elevate. Each of these is activated in our *testimonios* of decolonial alchemy.

Our methodology of *testimonio* is rooted in feminisms of color that grew from Indigenous roots in response to mainstream feminism's neglect of women of color issues (Bryant-Davis & Comas-Díaz, 2016). It is too often that BIPOC women and femmes experience disenfranchised grief as a product of continual harsh intersectional oppression. As feminists of color, womanists and *mujeristas* (Latinx womanists), we advocate for a collective liberation. As dissident daughters of theologies of liberation, we recognize the power of spirituality (Bryant-Davis & Comas-Diaz, 2016). Feminists of color aim to decolonize mainstream feminism by addressing the needs of Women of Color and those of women in the Global Majority (Comas-Díaz & Castaneda-Sound, in press; Espinosa Miñoso, 2020). As such, womanists and *mujeristas* promote the Indigenous precept that every living being is sacred. Indeed, compared to religion, spirituality promotes liberation (Comas-Díaz, 2008). The architect of liberation psychology Ignacio Martin-Baró (1994) stated that a connection with a higher power assists healing. The dual nature of alchemy, that involves both the material and the miraculous, is thus a particularly powerful descriptor of change processes with roots in feminisms of color.

We thus offer our *testimonios* as sacred stories in sacred voices. These offerings reflect lived experiences that are often held in silence and frequently invisible in our public-facing professional lives. They reflect the transformative power of voice and visibility, of bringing into the light what has been relegated to shadows. In alchemy, darkness is the starting point of all creation and transformation; it is the dark earth, the dark matter where stars burst into brilliance. Our testimonies come out of our darkness, our truth-telling transforms pain/suffering into holistic thriving. Transforming the field of psychology requires transmuting ourselves. We offer glimpses of our larger journeys of decolonizing our minds, our lives, and our work as psychologists. Our *testimonios* are more than disembodied monologues and they speak from voices beyond fact-based narrative statements. They contain ancestral longings for humanization and liberation. As we shared our stories with each other, we also recognized there was a sense of powerful resonance and affirmation. Collectively, they reflect an often unspoken base of evidence that informs the process of transformative change amid ongoing dynamics and expressions of coloniality and oppression. Our *testimonios* are invitations to bear witness, to hold space, to honor the experiential truths of our lived experience – and to accompany. Our *testimonios* are a protection and prayer to our sacred liberation praxis that have organically unfolded over time. Here, and after each testimonio, we offer a *Selah*, a sacred pause to hold space for a moment of presence, prayer, and praise, as well as to invite affirmation, reflection, and connection.

Selah.
Praise to the courage of vulnerability and truth-telling.
(Inhale) We breathe in, filling ourselves with love for each other and for the humanity of all people.
(Exhale) We breathe out and release the fear of visibility that coloniality has created within us.

Embracing an Ethic of Care: Surviving the Graduate School Gauntlet for the PhD

I, Andi, am a queer neurodiverse Taiwanese American daughter of immigrants who has been told that I "care too much." I am a liberation psychotherapist who stands for the freedom and self-determination of our Global Majority siblings in Palestine, Sudan, Congo, Haiti, Puerto Rico, Hawai'i, Turtle Island, and beyond, for the abolition of the prison industrial complex and policing, and who wants to dismantle carceral elements that are replicated in the practice of psychology. The barriers to entry in this field are high; they're even higher for those of us who envision something different for Global Majority members, particularly something that affords us the recognition of our humanity and right to wellness and joy amidst systemic racism and generational wounds. I entered this field with a vision: to become a clinical psychologist hoping to work with clients who are also children of immigrants, Asian American, members of the LGBTQIA+ community, survivors of trauma, and more. This vision has been challenged at every step of an oppressive path embedded in the ivory tower, obstacles that were hazing rituals disguised as requirements to sharpen my research and clinical skills. In moving from oppression to liberation, my path of decolonial healing justice required creativity, connection, and love for my survival alongside chosen siblings and comrades with a shared vision for psychology.

The core message of my *testimonio* is that we need to model, cultivate, and embrace an ethic of care for psychologists across all developmental stages, but especially for trainees in graduate school. When I say an ethic of care, I mean a commitment to the relational over renown, to trust, curiosity, and nurturing humanity rather than a culture of competition and scarcity, and to recognizing we need each other, that we cannot do any of this alone. I will share why this is so important to my heart, where I have experienced it, and some ideas for how we may continue to foster this as a field to decolonize training and research mentorship.

I had followed all the "right steps" to becoming a clinical psychologist - clinical psychology major, hired in a post-baccalaureate research position after completing my undergraduate degree, acceptance into a highly ranked doctoral program. Not in the "right steps": dropping out before completing my first year. It was March of 2018, and my research advisor at the time, a white male assistant professor, had told me I was not "cut out for research" and that I didn't "know how to critically think – you only how to follow orders." When I teared up at that feedback, he told me that I "internalize too much." My first week in his lab, in a moment of frustration, he stated that I was "not his first-choice student." Having just uprooted my life from my community, my partner, and mentors that supported me, this was a devastating start to an already financially, physically, and emotionally difficult transition. Throughout that first year, this advisor told me in numerous ways that I was "not enough" and was quick to point out my flaws, including minor spelling errors, meeting with other faculty across campus to hear about their work, and taking a two-week break from research to see my family in Taiwan over the university winter holiday. After leaving the lab,

I learned I'd been working under different conditions than my fellow first-year lab mates – shorter deadlines, longer work shifts, and had joined the pool of other Asian women this advisor had bullied and abused. I had to unlearn colonial mentalities (David & Okazaki, 2006) that prized and elevated white male cultural values and behaviors, which taught me there was no room for emotion, especially tears, and that I should gladly accept any type of mentorship I could get. Yet, in seeking approval from and attempting to meet colonial standards of success, I was the unhappiest and most uncertain of my purpose in this field that I've ever been.

My turning point was when a fellow graduate student of color saw my distress, listened to my story, and emphasized that I deserved better. He not only said this but also demonstrated it by advocating for my transition to a new lab with his advisor in counseling psychology, even going as far as writing a letter of recommendation for me to this advisor. This form of care – genuine, non-transactional, and timely – was so critical to my journey and survival as I was able to find restoration, clarity, support, community, and mentorship in leaving this former research advisor and joining Dr. Helen Neville's Liberation Lab. The Liberation Lab fostered not only healing but also immense hope and happiness. As a research mentor, Dr. Neville's style of person-first mentorship has not only encouraged me to move beyond those messages of not being enough but also build confidence in my ability to contribute as a researcher and clinician in this field. Critical mentorship moments that were not only decolonial but also liberatory include: first, after she heard why I left my former lab, she stated, "I am so sorry this happened to you. I know there will be moments in our work where frustration may come up, and it's okay to bring that up with me." This felt decolonial in this leveling of power (in her role as an advisor, she was willing to hear my feedback for her), but also in intentionally embracing conflict as a component of being in community with others with opportunities for repair. Second, I was holding a lot of shame for not having "produced" enough in my first year compared to others in my program. Dr. Neville not only explored my research interests with me but also offered numerous publication opportunities, collaboration with fellow lab mates, and research funding to support data collection. She never made me feel "behind" and instead supported research projects that aligned with my values and felt personally meaningful to me. And third, the Liberation Lab fosters intentional relationality. Whether through starting each lab meeting with honest "check-ins," or in having enthusiasm and curiosity about our peers' work, our lab members truly show respect and love for each other. Structurally, we have so much support for deepening our relationships, including lab dinners, hikes, dance parties, and regular celebratory group chat messages highlighting our labmates' numerous accomplishments. We feel seen, uplifted, and supported in moments of difficulty. The ongoing COVID-19 pandemic has encouraged us to acknowledge our oppressive conditions both in academia and outside of it. Though there are so many examples of when I have felt deeply held by this lab, one I want to share is, after the 2021 Atlanta Spa Shootings where six Asian women died (Lenthang, 2021), Liberation Lab members showed up with food, flowers, and friendship. These actions didn't further our research productivity or careers and instead were steps to model holding gentle and loving space for our humanities.

As trainees, we often feel that we don't have power as workers and students. However, we do have power in mutually offering care and letting ourselves be cared for – whether that is sharing institutional wisdom with newer students, breaking bread together, and being there for each other in moments of joy, grief, anger, and exhaustion. In 2020, amidst very public anti-Black and anti-Asian violence, our graduate students of color, frustrated by the lack of acknowledgment and care from our program faculty, formed a community care collective and wrote a letter asking for anti-racist change, detailing actionable steps, Diversity, Equity, Inclusion consultants faculty could hire, and were vulnerable in sharing how we had personally been impacted by the lack of action to date. While faculty responded with anger and apathy toward our requests, we students of color did experience decolonial psychology in this collective action by following our values and speaking up in the face of injustice, and recognizing our experiences were valuable to support change. The relationships that grew from our community care collective are some of my most cherished and largest contributions to my survival of this graduate program.

As I close my *testimonio*, an ethic of care was a key ingredient of decolonial alchemy that catalyzed my process of healing, being witnessed in my humanity, and cultivating hope. I probably still do "care too much," but despite this being used against me as a weakness, I find it a strength to stay connected and invested in our shared humanity. I hope my *testimonio* can reflect how caring is necessary for our liberation, why it is radical to care amidst so much pain, suffering, and apathy, and why this sensitivity and attunement to ourselves and each other is a necessary skill as healers, caregivers, and builders for the current and future generation of dreamers in this field. I acknowledge that, especially as trainees, we are constantly up against colonial forces of scarcity and rejection, as we have to apply for grants, submit publications, apply for internships just to get our degree, and more. To my fellow graduate students and healers-in-training: our values are our strengths, we belong in this field and have something to contribute, and we are enough.

Selah.
Praise to the courage of vulnerability and truth-telling.
(Inhale) We breathe in, grounding in connection, and care.
(Exhale) We breathe out, freeing ourselves from the chains of abusive and dehumanizing treatment.

Owning All of Me: Resuscitating My Heart and Spirit to Forgo the Ego

I (Mercedes) write my *testimonio* as a request from the people who continue to be inspired by my journey. I am an Afro-Latine queer cisgender femme and proud first-generation college graduate born as a guest on the Dakota lands of Turtle Island. My own survivance has created a fierce passion about ending the transmission of intergenerational trauma. I continue to become my *Quisqueya* ancestors' wildest dreams, simultaneously the colonizer's nightmare. As you can already tell, Western psychology was not meant for nor ready for me. Often, my professors found themselves taken aback by my persistent resilience against the pervasive forces of colonialism, seemingly diminishing the rich tapestry of my lived experiences prior to embarking on the journey of graduate studies. Nonetheless, my resistance to the field was persisting and continuing to trailblaze ways of thinking and doing with the sole reason of improving training, education, and clinical practice experiences for the people.

Training and education in psychology has continued to focus on applying a multicultural experience and knowledge base to serve the globe. Recently, scholars have highlighted my felt experience navigating multicultural prided graduate programs (Neville et al., 2021). Hence, I was decolonizing myself since my undergraduate psychology education. I learned early that questioning the "why" of practices, systems, and policies was always a threat and most often met with defensiveness at the least. Additionally, the environment taught me that asking to be contextually treated with respect, care, and tenderness as a student was inappropriate, especially within the confines of clinical practice. I vividly remember resigning from a practicum that directed my personal phone calls received in Spanish to be taken in the alley, as inclusivity was weaponized as "everyone knowing what is being said." This was a prized practicum site that remained on our list despite years of students prior having experienced the same mistreatment. Psychology's outward facing focus on trauma neglects what is happening in the class, clinical supervision, and internship experiences. I realized as a practitioner the same limitations of my trainers had become that of my own. Our liberation as students is bound to that of our preceptors. I was unable to identify, name, and heal trauma in my clinical practice. It is no coincidence the year I entered the field, a special issue dedicated to trainee harm was published which validated my experiences. Somewhere within the timeframe, the APA ethics code was edited to include students as a vulnerable population to harm (APA, 2017). The trauma was not only happening to me but also around me in the form of witnessing. I watched every other Black, Indigenous, and Person of Color trainee and staff experience microaggressions and other forms of coloniality on a daily basis in every clinical setting. Worse, I watched suffering Global Majority members receive inappropriate and harmful colonial clinical care devoid of context. My ancestors recalled and remembered entering battle many days entering clinical settings in the form of somatic pain. I recall driving to many places of clinical practice with a sense of battle in my bones and a fierce urgency to help my community. My vision was how to provide the necessary practices to a clinical population that continued through a revolving door seeking a higher ethic of care. It was defaulting to continue receiving raving reviews and harsh criticism of minuscule mistakes only to not provide sustainable care to oppressed peoples. These experiences coupled with feeling clinically incompetent and confused brought me to the point of almost leaving the field shortly after securing licensure. My personal mental health reflected many walking into my office. A sense of pure exhaustion, shame, pain, rage, and panic. My barrier was that nothing outside of psychology was appealing. I had been called to this work as a child, a conviction in my heart to serve and heal combined with a lineage of wisdoms and talents that fortified the calling. Though a weary warrior, my ancestors had a plan, and I decided to listen.

I fell into a time of deep reflection and (un)learning. I immediately stopped seeking training from "experts" in the field who all had the same thing in common: white person, middle age, wealthy, heterosexual, and Christian. Each one had an inability to provide consultation on cases involving members of the Global Majority upon my inquiry. In fact, most of them were unable to contextually follow my questions and struggled to communicate with me as a person of color in the conversation. I aligned with nature and in a season was able to slow down to uncover what was needed. I leaned toward my embodied epistemology of knowing and remembering. Multiculturalism propelled my clinical abilities, nevertheless it is and was not enough. I returned to fourth wave feminist works to uncover a pathway to decolonial and liberation-based psychologies a la Drs. Lillian Comas-Díaz and Thema Bryant – this fortified my decision to stay in the field and continue trying new ways of being. I started to challenge everything known. I looked at my pain of learning from all white American "experts" in psychology. I reached out and connected with decolonial practitioners and researchers at national conferences and via social media. I did not know the words; however, it became clear that understanding the impact of colonization in all its forms was my battle. The ways in which psychology would reinforce that something was either "wrong" (pathologizing) with me or my clients if progress was not happening fast enough (urgency) was now a red flag. When learning about complex trauma, my guide informed me that my clients were "scared" not displaying pathology and encouraged pacing. This learning resonated in my soul, as a survivor of complex trauma and colonization. It also allowed me to demonstrate a different ethic of care in the therapy room. I realized that multiculturalism is not enough. It is a necessary direction to follow, yet still is not enough. I needed to understand myself more as a guide than a power-yielding psychologist that was reinforced throughout my professional education and training.

My work came full circle when I called my power back. When I started to write, dream, envision, and hope again I became alive in psychology. My ancestral lineage promotes being in service, not servitude, to others. I have continued to seek out opportunities to challenge psychology and medicine to think about those needing care. I have been fortunate to serve on a working group with several other decolonial and liberation rooted psychologists. Through this process, I have been able to further reclaim myself while also being challenged to further my decolonization process. I do not attempt to decolonize Western approaches to psychology, but rather name what has been co-opted and (re)learn what has been stolen. I understand myself in connection to my current ancestors as well as those which have walked for centuries. I have (re)called my wisdom back and connection back to intuition. My spirit is no longer fragmented and I am a whole person in psychology. I am wrapped in love and surrounded by fellow double-agents who are working for and against the system to demand changes in all contexts. Sisterhood circles of fellow decolonial thinkers and practitioners are crucial to continuing the work and going deeper into the decolonial process. I understand decolonization is an ongoing process, one in which I wholeheartedly am open to the challenges, trials, and tribulations that come, knowing that the people get better when I divest.

Selah.
Praise to the courage of vulnerability and truth-telling.
(Inhale) We breathe in- opening to our wisdom, intuition, and ancestral resilience.
(Exhale) We breathe out- healing intergenerational trauma and becoming whole.

The Calling of Sankofa

It is not wrong to go back and retrieve what has been lost or forgotten.

—Akan proverb

The African wisdom of Sankofa ("go back and get it") is represented by two visual symbols and the proverb above. They are part of the representation of Akan wisdom through over 100 adinkra symbols with origins in the West African regions of Ghana and the Ivory Coast. Sankofa most broadly symbolizes reclamation, retrieval, and revitalization. I (Shelly) have been on a journey of Sankofa through much of my educational and professional life. I am a cisgender woman of African descent whose ancestors were trafficked primarily from Ghana, Ivory Coast, and Nigeria (based on ancestry testing). I am a Baby Boomer whose racial socialization was dominated with messages of education as savior. Succeeding in academic contexts was among the highest values in my family and was seen as necessary for our surviving and thriving. The expectation was to endure and overcome any challenges encountered along the way. I am the only child of parents who sacrificed tremendously for me. My father, a Black man who died at age 50 from chronic diseases resulting from "living while Black." My father, despite the daily indignities he faced, was an embodiment of love and laughter. He taught me the African American wisdom of "don't let nobody steal your joy." My mother was raised in the Appalachian mountains of West Virginia. She was one of three daughters of a Black coal-mining activist who fled Alabama with his young family after threats of violence subsequent to "standing up to a white man." She was the youngest daughter of my grandmother who had a sixth grade education, had a life-giving green thumb, did crossword puzzles daily, and could beat her three college educated daughters and all of their children in Scrabble until the day she died. My mother was a Black woman who broke barriers (received a master's of Foreign Languages from a high-status, predominantly white university in the early 1950s and taught four languages as a high school teacher). She was also a woman who battled colorism, and who was able to cast her vote for a Black man for President just months before she died. I carry not only my own losses and forgettings but also the losses of my ancestors – what was denied, silenced, and stolen from them.

Whispers of Sankofa began in childhood and adolescence, from the late 1960s to the mid-1970s where I was one of very few Black students at private schools outside of Detroit Michigan. Post 1967 riots – Detroit was a vibrant hub of Black Pride and Black Power. Each day that I left my Black community and rode the bus to a "different world," I began to lose things that I didn't realize were getting lost until years later. It was there where I first began to contort myself to be approved of and accepted. It is there where I began to hear the inner critic of anti-Blackness, and where colonial performativity began. The Sankofa calling got louder in college at Harvard/Radcliffe in the late 70s, as it became clear that Black people were invisible in my psychology courses. Through my increasing global awareness during protests demanding US divestiture from South Africa, and through experiencing racism in multiple forms (peers, in Harvard Yard by a white man with a knife yelling racist obscenities, medical trauma experiences seeking care at the university health center, etc.), Sankofa kept calling me to remember what my settings would have me forget and silence. My senior honors thesis explored "fear of success" among Black students. During graduate school in the early 1980s at UCLA, the Sankofa calling took the form of increasing emphasis on race, culture, and community-based practice. However, despite an emphasis on racism in my research, I generally followed a career path of what was expected and acceptable. The internalized racism and coloniality were powerful and reflected in both overt and subtle ways in my professional socialization. It wasn't until mid-career that I more fully answered the call return, reclamation, retrieval, and revitalization.

Sankofa Theory and Practice (Harrell, 2023) conceptualizes the psychological-relational-collective impact of colonialism and oppression through the profound disconnections that occur. Sankofa theory names these disconnections as dehumanization, detachment, domination, delusion, disharmony, demoralization, and destruction. Recognizing the overt and subtle ways that each of these showed up in my own journey has been a significant part of my healing. For example, when I was teaching research methods with a commitment to illuminating critiques of the status quo, I reached out to a former professor to chat about the limitations of the randomized controlled trial (RCT) design as the sole determinant of "evidence," particularly in the context of diversity. She stayed on script and dutifully recited the default party line of RCTs being the "gold standard" of proof, and how randomization guarded against bias. She clearly didn't want to hear any of what I had to say. Noted.

Sankofa Theory and Practice also offers seven reconnection processes (phases) of a Sankofa Journey that unpack and illuminate the deep wisdom of Sankofa. The processes move from recognition, through reclamation, return, remembrance, and release, to retrieval and revitalization (Harrell, 2024). The first process of Recognition can be an experience of realization and reckoning. For me, it involved some of both as the nuanced ways that I colluded with the status quo of our profession became clearer and clearer to me over time. As I interrogated the layers and various expressions of anti-Blackness and coloniality, I began mining my own life, work, and mind. I am very proud of my early conceptual work on racism (Harrell, 2000), and development of the Racism and Life Experience Scales (RaLES; Harrell, 1997). However, particularly with the latter, I began to see the ways that psychology's love affair with statistical/numeric data, and orientation toward reduction and categorization perpetuated the exclusion and erasure of "minority" experience. I taught statistics and research methods in the doctoral programs of two institutions of higher education for over 20 years. I drank some of that kool aid for several of those years until the Sankofa calling brought me into deeper "recognition" that the master's tools will never dismantle the master's house (Lorde, 2007). Despite my focus and commitment throughout my career to understanding and documenting racism-related stress and trauma, it hit me that this approach was not fundamentally designed to change or heal the impacts of racism. In addition, although I had begun dismantling my own internalized racism more than 40 years ago, it wasn't truly until mid-career (about 15 years ago) that I more deeply realized the intricate and nuanced work of decolonizing my own mind and psyche. Vestiges of racism, intersectional oppression, and coloniality can hide-out and mask themselves such that it is difficult to see unless one is looking intentionally. As musician and ancestor Prince sang to us "the voice you hear is the alchemy of your mind" (Rogers Nelson, 2004). As I continue this journey of life, the voices (ancestral, experiential, spiritual, relational) of my Sankofa callings have become stronger and clearer. I am embodying them more fully, and working more intentionally with their alchemical potential for transformative liberation of minds, bodies, and communities. The elements of Nixon's (2020) BRACE model of decolonial transformation resonate with the process of my own decolonial alchemy.

I BURN. I am a Phoenix. I have been burned by loss, silencing, performativity. I have burned down the internalized frames of racism and colonialism. I have laid in the ashes of grief and disconnection. I have soothed the wounds and recognized the scars. I have reclaimed myself, my soul, my people, and the souls of my people. I have recommitted to the ongoing work of restoration, regeneration, and revitalization. I have risen and re-risen. I will burn and rise again.

I RESIST. I see. I refuse to close my eyes. Resistance requires seeing clearly what has happened and what is happening now, so that there is not unconscious collusion. I listen. I hear the voices of my ancestors telling me what happened to them, guiding me, protecting me, lifting me up. I resist all that seeks to bring me down.

I ACT. I engage in intentional acts of connection. I reconnect, over and over and over again – to myself, my blessings, and the truth of my lived experience. I reconnect to community, to culture, to nature, to God/Spirit. I reconnect to the temporal interconnectedness of past, present, and future (ancestors-myself-descendants) which inspires my actions.

I CARE. I love. I love fiercely and feel deeply. I open my heart and my mind to the struggles and concerns of others. Love is my ground and my guide.

I ELEVATE. I reach above and beyond what I can see. I inspire and am inspired. I receive and share knowledge. We heal. We flourish. We fly. We soar.

> *Selah. Praise to the courage of vulnerability and truth-telling.*
> *(Inhale) We breathe in- remembering, reclaiming, retrieving what we have forgotten.*
> *(Exhale) We breathe out- rebirthing and revitalizing what we bring forward for our descendants.*

Inhabiting *Nepantla*, Embracing Spirit

As I (Lillian) witness my present, I embody my future. I experienced oppression most of my life. Born in the continental United States and raised in Puerto Rico – the oldest colony in the world (Trias Monge, 1997) – poisoned me. An Afro-Latinx female, I became a victim of intersectional oppressions such as colonization, imperialism, gendered racism, sexism, classism, elitism, and other forms of dehumanization. Paradoxically, oppression conjured opportunity. Due to colonial oppression, my parents journeyed circular migrations between the island and the continental US. Following their example, I returned to El Norte during my early adulthood and nursed a harbor mind – the ability to manage multiple realities resulting in pluralism (Nicolson, 2023). Like geographies of the self (Anzaldúa & Keating, 2013), a harbor mind helped me integrate every place I lived into my identity. These *vivencias* (life experiences) awakened my critical consciousness (Anzaldúa & Keating, 2013).

An avid reader since childhood, I voraciously read about colonization, decoloniality, and liberation. One of my impacting readings was the poem "*Yo misma fui mi ruta (I was my own route)*" published by Puerto Rican writer Julia de Burgos in 1938 (see de Burgos, 1938). This poem is a feminist ode to self-empowerment, decoloniality, and liberation. Although reading inspired me, however, reading was insufficient. I yearned for spirit. Reconnecting with ancestral wisdom, I birthed, or rather received, *Spirita* (Comas-Díaz, 2008) – a feminism of color that proclaims sacredness as a collective right to be free and well. *Spirita* echoes Gloria Anzaldúa's (1987) construct of *Nepantla* (being in between-ness or in the middle). Therefore, *Nepantleras* (females who inhabit Nepantla) belong nowhere, dwell in liminal spaces, and simultaneously are part of every group. Both Spirita and Nepantla summon a shamanistic power for healing, transformation, liberation, and illumination. Likewise, *mujeristas* reclaim their right to freedom and to *buen vivir*. An Aymara concept, *buen vivir* consecrates every living being as sacred. A *mujerista* and a liberation psychologist, I uncovered a buried mirror – one that reflects the real meaning of *acompañamiento* (accompaniment). A mutual process grounded in love, *acompañamiento* announces a vision of liberation – one that is either latent or manifest (Freire, 1970). Likewise, I learned that when you accompany the oppressed, you connect with a powerful sacred force to heal. Hence, armed with Spirita and grounded in *Nepantla*, I engaged in decolonization and anticolonization. Following a *mujerista* path led me to embrace *la lucha* (the struggle), syncretism, psycho-spirituality, and collective solidarity. Drinking from these fountains, I committed to enhance my spiritual faculties, including l*a facultad* – a spiritual intuition about knowledge, especially regarding power differentials (Anzaldúa, 1987). Through this process, I connected with ancestxrs to transmute oppression into resistance. I remembered my mother's words: *Healing others heals you*. Likewise, my maternal grandmother counseled me to embrace the spirits, while my paternal grandmother taught me to listen to spirits' messages and to work with them. In other words, ancestral spirituality uncovered my dharma – an alchemical feminist decolonial liberation.

Today, I labor as a healer, scholar, and social justice activist. I continue to bond with ancestral wisdom/spirituality and integrate new/old *conocimiento* (knowledge) into my life and work. Instead of authoring *conocimiento*, I welcome visions that assist me in my healing practice. Moreover, I aspire to become a Warrior of the Light (Coelho, 2002) – an instrument of healing, peace, and *buen vivir.* Like the Chilean women who weave together pieces of fabric to denounce and combat their oppression (Triani, 2013), Andi, Mercedes, Shelly, and I composed our testimonios as a liberation *arpillera*.

Selah. Praise to the courage of vulnerability and truth-telling.
(Inhale) We breathe in- opening to ancestral spirituality, messages, and visions.
(Exhale) We breathe out- healing in the light.

Closing Questions and Invitations

We hope and pray that our collective *testimonios* have sparked decolonial alchemy within you as it has within us. We are grateful for the interpersonal relationships we have woven together and forged into the gold of liberation, healing, and thriving. It isn't often that we are able to convene with others with shared identities, as we are all women of color with experiences and histories of surviving and fighting colonial oppression, but shared values and dreams for how psychology can be. In sharing our stories, we aim to not only cleanse ourselves of the toxins of colonialism but also bear witness to each other in these unique and shared journeys toward psychological freedom and wellness. We are grateful for kindred sisterhoods who gather to braid and weave lived experience through multi-vocal, embodied, and emancipatory testimony and *testimonio*. By "writing differently" (Einola et al., 2021, p. 1602), we engage in acts of solidarity, love, and "epistemic disobedience and resistance" (Fernandez et al., 2022, p. 400). We invite you to join us in witnessing and being in relationship with us through your responses, whether in resonance, *acompañamiento* (accompaniment) (Martín-Baró, 1994), surprise, sadness, grief, anger, and/or curiosity with our stories.

Some themes that emerged as guideposts and core ingredients across our *testimonios* encircle the importance of relationships and how we infuse love into these relationships as a form of guidance, knowledge, resistance, and truth-telling to catalyze decolonial alchemy. **Guidance**, such that an ethic of care – for ourselves, each other, and those who come after us – means that we hold space for this as part of how we move in all spaces, as therapists, mentors, students, researchers, and colleagues. Even if the academy tells you otherwise, to care about others only brings us all toward our goals and healing – there is no "getting ahead" or "falling behind" when we operate from a foundation of respect for each other's dignity, humanity, and dreams. Building upon this is the importance of trust, trusting our hearts, intuition, and our ancestral wisdom over the "European American mainstream written word" as ways to promote healing in psychology. Heart intelligence is something we carry with us, deep in our souls from our ancestors, and as a compass for teaching us to identify, heal, and transform trauma within ourselves and our Global Majority siblings. It affords us clarity and the opportunity to engage in de-ideologization of our daily experiences and keeps us from acclimating to our oppressive conditions, and instead have the energy to resist and connect with others in our fight toward a better world for ourselves and the generations to come. Among our collective, we highlight the power of **Sankofa**, which symbolizes reclamation, retrieval, and revitalization as a pathway to our authenticity and acceptance of ourselves and each other. It affords us access through recognition of our wounds, our energy to resist continued harm, connection and reconnection with our communities, and the importance of sharing our lessons with each other to heal and thrive.

As we close, we call back to our opening epigraph and reflect on the importance of love as the foundation for dialogue, relationality, and humanization. Through our testimonios, we recognize the most active and necessary ingredient of decolonial alchemy as love, love for ourselves, love for others, love for life, love for the world. The "gold" of liberation cannot be created in the absence of love. The decolonial transmutations that happen in the alchemizing of our ancestral, personal, and collective experience are fueled and flavored by love. Black feminist ancestor bell hooks (1994) teaches:

> Without love, our efforts to liberate ourselves and our world community from oppression and exploitation are doomed. As long as we refuse to address fully the place of love in struggles for liberation we will not be able to create a culture of conversion where there is a mass turning away from an ethic of domination.
>
> (p. 289)

The sharing of our testimonios is done from a ground of love that has supported us to engage inner, relational, and collective alchemies of decolonization. As appropriate timing and resourcing are presented, we invite you to explore engagement with your own decolonial alchemy processes and leave you with a few questions for consideration:

1. Honor your voice and uncover its sacred function. What have you been wanting to say that you have not, and who can you share your story with?
2. What wounds and core beliefs from psychology are interfering with your decolonial dharma?
3. How do you incorporate spirit into your life? What knowledges and wisdoms do you bring?
4. What are the "ingredients" of decolonial alchemy that you can incorporate into your life as well as those of others?
5. What are three ways you can begin to practice decolonial love in your relationships within yourself, with your loved ones, and with those who are hard to love?

References

American Psychological Association. (2017). *Ethical principles of psychologists and code of conduct*. https://www.apa.org/ethics/code/

Anzaldúa, G. (1987). To live in the borderlands. In A. G. Melendez, M. J., Yong., P. Moore, & P. Pynes (Eds.), *The multicultural Southwest: A reader* (pp. 139–140). The University of Arizona Press.

Anzaldúa, G., & Keating, A. (Eds.). (2013). *This bridge we call home: Radical visions for transformation.* Routledge.

Bernal, D. D., & Villalpando, O. (2002). An apartheid of knowledge in academia: The struggle over the "legitimate" knowledge of faculty of color. *Equity & Excellence in Education*, *35*(2), 169–180. https://doi.org/10.1080/713845282

Breitbart, W. (2017). Alchemy and psychology. *Palliative and Supportive Care, 15*, 146–147. https://doi.org/10.1017/S1478951517000189

Bryant-Davis, T. E., & Comas-Díaz, L. E. (2016). *Womanist and mujerista psychologies: Voices of fire, acts of courage*. American Psychological Association.

Carmona, J. F., & Luciano, A. M. (2014). A student-teacher testimonio: Reflexivity, empathy, and pedagogy. *Counterpoints*, *449*, 75–92. https://www.jstor.org/stable/42982066

Cervantes, A. (2020). *Testimonios*. In L. Comas-Díaz, & E. Torres Rivera (Eds.), *Liberation psychology: Theory, method, practice, and social justice* (pp. 133–147). American Psychological Association. https://doi.org/10.1037/0000198-008

Coelho, P. (2002). *Manual of the warrior of the light*. Harper Collins.

Comas-Díaz, L. (2006). Latino healing: The integration of ethnic psychology into psychotherapy. *Psychotherapy: Theory, Research, Practice, Training, 43*(4), 436–453. https://doi.org/10.1037/0033-3204.43.4.436

Comas-Diaz, L. (2008). 2007 Carolyn Sherif award address: Spirita: Reclaiming womanist sacredness into feminism. *Psychology of Women Quarterly*, *32*(1), 13–21. https://psycnet.apa.org/doi/10.1111/j.1471-6402.2007.00403.x

Comas-Díaz, L. (2020). Liberation psychotherapy. In L. Comas-Díaz, & E. Torres Rivera (Eds.), *Liberation psychology: Theory, method, practice, and social justice* (pp. 169–185). American Psychological Association.

David, E. J. R., & Okazaki, S. (2006). Colonial mentality: A review and recommendation for Filipino American psychology. *Cultural Diversity and Ethnic Minority Psychology*, *12*(1), 1. https://doi.org/10.1037/1099-9809.12.1.1

De Burgos, J. (1938). *Yo misma fui mi ruta*. Ciudad Seva. https://ciudadseva.com/texto/yo-misma-fui-mi-ruta/

Delgado Bernal, D., Burciaga, R., & Flores Carmona, J. (2012). Chicana/Latina testimonios: Mapping the methodological, pedagogical, and political. *Equity & Excellence in Education*, *45*(3), 363–372. https://doi.org/10.1080/10665684.2012.698149

Einola, K., Elkina, A., Gao, G., Hambleton, J., Kaasila-Pakanen, A. L., Mandalaki, E., & Pullen, A. (2020). Writing multi-vocal intersectionality in times of crisis. *Gender Work & Organization, 28*(4), 1600–1623. https://doi.org/10.1111/gwao.12577

Espinosa Miñoso, Y. (2020). *Why we need decolonial feminism: Differentiation and constitutional domination in western modernity*. Afterall Articles. https://www.afterall.org/articles/why-we-need-decolonial-feminism-differentiation-and-co-constitutional-domination-in-western-modernity/

Fernandez, J. S., Fine, M., Madyaningrum, M. E., & Ciofalo, N. (2022). Dissident women's letter writing as decolonial plurilogues of relational solidarities for epistemic justice. *American Journal of Community Psychology, 69*(3–4), 391–402. https://doi.org/10.1002/ajcp.12567

Freire, P. (1970). Cultural action and conscientization. *Harvard Educational Review*, *40*(3), 452–477. https://doi.org/10.17763/haer.40.3.h76250x720j43175

Freire, P. (1978). Pedagogy of the oppressed. In J. Beck, C. Jenks, N. Keddi, & M. F. D. Young (Eds.), *Toward a sociology of education* (1st ed., pp. 374–386). Routledge. https://doi.org/10.4324/9780429339530

Harrell, S. P. (1997). *Racism and life experiences scales: Racial hassles (RaLES) [Database record]*. APA PsycTests. https://doi.org/10.1037/t09928-000

Harrell, S. P. (2000). A multidimensional conceptualization of racism-related stress: Implications for the well-being of people of color. *American Journal of Orthopsychiatry*, *70*(1), 42–57. https://doi.org/10.1037/h0087722

Harrell, S. P. (2023, July). *Introduction to Sankofa theory and practice* [Conference presentation]. Annual Convention of the Association of Black Psychologists.

Harrell, S. P., Henderson, I. S., Meng, C., Reyburn, L., Smith, B., & Williams, R. (2024, January). *Sankofa theory and practice: Centering the alchemy of reconnection in our healing interventions* [Poster Presentation]. National Multicultural Conference and Summit.

hooks, b. (1994). *Outlaw Culture: Resisting Representations.* Routledge.

LaFromboise, T. D., & Fine, M. (2021). The public psychology for liberation training model: A call to transform the discipline. *American Psychologist, 76*(8), 1248–1265. https://doi.org/10.1037/amp0000887

Latina Feminist Group. (2001) *Telling to live: Latina feminist testimonios*. Duke University Press.

Lenthang, M. (2021, March 21). Atlanta shooting and the legacy of misogyny and racism against Asian women. *ABC News*. https://abcnews.go.com/US/atlanta-shooting-legacy-misogyny-racism-asian-women/story?id=76533776

Lorde, A. (2007). *Sister outsider: Essays and speeches.* Crossing Press.

Martín-Baró, I. (1994). *Writings for a liberation psychology: Ignacio Martín-Baró* (A. Aron & S. Corne, Eds. and Trans.). Harvard University Press.

Merriam-Webster. (n.d.). *Alchemy*. Merriam-Webster.com dictionary. Retrieved June 4, 2024, from https://www.merriam-webster.com/dictionary/alchemy

Mosley, D. V., Neville, H. A., Chavez-Dueñas, N. Y, Adames, H. Y, Lewis, J. A., & French, B. H. (2020). Radical hope for revolting times: Proposing a culturally relevant psychological framework. *Social and Personality Psychology Compass*, *14*, e12512. https://doi.org/10.1111/spc3.12512

Neville, H. A., Ruedas-Gracia, N., Lee, B. A., Ogunfemi, N., Maghsoodi, A. H., Mosley, D. V., LaFromboise, T. D., & Fine, M. (2021). The public psychology for liberation training model: A call to transform the discipline. *American Psychologist, 76*(8), 1248–1265. https://doi.org/10.1037/amp0000887

Nicolson, A. (2023). *How to be: Life lessons from the early Greeks.* Farrar, Straus, and Giroux Publishers.

Nixon, A. (2020, November). *The elements of decolonial healing justice* [Video]. TED conference YouTube. https://www.youtube.com/watch?v=7J_BD0Jjk5c&t=202s

Ratele, K., Cornell, J., Dlamini, S., Helman, R., Malherbe, N., & Titi, N. (2018). Some basic questions about (a) decolonizing Africa(n)-centred psychology considered. *South African Journal of Psychology*, *48*(3), 331–342. https://doi.org/10.1177/0081246318790444

Robertson, R. (2017). Alchemy as a psychological model. *Psychological Perspectives, 60*(2), 240–254. https://doi.org/10.1080/00332925.2017.1314709

Rogers Nelson, P. (2004). Magnificent [Song]. Musicology [Album]. NGP Records.

Silva, J. M., Fernández, J. S., & Nguyen, A. (2021). "And now we resist": Three testimonios on the importance of decoloniality within psychology. *Journal of Social Issues*, *78*(2), 388–412. https://doi.org/10.1111/josi.12449

Torres Rivera, E., & Torres Fernández, I. (2024). Decolonization is liberation: Operationalization of decolonial model of counseling using liberation psychology principles with the Latine population(s). *Journal of Multicultural Counseling and Development*, 1–13. https://doi.org/10.1002/jmcd.12310

Triani, S. (2013). Unforgotten to the unforgettable: How *arpilleras* contributed to the Chilean history informing everyday occupations and social change. *School of Occupational Therapy, 44*(1), 93–96. https://doi.org/10.3233/WOR-2012-01568

Trías Monge, J. (1997). *Puerto Rico: The trials of the oldest colony in the world.* Yale University Press.

Walsh, C. (2010). Development as Buen Vivir: Institutional arrangements and (de) colonial entanglements. *Development*, *53*(1), 15–21. https://doi.org/10.1057/dev.2009.93

6 Decolonial Voices in Education

Resistance, Critical Epistemology, and Shaping of the Psychology of Education in India

Chetan Sinha

The decolonial psychology is an update on the working of decolonial in the specific socio-geographic boundaries comprising the site of resistance, politics, and movements. It is the advanced movement of collective as well as critical consciousness facilitating the praxis of dialogues (Freire, 1970; Kincheloe et al., 1999). It is a praxis of resistance and movement for change (Adames et al., 2024; Bhatia et al., 2024; Comaz-Diaz et al., 2024) and annihilation of something oppressive existing in the action and consciousness such as caste-based discrimination. It symbolizes the revolution critical to the status quo and dominance that overpowered existence and reverberated through generations. It is a way forward towards anticolonialism, anti-classism, anti-casteism, etc.

The research on the psychology of oppression in India has taken a pace in recent times (Fatima et al., 2024; Jogdand, 2024; Mukherjee et al., 2024; Pal, 2024). This was possible when the social movements for their rights and emancipation expanded as mass movements. Though the struggle against colonialism was active in different regions and cultures throughout India, at the broader level, this was more directed towards the rise of modern education, which was considered dangerous to traditions and cultural practices (see also Kumar, 2007; Kumar et al, 2013; Rao, 2016; Sadgopal, 2021; Tschurenev, 2019). In those phases of colonialism, the deep divide based on purity and impurity construct had occupied the minds of people. They were mindful of their loss of cultural memories. At the same time, the schools and institutes of higher education were established to enhance Western (e.g. British, English) education, which was ready to provide education to both boys and girls by having separate schools. The sidelining of the Gurukul system created much furore and emotional upheaval in the established order and its followers. In this chapter, I will embark on the meaning of resistance, which has shaped the voices nurturing critical pedagogies, decolonizing educational psychology, and situating the working of decolonial against the oppressive power relationship. The idea is to critically engage with educational psychology[1] that has impacted the social process of schooling and Indian society at large. The chapter is divided into three sections: (I) Enactment, (II) Issue and Problems, and (III) Agenda and Strategies.

Enactment

British Colonial Structure of Education

Colonialism is also about the creation and sustenance of social order in terms of the colonizers. It is worth noting that schools were the institutions for educating the people and social control, facilitating uniformity and compliance needed for developing nationhood. Formal education was not always encouraged before the 18th century as it was ignored because of the fear pertaining to the ongoing agenda of trading and establishing (Basu, 1935). The colonial agenda later to establish schools for the people in India was to make them civilized and make the working facilitative.

DOI: 10.4324/9781003492214-7

This started around the first colonial phase of the Portuguese, who were considered 'originators of modern education in India.' Though education was not the primary agenda except for trading, the momentum in educating the Indians started later through English medium (e.g. Anglo-Vernacular schools) (Venkatanarayanan, 2013). Other schools of French or Danish origin were permitted as charity schools. Earlier, the primary agenda was to educate their employees' children. The initiatives of missionaries in spreading modern education apart from Christianity, which can bring some social change, started sporadically but later gained full momentum as it was also necessary to establish the working of the government. Linguistic imperialism had a grounding in the colonial countries through these experiments of coercive ruling in order to control the Indian masses and create a workforce for the government.

This chapter does not take a passive stance as it is depicted in the texts on colonial education. The masses were not without their culture, languages, emotions, and socializations; they were active agents of their cultural practices and deeply involved in those states of affairs. Nandy (1988), in his book *The Intimate Enemy*, communicated how colonization systematically snatched a cultural memory and imposed it with the will of the state. Education is not apart from this colonized influence on human experience and cultural knowledge. Some missionaries and Anglicists' agenda was to reform and make people civilized against the cultural truism that has self-immolated their sensibilities.

The precolonial history of education, although some scholars called it equal to all the classes and castes through three universal subjects (Akshara Gyan, Bhasha Gyan, and Arithmetic) (Roy, 2024), the modernization of education with its limitations of overemphasis on Anglicization created a platform of modern education without much discriminations on the basis of Varna system. It is another matter that the privileged classes were more influenced by English education, keeping their traditional knowledge as part of their everyday discourses and practices. As we see that Urdu was the prevalent official language, the Sanskrit and other communal languages were of less everyday use in the schools and other institutions. Even today, the use of Urdu and Hindi words is common in official registers. The concern here is the voice of resistance raised from different social groups within the same socio-geographic context. Some found the colonial intervention through educational praxis innovative and rehabilitating, and some found it antithetical to the deep-seated cultural values.

Democracy and its practices are a postcolonial construction of social reality. Earlier, even during the British colonial times, democracy may have been in the process of intellectual discussion, was not part of the everyday people's reality, and was never part of education, curriculum, and pedagogy. The dialogues on democracy in colonial times can be considered an approach to amending the formal educational system. It is not a critical pedagogical framework, but it is certainly nearer to the agenda of social reformation as an educational system responsible for change through the critical consciousness (Freire, 1970). Apart from formal schooling, many reformers from different social sections and religions tried to run their community schools based on their traditions or keep traditions alive in the colonial educational climate (Rao, 2016). The politics of culture finds its route through the politics of education and social identities of community affiliation. This is a divergent disciplinary pathway that seems not to do anything with educational psychology's neutral and scientific vendetta that has overpowered the modern educational praxis. However, not clinging to the neutrality of educational psychology and rooting in the sociohistorical domain seems more fulfilling to the agenda of decolonizing educational psychology through critical pedagogies, integral education, and curriculum (see Elder, 1971; Huppes, 2014; Kincheloe et al., 1999; Nichol, 2012; Rivera & Fernandez, 2024; Sharma & Mir, 2019; Sibia, 2014). However, the West's superiority was communicated despite several attempts by the teachers and cultural workers. In one study, Elder (1971) noted how the teachers emphasize their cultural heroes, and literature found the deep quest to know one's culture and live by but school process, Western awareness, and the need of the time to achieve make them cognizant subtly their colonized self.

Issues and Problem

Educational Psychology and Its Epistemology: Whose Politics?

The systems of educational psychology formed the core of formal schooling. Though educational psychology has transitioned from its epistemological stance of individual improvement to social constructivism, it needs further to respond to the critical interdisciplinarity and power dynamics (Sinha, 2023). Introducing self-reflexivity and self-criticism shall further refurbish the metatheory on which modern educational psychology depends. In the times of neoliberalism, misinformation, the rise of cognitivism in education, and neglect of emotions keep reverting to the marketization of education under the aegis of corporate capitalism (e.g. Kasser & Linn, 2016). The educational system has become a contributor to the market by shaping the mindset of children, focusing on individual achievement, a departure from the community, nuclearization of self, and developing mini-programmes to cure mental health issues.

The resistance approach to thinking about the existing education system has to be linked with the history of struggle and emancipation. The dissent towards the systems of culture that were oppressive and unconcerned with the voices of the people was a new system of thought. The oppressive constructs that are systematically insinuated into the discursive practices have shaped the structure of society and, hence, the formal education system. Educational psychology is a colonizer connotation adopted by the powerful identities within the cultural system. The citadels of concepts on which the idea of educational psychology is built demand obedience and conformity on the part of receivers, who are usually students. The system of offering a curative mechanism is dominant as well as banal. Since subjectivity can be understood in various ways and communicated, the intimidating illusions of personal objectivity (see Pronin et al., 2004) imposed in formulating others' agency are non-representative. The voice of the colonizer and the powerful identities were both dominating and eroding the self of the colonized in the high times of neoliberalism (see also Vassallo, 2021). The double discrimination of the oppressed didn't fit into the existing models and framework of educational psychology. This demanded resistance to something that was regulating and depriving, leading to chronic disadvantage.

The general trends in the working of educational psychology in India during colonial and postcolonial periods were conforming to the status quo and fitting the students into the formal schooling systems designed as per the colonial legacies. There were systematic attempts to streamline the history of educational psychology, its place in psychology curricula and how in-depth it corresponds to the actual research problem and interdisciplinary collaborations, and improvement of school psychology in India (e.g. Khan, 2021; Raina & Srivastava, 1997; Ramalingam & Nath, 2012). Recently, Srivastava (2021) discussed the dynamics of teaching and learning, considering it as a hopeful engagement, character-building enterprise using context-specific research problems and innovative methodology. The quest to decolonize the received knowledge that has become part of our affective self is ever daunting. It is a matter of searching for hidden identity in the educational domain. The different approaches to connecting with one's social identities, whether language, religion, or any domain, found their way through the educational system, circumventing unique pedagogy and curriculum. This was the marker of identity assertion and a movement towards establishing one's social standing via systematic education.

Agenda and Strategies

Transformative Education in the Colonial Context

The modern education in the colonial and postcolonial periods has impacted socioreligious educational enterprises such as Sanskrit schools (Rao, 2020; Kumar, 2000) and madrasas (Ahmad, 2012;

Riaz, 2011). The legacies of these schools were much established among the masses attached to their religions. The colonial system of education and parallelly missionary education had their interventions to the people consciousness. The result was mix in the adoption of the modern education and much of the time the larger nationalistic agenda shaped the direction of these schools. For example, the role of madrassas is to conserve their educational system and to promote national movement. The Sanskrit schools preserved their schooling through the establishment of various Vidyalaya dedicated to the education of the Hindu sastras in Sanskrit. Britishers seem to be under the impression that India is Hindu which is why they established oriental colleges and Sanskrit schools to know more about Indian-Hindu culture. Muslim social reformers and loyalists like Sir Syed Ahmed Khan[2] started the Aligarh reformation as a movement to reconcile modern values with the Muslim culture. In terms of formal education, it was the British takeover. Parallelly the Indigenous and tribal way of education and cultural embeddedness was also impacted much (Shah & Bara, 2021). The 'moral civilising mission' of colonial education in India was based on their apathy towards the Indians lacking moral responsibility to fit into their ways (Singh & Maheshwari, 2024). This is directly situated in the power relationship where the superiority of race was manifested in the perceptions of colonials towards decolonial (e.g. Rao, 2016; Upadhyay, 2012). However, as indicated earlier, this perception of Indians was not as homogenous as conjectured in the historical documents and highlights of discursive practices.

The colonialists' views resonated with the upper castes, men, and elites of India instead of marginalized and oppressed. Their approach was Western, educated, industrialized, rich, and democratic (e.g. Henrich et al., 2010) rather than decolonial, whose voices were subjugated. The pedagogical adaptation to the working-class demand also added to the reorganization of Indigenous education and the structure of educational provision (Laqueur, 1976; Tschurenev, 2019). The schools started in the city area, and the rural areas were handled under the supervision of different supervisory groups. Rural education was the responsibility of missionary groups, and the municipalities administered the city schools. Though Indigenous education was prevalent in the rural Pathshalas, the government control of education through schooling gradually sidelined it (see Jha, 2011).

Educational psychology has also gone a long way from adjusting and proposing the colonial demands of individualism to a new psychology of education, bringing the relevant social issues and challenges to the forefront. The idea of educational psychology for social justice culminates in social theory and a critical interdisciplinary approach to address challenges related to the classroom learning process, diversity, social justice, racism, casteism, gender dynamics, and classism. It was an aloof subdiscipline of psychology controlling the students' behaviour to the demand of the powerful towards the critical response to the dominant psychological model and taking the grounded perspective and the narratives of the powerless. This new way provides an action-oriented approach to developing critical consciousness and an improved way of teaching, learning, and social justice-oriented curriculum and pedagogy. This shows how any discipline is opening its boundary and its readiness to be interdisciplinary with social justice-oriented metatheory (e.g. Claiborne, 2014; Muis & Chen, 2025; Prilleltensky, 2014; Vassallo, 2014). So, with these prospects, teachers are no longer the teaching machine, and students are no more individual robots who are banked with information.

In India, the first decolonial movement against the internal caste hierarchy and patriarchy seems to originate in the social movements taken forward by Savitri Bai Phule and Jyoti Rao Phule. The decoloniality paradox is sometimes observed regarding the politics of nativity and its origin in the history of the Indian education system. The politicization of indigeneity into the homogeneity of the Hindutva self in India has deprived marginalized minorities of their history, cultural expression, and the idea of compositeness. The divide into traditional, historically authentic and native has transcended what was collective into fragmented identities. This has affected education, where there are regular interventions from the state regarding unbalanced policies of dos and don'ts. The colonialist agenda seems to be twofold: one to educate the masses about their means and end and to keep the divisions in the society based on caste intact. This was aptly elaborated in the context of the subalterns who aimed to 'break the tradition of slavery' by not imbibing what upper-caste reformers adopted to improve their 'habits' and 'morality' (see Tschurenev & Mhaskar, 2021). The decolonial who were doubly victimized by colonialism and casteism took an active stance to counter the deep-seated resentment and prejudices based on caste and gender.

The following two cases discuss the 'actionable strategies for decolonizing educational psychology and develop the pathways regarding how resistance and critical pedagogy can be implemented in everyday schooling practices.' Two cases are elaborated ahead:

Cases 1: Critical Pedagogy as a Method of Educational Psychology

One of my studies (see Sinha, 2023) on the application of critical pedagogy in school education shows the role of teachers in facilitating resistance to the dominant ideologies based on gender, religion, and caste. The students were treated equally and encouraged to ask questions and express their views freely without any fear. The role of teachers as a critical pedagogue was collective and engaging in the sociocultural experiences of the students (see also Baveja, 2014; Cowden & Singh, 2013; Rogoff & Lave, 1984). The students from the marginalized communities were given special attention, and maximum care was taken to empower them with skills that would take them out of their working-class status. The meaning of being marginal can be taken as voiceless and powerless in the dominant social system. Their vocality depends upon the leadership stand taken by someone like them who is the authentic representative of their sociopolitical and socioeconomic needs. Their resistance is towards the ascribed identity, which doesn't allow them to cross the boundary of oppression and inequality. In colonial times, the marginalized were castes identified as apprehensive of their cultural erosion and not completely free to exercise their discretion and dominance as there was intervention by the government in matters that showed irrationality and superstition. However, many believed modern education was propagated through establishing government schools with Englishmen/British as headmasters and school inspectors. These schools were reformed/colonized to such an extent that it was deemed to fit carrying forward the administrative agenda of British rule.

Parallelly, the major population was comprising lower castes and other marginalized community members who were facing the double impact of colonialism and casteism. They were tribals, manual scavengers, iron smiths, butchers, carpenters, gardeners, loaders, and many others unfamiliar with the modern agenda of British benevolence. It was mediated by the upper and middle castes. So, in most cases, these identities acted as mediators who took the role of decolonial. Their approach was paradoxically situated in the British system as conformists or silent dissenters. Few crossed the boundaries of silence and acted as revolutionaries against the oppressive policies. Among the masses, forbidden castes considered untouchables were not even in the political calculations of colonial psychology. They were the hardest victim on the continuum of oppression, first, as a victim of casteism and second as voiceless stakeholders in the colonial regimes. In both cases, the decolonial needed a platform to express themselves, form movement, and represent themselves. However, impermeable boundaries needed a social context to cross through the representative of their experiences and identities. Leaders like Savitri Bai Phule, Jyoti Rao Phule, and BR Ambedkar were the representatives of decolonial voices (see also Bhatia & Ram, 2023), whose epistemological stance was resistive towards the oppressive ideology and strife for social equality. They crossed the boundaries of dominance through activism, empowerment, and suffering. Their approach was authentic and meaningful to the social justice needs of the marginalized.

The emancipatory/liberation psychology project was to make a culture fair and equitable through education (e.g. Martín-Baro, 1994). Observing the act of decolonization, there were decolonized who were against external colonialism where being under the rule of a foreigner who has a different language, culture, habits, and beliefs was threatening to one's cultural identity. The cultural identity was seen as homogenous with its vertical system of practices and rituals. The other act of decolonization done by the historically oppressed seems to pass through different terrains, from acceptance to awareness to collective movement. In all these processes of collective response, the role of visionaries was immense in representing the collective need for emancipation from the dominant sociocultural system. It is the system which was fuelled by the dominant caste's oppression towards the people and forcing the lower castes to serve them for their daily needs. Civic management was impossible without the interventions of the lower caste, for which they were hardly given credit and taken as their natural duty. This was the kind of humiliation that incited rage and movement to disregard the whole system of cultural dominance which is passed from generations. The ascribed demeaning social identity became meaningful and valuable when leaders intervened and creatively crafted them as meaningful and assertive identities, infusing a sense of positive emotions such as pride (e.g. Jogdand & Sinha, 2015; Sinha, 2020). This becomes necessary from two points of view: first, as a response to social threats, atrocities, and epistemic violence (e.g. Sinha, 2023; Tiwari, et al., 2017), and second, as a resistance towards the received culture, which historically regulated and dehumanized their agencies at the individual and collective levels. For example, in the second case, the struggle of Savitri Bai Phule to educate the girls was one of the authentic resistances to the dominant value system directed towards liberation. The model of education symbolized resistance and methods through the consciousness of one's group. The ethical agenda of education was a collective struggle to imbibe modern values. It was based on one's right to learn and cross the power dynamics based on caste and gender. This was emblematic of the politics of the oppressed and pragmatic in its approach.

The method to empower the most alienated and neglected people was a kind of education needed in the present times. Though in the post-independence times, educationist expressed their education concerns through different metaphors, the primary agenda to empower marginalized students is still unfulfilled. Metaphors like road maps, steps, promises, and networks (see Kumar, 2006) were the driving force behind educational committees, policymakers, and educationists. However, these metaphors were also the buzzwords or paradigmatic keywords frequently displayed in the discourses of the above stakeholders. How much they helped empower the marginalized is a matter of alignment with the latter's everyday needs, both socioeconomic mobility and social change. The rise of the culture of educational entrepreneurs, online learning, and coaching systems has also, to some extent, adversely affected the true spirit of school education. The idea of school education was based on the relationship between trust and teaching. It was the platform where teachers and students engaged with the phenomenon despite the relationship manifested in a power relationship (e.g. Nawani, 2016; Rajan, 2021). The new flat system has taken over this hierarchy, which occupied the thinking mind into an algorithmic system of data processing. The rise of AI has extended cognition but separated it from the needed social network, which requires emotional and cultural connectedness.

The value system to which education has confined itself is the individual achievements and excellence as per the neo-liberalization agenda of individualism, meritocracy, and apathy towards community feeling. This trend has taken shape in the last few decades and even came into the discursive practices of the community, working class, and middle class. Taking lessons from the decolonial approaches to address blatant colonialism, educational psychology calls for multicultural education, representation, respecting the experiences of students, and helping them cross the barriers related to caste, gender, and social class. Schools need a balancing and equitable stance where students' culture is not demeaned or devalued, so schools become the space for embracing and taking students out of their sociocultural, psychological, and political inferiority. It also requires problem-solving of the concepts taken for granted in educational psychology. For example, despite the established concepts like intelligence, academic achievement, aspirations, aptitudes, instructional design, etc., form the structure of educational psychology, the critical responses derived from the decolonial psychology help in their deconstruction and offer a constructive disruption through new discursive practices as a result of dialogical engagement between community, teachers, educational leaders, policy designers. These concepts are developed in the social context of colonialism and mobilized, keeping the oppressive structure of society intact. The need for an inclusive and revolutionary psychology of education culminates in the perspective of decolonial and oppressed as a critical response to power, and it is a continuous process. Educational psychology operating on the rigid understating of social categories and concepts is unrepresentative of the experiences of the Dalits, Adivasis, Muslim minorities, and different marginalized groups such as underrepresented workers, labourers, scholars, and middle classes.

Case 2: Students as an Agent of Change

In one of my field explorations in Varanasi, where I engaged with the primary and elementary school children, staff, and principal, the agenda was to understand the role of schooling in the children's lives, how meaningful it is to them, and what hope they drive out of schooling. Usually, the schooling structure was based on deep engagement with the students, providing children and staff proper breakfast and lunch, creative education, revisiting the diversity of students, nurturing their aspirations and empowering them with the necessary skills to survive on their career pathways. Since most of the children were from working-class, socially marginalized and minority backgrounds who were dependent on ancestral jobs, both or one parent didn't complete their primary schooling, lived in a Mohalla (old urban areas), studying in government schools or private schools where low-income students take their education. The general view about the meaning of education and academic success seems as linear as it is in the discursive practices of children, parents, and teachers. The notion of good students showed in the children's attributes of being sincere, intelligent, high achievers, helpful, and hardworking. These were the characteristics within the individual that make them successful. From the observation and interaction, it was clear that these children come from backgrounds with little formal education. They were straight in their responses, where the meaning of success was directly connected to formal schooling. For them, school was the symbol of hope and, paradoxically, one of the important platforms for achievement. The engagement with the schooling process was a matter of honour, despite alternative narrations from the teachers and principal that the school is meant to have food and compensation.

In the children's worldview, the ascribed rules make them successful and achieve better status. They themselves wanted to be relieved from the cultural hindrances that have become part of their everyday lives. In their response, they explicitly mentioned the school's contribution to their social status enhancement. This seems theoretically founded in progressive educational psychology, which demands improving children through training and fitting into the educational system. This is another matter: these colonial turns in the educational system were only captured by the upper and middle classes, and most children fell back into their working-class status. The schools for students from Dalit backgrounds are important emancipating spaces where they like to study and are appropriate to the education system. They study to gain new knowledge and go to school routinely. Parents of these children, who are mostly engaged in jobs like manual scavenging, prefer schooling for their children. Due to socioeconomic needs, students are forced to return to their ancestral occupation since available schools lack a platform for their transition into the middle class. The available private schools are either costly or don't have sufficient resources and funds to fulfil the aspirations of the students. They are deprived of the dignity that any worker should have. So, formal education is the only source of achievement despite their understanding that they face caste-based discrimination (see Krishna, 2012).

Along with this, there were responses of the girl child who preferred education as a means to be educated. Their concern for education was connected to their familial concern about their future marriage. One girl said that people generally ask the bride about her education level and the number of classes she passed. This is one of the mobility concerns among the people since marriage is important for their girls and for achieving better alliances in their community. In all cases, the attainment of education seems an important benchmark. However, the percentage of girls and Dalits crossing the school levels to higher education is less as compared to the students from upper caste and middle classes. The Vidyashram school in Varanasi created hope among parents, guardians, and students by addressing their aspirations without overpowering them with the formal logic of mainstream educational psychology. The idea of this alternative school is to offer high-quality education at a lower fee compared to expensive schools catering to the needs of the better-income group. It is also important to note that these schools elevate the self-esteem and worth of parents and children and give them the courage to challenge the dominance of expensive schools for the systematic exclusion of the marginalized (Sinha, 2023).

School as Hope for Social Mobility

There is no doubt that colonial education, through its linguistic tools, created imposition and regulated at the cost of cultural loss, which is also like back seating the local-Indigenous language. The resistance from the decolonial who faced the oppression of colonialism, which was from outside the set cultural model, was facing the wrath of casteism from inside.

The time of coloniality and expressions has taken a new shape where the decolonial have to prove their agency. Ambedkar and Phule's approach to bringing social equality has turned into factions and toxic resistance from the upper-caste and other dominant groups, which, in some or another way, deprive the oppressed of expression against the oppressive policies conducive to the dominant identities. The voice of decolonial shaped the agenda of education. It is a condition for effective schooling, or it may be a dead end for the children with the right to be educated dignifiedly. The approach of colonial education was limited by many social psychological factors such as less representation of their own experiences and observations, stereotyping and prejudices towards the marginalized, violence both physical and epistemic, dehumanization and othering (see Pal, 2015; Sharma & Jogdand, 2024; Sinha, 2023).

There was a case in the government school of Uttarakhand where children from higher castes rejected the food prepared by the Dalit cook (*The Hindu*, December 27, 2021). These are the common observations across many schools in different states where caste-based discrimination is rampant. The point of resistance was that, in response, Dalit children did not eat food prepared by the upper-caste cook or Bhojmata. Both cases show how casteism, food, and education are mobilized in favour and disfavour of different social identities and reproducing the culture of disgust, hate, and violence. Even it is not unusual that Dalit children are discriminated against daily when it comes to having a need of democratic pedagogy and representative curriculum. The violence and prejudice have occupied the consciousness of dominant castes leaving marginalized students to everyday suffering and resistance. Though the pedagogical leadership of Phule's and Ambedkar inspire them to take education, follow Sarvajanik Satyadharma, resist oppression, and embrace rationality (e.g. Bagade, 2010, 2021). The colonialization of education has also a psychological meaning for the parents and children. As Jyoti Rao Phule noted earlier, education has also become a site of Brahmanical colonialism (see Mani, 2005). The legacy of colonialism is taken forward till it suits the agenda of revivalism of dead philosophy, and educational institutions like schools and universities are the medium to sustain these undemocratic practices.

It is necessary to proactively reframe the dominant discourses in taking the agenda of marginalized people forward. The wrath of the educational system has adversely affected many, especially the marginalized and Dalits. The reported rise of suicide in educational institutions from the marginalized community shows how education, despite being important for social change, is simultaneously the site of discrimination based on social identities. Schools are the means to become responsible citizens, become successful in the domains usually meant for upper castes and classes, possibilities of social mobility and gain knowledge. The response to colonization also focuses on pragmatism, which facilitates the subaltern self with Indigenous symbols, transformative education, inclusive sensemaking, decolonizing knowledge, and creating an eclectic model of nationalism. The making of the Indian constitution is an example of decolonization, as it keeps the spirit of the Indigenous self and the philosophies of democratic rights. At present, we need to overhaul education to sustain diversity. For example, Batra (2021) aptly noted the need to reimagine the curriculum to fit the needs of students who were victims of difficult times (e.g. COVID-19). She hinted towards the decolonizing movements integrative of perspectives of Gandhi, Tagore, and Sri Aurobindo as they envisioned a free India. Savitri Bai Phule and Jyotiba Phule's work and activism as critical decolonial activists can overhaul the colonial and caste-based dominant curriculum framework. The making of the nation with its symbols, identity, and collective memory of historical struggles suits the working of education (see Sharma & Mir, 2019). The workings of educational psychology require an integrative approach to cater to democratic principles and a decolonized psychology of education.

Conclusion

Today's schools are as segregated as they were in earlier postcolonial India. Many of the policies dedicated efforts to improve education, from increasing literacy to providing quality and equal education. However, on all the parameters, children of the marginalized suffered, and the cycle of systematic discrimination was maintained. Scholars speculated on different factors that are responsible, but most of them are inclined towards deficit agencies and situations such as lower social class. If that is the case, then the platform of schooling and agenda of education has failed, as data clearly shows social inequality. During the COVID-19 pandemic and afterwards, the picture of discrimination, prejudice, and inequality become clear.

The worldviews of the decolonial were reduced to invisibility whenever there was a catastrophe like COVID-19. They bear the brunt of being infectious, unclean, spreading viruses, and anti-social to the dominant idea of nationality. However, their engagement with education and aspirations to excel in the future showed the need to go beyond the construction of their ascribed agencies derived from colonialism, casteism, and classism. These children are aware of their history, which they confront on an everyday basis. The existential questions of survival, discrimination, and future mobility emerge in all social interactions. The resistance to the given appropriations through educational involvement, school identifications, and readiness constructs the decolonial selves. In the case of decolonial educational psychology, the metatheoretical assumption is based on a critical understanding of the theory of science and metascience. They are not without foundation or deprived of any structure and are deeply rooted in the philosophy of Indigenous psychology and non-Western metaphysics. They are based on the resistance to the dominant logic of understanding people in a homogenized way.

Notes

1 An applied field of psychology involved in controlling, shaping, and levelling the behaviour and thought processes of children of different age groups.
2 https://theprint.in/theprint-profile/sir-syed-ahmad-khan-for-whom-educational-reform-way-of-life/306520/.

References

Adames, H. Y., Chavez-Duenas, N. Y., & Comas-Diaz, L. (2024). Introduction: Decoloniality as a transformative force in psychology: An orientation to this book. In L. Comas-Diaz, H. Y. Adames, & N. Y. Chavez-Duenas (Eds.), *Decolonial psychology: Toward anticolonial theories, research, training, and practice* (pp. 3–12). American Psychological Association.

Ahmad, I. (2012). Muslim educational backwardness: Competing pressures of secular and religious learning. In C. Sleeter, S. B Upadhyay, A. K. Mishra, & S. Kumar (Eds.), *School education, pluralism and marginality: Comparative perspectives* (pp. 121–151). Orient BlackSwan.

Bagade, U. (2010). *Mahatma Jotirao Phule*. Gandharv-Ved Publications.

Bagade, U. (2021). Seeking freedom from slavery and ignorance: Phule's theorisation of knowledge and education. In V. Gupta, R. K. Agnihotri, & M. Panda (Eds.), *Education and inequality: Historical and contemporary trajectories*. Orient BlackSwan.

Basu, B. (1935). *History of education in India under the rule of East India Company*. Government Printing.

Batra, P. (2021). Re-imagining curriculum in India: Charting a path beyond the pandemic. *Prospects, 51*, 407–424.

Baveja, B. (2014). Situating teacher education in the Indian context: A paradigm shift. In M. Cornelissen, G. Misra, & Varma, S (Eds.), *Foundations and application of Indian psychology*. Pearson Education.

Bhatia, S., & Ram, A. (2023). Outsider at home: Reading Babasaheb Ambedkar as a radical, decolonial psychologist. *Journal of personality*, *91*(1), 14–29. https://doi.org/10.1111/jopy.12751

Bhatia, S., Long, W., Pickren, W., & Rutherford, A. (2024). Engaging with decoloniality, decolonization, and histories of psychology otherwise. In L. Comas-Diaz, H. Y. Adames, & N. Y. Chavez-Duenas (Eds.), *Decolonial psychology: Toward anticolonial theories, research, training, and practice* (pp. 61–86). American Psychological Association.

Claiborne, L. B. (2014). The potential of critical educational psychology beyond its meritocratic past. In T. Corcoran (Ed.), Psychology *in education. Bold visions in educational research* (pp. 1–16). Sense Publishers.

Comas-Diaz, L., Adames, H. Y., & Chavez-Duenas, N. Y. (Eds.) (2024). *Decolonial Psychology: Toward anticolonial theories, research, training, and practice*. American Psychological Association.

Cowden, S., & Singh, G. (2013). *Acts of knowing: Critical pedagogy in, against and beyond the university*. Bloomsbury Publishing.

Elder, J. W. (1971). The decolonization of educational culture: The case of India. *Comparative Education Review*, *15*(3), 288–295. https://www.jstor.org/stable/1187130

Fatima, I., Zafar, M., & Thangal, M. R. (2024). Social psychological explorations of caste: Unravelling challenges and discovering opportunities. *CASTE: A Global Journal on Social Exclusion*, *5*(2), 186–201. https://doi.org/10.26812/caste.v5i2.907

Freire, P. (1970). *Pedagogy of the oppressed*. Herder and Herder.

Henrich, J., Heine, S. J., & Norenzayan, A. (2010). The weirdest people in the world? *Behavioral and Brain Sciences*, *33*(2–3), 61–83. https://psycnet.apa.org/doi/10.1017/S0140525X0999152X

Huppes, N. (2014). Integral psychology: An application of Indian psychology. In M. Cornelissen, G. Misra, & S. Varma (Eds.), *Foundations and application of Indian Psychology* (pp. 293–302). Pearson Education.

Jha, H. (2011). Decay of village community and the decline of vernacular education in Bihar and Bengal in the colonial era: A sociological review. *Indian Historical Review, 38*(1), 119–137. https://doi.org/10.1177/037698361103800106

Jogdand, Y. (2024). Laying the ground for a critical psychology of caste. *Caste a Global Journal on Social Exclusion*, *5*(2), 49–72.

Jogdand, Y., & Sinha, C. (2015). Can leaders transform humiliation into a creative force? *Journal of Leadership Studies, 9*(3), 75–77.

Kasser, T., & Linn, S. (2016). Growing up under corporate capitalism: The problem of marketing to children, with suggestions for policy solutions. *Social Issues and Policy Review, 10*(1), 122–150. https://doi.org/10.1111/sipr.12020

Khan, F. (2021, April 26). *Psychology and its impact on education in India.* Oxford Research Encyclopedia of Education. https://doi.org/10.1093/acrefore/9780190264093.013.116

Kincheloe, J. L., Steinberg, S. R., & Villaverde, L. E. (1999). *Rethinking intelligence: Confronting psychological assumptions about teaching and learning*. Routledge.

Krishna, M. M. (2012). Pedagogic practice and the violence against Dalits in schooling. In C. Sleeter, S. B Upadhyay, A. K. Mishra, & S. Kumar (Eds.), *School education, pluralism and marginality: Comparative perspectives* (pp. 54–82). Orient BlackSwan.

Kumar, D., Bara, J., Khadria, N., & Gayathri, R. (2013). *Education in colonial education: Historical insights.* Manohar.

Kumar, K. (2006). *Metaphors of reform: Second J. P. Naik Memorial Lecture*. School of Social Sciences, Jawaharlal Nehru University. Educational Records Research Unit.

Kumar, N. (2000). *Lessons from schools: The history of education in Banaras*. Sage.

Kumar, N. (2007). *The politics of gender, community, and modernity: Essays on education in India.* Oxford University Press.

Laqueur, T. W. (1976). Working-class demand and the growth of English elementary education. In L. Stone (Ed.), *Schooling and society* (pp. 1750–1850). Johns Hopkins University Press.

Mani B. (2005). *Debrahmanizing history: Dominance and resistance in Indian Society*. Manohar.

Martín-Baro, I. (1994). *Writings for a liberation psychology.* Harvard University Press.

Muis, K. R., & Chen, J. A. (2025). Culture as practice: Three pillars for educational psychologist (incoming editors' statement). *Educational Psychologist, 60*(1), 4–6. https://doi.org/10.1080/00461520.2025.2439768

Mukherjee, A., Agarwal, G., Tandon, C., & Meena, A. (2024). Exploring narratives of victimization, resistance, and resilience among Dalits using thematic analysis. *CASTE: A Global Journal on Social Exclusion, 5*(2), 160–185. https://doi.org/10.26812/caste.v5i2.911

Nandy, A. (1988). *The intimate enemy: Loss and recovery of self under colonialism.* Oxford: Oxford University Press.

Nawani, D. (2016). *Teaching-learning resources for school education*. Sage.

Nichol, R. (2012). Growing up in the ashes: Theoretical and pedagogical issues affecting Indigenous education. In C. Sleeter, S. B Upadhyay, A. K. Mishra, & S. Kumar (Eds.), *School education, pluralism and marginality: Comparative perspectives* (pp. 415–436). Orient Blackswan.

Pal, G. (2015). Social exclusion and mental health: The unexplored aftermath of caste-based discrimination and violence. *Psychology & Developing Societies, 27*(2), 189–213. https://doi.org/10.1177/0971333615593446

Pal, G. C. (2024). Caste as a socio-psychological construct: Theoretical and empirical expositions. *CASTE: A Global Journal on Social Exclusion*, *5*(2), 121–142. https://doi.org/10.26812/caste.v5i2.913

Prilleltensky, I. (2014). Education as transformation. In T. Corcoran (Ed.), Psychology *in education: Bold visions in educational research* (pp. 17–35). Sense Publishers.

Pronin, E., Gilovich, T., & Ross, L. (2004). Objectivity in the eye of the beholder: Divergent perceptions of bias in self versus others. *Psychological Review, 111*(3), 781–799. https://psycnet.apa.org/doi/10.1037/0033-295X.111.3.781

Raina, M. K., & Srivastava, A. K. (1997). Educational psychology in India: Its present status and future concerns. *International Journal of Group Tensions*, *27*(4), 309–340. https://doi.org/10.1023/A:1021957718944

Rajan, J. (2021). The school teacher in India. In V. Gupta, R. K. Agnihotri, & M. Panda (Eds.), *Education and inequality: Historical and contemporary trajectories* (pp. 135–159). Orient Blackswan.

Ramalingam, P., & Nath, Y. (2012). School psychology in India: A vision for the future. *Journal of the Indian Academy of Applied Psychology*, *38*(1), 22–33.

Rao, P. V. (2016). *New perspectives in the history of Indian education.* Orient Blackswan.

Rao, P. V. (2020). *Beyond Maccaulay: Education in India, 1780–1860*. Routledge.

Riaz, A. (2011). Madrassah education in pre-colonial and colonial South Asia. *Journal of Asian and African Studies*, *46*(1), 69–86. https://doi.org/10.1177/0021909610387758

Rivera, E. T., & Fernandez, I. T. (2024). Decolonizing the high school and undergraduate curriculum. In L. Comas-Diaz, H. Y. Adames, & N. Y. Chavez-Duenas (Eds.), *Decolonial psychology: Toward anticolonial theories, research, training, and practice* (pp. 205–217). American Psychological Association.

Rogoff, B., & Lave, J. (Eds.). (1984). *Everyday cognition: Its development in social context.* Harvard University Press.

Roy, H. (2024). Indic education in pre-colonial India. *Indian Journal of Public Administration*, *70*(2), 345–355. https://doi.org/10.1177/00195561231221812

Sadgopal, A. (2021). Post-Independence political economy of education: From welfarism to neoliberalism in alliance with fascism. In V. Gupta, R. K. Agnihotri, & M. Panda (Eds.), Education and inequality: Historical and contemporary trajectories (pp. 642–707). Orient BlackSwan.

Shah, G., & Bara, J. (2021). *Social inclusion and education in India: Scheduled tribes, denotified tribes and nomadic tribes*. Routledge.

Sharma, N., & Mir, S. A. (2019). Decolonizing education: Re-schooling in India. *Sinéctica, Revista Electrónica de Educación*, *52*, 1–10. https://doi.org/10.31391/s2007-7033(2019)0052-007

Sharma, S., & Jogdand, Y. (2024). The nature of caste prejudice: A new look at prejudice, social identity, and casteism in India. *CASTE: A Global Journal on Social Exclusion*, *5*(2), 73–96. https://doi.org/10.26812/caste.v5i2.906.

Sibia, A. (2014). Education for life: The Mirambika experience. In M. Cornelissen, G. Misra, & Varma, S (Eds.), *Foundations and* application *of Indian psychology* (pp. 325–343). Pearson Education.

Singh, K., & Maheshwari, K. (2024). *Colonial discourse and the suffering of Indian American children: A francophone postcolonial analysis*. Palgrave Macmillan.

Sinha, C. (2020). Dalit leadership, collective pride and struggle for social change among educated Dalits: Contesting the legitimacy of social class mobility approach. *Contemporary Voice of Dalit*, *12*(1), 52–70. https://doi.org/10.1177/2455328X19898411

Sinha, C. (2023). *Power dynamics in education: Shaping the structure of school education in India* (1st ed.). Routledge. https://doi.org/10.4324/9781003378297

Srivastava, A. K. (2021). Perspectives on educational psychology in India. In G. Misra, N. Sanyal, & S. De (Eds.), *Psychology in modern India: Historical, methodological, and future perspectives* (pp. 393–403). Springer Nature.

The Hindu. (2021, December 27). Students of Uttarakhand school eat mid-day meal together after caste row. *The Hindu.* https://www.thehindu.com/news/national/other-states/students-of-champawat-district-secondary-school-in-uttarakhand-eat-mid-day-meal-together-after-caste-row/article38047827.ece

Tiwari, M. K., Kumar, S., & Mishra, A. K. (Eds.). (2017). *Dynamics of inclusive classroom: Social diversity, inequality and school education in India*. Orient BlackSwan.

Tschurenev, J. (2019). *Empire, civil society, and the beginnings of colonial education in India*. Cambridge University Press.

Tschurenev, J., & Mhaskar, S. (2021). "Wake up for education": Colonialism, social transformation, and the beginnings of the anti-caste movement in India. *Paedagogica Historica*, *59*(4), 630–648. https://doi.org/10.1080/00309230.2021.1920986

Upadhyay, S. B. (2012). Dalits and the modern education in colonial India. In C. Sleeter, S. B Upadhyay, A. K. Mishra, & S. Kumar (Eds.), *School education, pluralism and marginality: Comparative perspectives* (pp. 152–82). Orient Blackswan.

Vassallo, S. (2014). The entanglement of thinking and learning skills in neoliberal discourse. In T. Corcoran (Ed.), *Psychology in education. Bold visions in educational research* (pp. 145–165). Sense Publishers.

Vassallo, S. (2021). *Neoliberal selfhood.* Cambridge University Press.

Venkatanarayanan, S. (2013). Tracing the genealogy of elementary education policy in India till independence. *Sage Open, 3*(4), 1–10. https://doi.org/10.1177/2158244013510302

Part 2

Indigenous Retrieval and Community Building across Self, Body, and Place

Psychology of Healing Resistance, and Relationality

7 Decolonializing Hegemonic Psychology based on Indigenous Healing of the Pitaguary and Jenipapo-Kanindé Peoples in Northeast Brazil/Pindorama

James Ferreira Moura Jr., Larissa Niemann Pellicer, Sandra Patricia Acosta Salazar, Antonio Ailton de Sousa Lima, Juliana Murta de Lima, Marina Pereira Passos Campos, Socorro Taynara Araújo Carvalho, Rosa Pitaguary and Juliana Alves Jenipapo Kanindé

Introduction

This chapter emerges from a Participatory Action Research (PAR) project developed collaboratively with participants from the Pitaguary and Jenipapo-Kanindé communities. A significant feature of this project is the shared authorship between the researchers and the community participants, emphasizing a decolonial approach to knowledge production. This collaborative authorship is not a universal feature of all PAR efforts, making it a distinctive characteristic of this study. The writing also draws on contributions from researchers with diverse backgrounds, including those rooted in Latin American Community Psychology traditions and others with complementary perspectives. Acknowledging these contributions, we aim to highlight the plurality of voices and approaches that shaped this work.

While this chapter is rooted in the context of a PAR project, the primary focus is not on detailing the PAR process itself. Instead, the aim is to present the Indigenous healing practices of the Pitaguary and Jenipapo-Kanindé peoples, emphasizing their ancestral methods and ways of knowing. This chapter highlights how these practices challenge traditional psychological approaches by incorporating Indigenous perspectives on healing. We aim to contribute to a broader discussion on integrating Indigenous knowledge into psychological practice by presenting these alternative frameworks. This approach underscores the importance of expanding the field of psychology to include diverse ways of understanding health and healing rather than solely concentrating on the participatory research methods employed.

We recognize the legitimacy of Indigenous oral, ancestral, and spiritual knowledge from a counter-narrative perspective (Dutta et al., 2021). Thus, the Decolonial Indigenous Healing we envision and write about here is created in the encounters being woven with the Jenipapo-Kanindé and Pitaguary peoples in Aldeia Encantada and Aldeia Monguba, respectively their ancestral territories. Such encounters are part of the Indigenous mental health action research that has been taking place since 2020.

We adopt a perspective of counter-storytelling (Dutta et al., 2021), recognizing the legitimacy of their oral, ancestral, and spiritual knowledge. Pitaguary and Jenipapo-Kanindé resist in Northeast Brazil, in the state of Ceará. Brazil is an Indigenous land of Pindorama inserted in Latin America (Abya Yala). The term Pindorama originates from the Tupi language and was historically used by Indigenous peoples to refer to the land before European colonization. Rather than denoting a

DOI: 10.4324/9781003492214-9

specific geographic region within the state of Ceará, Pindorama is a broader ancestral and symbolic term that Indigenous peoples use to reclaim Brazil's Indigenous identity beyond the colonial imposition of territorial boundaries (Alves Carneiro de Lima, 2023). Within this perspective, Pindorama is not restricted to a political or administrative division but instead signifies a decolonial reclaiming of Indigenous lands and epistemologies. The state of Ceará has several Indigenous communities, such as these, who have faced various forms of violence since the beginning of colonization. These include the denial and invisibilization of their identities and cultures, exploitation, and the lack of complete demarcation of their territories by the Brazilian state.

The Colonial Bases of Psychology from the Indigenous Epistemicide

The processes of violence against Indigenous peoples in Brazil originated with colonization and persist to this day. Colonialism refers to the historical process of conquest and domination, marked by the political and economic subjugation of territories (Quijano, 2005). The history of Brazilian colonization reveals a complex interplay between Indigenous agency and colonial imposition. When the Portuguese arrived in 1,500, they encountered a vast and diverse Indigenous population, with estimates ranging from one to over five million individuals across the territory (Langfur, 2014). The early colonial period was marked by establishing mission villages (aldeias) by Jesuit missionaries, who sought to "civilize" the Indigenous peoples through conversion to Catholicism. These missions became tools for both spiritual domination and economic exploitation, with Indigenous labor redirected to serve the colonial economy (Miranda & Dantas, 2021).

Colonial policies were underpinned by the idea of tutelage, which framed Indigenous peoples as "incomplete" and incapable of self-governance. This led to their subjugation under the guise of religious and social education (Langfur, 2014). However, Indigenous communities were not passive subjects. They actively resisted, negotiated, and adapted to the colonial order, maintaining their cultural practices and asserting agency in various forms. Despite this resistance, the colonial framework systematically undermined Indigenous knowledge systems, contributing to the epistemicide—or systematic destruction—of Indigenous ways of knowing (Miranda & Dantas, 2021).

These repeated physical and symbolic violence are associated with what sociologist Aníbal Quijano (2010) calls coloniality. This is defined by a power system that updates colonialism in modernity through the control of resources, capital, labor, and knowledge through the ideological construction of cis-gendered hetero-patriarchal white superiority located in the Global North. It is an element founded on "the imposition of a racial/ethnic classification of the world's population as a cornerstone" (Quijano, 2005, p. 73). Coloniality extends beyond the colonial period, signifying the persistent structures of power, knowledge, and being that continue to shape societies long after formal colonialism has ended (Maldonado-Torres, 2016). Coloniality underscores how modernity and capitalism are inextricably linked to the racial and epistemological hierarchies established during colonization (Quijano, 2000).

From this perspective, coloniality is a powerful force in producing death, violence, and illness for those non-white people located in the Global South. Indigenous peoples are the historical target of the murderous force of coloniality (Grosfoguel, 2016). The imposition of lifestyles and values based on European culture created an environment of oppression and subjugation, which continues to impact the lives of traditional peoples, especially in the territories transformed by invasion and domination (Brighenti, 2015). Furthermore, the marginalization and dehumanization of Indigenous peoples and repeated invasions and violence in their territories cause ethical-political suffering. This consists of the anguish related to the mutilation of existence, arising from a "social situation of being treated as inferior, subordinate, worthless, a useless appendage of society" (Sawaia, 2017, pp. 104–105). In this sense, the death resulting from coloniality is not limited to the end of life. It includes social and cultural death, most often implemented by the destruction or seizure of the sacred territories of Indigenous peoples. By imposing a single model of development and progress, coloniality ignores and eliminates the diversity of knowledge and practices of Indigenous peoples that can contribute to a more sustainable and supportive world (Nascimento et al., 2021).

In this context, Psychology's theory was forged and determined by knowledge production based on the scientific rationality founded on coloniality (Guimarães, 2023). Specifically, the coloniality of knowledge (Quijano, 2005) decontextualizes Psychology, as a scientific discipline, producing knowledge and practices that do not correspond to a social reality marked by the colonial process. The scientific knowledge produced by hegemonic Psychology establishes that the criteria of truth and humanity are located in cis-gendered hetero-patriarchal white men from higher economic classes in universities in the Global North (Barbosa et al., 2023). This colonial matrix where psychological science is situated creates a social process of invalidation of ways of being and existing that end up labeled as those of savages (Fanon, 2008) or as abnormal (Carvalho et al., 2023). Thus, the "other" subjects, whose identities have been subordinated, have their historical and social representation shaped by the continuous legacy of colonial relations (Sonn & Cruz, 2011).

The relevance of coloniality in the contemporary era is evident in the enduring epistemicide of Indigenous knowledge systems and the marginalization of non-European worldviews. Unlike colonialism, which is tied to the physical occupation of territories, coloniality persists as a matrix of power that operates through social, cultural, and epistemic dimensions (Maldonado-Torres, 2016). This framework highlights that the colonial struggle is far from over; it is present in the continued devaluation of Indigenous practices, the dominance of Eurocentric epistemologies, and the systemic inequalities that perpetuate these dynamics.

Decoloniality, then, emerges as a critical response to this ongoing coloniality. It calls for dismantling the hierarchies of knowledge and embracing pluriversality—a recognition of the legitimacy of multiple ways of knowing and being (Mignolo & Walsh, 2018). Addressing coloniality requires not only an acknowledgment of historical injustices but also a proactive engagement with alternative epistemologies, as will be evident in the Indigenous healing practices discussed in this chapter. Based on what Quijano (2005) calls the coloniality of power, certain subjects' social validation or invalidation affects subjectivities (Veiga, 2019). The success of colonization is based not only on the ability to colonize geographic territories but also on the ability to colonize identity and social territories. Thus, violent experiences mark the subjectivity of subordinated subjects, such as the notion of inferiority described by Fanon (2008).

Psychology constitutes itself from these colonial patterns of subjugation. It is a practice of care based on the pathologization of life supported by diagnostic manuals such as the Diagnostic and Statistical Manual of Mental Disorders (DSM) (American Psychiatric Association, 2022) and the International Statistical Classification of Diseases and Related Health Problems (ICD) (World Health Organization, 2019), documents produced with a nosographic bias. Nosographic bias refers to the influence of cultural and epistemological frameworks on the categorization and diagnosis of illnesses, particularly within Psychology and psychiatry. This bias arises from the predominance of Eurocentric models that often fail to account for diverse cultural contexts, leading to the misrepresentation or pathologization of behaviors and experiences outside of these frameworks. In the context of coloniality, nosographic bias reflects the imposition of colonial frameworks on the understanding of mental health, marginalizing non-Western epistemologies. This perpetuates the epistemicide of Indigenous knowledge systems and reinforces systemic inequalities in mental health care. Addressing nosographic bias involves recognizing the cultural specificity of diagnostic categories and expanding these frameworks to include pluralistic and context-sensitive approaches, as demonstrated by the Indigenous healing practices explored in this chapter.

In them, the types of diseases and psychic sufferings are named through statistics, disregarding contextual and specific issues (Correa et al, 2020). Stemming from scientific rationality, subjectivity must be entirely understood based on hegemonic knowledge from the Global North (Maldonado-Torres, 2016). Based on coloniality, there is a separation between subject-objective, subjectivity-objectivity, and mind-body (Grosfoguel, 2016). Psychological practice develops without taking into account people's life contexts, internalizing care practices developed in historically marginalized territories, such as Indigenous territories. Specifically, by importing theoretical perspectives disregarding the population's sociocultural diversity, Brazilian Psychology reinforces colonial power/knowledge. It delegitimizes sensitivities and cosmologies specific to Brazilian society, imposing distant and disconnected standards and models from our reality (Moura & Teixeira, 2022, p. 170). Psychology has a recent history built from a colonial academic logic based on pathologizing subordinated ways of life (Moura & Teixeira, 2022).

From Colonial Psychology to Decolonial Healing: Reclaiming Indigenous Epistemologies

Thus, we emphasize that caring is designated from an academic and psychological perspective and as a social, historical, ancestral, and collective practice. We highlight that the term cure, from Latin, means "to care." "Cure, then, can be understood as care and, as a result of this care, the recovery of health" (Paiva, 2007, p. 100). Atallah et al. (2022) present the collective practice of healing as decolonial love, where not only do we fight for each other against colonial oppressions but we also love each other in the collective struggle. For the authors, human love is a potential enhancer of criticality, transforming colonial wounds and traumas into possible paths of healing from the sufferings generated by violence (Atallah et al., 2022). Traditional healing practices persist through generations through practice and orality.

It is necessary to understand and legitimize the traditional knowledge of Indigenous peoples. In this context of decoloniality, we must learn to unlearn (Spivak, 2010) to reformulate the conception of illness: Illness should be understood as the sufferings linked to colonial violence, coloniality, historical erasure, and the dispossession of Indigenous people's lands. Thus, to develop healing practices, we should make coloniality visible (Atallah et al., 2022) and establish counter-colonial resistance practices (Bispo, 2022). These healing practices must be based on recovering the historical memory (Martín-Baró, 2011) of Indigenous. Thus, this task can foster a change in the collective in historical violence, enabling an awareness of the various forms of violence (Adams et al., 2015). This process does not aim to erase or forget the historical violence they have endured but rather to confront and transform it. Recovering historical memory enables collective healing by fostering an awareness of historical violence and its ongoing impacts. It allows communities to reclaim their narratives and cultural resilience, challenging the silence imposed by colonial structures and preventing the perpetuation of historical trauma.

Healing practices must also highlight the possibility of rescuing resistance strategies historically developed against oppression and intersecting class with race/ethnicity (Bernardino-Costa, 2015) and gender (Castro & Mayorga, 2019), since social hierarchies and economic disparities are deeply intertwined with racial and ethnic identities. Thus, through popular revolt movements and Indigenous struggles, emphasis is placed on the possibility of recovering historical memory with a focus on community and social care practices based on culturally significant relational approaches (Atallah et al., 2018).

These healing practices include understanding reality from the people's perspective (Martin Baró, 1996). Such a task requires an ethical-political stance and commitment to Indigenous peoples (Goes et al., 2015). Thus, these tasks are believed to represent a revolutionary paradigm shift and affirm their commitment of the Indigenous Territories and care for the popular majorities (Adams et al., 2015). Therefore, it is necessary to decolonize Psychology itself (Atallah, 2016; Lykes & van der Merwe, 2017) and dismantle the existing coloniality in the relations between academia and traditional communities (Atallah et al., 2018). When jointly facing violent and oppressive processes, this decoloniality provides self-liberation and healing as an integral part of decolonial praxis (Atallah & Dutta, 2021).

The mention of people's physical and mental suffering and the possibilities of healing practices for such sufferings, of spiritual, biological, and bodily order, is ancestrally present in several Indigenous nations (Ciofalo, 2019). In this sense, Africans, Indigenous people, and *mestizos* were the great healers of colonial Brazil with the "knowledge they had of herbs and specific ritual procedures" (Souza, 2005, p. 166). Traditional healing practices persist, then, through generations, and although modern Psychology and Medicine have constructed another logic of conceiving health-cure-disease, both share principles, "such as empiricism; specific rituals; and the mediation of forces and energies according to the type of practice and historical context, for the realization of cures" (Gewehr et al., 2017, p. 33).

Indigenous peoples have developed resistance and healing practices for colonial violence through counter-colonization practices. Counter-colonization comprises ancestral resistance practices developed by the colonized peoples to face violence, discrimination, and epistemicide (Bispo, 2022). Thus, traditional healing practices are essential counter-colonial tools for constructing Decolonial Indigenous Healing.

Decolonial Indigenous Resistance and Ancestral Healing Practices from the Northeast of Pindorama

To discuss localized Indigenous resistance practices, we cite the experience of the Pitaguary and Jenipapo-Kanindé peoples in Northeast Brazil. First, we will call Brazil Pindorama when rescuing historical memory. The land that the Portuguese and Spanish colonized was called the land of palms, which in the ethnic Tupi language of the Tupi-Guarani Indigenous people translates as Pindorama (Alves Carneiro de Lima, 2023). Reflecting on the experiences of Indigenous peoples in Pindorama, it is noteworthy that the Jenipapo-Kanindé and Pitaguary peoples still experience colonial traumas which arise from the colonization of being, power, and knowledge (Quijano, 2005). However, they resist, creating new possibilities for healing and decolonial existences based on their ancestral knowledge rooted in herbs, dances, music, rituals, and prayers. Understanding the effects, as well as the symptoms of this "colonial ailment," which has historically caused illnesses, especially among Indigenous populations, we point out the practices of exploitation, domination, and indoctrination in Brazil as their main causes (Battestin et al., 2019). Thus, these practices have been reflecting and influencing the identity, culture, language, and many other practices of these peoples' material and immaterial culture. Therefore, in building care and resistance practices against these and other forms of psychosocial illness, the Pitaguary and Jenipapo-Kanindé peoples reclaim their traditional knowledge and healing practices transmitted through generations.

The notion of healing from the Indigenous perspective, whether Pitaguary or Jenipapo-Kanindé, is understood as collective, ancestral, communal, spiritual, territorial, embodied, and political. Each of these dimensions is further elaborated below, maintaining the order and terminology introduced:

- Collective: Healing is not an individual endeavor but one deeply rooted in the community, where shared experiences and mutual support play a central role in restoring well-being.
- Ancestral: The process draws upon the wisdom and practices handed down through generations, recognizing ancestors' spiritual and cultural knowledge.

- Communal: Emphasizing the importance of togetherness, healing occurs in spaces that foster connection and solidarity among community members.
- Spiritual: Spirituality is a cornerstone, with rituals and ceremonies connecting individuals to their cultural and metaphysical roots.
- Territorial: The land is integral to healing, as it is deeply tied to identity, history, and the sustenance of life itself.
- Embodied: Healing acknowledges the lived experiences of the body, where trauma is held and must be released through practices that honor physical and emotional realities.
- Political: The healing process is inherently political, as it challenges systemic injustices and asserts the right to self-determination and cultural sovereignty.

With their worldview based on the principle of collectivity, the Pitaguary and Jenipapo-Kanindé peoples seek their healing and strengthening processes from community experiences and their relationship with the territory itself.

Collectivity is a value in Indigenous cosmology, not just about an individual. In Pindorama, all Indigenous people are considered relatives (Munduruku, 2009), intimately connected like the blood ties of the same family. Through our observations and immersions in PAR, both in the Encantada Village of the Jenipapo-Kanindé people and in the Munguba Village of the Pitaguary people, it was possible to perceive that collectivity is a central perspective. For example, the entire community gathers during celebrations and rituals, and Indigenous peoples from other ethnicities and villages are also welcomed for community celebrations. Different Indigenous peoples recognize themselves as part of a single family that crosses the lands of Pindorama because all Indigenous peoples are connected by ancestry and spirituality (Feitosa, 2019).

Highlighting the foundations of Indigenous healing, we also mention spirituality as a primordial aspect in the ways of life of the Pitaguary and Jenipapo-Kanindé peoples. According to Krenak (2020), since the appearance of the first human beings, there is knowledge that regulates our lives which is based on spirituality, nature, and the community and ancestral territory. Thus, whether through rituals or even contact with Mother Earth, spirituality is experienced and exercised.

We highlight nature as their primary source of healing. Contact with nature serves as a bridge for connection with spirituality, which is materialized in the figure of enchanted beings, who are the spiritual protectors of life (human and extra-human). However, this relationship is not hierarchical. Indigenous peoples also protect the enchanted beings' dwellings in nature. Thus, we must also care for and protect them. Healing occurs by strengthening these spiritual connections with nature, the territory, and the enchanted beings (Farias & Hennigen, 2019).

That said, according to Portela (2015, p. 6), spirituality is understood as "energies and entities" that generate and guide life and the world, whose presence can be read and detected in different ways, whether by the air we breathe, climatic changes, or even by the signs present in the winds, tides, and forests. Thus, we point out that spirituality "materializes" from sacred places within the territory, becoming spaces for rites, celebrations, and healing. For example, we cite the Encantada Lagoon, the Sacred Mango Trees of Uncle Odorico, the Culture Point of the Enchanted Women Artisans Jenipapo-Kanindé (AMEJK), among other sacred places in the Jenipapo-Kanindé territory, as well as the Bica, the Sabiá Forest, the Bamboo Grove, the courtyards, and the mountain in the Pitaguary territory.

In this sense, by pointing out the (spiritual) relationship between the enchanted beings and nature, we understand the body as the conduit responsible for manifesting connections. Thus, embodiment presents itself as an indispensable tool for the Jenipapo-Kanindé and Pitaguary peoples, where through dances, rituals, and the handling of herbs, they produce healing practices that reach dimensions such as body-mind-spirit. "Some people understand that our bodies are related to everything that is life, that the Earth's cycles are also our bodies'. We observe the Earth and the sky and feel we are not dissociated from other beings" (Krenak, 2020, p. 24).

Finally, we emphasize that, concerning healing practices, the Indigenous worldviews of Jenipapo-Kanindé and Pitaguary integrate community life factors such as Indigenous body painting through the ancestral practice of graphics, spirituality, and dance manifested in the Toré ritual, bringing circularity and the body in movement as a producer of energy. Furthermore, when pointing out expressions of Indigenous embodiment, we highlight the different manifestations of the *Toré*. This is a cosmological system incorporated by the Indigenous movement of Northeast Pindorama as a strategy of daily resistance against the physical and symbolic violence experienced since the colonial period (Oliveira, 1999). Thus, the Torés for the Jenipapo-Kanindé and Pitaguary peoples express culture and ancestral sacredness, which are fundamental for continuing and strengthening ways of living.

The Toré expresses the process of a repeated exercise of creativity conceived as a historical practice of self-affirmation of Indigenous collectivities (Grünewald, 2005). Toré, a sacred ritual dance performed by Indigenous communities in Brazil, holds profound spiritual and cultural significance. It serves as a means of connecting with ancestral spirits, reaffirming communal bonds, and preserving cultural heritage. Led by *pajés*, spiritual leaders, chiefs, and reference people in the villages, the Torés are sung by maracas and drums. In Brazilian Indigenous traditions, pajé refers to spiritual leaders, often equivalent to shamans in other cultural contexts. However, it is essential to note that while all pajés are spiritual leaders, not all spiritual leaders take on the role of a pajé. Indigenous healing practices often involve a variety of roles, including pajés, ceremonial leaders, and other figures who fulfill spiritual or communal functions. Thus, throwing the body into a Toré circle makes it possible to feel, vibrate, and share the union to achieve harmony. Indigenous peoples see in the Toré the possibility of mobilizing energies for the practice of healing, as well as for recharging. Thus, it is common to have expressions of crying and pain similar to catharsis during the ritual. In this way, healing occurs not only through the body but also through the mind and spirit.

Beyond the rituals of spirituality in the territories, these are also performed as political acts in struggles, public spaces of power, and decision-making, whether for demanding rights and political reaffirmation of Indigenous identities or celebration of the land demarcation. The Toré also reveals the growing internal organization of Indigenous communities based on their cultural repertoire, not only to position themselves in the arenas of political-social interaction but to reinvent their way of positioning themselves in the world. These spiritual leaders in the territories also have ancestral knowledge about the power of plants in Indigenous communities. The care performed through medicinal plants is favorable to human health, requiring prior knowledge of its handling and its effects, risks, benefits, and purposes. Therefore, those who perform this work are usually the *pajés* of the villages, responsible for collecting and preparing teas to be served. These healing practices focus on the body, which is sacred (Munduruku, 2009). In this way, speech would not be the only healing practice, but it must be involved in a series of practices that centrally affect the body through rituals, blessings, contact with nature, ingestion of teas, and dance.

Paying greater attention to Indigenous conceptions, we expand our ways of interpreting and seeing the world and relating and acting with/in Indigenous villages. Thus, we must understand therapeutic action and its healing practices from notions of collectivity, ancestry, community, spirituality, territory, body, and politics. These are the foundations of healing that the Jenipapo-Kanindé and Pitaguary peoples constantly seek to maintain harmony. With this, we emphasize that ancestry, as well as its knowledge which is revived daily, are the result of their histories guiding their way of living, existing, and resisting (Pinho Burlamaqui & de Souza Aguiar, 2023). Ancestry is, therefore, the foundation of Indigenous knowledge, supporting and signifying their ways of life. Despite the numerous attempts to deny their existence, the Jenipapo-Kanindé and Pitaguary peoples affirm themselves through the differences and similarities of cultures and ancestry.

Indigenous Healing Practices from a Decolonial Psychology

With these understandings of ancestral and Indigenous healing, it is necessary to question Psychology and its forms of practice so that it can be sensitive to ancestral knowledge and practices and the ways of life produced in these spaces. When psychologists enter and insert themselves into Indigenous contexts, they must recognize the plurality of worldviews and legitimize Indigenous communities' everyday knowledges and practices (Ciofalo & Ortiz, 2024). Considering such worldviews means understanding and legitimizing the relationships with spirituality, the land, ancestry, and the collective dimension as part of the therapeutic, prevention, and care processes of psychosocial health and, consequently, healing.

Regarding Psychology in the health context, professionals often need help understanding or valuing the knowledge and healing practices among Indigenous populations. This results in a devaluation and rejection of the rituals performed by pajés, healers, and *benzenes*, demonstrating how limited the training process in Psychology has been. This situation highlights the need to incorporate understanding and action in different cultures during training, allowing professionals to know the rights of these people and the healing practices of specific ethnic contexts (Carvalho et al., 2023; Luna et al., 2020).

From this perspective, it is essential to integrate the psychological practices into traditional and cultural health practices based on the participation of Indigenous communities, enabling the prevention and care of psychosocial health in these communities in their own way or integrated with Western knowledge. Therefore, it is necessary to understand the ways of life of Indigenous communities, even if our points of reference are Western and colonial. This requires a cognitive exercise of reworking our cultural references and seeking to promote a constant dialogue between Western and traditional knowledge. It is relevant, therefore, to talk about "a partnership approach to help a community generate more humanizing knowledge and practices from their body of knowledge" (Ndagijimana & Taffere, 2020, p. 20) so that the community can "shed light" on their healing processes from their experiences.

While recognizing the importance of Western medicine, of which Psychology is an heir, we emphasize that in intercultural encounters, Psychology must shed their centrality to effectively dialogue and learn from every person's complex and diverse knowledge systems. Otherwise, we will be merely reproducing another type of colonial violence. In other words, biomedical/Western care often does not consider individuals and their integration with culture, which we understand today as necessary and urgent (Scorsolini-Comin, 2023). Furthermore, there is a lack of appreciation for ancestral ethnic health, from which communities practiced care and community healing long before the formal and Western health networks arrived in their territories.

Listening to colonial sufferings and counter-colonial powers can be conceived as humanizing practices. With different theoretical-clinical contributions, we understand that it is necessary to listen from a posture of valuing the experience of those who narrate, thus promoting an atmosphere of welcome, understanding, and human warmth (Araújo & Freire, 2014). By listening, we reiterate the importance of valuing ancestral memory. After all, revisiting the stories told and shared constitutes a practice of affirmation and creation of meanings and facilitates understanding experiences shaped by coloniality that need to be re-signified.

Listening focused on an Indigenous healing practice must be open not only to the content manifested through words and feelings but also to the meanings produced by nature and the presence of the enchanted beings. It should occur in nature, such as under trees in sacred spaces of the territory.

Thus, we can hear nature and hear from nature through the sounds of other animals and the dance of the trees, the colorful butterflies that pass by sight and speech, the light and warmth of the sun, the wind that touches our skins, the smell of the rain, the temperature changes throughout the afternoon. In this way, we can connect on a symbolic level, as many of the Pitaguary ways of interpreting the world pass through nature and its spirits. Thus, they understand that we are part of nature, that the sounds of birds, crickets, and rain tell us something, that we can be like a branch of a tree, and that we can share their wisdom and state of harmony.

In this sense, as Indigenous leaders have summoned Indigenous people to collaborate in strengthening Indigenous processes, they must also strive to listen and learn from the traditional knowledge and practices developed in the Indigenous territories. To build possibilities for a decolonial practice based on our experiences and learnings in the context of the previously mentioned PAR, researchers-psychologists, along with Indigenous leaders, pajés, and the Indigenous health team from the Pitaguary territory, designed an intervention to meet the demands of the Pitaguary villages. We planned and aligned knowledge and practices to provide healing practices. Thus, we emphasized that this healing must align with three essential dimensions: body, mind, and spirit, which are understood as a unit, as there is no way to conceive one without the existence of the other. As Munduruku (2009) points out, understanding body-mind-spirit at first glance may seem contradictory or discordant. However, for some native peoples, this unity corresponds to how the mind operates, its way of thinking, and its way of living.

Psychology must be recognized as an ally in strengthening Indigenous decolonial healing, but it should not be the only existing practice (Ciofalo et al., 2022). It must be aligned with the practices of reference people and historical promoters of these healing practices in Indigenous territories. To effectively bridge the gap between Indigenous knowledge and mainstream psychological practice, it is necessary to go beyond acknowledging the importance of Indigenous practices and actively engage with strategies to achieve this integration. Below, we outline key challenges faced when integrating Indigenous epistemologies into Psychology and propose practical steps to address them, based on the experiences of those who worked directly with Indigenous communities.

1 **Epistemological Dominance**

- **Challenge:** The prioritization of Western frameworks in Psychology marginalizes Indigenous epistemologies and limits their inclusion.
- **Solution: Decolonizing Curricula**—Training programs should include courses on Indigenous epistemologies, methodologies, and healing practices. This includes inviting Indigenous healers and leaders to co-develop and deliver content.

2 **Lack of Training**

- **Challenge:** Professional training often overlooks Indigenous healing practices, leaving practitioners unequipped to engage with or respect these approaches.
- **Solution: Cultural Immersion & Capacity-Building**—Programs should incorporate immersive learning experiences where Psychology professionals spend extended periods in Indigenous communities to build trust and understand healing practices in their cultural context.

3 **Institutional Resistance**

- **Challenge:** Institutions may resist change due to entrenched biases or structural limitations that prioritize efficiency over relational and contextual practices.
- **Solution: Dialogue and Advocacy**—Persistent engagement with institutional stakeholders can help integrate Indigenous perspectives into mainstream frameworks. Advocacy efforts should focus on demonstrating the validity and effectiveness of Indigenous healing practices.

4 **Absence of Community-Led Partnerships**

- **Challenge:** Knowledge is often extracted from Indigenous communities without reciprocal collaboration, leading to exploitative research practices.
- **Solution: Community-Led Partnerships**—Research and interventions should be co-designed with Indigenous communities, ensuring that knowledge is shared rather than extracted. This requires long-term relationship-building and shared decision-making.

5 **Colonial Bias in Psychological Practice**

- **Challenge:** Many psychologists and practitioners approach Indigenous healing with skepticism, viewing it as "non-scientific" due to entrenched colonial biases.
- **Solution: Self-Reflection and Unlearning**—Psychologists must critically examine their own biases and actively work to unlearn colonial perspectives. Training should include reflective practices that encourage professionals to recognize the validity of Indigenous worldviews.

6 **Methodological Rigidity**

- **Challenge:** Conventional research methods often fail to adapt to Indigenous ways of knowing, making it difficult to fully integrate these perspectives into psychological practice.
- **Solution: Flexibility in Methodologies**—Researchers should adopt more fluid and participatory approaches that align with the rhythms, priorities, and relational structures of Indigenous communities, emphasizing co-creation rather than extraction.

By addressing these challenges with intentional strategies, we move toward a more inclusive and decolonized Psychology that respects and integrates Indigenous knowledge systems. For meaningful integration, it is essential to foster environments of mutual respect where Indigenous knowledge is recognized as equal to Western epistemologies. This involves creating institutional spaces for dialogue, encouraging cross-disciplinary collaborations, and investing in long-term relationships with communities. By addressing these barriers and implementing these strategies, psychologists can contribute to decolonizing the discipline and fostering equitable practices. Thus, considering their specificities and worldviews, it is essential to (re)think and (re)assemble therapeutic spaces and moments that integrate the ancestral and traditional practices of the most diverse peoples.

Final Considerations

The healing practices of the Pitaguary and Jenipapo-Kanindé peoples point to an ancestral resistance to the colonial traumas that permeate the Indigenous history of Pindorama. These Indigenous peoples have not only preserved their ancestral traditions but also continued to practice their healing rituals through spirituality, medicinal herbs, dances, music, and prayers, living in an integrated and communal way with the territory. By recognizing the healing practices of the Pitaguary and Jenipapo-Kanindé, we emphasize the value of cultural diversity and knowledge but also highlight the continuous processes of resistance in Indigenous territories. In a modern context where Psychology based on colonial scientific epistemicide is dominant, Indigenous healing practices point to decolonial forms of care and make us reflect on how traditional knowledge can/should be integrated into decolonial ways of practicing Psychology.

References

Adams, G., Dobles, I., Gómez, L. H., Kurtiş, T., & Molina, L. E. (2015). Decolonizing psychological science: Introduction to the special thematic section. *Journal of Social and Political Psychology, 3*(1), 213–238. https://doi.org/10.5964/jspp.v3i1.564

Alves Carneiro de Lima, L. (2023). Rotas e Desvios: Mulheres artistas, leitura selvagem. *Visualidades, 20*, 1–23. https://doi.org/10.5216/v.v20.71312

American Psychiatric Association. (2022). *Diagnostic and statistical manual of mental disorders*. American Psychiatric Publishing.

Araújo, I. C., & Freire, J. C. (2014). Os valores e a sua importância para a teoria da clínica da abordagem centrada na pessoa. *Revista da Abordagem Gestáltica, 20*(1), 94–103.

Atallah, D. G. (2016). Rumo a uma virada decolonial no pensamento de resiliência em desastres: Exemplo dos mapuches do sul do Chile nas linhas de frente e nas falhas. *International Journal of Disaster Risk Reduction, 19*, 92–100.

Atallah, D. G., & Dutta, U. (2021). "Creatively in Coalition" from Palestine to India: Weaving stories of refusal and community as decolonial praxis. *Jornal de Assuntos Sociais*, *78*(2), 434–451. https://doi.org/10.1111/josi.12460

Atallah, D. G., Dutta, U., Hana, M. R., Bernal, I., Robinson, R., Del Rio, M., Voyard, C., Al-Ajarma, Y., Antilef, I., Azad, A. K., Bivens, D., Darwish, A., Painemal, C. C., Hakim, C., Hussain, K. S., Jones, D., Marrero, W., Mervin, A., Mitchell, S. S., Mullah, M., Musleh, A., Lizama, E. P., Rosa, M., Tang Yan, C., & Jara, G. C. T. (2022). Transnational research collectives as "constellations of co-resistance": Counterstorytelling, interweaving struggles, and decolonial love. *Qualitative Inquiry*, *28*(6), 681–693. https://doi.org/10.1177/10778004211068202

Atallah, D. G., Shapiro, E. R., Al-Azraq, N., Qaisi, Y., & Suyemoto, K. L. (2018). Descolonizando a pesquisa qualitativa por meio do engajamento comunitário transformador: investigação crítica da resiliência com refugiados palestinos na Cisjordânia. *Pesquisa Qualitativa em Psicologia, 15*(4), 489–519.

Barbosa, V. N. M., Holanda, R. R., Lima, A. A. S., Moura Júnior, J. F., Negreiros, D. J., Antunes, D. C., & Mesquita, N. M. (2023). Relações entre psicologia e pobreza: Propostas de atuação decolonial. *Revista Polis e Psique, 12*(3), 90–110. https://doi.org/10.22456/2238-152X.116537

Battestin, C., Bonatti, J., & Quinto, J. R. (2019). A colonização e resistência dos povos originários da América Latina. *Revista Fórum Identidades, 30*(1), 13–27. https://periodicos.ufs.br/forumidentidades/article/view/13495

Bernardino-Costa, J. (2015). S*aberes subalternos e decolonialidade: os sindicatos das trabalhadoras domésticas no Brasil*. EdUnB.

Bispo, N. (2022). *Colonização, Quilombos: Modos e Significações*. Editora Jandaíra.

Brighenti, C. A. (2015). Colonialidade do poder e a violência contra os povos indígenas. *PerCursos, 16*(32), 103–120. https://doi.org/10.5965/1984724616322015103

Carvalho, S. T. A., Júnior, J. F. M., & Vasconcelos, A. F. (2023). Círculo de cultura sobre estratégias de Indigenização da saúde mental com povos Indígenas do Ceará. *Acta Scientiarum. Human and Social Sciences, 45*, e69728. https://doi.org/10.4025/actascihumansoc.v45i3.69728

Castro, R. D., & Mayorga, C. (2019). Decolonialidade e pesquisas narrativas: Contribuições para a psicologia comunitária. *Revista Pesquisas e Práticas Psicossociais, 14*(3), 1–18. https://www.seer.ufsj.edu.br/revista_ppp/article/view/e3178

Ciofalo, N. (2019). Indigenous psychologies: A contestation for epistemic justice. In N. Ciofalo (Ed.), *Indigenous psychologies in an era of decolonization* (pp. 1–38). Springer.

Ciofalo, N., Dudgeon, P., & Nikora, L. W. (2022). Indigenous community psychologies, decolonization, and radical imagination within ecologies of knowledges. *American Journal of Community Psychology*, *69*(3–4), 283–293. https://doi.org/10.1002/ajcp.12583

Ciófalo, N., & Ortiz-Torres, B. (2024). Toward decolonial community psychologies from Abya Yala. *American Journal of Community Psychology*. Advance online publication. https://doi.org/10.1002/ajcp.12746

Corrêa, H. P., Moura, C. C., Azevedo, C., Bernardes, M. F. V., da Mata, L. R. F. P., Costa, P. H. A. D., & Mendes, K. T. (2020). Colonização, guerra e saúde mental: Fanon, Martín-Baró e as implicações para a Psicologia brasileira. *Psicologia: Teoria e Pesquisa, 36*(spe), e36nspe14. https://doi.org/10.1590/0102.3772e36nspe14

Dutta, U., Azad, A. K., & Hussain, S. M. (2021). Counter storytelling as epistemic justice: Decolonial community-based praxis from the Global South. *American Journal of Community Psychology*, *69*(1–2), 69–70. https://doi.org/10.1002/ajcp.12545

Fanon, F. (2008). *Peles negras Máscaras Brancas* (Trad. Renato da Silveira). EDUFBA.

Farias, J. M., & Hennigen, I. (2019). A Tekoá Ka'aguy Porã: Espaço Ancestral e Produção de Subjetividade Mbya-Guarani. *Psicologia: Ciência e Profissão, 39*. https://doi.org/10.1590/1982-3703003221659

Feitosa, M. Z. S. (2019). *Lideranças Pitaguary de Monguba: Estratégias do bem viver e de compromisso ético-político* [Tese de Doutorado em Psicologia, Universidade Federal do Ceará]. https://repositorio.ufc.br/handle/riufc/57582

Gewehr, R. B., Baêta, J., Gomes, E., & Tavares, R. (2017). Sobre as práticas tradicionais de cura: subjetividade e objetivação nas propostas terapêuticas contemporâneas. *Psicologia USP, 28*(1), 33–43. https://doi.org/10.1590/0103-656420150092

Goes, M., Ximenes, V. M., & Moura, D. (2015). Relações da psicologia comunitária com a libertação a partir da dialética dominação-opressão. *Revista Psicologia de la Liberación, 6*(Número especial), 25–45. https://www.teocripsi.com/ojs/

Grosfoguel, R. (2016). A estrutura do conhecimento nas universidades ocidentalizadas: Racismo/sexismo epistêmico e os quatro genocídios/epistemicídios do longo século XVI. *Revista Sociedade e Estado, 31*(1), 25–49. https://doi.org/10.1590/S0102-69922016000100003

Grünewald, R. A. (2005). *Toré: regime encantado do Indio do nordeste*. Fundação Joaquim Nabuco, Editora Massangana

Guimarães, D. S. (2023). Indigenous psychology as a general science for escaping the snares of psychological methodolatry. *Integrative Psychological & Behavioral Science, 57*(2), 381–389. https://doi.org/10.1007/s12124-022-09724-1

Krenak, A. (2020). *Caminhos para a cultura do bem-viver. Editora Cultura de Paz.*

Langfur, H. (2014). *Recovering Brazil's Indigenous pasts*. University of New Mexico Press.

Luna, W. F., Malvezzi, C., Teixeira, K. C., Almeida, D. T., & Bezerra, V. P. (2020). Identidade, cuidado e direitos: A experiência das rodas de conversa sobre a saúde dos povos Indígenas. *Revista Brasileira de Educação Médica, 44*(2). https://doi.org/10.1590/1981-5271v44.2-20190309

Lykes, M. B., & van der Merwe, H. (2017). Exploring/expanding the reach of transitional justice: Editorial note. *International Journal of Transitional Justice*, *11*(3), 371–377. https://doi.org/10.1093/ijtj/ijx026

Maldonado-Torres, N. (2016). Colonialism, neocolonialism, internal colonialism, and decoloniality. In Y. Martínez-San Miguel, B. Sifuentes-Jáuregui, & M. Belausteguigoitia (Eds.), *Critical terms in Caribbean and Latin American thought* (pp. 67–75). Palgrave Macmillan.

Martín-Baró, I. (1996). O papel do psicólogo. *Estudos de Psicologia (Natal), 2*(1), 7–27. https://doi.org/10.1590/S1413-294X1997000100002

Martín-Baró, I. (2011). Desafios e perspectivas da Psicologia Latino-Americana. In R. S. L. Guzzo, & J. F. Lacerda (Eds.), *Psicologia Social para a América Latina: o resgate da Psicologia da Libertação* (2nd ed., pp. 199–220). Alínea.

Mignolo, W., & Walsh, C. (2018). *On decoloniality: Concepts, analytics, praxis*. Duke University Press.

Miranda, B. R. F., & Dantas, M. A. (2021). A government of Indigenous peoples: Administration, land, and work in the state of Brazil during the Portuguese Empire (1548–1822). *e-Journal of Portuguese History, 19*(2), 25–30. https://doi.org/10.26300/5bt0-4s02

Moura, E. P. G. de., & Teixeira, L. F. (2022). Descolonizar o pensamento: sobre a colonialidade da psicologia. *Revista Científica Multidisciplinar Núcleo do Conhecimento, 7*(12), 98–111. https://www.nucleodoconhecimento.com.br/psicologia/colonialidade-da-psicologia

Munduruku, D. (2009). Educação Indígena: do Corpo, da Mente e do Espírito. *Revista Múltiplas Leituras, 2*(1), 21–29.

Nascimento, V. A., do Nascimento, V. A., Tenório, L. R. R., de Assunção, A. V. P., & dos Santos, L. F. (2021). Saúde mental e os indígenas brasileiros. In V. A. Nascimento, & I. D. Souza (Eds.), *Transtornos mentais e sociedade: vãos e desvãos do sofrimento psíquico em perspectiva multidisciplinar* (pp. 76–83). Editora Científica.

Ndagijimana, J. P., & Taffere, K. (2020). Re-envisioning trauma recovery: Listening and learning from African voices in healing collective trauma. *International Journal of Human Rights Education, 4*(1), 1–15. https://repository.usfca.edu/ijhre/vol4/iss1/8

Oliveira, J. P. (1999). *A viagem da volta: etnicidade, política e reelaboração cultural no Nordeste indígena.* Contra Capa.

Paiva, G. J. D. (2007). Religião, enfrentamento e cura: Perspectivas psicológicas. *Estudos de Psicologia*, *24*, 99–104. https://doi.org/10.1590/S0103-166X2007000100011

Pinho Burlamaqui, A. K., & de Souza Aguiar, J. V. (2024). Corpo-Afeto e Ancestralidade no Processo Educativo dos Povos Indígenas e Quilombolas: Saberes-Vivências de Docentes Atuantes na Região Amazônica. *Diversidade e Educação*, *11*(1), 807–832. https://doi.org/10.14295/de.v11i1.15268

Portela, H. G. (2015). *Cuerpo y Cosmos en el rito*. Academia.edu. https://www.academia.edu/7326688/Cuerpo_y_Cosmos_en_el_rito_Autor_Hugo_Portela_Guarin

Quijano, A. (2000). Coloniality of power, Eurocentrism, and Latin America. *Nepantla: Views from South*, *1*(3), 533–580. https://muse.jhu.edu/article/23906

Quijano, A. (2005). Colonialidade do poder, eurocentrismo e América Latina. In E. Lander (Ed.), *A colonialidade do saber: eurocentrismo e ciências sociais perspectivas latino-americanas* (pp. 38–51). Clacso.

Quijano, A. (2010). Colonialidade do poder e classificação social. In B. Sousa Santos, & M. P. Meneses (Eds.), *Epistemologias do Sul* (pp. 84–130). Cortez.

Sawaia, B. (2017). *As artimanhas da exclusão: análise psicossocial e ética da desigualdade social.* Editora Vozes Limitada.

Scorsolini-Comin, F. (2023). Escuta é Perfume: por uma clínica etnopsicológica. In F. Scorsolini-Comin, & J. F. M. H. Bairrão (Eds.), *Etnopsicologia e Saúde* (pp. 55–78). Editores Pedro e João.

Silva Guimarães, D. (2023). Indigenous psychology as a general science for escaping the snares of psychological methodolatry. *Integrative Psychological & Behavioral Science, 57*(2), 381–389. https://doi.org/10.1007/s12124-022-09724-1

Sonn, C. C., & Cruz, M. R. (2011). (De)colonizing culture in community psychology: Reflections from critical social science. *American Journal of Community Psychology, 47*(1–2), 203–214. https://doi.org/10.1007/s10464-010-9378-x

Souza, L. de M. (2005). *O Diabo e a Terra de Santa Cruz*. Companhia das Letras.

Spivak, G. C. (2010). *Pode o subalterno falar?* (M. C. C. Costa, Trad.). Editora UFMG.

Veiga, L. M. (2019). Descolonizando a psicologia: Notas para uma psicologia preta. *Fractal: Revista de Psicologia*, *31*, 244–248. https://doi.org/10.22409/1984-0292/v31i_esp/29000

World Health Organization. (2019). *International statistical classification of diseases and related health problems* (11th revision). WHO.

8 Decolonial Love in Action

Centering Spiritual Solidarity in Restorative and Transformative Justice

Jenny Escobar

> Ubuntu: a person is a person through their relationships.
>
> (Davis, 2019)

> We don't have a word for 'offender' in our language; the word we use means 'un-healed.' Faith Tait, Nisga'a Nation.
>
> (Shah et al., 2017)

Introduction

In his essay titled "Outline of Ten Theses in Coloniality and Decoloniality," Maldonado-Torres (2016) describes our current state of coloniality as one where dehumanization and the naturalization of war is the basis for how power is imposed upon, knowledge is built, and a sense of being is defined. The colonization of power, knowledge, and being, as he referred to them, are consequences of what he termed the catastrophe of modernity. To change these current dehumanizing practices, he proposes a decolonial turn, where decoloniality can occur through the centering of love. Decolonial love, as proposed by Sandoval (2000), is the antidote to the consequences of coloniality due to its power to (re)focus back to relationality and understanding. Decolonial love has the power to "'breaking' through whatever controls in order to find understanding and community" (Maldonado-Torres, 2016, n.d.). This type of love can be seen in the types of relationships and web of relationalities among beings, particularly in Indigenous relational paradigms that include building connections of interdependence and reciprocity with all sentient beings. In this reflexive piece, I join in with other decolonial psychologists (Atallah, 2022; Bhatia & Priya, 2021; Ciofalo, 2022; Fernández, 2022; James, 2017; Sonn & Stevens, 2021) to reimagine how psychology as a field of praxis with the liberation movements of the oppressed can center its focus on decolonial love through the lens of spiritual solidarity and restorative justice (RJ) and transformative justice (TJ).

In this chapter, I offer spiritual solidarity (Escobar, 2022) as a framework that can help us integrate the often-ignored relationships that those fighting for healing and justice have with loved ones no longer physically present. Spiritual solidarity attends to the role of ancestors/loved ones who are deceased but continue to guide the actions of those still alive. I particularly examine these relationships in RJ and TJ processes in my experience as a facilitator of these processes. Specifically, I propose three ways that spiritual solidarity and RJ and TJ interconnect for the sake of building relationships based on decolonial love, reciprocity, and accountability. (1) Circles as spaces for memory practices to emerge; (2) memory practices, such as storytelling that conjure up memories of loved ones to whom people feel connected and accountable, can strengthen individuals' and communities' commitment to relationship building; and (3) spiritual solidarity can support accountability by focusing on the relationships with those no longer here but whose presence helps

DOI: 10.4324/9781003492214-10

move individuals and communities into justice-oriented actions. This exploration is critical at this moment as RJ and TJ practices are being misused and co-opted by institutions who are using their practices to maintain the status quo, and not for social justice transformation and as a decolonial praxis. By recentering the essence of RJ and TJ as two separate community-driven justice practices that share some similar values, this chapter seeks to further develop the potential of these justice models as decolonial practices through spiritual solidarity. Lastly, the lessons that emerged from centering spiritual solidarity in justice endeavors can contribute to building a psychology of healing, resistance, and relationality.

This chapter is comprised of my experiences as an RJ and TJ facilitator in educational and community settings and the collective wisdom that participants of these practices bring to building collective remembrance and decolonial ways of relating. The specific experiences dovetailed in this chapter come from working overtime with schools' communities in Southern California in my capacity as an RJ trainer. I offer memories of particular circles with school administrators and teachers, where I witnessed circle participants' storytelling demonstrates decolonial love in action through the embodiment of remembrance of loved ones no longer physically present. I also weave in the public testimony of a survivor of state violence whose ongoing love for his assassinated son transformed his approach to addressing structural harm. These experiences are dovetailed to show the powerful matrix that decolonial love and spiritual solidarity can have in building a praxis of healing, justice, and transformation.

Relational Justice: Restorative and Transformative Justice

Contemporary RJ, as implemented within a Western, settler-colonial context, emerges out of the necessity to find "alternative ways" to the existing punitive model of justice (Valandra & Wapȟáha Hokšíla, 2020). The impacts of Eurocentric justice frameworks where colonial values of vengeance, retribution, and individualism (the focus solely on the person who caused harm/broke the law) have resulted in an ongoing dehumanization crisis. From the school-to-prison to deportation pipeline (Ríos Vega, 2020; Rodriguez, 2022), to the prison industrial complex (Cullors & Dorriz, 2022; Meiners & Winn, 2010), where mostly communities of color take the brunt of punitive policies and practices, RJ seeks to bring forth values of centering relationships and healing instead of laws and rules in how harm is addressed. In essence, RJ seeks to strengthen relationships so that when a conflict or harm occurs, the focus is on repairing the relationships at stake. This relationality approach to justice is not new, nor does it originate with RJ. It is found in the essence and practices among many Indigenous communities across the world whose understanding of harm is rooted in a cosmovision of reciprocity, relationality, and justice as healing. As scholar and RJ practitioner Fania Davis (2019) recounts, "...restorative justice arises along the historical backdrop of heightened international awareness that Indigenous knowledge, grounded in an ecological ethos of interrelatedness and collaboration, have much to offer today's fractured world" (p. 21). As a result, RJ is seen by many as a way to bring similar relational orientations into existing institutions, such as schools and criminal justice procedures, and community-driven initiatives, such as non-profit organizations and collectives, to mitigate some of the harmful effects of punitive measures.

Yet, the Indigenous origins from which RJ derives its values and set of practices are not always acknowledged nor integrated fully, particularly by those who see RJ as a "violence prevention program" or "an alternative to suspension" for "bad kids" "initiative," instead of what it is meant to be: a lifelong re-orientation to honoring relationships and kinship in every aspect of our lives. For some RJ practitioners, particularly those who are settlers and do not have a direct link with Indigenous teachings and ancestry, acknowledging the connection between RJ and Indigenous origins can be superficial and almost risk being a co-optation of Indigenous practices. In this case, Davis

(2019) invites RJ practitioners to seek their ancestral lineages for relational accounts and practices and integrate those into their RJ efforts. But that is not enough. Indigenous scholars, activists, and justice leaders who participated in a "listening tour" to document the history and impacts of RJ nationwide (Shah et al., 2017) warned about the erasure and co-optation of their cultural and ancestral ways of being in the RJ movement, particularly the use of circles and peacemaking practices akin RJ. These practices come from a particular context and history and vary in the way they are done depending on the Indigenous nations. Thus, one cannot use RJ interchangeably with peacemaking, for example. As the report summarized,

> Several people in the Navajo Nation felt that peacemaking and restorative justice were not the same thing, and you cannot in the Diné language simply replace one word with the other. Language is critical to reclaiming identity and dismantling shame.
>
> (Shah et al., 2017, p. 20).

It is important then that the Indigenous relational paradigm be differentiated from the orientations of RJ, which although share some similarities, derive from a different context and histories, and thus cannot be equated as being the same. Nevertheless, the disruptive impact that RJ can have on punitive, dehumanizing practices if applied with fidelity to its justice goals, can help shift individuals and structures toward a healing and justice approach to harm and conflict.

Similar to RJ, TJ centers relationships and a community's resources and wisdom, as the basis for addressing harm to promote safety, healing, and transformation for all those involved. Given its emergence from the anti-violence movement led mainly by Black women, women of color, survivors of domestic violence, and queer communities (Dixon & Piepzna-Samarasinha, 2020; Rasmussen & Shah, 2022), TJ emerges as a response to witnessing first-hand the punitive violence inflicted by a carceral system which has resulted in the over-incarceration of Black, Indigenous, People of Color and the ongoing use of violence perpetrated by the state. As a result, TJ seeks to build collective accountability processes that rise from collective efforts and initiatives and not from state-sanctioned responses to violence. This departure from what exists to something different is one of the ways that communities targeted and impacted by state-sponsored violence can keep each other safe and create avenues for healing and transformation that break the cycles of violence resulting from the ongoing colonial project. In essence, TJ positions interpersonal violence as a symptom and direct product of ongoing state violence, which most existing institutions have been created to support, and thus does not seek to work within existing systems. This separation goes beyond what RJ efforts have focused on, to change the system within, and thus RJ has been critiqued as a reformist project.

Despite their different approaches to undoing punitive violence, RJ and TJ as two paradigms of justice when bridged together can offer a clear political and practical foundation to implement a decolonial approach to justice. As practitioners of this work, Rasmussen and Shah (2022), explain:

> RJ has offered us a philosophy of justice that prioritizes relationships, healing, and care, and TJ has helped us to understand that addressing interpersonal harm without addressing systemic harm will always be insufficient...From our respective RJ and TJ efforts, we strongly believe that the work of supporting the right relationships between people and communities is only effective when done in connection with larger social movements struggling for a society in which these relationships and communities can flourish.
>
> (n.d.)

As an RJ practitioner who has worked within and outside institutions with a TJ political commitment to create something different than what exists, I have witnessed the power of merging these two orientations in both practice and approach. I have also experienced the power of centering relationships to deal with conflict in my own life. As a former undocumented person, it was clear to me and my family that calling the police when there was a family or community conflict was not the best option. As we feared that instead of bringing safety, it would result in further victimization and deportation. As a result, we had to figure out how to address familial and community harms on our own. Although we did not have access to a political and healing justice movement such as RJ and TJ at the time, and oftentimes we fell back on punitive ways of dealing with harm, we created conditions of safety the best way we knew by relying on familiar relationships that we respected and felt accountable to.

Spiritual Solidarity in Restorative and Transformative Justice Practices

One type of relationship that evokes love, safety, and accountability is the relationship with those no longer physically present. In my previous work, I have explored the relationships between survivors of state violence and their loved ones who have been disappeared or killed by the state (Escobar, 2013, 2022). This relationship has played a pivotal role in guiding and strengthening survivors' quests for justice and healing from state violence. Spiritual solidarity, as I was called to name this relationship, captures the love that transcends human/spirit dichotomies and sheds light on relationships with spirits/ancestors that support everyday acts of justice. In the context of RJ and TJ, the role of spiritual beings is palpable through the stories that emerge in circles, and in individuals and communities honoring the lives taken by state-sponsored violence.

Chicanx feminist writer Gloria Anzaldua offers a way in which the spiritual can be integrated into co-creating knowledges and other ways of being (Anzaldua, 2015). Spiritual activism, she declares is a *conocimiento*, a way of knowing that comes from within our connection to spirit, to the otherworldly and we connect this knowledge to the political visions for social transformation (Anzaldua, 2015). Similarly, Maldonado-Torres (2016) defines the spiritual as "a way of relating to the world in its totality, and through that, to each of its parts" (n.d.). Spiritual solidarity, when connected to RJ and TJ movements, centers the relationality of the human and non-human as not just a personal relationship of reverence and remembrance, but as part of the political project of justice and healing. From this place, ancestral, spiritual knowledge emerges guiding humans in how to connect spiritual knowing or as Anzaldua states *conocimientos* into political acts of social transformation. Ultimately, at the heart of these relationships is love, a decolonial love. One of the impacts of colonialism has been to declare love between humans and non-humans as insignificant, impossible to prove in the logic of scientific imperialism, and non-existent. In the sections that follow, I provide specific examples of RJ and TJ practices that shed light on the relational, healing, and justice possibilities that emerge from centering the spiritual in how we build relationships.

Circles as Memory Practices

Circles are at the heart of how RJ and TJ are practiced. This practice of convening allows for presence, vulnerability, and connection to emerge. First, the physical act of sitting in a circle without any tables or other objects around exposes the full body for others to see. This somatic exposure, although uncomfortable for some, supports the process of showing up fully without any distractions or a place to hide. The rituals that are implemented in circles such as taking turns talking and listening using a talking piece, placing a centerpiece in the middle of the circle (usually a fabric with objects of significance for the community), and a set of community agreements to guide the sharing, indicate the transition between everyday ways of convening into a more intentional, dedicated time to connect. Circles become portals that disrupt the productivity wheel of relationality set out by capitalism and set forth a time portal for relationship building and accountability to take place.

Circles can also be conduits for remembrance. Memories of the past can be conjured up through specific circle prompts and the sharing from circle participants that provoke individual and collective memories of past events and experiences. These memories time travel to the present, and at times well into the future as the storytelling that emerges in the circle transforms into a portal of remembrance where linear time constructs cease to exist, and instead access to a decolonial sense of remembering can emerge. For example, as a circle facilitator, I invite individuals to look back at their younger selves and to think of advice they would give themselves knowing what they know today. I instructed circle participants to "make room" for their younger selves to join them in a circle by physically moving to one side so their past selves could join in. I further prompt them to describe what their younger selves look like. What are they wearing? How do they smell? What body and facial expressions did they show up with? I conjured up the specifics of this version of themselves not only for individuals to have better access to their memories of their past selves but also to have their younger version take up space in the present moment, and in the circle process of remembrance we are undertaking. As circle participants give their past selves a place in the circle, the storytelling emerges. These stories contain specifics of that time in their lives, giving voice to their past selves as they (re)introduce themselves in the circle and provide others with a sense of who they were and what was going on for them during that time. With the stories, emotions also arise. Tears and laughter filled the room as individuals recalled the specifics of that time. When it comes to offering advice to their past selves, the energy often shifts. Things get quieter and more serious. The wisdom that comes from hardships and time is shared, sometimes with regret and often with increased understanding and empathy for themselves and each other.

This process of remembrance is collectively built by circle participants who choose to share themselves with others opening up the possibility for healing to emerge as individuals recalled all they have endured. As a facilitator, I bring the invitation to circle participants to build a portal of remembrance, but this container is only built if participants accept and embody the invitation. The presence of a past self also opens up the possibility for other than physical bodies to be part of the circle process. The remembrance that takes part in the circle allows for the embodiment of memories to go beyond a retelling of memory and transform into a symbolic and sensory experience of witnessing oneself and each other in different times, breaking away from colonial linear time constructs separating the past, present, and future. This remembrance aligns with Indigenous scholar Linda Tuhiwai Smith's (2013) description of remembrance as "…not so much to an idealized remembering of a golden past but more specifically to the remembering of a painful past, remembering in terms of connecting bodies with place and experience, and, importantly, people's responses to that pain." (p. 167). This process of active remembering expands the purpose of circles from a way to gather to a container where openings for healing can emerge within a context of justice. As individuals share their experiences, a collective witnessing takes place, and these experiences are then connected to structural, historical, and social-political contexts that help (re)shape the individual stories into one of collective visions of justice. For communities who have endured structural violence, this collective witnessing can be a pivotal healing moment where their stories disrupt the dehumanizing narratives surrounding their experiences. In essence, circles can embody an ethos of healing and justice by being implemented as an ongoing tool for bearing witness to the memories of those no longer alive and those still present who are intentionally excluded. The following section describes how circles can be portals of remembrance that invite the spiritual in and expand the relational possibilities stemming from decolonial love.

Relationality through Spirit and Decolonial Love

As a circle facilitator, I have found that paying attention to the spiritual before, during, and after circles is an opportunity to witness the intangible and sacred forces that support the collective ethos of coming together. My practice of evoking and speaking to the ancestors of circle participants as I prepared the space comes from my spiritual practice that was passed down by my lineages and is fortified by spiritual elders and community. There are protocols that I am accountable for following, and a spiritual community that holds me accountable for the way I navigate the spiritual realm. As I create the container for participants' full selves to show up, I have to account for not only their lived experiences to fill the circle but that of their families, communities, and ancestors to emerge.

When I first began facilitating circles, I did not start by preparing the space. I was hesitant to bring the spiritual into the mundane, into a workspace, fearful of my work being seen as unprofessional, woo-woo, and not legit. A concern that stems directly from the impacts of coloniality that promotes and rewards the compartmentalization of ourselves, where the body, mind, and spirit are separate. But I quickly realized that whether I acknowledged it or not, I prepared or not, the presence of those no longer physically present would show up in the RJ and TJ work I was doing. This led me to be spiritually accountable to acknowledge the spiritual elements of this work, with clear intentions, in the way I facilitate and create containers for relationality to emerge. Below is a recount of the ways the spiritual has shown up during this practice in my experience as a circle facilitator, and the way that circle participants bring their spiritual embodiment into the collective experience.

I turn on the lights in the cold, dark room. It is the same as the countless rooms I have been assigned to, surrounded by gray, big, plastic foldable chairs and tables, the lingering smell of sweat and cleaning supplies, and a bright neon red sign indicating the emergency exit. I get straight to it. Moving the tables to the periphery of the room and pulling the chairs closer to touch side by side forming a circle. I exhale before digging in my bag, slowing my breath to transition worlds. I find the ziploc bag with the ingredients that I need. I take another deep breath. I look toward the door to make sure no one is around and then slowly I start walking around the circle, letting my fingertips drop the sacred white powder, *cascarilla*, harnessed in my hands, and delivering my words to the earth and heavens. My prayers are first full of gratitude for the people, ancestors, and beings that live in this school, this community, this land, *agradeciendo y pidiendo permiso a todos los espiritus de este territorio que vinieron antes de todos nosotros*. I thank my lineage and beings for letting me be here to do the heart's work. I then proceed to imagine each person who is going to be sitting in this circle. Although I do not know them yet, I see their tired looks, their stressed energy from teaching and giving, and their lingering rush to get to the next thing. I speak to them and their ancestors my intentions and my prayer for healing and service that I bring, *vengo con intenciones de amor y sanacion para que juntes encontremos apoyo, esperanza y un deseo por un buen vivir*. As the *cascarilla* flows out of my fingerprints creating a thin line around the circle, my words get louder with each round and I listen for what else is needed, perhaps some music, more games and activities, or slowness and nourishment. This is how I prepare. This is how I bring spirit to circles with me.

After warming up with some games and a check-in question, I asked the teachers and school administrators in the circle to share a fond memory about themselves through the voice of someone they felt supported growing up. Stories about childhood teachers, favorite aunties and uncles, grandparents, and parents fill the space turning the gray in the room into shades of yellow and blue. As we are approaching the end of the circle, one of the teachers who has been quietly listening takes the talking piece into his hands and proceeds to transport us back to his kitchen table, in the late seventies, across the country in Boston. His voice gets coarser and slower, and before he speaks, he smokes his pretend cigar, lounges back in the chair, and with a heavy Boston accent starts, "Let me tell you about my boy here...." The room still in anticipation remains silent for the duration of the story. Collectively, we honor this new guest, the father of one of the teachers, who shares with us the last words he said to his son before dying. There are tears and a collective sense of reverence for the presence in the circle, and for the teacher who has allowed for his deceased father to come in and share with us. He takes a breath after finishing his account and passes the talking piece to the person to his left. This is how spirit shows up through participants in a circle.

The presence of loved ones who are no longer present in RJ and TJ processes is very much alive. Circle participants, when given the space and time, will often evoke the memory of loved ones no longer alive. The teacher who spoke about his father, through his father's voice and mannerisms, is an example of how circles can be a vehicle for spiritual solidarity to emerge. That is, for the lines between the human and spirit to be blurred within a container intentionally acknowledging the role of ancestors. In institutions such as schools, where there is minimum time and space for intuition and spiritual connections to emerge, circles can be rituals that give participants access to the fullness of their relational humanity and co-create containers for sacred connections to cohabit in the present moment. Situating love in remembrance, Attallah (2022) proposes that "through radical grief and remembrance, we can be engulfed by love so powerful and transformative that new understandings and pathways toward freedom are forged as we actively and defiantly remember and resist" (p. 78). Similarly, decolonial love that emanates from remembering loved ones no longer alive during circles are openings for collective visions of healing and justice to emerge in contexts often plagued with mistrust, apprehension, and injustices such as seen in institutions and communities experiencing ongoing structural violence. In this context, circles and remembrance become an antidote to historical amnesia of injustices, and instead open up the possibilities for accountability, repair, and justice to take place.

"I am my ancestors' wildest dream": Accountability to Spirit as a Way toward Justice

"I am my ancestors' wildest dream" is a statement I have heard in many social justice spaces. I do not know who first coined this phrase nor in what context it came from, but it captures the duty to remember who and where we come from, and how we are accountable to those no longer here. Similarly, accountability to deceased relatives whether blood-related or not can play an important role in how we address conflict and harm. When spiritual entities, as one-way ancestors can be perceived, become part of accountability processes, there is space to expand the relational nature of harm restoration in RJ and TJ processes.

When harm occurs, an RJ approach to righting the wrong committed consists of bringing people together to explore the impact of harm, reasons for why harm occurred in the first place, and agreements from all those involved on how to move forward and best repair after the harm. This approach to harm can also be applied at a collective level, where communities who have caused harm and structures that support it go through a similar accountability process, attempting to right a wrong to the best of their ability by honoring the requests of those most impacted by the harm. Some tenets of this model can be found in transitional justice mechanisms such as truth commissions (MacDonald & Garcia-Moores, 2024) and culturally rooted models of conflict mediation such as gacacas in Rwanda (Nowotny, 2020). At the heart of these approaches to harm is the presence of those no longer present as a direct result of being killed or disappeared during the collective harm taking place such as in the case of wars and genocide. Memory work done by survivors of the violence on behalf of loved ones allows for the lives and teachings of those no longer present to continue to shape the fabric of healing and justice.

In other contexts, the role of the spiritual when addressing conflict and harm attends to the rituals of a particular community. RJ scholars Wielenga et al. (2020) describe the spiritual cleansing that happens in various African traditions as a way to prepare individuals and collectives for the process of reconciliation and repair, as they state,

> The intrinsic importance of the intersection of the physical and metaphysical is most visible in the cleansing rituals that characterize most African systems of justice (see, for example, Banies

> 2010). Even were a conflict to be resolved between individuals through the formal state system, on returning to their community, these individuals would need to engage in a cleansing ritual that involves the whole community in the cosmological sense…
>
> (p. 49)

This demarcation of the different ways communities integrate the spiritual into the work of justice is important to highlight when a decolonial approach to justice is being co-created with ancient traditions. Accountability, in this sense, points to an accountability to the unseen and often silenced, the rituals, ceremonies, and everyday acts of enacting spiritual solidarity with those no longer physically present. As a facilitator of harm restoration, I find that experiences of loss, grief, and unending love with those deceased can function as a meeting place, that is a set of memories that help individuals and communities connect to the most vulnerable parts of their humanity. It is from this place that true accountability can emerge.

In my previous work with survivors of state violence in Colombia (Escobar, 2013), I formed a relationship with one father whose 15-year-old son had been assassinated by the riot police. In one of our many walks/talks we would do around Bogota, this father described his desire for revenge rooted in anger and grief for the loss of his son. He confessed that soon after his son's death, he would observe and take detailed notes of the coming and going of police officers at a nearby police station. He remembered how every day he would wake up and plan to blow himself up inside the station. He did not express any fear or concern about this plan; instead, he wanted to be meticulous in his observations so that his revenge would be successful. One day, as he retells the story, he meets a young man in one of his workshops about the history of the police force in one of the many schools he visited. This young man reminded him a lot of his son, and as he was conversing with him the young man told him that whatever he was thinking of doing, it was not worth it, and that instead, he should dedicate his time to doing things from a place of love. The father never told anyone what he was thinking of doing during that time, and although it was inexplicable how this young man knew what he was up to, his warning hit home. From that day forward, the father decided to act out of the unconditional love he has for his son and not from the anger and grief that burden him. Although he still carried the feelings of revenge, his commitment to loving his son in memory practices provided him with the anchor of his action toward love. This is an example of accountability to those loved ones who although not present physically guide the healing and justice actions of those left behind, this is spiritual solidarity in action. This is living and embodying our ancestor's wildest dreams.

Building a Decolonial Psychology of Healing, Resistance, and Relationality

An epistemology of spiritual solidarity is my love offer to psychologists who are committed to the decolonial turn. This epistemology lends a lens by which to understand the healing possibilities that can emerge through the inclusion of relationships with those no longer alive. As seen through the stories shared, spiritual solidarity can take place when relational containers such as circles are co-built. Decolonial love as acts of love for ancestors and those no longer alive can emerge within RJ and TJ practices by centering the non-human, the spiritual. These spiritual solidarity relationships support the rehumanization and accountability processes that RJ and TJ seek to do. Through memory practices such as storytelling, the presence of past, present, and future selves and loved ones no longer alive, provides a vehicle for vulnerability and affect that extends the logic of time and space to create a decolonial relational paradigm. These examples show the symbiotic relationship between community justice models and spiritual solidarity wherein RJ and TJ practices are a vehicle for spiritual solidarity to emerge, and spiritual solidarity strengthens circles and harm and conflict accountability processes through the presence of ancestors and loved ones no longer physically present.

Psychologists building critical spaces for relationality can commit to weaving in the spiritual aspects of relationships. This requires a trust in the process of decoloniality which leads to a letting go of an ingrained suspicion of anything related to spirit, which is understandable given its misuse in the justification of violence. An epistemology of spiritual solidarity invites psychologists and others to lean into the legitimacy of otherworldly teachings that can emerge in reciprocal relationships with spirits and ancestors. These other ways of knowing can contribute to the existing *saberes decoloniales* (decolonial knowledges), dismantling the silencing and exclusionary preference for only the tangible and measurable. Giving strength and validity to the everyday acts of spiritual solidarities can transform the way we understand and perceive a decolonial vision forward.

My other love offering to psychology has to do with *amor eterno* (eternal love), derived from the famous Mexican composer and singer Juan Gabriel's song *amor eterno* which he wrote after the passing of a loved one. *Amor eterno* describes the grief and sadness that is left behind after a loved one dies. But it is also a declaration and centering of love as never-ending, as a feeling and action that do not conform with colonial dichotomies of life and death, human and spirit. The invitation is for psychologists to embrace this kind of love in their understanding of the relationships that exist within and outside communities fighting for liberation and toward decolonial futures. *Amor eterno* contributes to decolonial love in that it offers a way of including ancestral love in the way we *feel* our way into the decolonial turn in the field and world at large. The centering of "afectos" or the feeling toward the decolonial is similar to the sentipensar paradigm offered by Colombian sociologist Orlando Fals Borda (2009), who as described by Victor Manuel Moncayo situated the role of the heart as the place to think from, and the head as the place to feel from centering the emotive wisdom in his work with Indigenous and fishing communities in the coastal region of Colombia. In the *amor eterno* present in the memories of loved ones no longer alive, we witness the centering of the heart, of a decolonial love, that creates and imagines justice possibilities through transformative relational ways of being. I offer a set of questions that can aid psychologists in the strengthening of love and centering of their hearts in their decolonial commitments: what is love in action asking of you right now? How is *amor eterno* present in your work? What do you have to undo and let go to embody an ethos of *amor eterno*?

For RJ and TJ practices, an epistemology of spiritual solidarity and the presence of *amor eterno* exist, although not always visible. They are at many times doing the behind-the-scenes work for relationships of reciprocity and justice to emerge in these processes, and I propose that as psychologists, we are well equipped to bring forth these elements often silenced and invisible through the colonial lenses that still plague the field. May we be guided to change the lens and instead put on the pluriverse lenses of decoloniality in action.

References

Anzaldua, G. E. (2015). *Light in the dark/luz en los oscuro: Rewriting identity, spirituality, reality* (A. Keating, Ed.). Duke University Press.

Atallah, D. G. (2022). Reflections on radical love and rebellion: Towards decolonial solidarity in community psychology praxis. In: S. Kessi, S. Suffla, & M. Seedat (Eds.), *Decolonial enactments in community psychology*. pp. 75–97. Community Psychology. Springer.

Banics, E. (2010). Spirits and social reconstruction after mass violence: Rethinking transitional justice. *African Affairs*, *109*(436), 409–430. https://doi.org/10.1093/afraf/adq023

Bhatia, S., & Priya, K. R. (2021). Coloniality and psychology: From silencing to re-centering marginalized voices in postcolonial times. *Review of General Psychology*, *25*(4), 422–436. https://doi.org/10.1177/10892680211046507

Ciofalo, N. (2022). Making the road *caminando de otra manera*: Co-constructing decolonial community psychologies from the Global South. *American Journal of Community Psychology, 69*(3–4), 426–435. https://psycnet.apa.org/doi/10.1002/ajcp.12562

Cullors, P., & Dorriz, A. A. R. (2022). Abolitionist aesthetics and the abolitionist movement: Los Angeles grassroots organizations and the aesthetic foundations of real-time abolition. *UCLA Law Review*, *69*, 1488.

Davis, F. (2019). Ubuntu: The indigenous ethos of restorative justice. In Fania E. Davis (Ed.), *The little book of race and restorative justice: Black lives, healing, and US social transformation* (pp. 17–29). Living Justice Press.

Dixon, E., & Piepzna-Samarasinha, L. L. (2020). *Beyond survival: Strategies and stories from the transformative justice movement*. AK Press.

Escobar, J. (2013). *Memoria Viva: State violence and the movement for memory in Colombia* [ProQuest Dissertations and Theses database].

Escobar, J. (2022). The role of memory practices in building spiritual solidarity for survivors of state violence. *American Journal of Community Psychology*, *69*, 403–414. https://doi.org/10.1002/ajcp.12570

Fals Borda, O. (2009). *Una sociología sentipensante para América Latina, compilado por Víctor Manuel Moncayo*. Siglo del Hombre.

Fernández, J. S. (2022). A mujerista liberation psychology perspective on testimonio to cultivate decolonial healing. *Women & Therapy*, *45*(2–3), 131–156. https://doi.org/10.1080/02703149.2022.2095101

James, S. (2017). Indigenous epistemology explored through Yoruba Orisha traditions in the African diaspora. *Women & Therapy*, *41*(1–2), 114–130. https://doi.org/10.1080/02703149.2017.1324192

MacDonald, D. B., & Garcia-Moores, J. (2024). Truth commissions and truth-telling. In S. Lightfoot, & S. Maddison (Eds.), *Handbook of indigenous public policy* (pp. 332–350). Edward Elgar Publishing.

Maldonado-Torres, N. (2016). *Outline of ten theses in coloniality and decoloniality*. Foundation Frantz Fanon. https://frantzfanonfoundation-fondationfrantzfanon.com/IMG/pdf/maldonado-torres_outline_of_ten_theses-10.23.16_.pdf

Meiners, E. R., & Winn, M. T. (2010). Resisting the school to prison pipeline: The practice to build abolition democracies. *Race Ethnicity and Education*, *13*(3), 271–276. https://doi.org/10.1080/13613324.2010.500832

Nowotny, J. (2020). The limits of post-genocide justice in Rwanda: Assessing gacaca from the perspective of survivors. *Contemporary Justice Review*, *23*(4), 401–429. https://doi.org/10.1080/10282580.2020.1719365

Rasmussen, C., & Shah, S. (2022, September 9). Growing justice: Why understanding restorative and transformative justice on their own terms, and at their best and worst, will help us build more of both. *Inquest: A decarceral brainstorm*. https://inquest.org/growing-restorative-transformative-justice/

Ríos Vega, J. A. (2020). School to deportation pipeline: Latino youth counter-storytelling narratives. *Journal of Latinos and Education*, *22*(1), 258–270. https://doi.org/10.1080/15348431.2020.1745642

Rodriguez, S. (2022). "Immigration knocks on the door… we are stuck…": A multilevel analysis of undocumented youth's experiences of racism, system failure, and resistance in policy and school contexts. *Teachers College Record*, *124*(6), 3–37. https://doi.org/10.1177/01614681221093286

Sandoval, C. (2000). *Methodology of the Oppressed*. University of Minnesota Press.

Shah, S., Stauffer, C., & King, S. (2017). *Restorative justice listening project final report*. Zher Institute for Restorative Justice. https://zehr-institute.org/images/Restorative-Justice-Listening-Project-Final-Report.pdf

Sonn, C. C., & Stevens, G. (2021). Tracking the decolonial turn in contemporary community psychology: Expanding socially just knowledge archives, ways of being and modes of praxis. In G. Stevens, & C. C. Sonn (Eds.), *Decoloniality and epistemic justice in contemporary community psychology* (pp. 1–19). Springer Nature Switzerland AG.

Tuhiwai Smith, L. (2013). *Decolonizing methodologies: Research and indigenous peoples* (2nd ed.). Zed Books.

Valandra, E. C., & Wapȟáha Hokšíla, W. (2020). Undoing the first harm: Settlers in restorative justice. In Edward C. Valandra & Waŋbli Wapȟáha Hokšíla (Eds.), *Colorizing restorative justice: Voicing our realities* (pp. 325–370). Living Justice Press.

Wielenga, C., Batley, M., & Murambadoro, R. (2020). Beyond restorative justice: Understanding justice from an African perspective. *Ubuntu: Journal of Conflict and Social Transformation*, *9*(1), 43–69. https://doi.org 10.31920/2050-4950/2020/9n1a3

9 The Black MAP Project

An Online Installation of Afrodynamic Healing Ways

Britton Williams

Introduction

> Lucille Clifton gives us an invitation to join her in celebration… Against the backdrop of brutality and denigration…. Like Maya Angelou said: and still, we rise… And truth be told this is no surprise… because one thing Black folx know how to do…. Is be between a rock and a hard place and still come through… As a people we are adept at making a way out of no way… with detailed maps and potent recipes of our healing ways… –celebrate.[1]

When my grandmother was alive, she shared many times with clarity and confidence: *I don't need to see a therapist. God is my therapist.* A few of those times, I implored her to (re)consider and imagine a world where she could attend church and recognize God as an element of her healing *while also* seeing a therapist. She always declined. I look back at the times I tried to convince my grandmother to see a therapist and recognize now how—through my academic and societal socialization—I was severed from my own cultural healing ways. As a drama therapist, I understand the ways in which the churches my grandmother attended—and that I grew up in—echo much of what I know to be healing. The gathering of community, the collective singing, the moving to music, being roused by an inspiring word from the preacher and relational support. These elements, in fact, share pieces of what makes drama therapy groups so impactful. What is readily apparent is that drama therapy—and the creative arts therapies—has appropriated creative and ritual practices from Indigenous, Black, Latinx, and Asian communities (Williams, in press).

It has long been a belief that *Black people do not go to therapy*. However, as I think about my grandmother and her wisdom, I wish to unsettle this myth. Black people engage a myriad of creative and communal practices that have carried us through trials and sustained us amid tribulations. We have sung/stitched/painted/danced/written/spoken/cooked/created/spun/[and…] our healing individually and collectively. And yet, Black healing ways remain illegible as legitimate and valuable forms of mental health care by whitestream[2] care systems.

As a drama therapist, I am interested in the ways in which the arts and creative expression support healing. As a Black woman I know that healing is inextricably connected to liberation. Anti-Blackness is injurious to mental health. And yet, whitestream mental health care systems do not have diagnoses or approaches that meaningfully and intentionally consider the deleterious impact of oppression or the dehumanizing brutalities of enduring racial violence (Fanon, 2020; Williams, 2023). Furthermore, Western-European perspectives of mental health care locate healing as an individual endeavor and speak in the language of pathology, coping, and individual (un) wellness. Alternatively, an Afrocentric viewpoint considers and centers ancestral, spiritual, familial, communal, environmental, societal, and historical connections in healing and care processes. Healing cannot be disentangled from culture, history, and identity. Amid enduring coloniality and

DOI: 10.4324/9781003492214-11

racial oppression—forces that inevitably seep into conventional mental health care systems—decolonial approaches to healing are essential (Bhatia, 2018; Mullan, 2023).

There are movements and practices that recognize and center the inextricable connectedness between healing and liberation, including liberation psychology (Martín-Baró, 1994), liberation-based healing (Almeida, 2018), liberation health (Belkin-Martinez & Fleck-Henderson, 2014), and just practice: a social justice approach to social work (Finn, 2021). The Black Music and Performance (MAP) Project (BMP), in conversation with liberatory care approaches, lifts Black healing ways and freedom practices as a contribution to the conversation around decolonizing mental health care practice and education. This work (re)conceptualizes and acknowledges the long history of Black healing as an individual and collective pursuit of aesthetics and community, inextricably tied to liberation. This work seeks to benefit artists, activists, psychologists, social workers, and creative arts therapists.

I should note that this work is grounded in knowing that the [interconnected] histories of the mental health field—including psychiatry, psychology, social work, counseling, and the creative arts therapies—are rooted in oppressive and anti-Black beliefs and practices (Auguste et al., 2023; Cartwright, 1851; Eidelson, 2017; Faber et al., 2023; Fadus et al., 2020; Fanon, 2020; Finn, 2021; Mayor & Williams, 2024; Meerai et al., 2016; Metzl, 2009; Pilgrim, 2008; Yakushko, 2019). I do not indulge in the work of proving that anti-Blackness exists in society and mental health care as I resist distractions[3] from centering liberatory practices and possibilities.

Concurrent with reimagining mental health care through a liberatory lens, this work focuses on decolonizing mental health care education and practice within psychology, social work, and creative arts therapies. It builds on the foundational and enduring work(s) of Black and Indigenous activists/cultural workers/scholars/artists/theorists who have long critiqued the colonial mission of whitestream institutions—including conventional mental health care systems—and called for decolonial and liberation-focused approaches to academia, research, and the mental health care field (Absolon & Dion, 2018; Martín-Baró, 1994; Mullan, 2023; Patel, 2021; Wilson, 2008).

Rooted in Black healing and knowing practices, this work emphasizes the necessity of *poets*[4] and poetry (Baldwin & Kenan, 2010; Lorde, 2007), the importance of Black storytelling (Toliver, 2021), the power of freedom dreams (Kelley, 2002), and the aesthetics of Black way-making (Taylor, 2016) and theorizing (Christian, 1987; hooks, 1991). It draws deeply from Black and Indigenous knowledges that center cultural histories, ancestral practices, and generational healing traditions (Toliver, 2021; Wilson, 2008). These epistemologies challenge dominant therapeutic and epistemological frameworks and insist on wholeistic,[5] culturally grounded approaches to mental health and well-being.

In line with these commitments, Black aesthetics are steeped throughout the BMP and embedded, via poetic reflexivity and inquiry, throughout this chapter. Every aspect of the BMP—and its dissemination—is grounded in Black onto-epistemologies. The project, a public-facing initiative, lifts the knowledge of everyday Black folx, recognizing conversation and creative practices as forms of knowledge sharing and co-creation (Collins, 2006). By returning to these commitments, the BMP resists colonial commitments often upheld/expected/exalted in research.

The Black MAP Project

Foundationally, the BMP seeks to lift and re/cover the ways in which Black healing has been a fugitive one, a creative one, a communal one. The BMP was/is an emergent creation I never set out to do. Long before I would even begin working on my dissertation, I visited Dr. Willie Tolliver to discuss my re:search[6] ideas. My ideas were focused on understanding anti-Black racism across education, mental health care, and medical health care. Foundationally, I was concerned with how Black people were enduringly harmed across so-called "care" systems and "helping" professions that were meant to offer support. During our discussion, Dr. Tolliver asked me if I knew Mary Turner's story… that she was brutally murdered while eight months pregnant in 1918 for publicly speaking against the unjust lynching of her husband. He then asked me, "what does therapy look like for the descendants of Mary Turner?" That question (re)shaped the trajectory of my work and re:search and became the core question of my project (Williams, 2023). The BMP takes seriously this question and seeks to lift healing practices that hold the descendants of Mary Turner [i.e., Black people] centrally and intentionally in mind (Williams, 2024). I believe this was/is a work born out of desire of my ancestors. I believe this is a [spiritual] calling and—with the help of my wise ancestors, elders, and guides—the BMP is the response.

Creating the Black MAP Project: Three Phases

Conducted across three phases, the BMP lifts Black peoples' enduring experiences of emotional injury/strain and remedies for healing—which is understood as inextricably connected to liberation—through Black cultural practices. The three phases are outlined below.

Phase one: During the first phase of this project, I turned to Black [creative-arts | social-societal] histories from Middle Passage to present. This allowed me to assemble representations of ways in which society informed Black creative practices and how Black creative practices influenced society. I gathered an expansive assemblage, whereby I identified three themes which included: (1) Expression and cultural memory; (2) Resistance, Activism, Disruption, and Subversion (RADS); and (3) Freedom dreams, Radical Hope, and the Black radical imagination (Williams, 2023, 2024).

Phase two: I was mindful not to reproduce the colonial practice of having one person be the voice that speaks for/over/about Black folx. I wanted to be in conversation with as many Black people as possible to consider and explore the depth and breadth of our creative healing and liberatory practices. Therefore, I created the Black MAP Project Community Archive. The BMP Community Archive welcomes submissions from Black people across the diaspora who are 18 years old and over to submit photos, images, stories, poems, videos, songs, and/or other materials that represent Black creative healing.

Phase three: In the third phase of this work, 15 oral history dialogues were conducted with Black artists/scholars/practitioners engaged in Black healing and liberation. This allowed me to speak with Black folx across a range of experiences and positionalities to hear and understand their articulations of Black creative healing.

The BMP—informed by a collective well of Black wisdom—critiques and reimagines the process of (individual/internal) therapy as an expansive healing endeavor and offers counter-possibilities to core assumptions in whitestream mental health care. This work traces and lifts the ways in which Black embodied and enacted practices—including song, dance, poetry, visual arts, performance arts, hair practices, birthwork, culinary arts, body work, spiritual practices, and […]—have been at once healing and freedom practices. This work lives in what I articulate as an Afroparadox which can be understood as a blend of Afropessimism and Afrofuturism… a contradictory reality that holds *both and*… Furthermore, "I recognize what I am calling Afroparadox as a theory of Black navigation. Black folx have long had to both endure and resist the conditions of anti-Blackness… and yet, as Maya Angelou said, *we rise"* (Williams, 2024, p. 190). Ancestors, elders, and guides have created and shared roadmaps for Black creative healing practices. This work is about re/covering severed histories and wisdom and drawing from [communal | collective] wells of care that are disentangled from oppressive/colonial/capitalist *care* systems.

Call and Response as Epistemology and Methodology

> Call-and-response patterns, developed in spirituals and play and work songs, are related to the group or communal nature of art; these patterns both value improvisation and demand that new meanings be created for each particular moment. The valuing of these characteristics suggests that importance lies not only in what is said, but also in how it is said. The assumption is that a story will be repeated and will change with every telling, and that the success of the telling, and so of the particular story, resides not so much in its similarity to the original as in its individual nuances and its ability to involve others.
>
> (Sale, 1992, p. 42)

It was important to this project to engage Black epistemologies and methodologies. So much of this work felt like conversation.... improvisational riffs with the songs, literature, materials, and people that I engaged. Therefore, I developed and incorporated Call and Response (CaR) as epistemology and methodology across every phase and context of the project (Williams, 2023). To implement CaR is

> [...]to be in relationship...it is to contribute to the tone and trajectory of a story. I am introducing CaR method, which centers the [existent | emergent] relational dynamics at every stage of research–dynamics between me and the archive, ancestors, Black people who read and submitted their narratives, and dynamics between me, the writer and you the reader.
>
> (Williams, 2023, p. 65)

In other words, I approached the work as a spontaneous, dynamic, and deeply relational endeavor across every phase of the study.

An element of CaR methodology is an investment in sharing openly the riffs and remixes of the re:search process. When I first conceptualized a CaR process, I articulated it as CaR method (Williams, 2023). However, as the work continued, I realized that CaR was a methodology in which I engaged multiple methods. While the scope of this paper does not allow for me to outline those specific methods, it is important to explicitly update the written record in alignment with CaR commitments. The poem I wrote below articulates how CaR is understood as a cultural, relational, methodological process.

Can I get an Amen

Preacher in the pulpit
Wanna make sure you heard what was said
Give him an amen while you nod your head
And if the message is really hittin'
Stand up from where you sittin'
And in the middle of his phrase
You shout out and give praise
Can I get an Amen
That's what we do
To let you know the message has come through

Call and response
A practice
A way of life
Helps us speak in the daylight
And *steal away* at night
Gives us ways to talk in code
Helps us lift back breaking loads
It's a practice that sustains
Its, in part, why we remain

Call and response is embedded
In the way that we move
It's the way Black kids learn
They practice at home and in school

It's when Poet/Wise Guide and me
Laugh out loud and feel free
With our expression, and no words
We say, I get you, *heard!*
It's how Freedom Singer/Wise Elder
Tells a story from her life
As they dragged her up the stairs
She held her body still and tight
She looked at me stern, with her brow in a furl
She says of that moment, "and not one bruise, *girl!*"
I know that *girl*… so much was said in that word
An older Black woman to a younger Black girl
The tone in her voice asked, did you hear what I said
Did you pick up that message, did it sink in your head
It's the mmm hmmms in the background as we sit and converse
It's the *yesses* and *okayyys* that we almost sing as if verse
Silent facial expressions that say so very much
Nods and acknowledgements from a distance that still touch

We repeat so that we understand,
Repetition has its purpose says the Drummer man
Call and response is a praxis that has helped us connect, collaborate and survive
Call and response is a practice embedded in all areas of our lives
A dynamic way of expression whether improvised or planned
It's hard to define this magic… can I get an Amen?

(Williams, 2024, pp. 191–192)

Black Cultural Production as Theory and Praxis

For women, then, poetry is not a luxury. It is a vital necessity of our existence. It forms the quality of the light within which we predicate our hopes and dreams toward survival and change,

> first made into language, then into idea, then into more tangible action. Poetry is the way we help give name to the nameless so it can be thought. The farthest external horizons of our hopes and fears are cobbled by our poems, carved from the rock experiences of our daily lives.
>
> (Lorde, 2007, p. 37)

Engaging creative practices as a way of knowing and doing is grounded in Black theoretical processes and onto-epistemological stances. Black creative practices serve as a decolonial approach to knowledge. The poem I've written below exemplifies how poetic reflexivity is used in the BMP to understand, elevate, reveal, and communicate information (Williams, 2023). Poetry—i.e., art (Baldwin & Kenan, 2010)—functions as a form of thinking (Lorde, 2007) and knowing, allowing multiple contexts, expressions, and meanings to be shared simultaneously.

Freedom: Our Creativity, Our Practices

Lorde[7] knows that poetry is not a luxury
That we must get our hooks[8] in liberatory theory
Black folx have engaged freedom "as a practice[9]"
Our creativity is a liberatory praxis
Bodies bound by white enslavers
Flesh burned by the engraver
Trying to collapse us into anonymity[10]
But our spirits still fought for free
Maybe we didn't speak in the same tongues
But we had our moans, and we had our hums[11]
We made new ways to convey
That which we needed to say
In plain sight we speak in code[12]
Through the arts our truths are known

Re/turning to History

The first phase of this work involved engaging Black [social-societal | creative] histories. What began as an independent study with my dissertation chair, Dr. Michelle Fine, to gather supportive information evolved into a rich exploration of Black expression, memory-keeping, resistance, and freedom dreams through digital archives, music, reading, and viewing. At one point, Dr. Fine suggested indexing the materials (Williams, 2023), which inspired the creation of the BMP Community Archive. Through this process, I group[ed] the creative pieces I had gathered informed by the conversation between the extensive histories, literatures, movements, archives, and other materials I engaged. This process of assemblage was a CaR. The bricolage of themes include: (1) Expression and cultural memory, (2) RADS, and (3) Freedom dreams, Radical Hope, and the Black radical imagination. It is not my contention that these three themes are an exhaustive or definitive list. Rather, this is an emergent story from the materials I gathered at a moment in time—marked by the shadows of COVID-19, swells in the movement for Black lives, demands for police accountability amid a deluge of anti-Black violence and Black death… and yet, still with a spirit of Lucille Clifton and Maya Angelou… *everyday something has tried to kill us and has failed… And Still We Rise* (Williams, 2023, pp. 69–70).

I found engaging these histories to be an inspiring, encouraging, and therapeutic process—especially as I was doing this as a time where we were experiencing the global COVID-19 pandemic, swelled [societal | global] fracture and [enduring] racial oppression. Engaging these histories served as a process of re/membering myself (Williams, 2021, 2023). However, I knew there were erasures in the histories I was engaging. I wanted everyday Black folx to write themselves into this story of Black creative healing I was seeking to lift (Williams, 2023). To be clear, I was/am also aware that no one archive would be able to assemble a complete story and that is not what this work asserts or intends to do. This work seeks to tell *a* rich and expansive story.

Endarkened[13] *Archives*

> Black women continue to work as community archivists, dedicated to the political project of gendered memory-keeping. The personal archives kept and curated by everyday Black women—often a multimodal assemblage of handwritten letters, photograph albums, oral histories, and family heirlooms—illuminate their collective struggle to memory-keep within and against archival silences. In doing so, they boldly challenge whose lives, movements, and resistance stories are worthy of being remembered.
>
> (Tanksley, 2023, p. 560)

Blassemblage…

Archives, which can be understood as "repository[14]"
Allowed for complicated and multimodal story
A collection of various texts, videos, images, and materials
That allowed me to share Black histories through visuals
The US and it's history of Anti-Blackness and racial capitalism, for instance
At the intersection of a persistent history of Black creative resistance
The archives of course have been known to erase, dismiss, and appropriate[15]
So, I recognized archives do not guarantee an inherently decolonial space

To build on the Black [social-societal | creative] histories I accessed through digital archives, I created the BMP Community Archive so that everyday Black folx could write themselves into a narrative of Black creative healing (Williams, 2023). I wrote the poem "Blassemblage" above to reflect on and share the commitments/complexities/contradictions of the BMP Community Archive. The archive accepts submissions from Black folx 18 years and older. Submissions may include images, videos, songs, poetry, and other creative representations that are accompanied by a narrative reflection that shares how/why the submission represents Black creative healing. The intention of the archive is to co-create a narrative of Black creative healing

> …formed and framed in community. I also want to honor the many minds that inform my research and allow this [co-thinking | co-creating] to be reflected publicly. It was/is also a commitment of this work that Black folx outside of academia be recognized for their [valuable | meaning-full] contributions to this work [and beyond]… dis/rupting and expanding *who* is considered a scholar.
>
> (Williams, 2023, p. 77)

I envision(ed) the BMP Archive as a free and accessible resource of Black care praxes. Welcoming submissions from across the diaspora "was an intentional choice meant to re/member that which has been severed and broken apart and to reweave conversations and connections across histories/experiences/locations/kin that have always been interconnected" (Williams, 2024, p. 117). The archive remains open to submissions and is publicly accessible on the BMP website (www.thebmp.org).

Conversation as Knowledge Sharing and Co-Creation

> For Black women, new knowledge claims are rarely worked out in isolation from other individuals and are usually developed through dialogues with other members of a community. A primary epistemological assumption underlying the use of dialogue in assessing knowledge claims is that connectedness rather than separation is an essential component of the knowledge-validation process.
>
> (Collins, 1989, p. 763)

Black feminists have long recognized conversation as a rich and powerful method for sharing and co-creating knowledge (Collins, 1989). Additionally, dialogue "has deep roots in an African-based oral tradition and in African-American culture" and engages the practice of "call and response discourse" that is prevalent among Black folx (Collins, 1989, p. 763). Dialogue is a tool for resisting dominant narratives that misrepresent and invisibilize marginalized others (Lorde, 2007). This important aspect of liberation work allows us to confront our assumptions and learn from those who have experiences different from our own (Smith, 1983). Practices of resistance in the struggle for liberation require a blend of acquiring and sharing knowledge, therefore, conversation is necessary (Davis, 1998).

To honor the wisdom of Black feminist thinkers that have shaped my scholarly identity, I took seriously the contribution of conversation. Therefore, instead of conducting interviews, I engaged in oral history dialogues (Williams, 2023). I spoke with 15 discussants including an original freedom singer, jazz musicians, Black culinary historian, doula, oral historian, drummer, storytellers, scholars, and teachers. In our discussions, I did not seek to separate myself from those I spoke with, rather I sought to be in connection with them. When they mentioned cultural references that were resonant with my own experiences, I noted it. This opened rich relational discussions that this project recognized as important. To be clear, subjectivity was not recognized as an obstacle to overcome; rather, it was engaged as a truth to meaningfully acknowledge and lift (Williams, 2023).

Being that the conversation itself was understood as knowledge co-generation, I considered the "mms," the "ahhs," bursts of knowing laughter, looks, and other nonverbal cues of communication as information (Williams, 2023). Additionally, I was cognizant of my own embodied and affective responses in these conversations and recognized those experiences as meaningful points of information and inquiry. Much like therapy—with the concept of the blank slate (aka la tabula rasa)—academia asserts objectivity as the right and ethical way to do research. However, this work troubles the myth of objectivity and recognizes it as an elusive form of dominance, othering, and oppression (Williams, 2023).

This work additionally troubles the idea that confidentiality is inherently protective. Therapy relies heavily on the practice of confidentiality and privacy. While this can certainly serve beneficial to care practices, so too can public facing, community centered care that is not bound to confidentiality and anonymity. Everyone who contributed to the BMP Community Archive or participated in an oral history dialogue decided if/how they wished to be identified as a contributor to this project. The consent processes for the oral history dialogue participants were ongoing. Discussants were able to make changes to how their dialogues would be shared or not to the archive at every step of the process. They were additionally invited to make any shifts/changes/amendments to how their words, voice, and/or images were represented. I did not want to participate in the colonial practice of extracting wisdom from Black people without due attribution; therefore, I recognized that anonymity should not be assumed best practice for this work. This commitment sits in alignment with an Indigenous axiology which centers "relational accountability" (Wilson, 2008, p. 77). Many Black care and liberation practices are public facing and community centered... perhaps the

BMP can be understood as communal conversation concerned with social change and [individual | collective] emotional well-being.

The Black MAP Community Archive: Snapshots

The submissions shared below from the BMP Community Archive represent practices that Black people have engaged in to heal and practice freedom in the face of ongoing racial violence and oppression. They are presented and named as they appear in the BMP Archive. This archive assembles snapshots/pieces/fragments of how healing is recognized as creative and communal and unsettled from institutions and endeavors driven by capitalism, consumerism, carcerality, and transactional care. Figures 9.1 and 9.2 illustrate the photos submitted to the community archive.

These are not prescriptions in the conventional sense; rather, they are healing *notes* in the cultural sense—salves for soul wounds, songs for sorrow… reflections on how we stitch history, memory, and joy with threads of love and care… reverence to how we water and wash our spirits, and dance through good times and bad… These archive submissions unsettle conventional notions and assumptions of what constitutes mental health care, while lifting the potency of Black healing practices and survivance strategies.

The Plantation

The "Plantation" I was invited to visit was called "Totomoi" in Virginia. I walked the entire grounds alone… It was a horrific vista stroll. A member of the plantation family joined later and my walk

Figure 9.1 The Plantation, submitted by Professor Dale Ricardo Shields

ended in the small, gated family graveyard. He broke down and explained the family tree. I found this tree there to reflect on the moment. He shared the slave master's "Slave" log and that this slave master reserved Tuesdays to beat his slaves... I silently cried on the way back to my hotel. This experience continues to haunt my soul and spirit. I am an activist, historian, and professor of Black Theatre History and Black Studies. I post free Black History... Facts... in their historical context daily. An exercise and gift of critical thinking. Researching and sharing Black History is my only intellectual freedom, from the tragic past of my African and Native Indian ancestors. *Finding and sharing light for my people. * Professor Dale Ricardo Shields Iforcolor.org.

Insidious [song submission]

"insidious!" is an unapologetic expression of Black rage at the corrosive effects of White supremacy. Additionally, this song is a recognition that systemic oppression plays out intimately and interpersonally, causing particular depths of heartache. This track supports Black emotional health by providing Black folks a space to safely and fully feel the rage and heartache engendered by White supremacy, so that we all might be one step closer to liberation. Link to song on Spotify: (https://open.spotify.com/track/6WZYtm2jPvS9TocGpxqkiB?si=6e620a3e3c944153&nd=1)

*Submission by Grant Jones

Family Quilt

Family Quilt—Where there is hope, there is life. My mother and I made this family quilt together years ago. I sat at her feet as she instructed me to measure and cut the slivers and patches of fabric. We mapped our family story through family photos, memories, colors, and textures. This quilting of memories was an enacted practice of connection, remembrance, and celebration of nearly a century of Black love and liberatory practice. The finished quilt is an embodiment of mutual aid and emotional health within my family. In my family, we love on each other through our hands, making art, food, gardening, and fixing things. Love is a verb. This quilt sits on my 95 year old Grandmother's (Alfreda Johnson) couch in my hometown West Chester, PA. Although I live in Brooklyn, NY I hope to retire there one day and to possibly inherit this piece from her as a reminder of the many shoulders I stand upon.

*Submission by Tyese Alfreda Brown

R. Lepere

"The wild idea that animates this... is that black women are radical subjects who tirelessly imagined other ways to live and never failed to consider how the world might be otherwise" (Hartman 2019, p. 8). Telling the story of my Grandma and water; I want to assert a political and ideological utility, that story is both an idea and material space. The story is a container, a space for making and creating. I want to suggest a broader story of black women and how their everyday lives and their engagement in life is a fight for decency and freedom. When one comes to learning about art and art-making in school it has always been about the power that the right frame can have in presenting and enhancing work. In my earliest memory of art-making and creating, it was situated in borders and frames or lines of demarcation. The modern sense of healing and art-making is always associated with some sort of border. These borders are there to contain, divide, and focus our attention. Participating in the process of disrupting, and interpreting the frame of my artistic practice. I am hoping my contribution to this conversation will help us see where borders can be crossed, frames removed, and stories told. When exploring my grandma's voice, a new way of framing and understanding

Figure 9.2 Family Quilt, submitted by Tyese Alfreda Brown

the world had to come through. What materials are there? What are the everyday acts that touch something deeply hidden and ineffable? What snatch of life brought healing, what riff of music illuminated a moment, what words do we miss that say so much? This is a story about a moment I had missed, but a process of healing that I carry with me. It is a vision of my snuff-smoking granny who works and heals with water. It is a story of arranging, plotting, planning, and checking, cups, glasses, bottles, baths, and buckets. A performance of the repeatable and embodied activities, and how these bodily encounters heal us. Link to Audio https://youtu.be/jWNWHiumX20.

Reflections

The BMP Community Archive lifts and stitches a conversation within and across the African Diaspora, centering everyday healing and freedom practices of Black folx. In this work, I do not seek to analyze the contributions of research collaborators, as that would feel dismissive and reductive to the thoughts/reflections/wisdom they offer. Instead, I present "an analytic" that does not claim objectivity or neutrality (Williams, 2023, p. 79); rather, I recognize the subjective understanding of the work as a site of meaning and knowledge-making. The poem below engages poetic reflexivity to honor the wisdom of contributors to the BMP Community Archive and seeks to lift truths about Black healing and liberatory practices—without claiming them to be *the* truth—resisting the colonial desire for expertise and definitive answers.

[Black | Creative*] Healing is…*

Healing… is re/turning to history
Free, with attention to accessibility
Revisiting the past and dreaming of times to come
And gratitude for paths walked so that I might run

Healing is unapologetic expression of rage
Allowing for room to feel the ache(s)
Lifting our voice and letting it sing
Believing that the bell of freedom will ring

Healing is… singing with my *whole* heart
Meaningful engagement in the expressive arts
Participation in the movement for liberation
Being supported and held by my community's vibrations

Healing is sitting at my mother's feet
Stitching our history as a practice of re/memory
Honoring the legacies of family history
Paying homage to the ways we have practiced free

Healing is… re/membering cultural roots
Imagining radical futures and believing in new truths
Healing is crossing borders… sharing and telling our stories
And everyday living as if we were already free

In engaging poetic reflexivity, I make connections that might not otherwise emerge, offering a more complex and robust reflection. Poetic reflections—such as the poems I have shared herein—resonate more deeply for me than conventional distillations of research. Poetic reflexivity allows me to make sense of expansive experiences and information, honoring the nuances and complexities of what is shared, while acknowledging the limitations of any singular reading. In other words, poetry is [an] episteme. Through the poem above, I engage poetic reflexivity to reflect on what the archive submissions reveal about Black healing and liberation, without claiming to present a definitive or final truth. It is also my hope that presenting poetry as information offers a more engaging and accessible way for a wider audience, beyond the academy, to connect with and be impacted by the work.

Implications

Informed by the wisdom shared in the BMP Community Archive, oral history dialogues, and my reflections on the [embodied | affective | relational | cultural] learnings from this study, I offer the following questions for practitioners, educators, and researchers committed to decolonial practices. For context, I have come to see the Back MAP Project as cultural-spiritual work in addition to re:search. Before embarking on this journey, I never fully resonated with the role of researcher. I now understand that this was because the research I had been taught overwhelmingly lacked cultural resonance/relevance. The questions below arise directly from the BMP process and my subsequent reflections on decolonial approaches to practice, education, and research.

I must [responsibly] note that while I challenge oppressive institutions, I also remain—across multiple contexts—embedded within them. This creates a tension wherein I engage in a both-and approach, in which I dream of and strive for *otherwise*[16] spaces of knowledge creation, healing, and practice, while also working to unsettle colonial practices within the institutions that currently stand. I hold this commitment because communities I am committed and accountable to continue to receive services from these spaces—and they deserve better. Therefore, the questions below aim to encourage researchers and practitioners to dream both within and beyond our current institutions. I offer open questions for anyone interested in incorporating decolonial practices in their work; additionally, I offer endarkened questions for Black folx working with Black folx, following the wisdom of Toni Morrison, who imagined and centered the Black reader(s) on the other side of her work.

Open Practice Questions

- How/do you embed questions about culture, ancestry, family, and community into intake and assessment practices?
- How/do you engage discussions about how clients define healing as informed by their cultural and identity intersections?
- How/do you explore culturally resonant healing practices that can be engaged within and/or outside of clinical treatment?
- How/do you trouble the idea that mental health care is an individual endeavor?
- How/do you connect client to creative and culturally resonant practices with/in their community?

Endarkened Practice Questions

- How/do you actively support individuals and/or communities in accessing culturally resonant forms of healing outside of conventional health care systems (e.g., herbalism, music, dance, drumming circles, or spiritual practices)?
- How/does your practice center Black healing ways—such as ancestral rituals, storytelling, and community gatherings, as central to the healing process—and resist/refuse subsumption by institutional frameworks and colonial systems?
- How/do you cultivate and sustain collective healing spaces (e.g., community circles, mutual aid networks) that prioritize community well-being and center Black cultural practices rooted in reciprocity, collective care, and liberation?
- How/do you resist the medicalization and pathologization of Black healing traditions—ensuring they remain rooted in cultural, spiritual, and community-based practices—and shed colonial assertions/definitions/frameworks?

Open Education Questions

- How/are Black aesthetics and Black onto-epistemologies centered in curricula?
- How/are discussions about culture and intersectional identities centered throughout every class?
- How/are the voices of racialized and marginalized others mindfully and intentionally centered?
- How/does the program highlight the necessity of connecting people to community-based and culturally resonant experiences that extend outside of clinical practice?

Endarkened Education Questions

- How/do you engage educational practices outside of the academy, that lift Black wisdom and experience(s), and prioritize community-based knowledge, ancestral teachings, and non-institutional learning spaces?
- How/do you participate in study groups, community circles, and/or fugitive learning practices to support and share Black knowledges, fostering spaces of resistance that not only preserve but also (re)envision *otherwise* futures?
- How/do you create or participate in spaces that foster collective learning—such as community workshops or informal study groups—where Black healing practices and cultural wisdom(s) are shared and passed down intergenerationally?
- How/do you center collaborative, non-hierarchical learning processes that move beyond individual knowledge acquisition and toward collective empowerment, cultural preservation, and liberated futures?

Open Research Questions

- How/do knowledges that unsettle colonial assumptions and assertions inform your research?
- How/do you recognize the ways in which culture and intersectional identities impact your research?
- How/does your research resist the tendency to extract knowledge from racialized and marginalized others without offering meaningful attribution and/or centering those voices a (co) researchers on the project?
- How/do you meaningfully assess if you are the right person(s) to do the research you are engaging?

Endarkened Research Questions

- How/do you engage in research—beyond the constraints of academic institutions—that turns to community review boards and prioritizes Black community needs, collective empowerment, and knowledge creation that supports liberation?
- How/do you engage in participatory or collaborative research practices that center Black people as co-creators of knowledge, ensuring they are active participants rather than merely subjects of study?
- How/do you center the voices, priorities, aesthetics, and lived experiences of Black communities in your research, ensuring that the knowledge produced is shared with the community in ways that are actionable and accessible?
- How/does your research center outcomes that foster healing, community-building, and tangible change for Black people(s), while engaging decolonial methodologies that resist the extraction of knowledge without reciprocity and meaningful engagement?

A question changed the trajectory of my re:search: *What does therapy look like for the descendants of Mary Turner?* This question, posed by Dr. Tolliver, (re)aligned my path, allowing me to walk a journey that was meant for me… it (re)adjusted my *vision*, so I could *see* how I had been trained [elusively] to view my work and research through a colonial lens. I offer the open questions above for those of us working in conventional/hegemonic/whitestream spaces, seeking to unsettle/trouble/dismantle from within. The endarkened questions, shaped by my work in the BMP study, are intended as guideposts/pathways/portals for freedom dreams that believe beyond these systems. I invite others to build on, amend, and expand these questions to chart transformative pathways toward a future *otherwise*.

In-Conclusive

The BMP is an ongoing work, and the BMP Community Archive continues to receive submissions. It is my hope that this work will serve to unsettle colonial practices in mental health practice, education, and research while also being a supportive tool for individuals and communities seeking to implement and/or expand on culturally resonant care practices that support liberation. The BMP is a public-facing work; therefore, those interested in following the project or engaging the freely accessible resources emergent from this work are encouraged to visit the project website (www.thebmp.org).

Notes

1 I wrote this poem as a response piece to the Black [creative arts | social-societal] histories I engaged through the Black MAP Project (BMP).
2 Canadian sociologist Claude Denis (Grande, 2003) introduced this term to underscore the [assumed | asserted] association between whiteness and societal convention.
3 This is a nod to Toni Morrison (1975) who noted racism as a "distraction."
4 This is a nod to James Baldwin's framing of poets as "all artists" (Baldwin & Kenan, 2010, p. 51).
5 I use "wholeistic" intentionally here to speak to the [multi-contextual] cultures, histories, identities, and ecologies that shape human experience(s), and inform healing processes and needs.
6 There is a long and troubling history of research exploiting and extracting from Black people and communities. I spell "re:search" in this way to trouble conventional interpretations and histories of research, re/imagining it as "regarding or concerning search" (Williams, 2023, p. 66).
7 This is a reference to Lorde's (2007) Poetry is Not a Luxury.
8 This is a reference to hooks (1991) Theory as Liberatory Practice.
9 This reference Gumbs (2018) and hooks (1994) who articulated freedom as "a practice."
10 I am informed by a truth of the slave state, which is animated in the movie, Middle Passage (Deslauriers, 2000). The opening scene depicts enslaved Africans being chained, branded, and forced overcrowded boats and into a system that sought to strip them of their humanity and identities.
11 Taylor (2016) noted that from the moment of contact with white enslavers, enslaved Africans found ways to communicate across cultures and language. Song, sound, and tradition emerged as enslaved Africans found ways to communicate across the Middle Passage.
12 This speaks to the ways in which music was used to send coded messages about plans to escape during slavery. See Berry (2017), Williams (2021).
13 I use endarkened here inspired by the work of S. R Toliver (2021), who calls for a "recovering" of Black storytelling traditions in qualitative research (p. xv) because The BMP archives engage Black storytelling traditions.
14 See Moore et al. (2016, p. 1).
15 Tanksley (2023) speaks to this tension.
16 This is inspired by Ashon Crawley's (2014) piece, Otherwise, Ferguson where he writes "Otherwise. Otherwise than this. To begin here in the otherwise, as the otherwise, is to pose a question about tears born in dreams" (para 1).

References

Absolon, K., & Dion, S. (2018). Doing indigenous community-university research partnerships: A cautionary tale. *Engaged Scholar Journal: Community-Engaged Research, Teaching, and Learning, 3*(2), 81–98. https://doi.org/10.15402/esj.v3i2.334

Almeida, R. V. (2018). *Liberation based healing practices*. Institute for Family Services.

Auguste, E., Bowdring, M., Kasparek, S. W., McPhee, J., Tabachnick, A. R., Tung, I., Scholars for Elevating Equity and Diversity (SEED), & Galán, C. A. (2023). Psychology's contributions to anti-Blackness in the United States within psychological research, criminal justice, and mental health. *Perspectives on Psychological Science: A Journal of the Association for Psychological Science, 18*(6), 1282–1305. https://doi.org/10.1177/17456916221141374

Baldwin, J., & Kenan, R. (2010). *The cross of redemption: Uncollected writings* (1st ed.). Pantheon Books.

Belkin-Martinez, D., & Fleck-Henderson, A. (Eds.). (2014). *Social justice in clinical practice: A liberation health framework for social work* (1st ed.). Routledge. https://doi.org/10.4324/9781315813073

Berry, K. D. (2017, January 25). *Singing in slavery: Songs of survival, songs of freedom*. PBS. https://www.pbs.org/mercy-street/blogs/mercy-street-revealed/songs-of-survival-and-songs-of-freedom-during-slavery/

Bhatia, S. (2018). *Decolonizing psychology: Globalization, social justice, and Indian youth identities*. Oxford University Press.

Cartwright, S. (1851). *Diseases and peculiarities of the Negro race*. PBS. https://www.pbs.org/wgbh/aia/part4/4h3106t.html

Christian, B. (1987). The race for theory. *Cultural Critique*, *6*, 51–63. https://doi.org/10.2307/1354255

Collins, P. H. (1989). The social construction of Black feminist thought. *Journal of Women in Culture and Society, 14*(4), 745–773. https://www.jstor.org/stable/3174683

Collins, P. H. (2006). *Patricia Hill Collins: Intersecting oppressions*. Sage Publications. https://uk.sagepub.com/sites/default/files/upm-binaries/13299_Chapter_16_Web_Byte_Patricia_Hill_Collins.pdf

Crawley, A. (2014, October 24). *Otherwise, Ferguson*. Interfictions Online. https://interfictions.com/otherwise-fergusonashon-crawley/

Davis, A. (1998, September 10). *Masked racism: Reflections on the prison industrial complex*. Colorlines. https://www.colorlines.com/articles/masked-racism-reflections-prison-industrial-complex

Deslauriers, G. (Director). (2000). *Middle passage* [Film]. Les Films du Raphia

Eidelson, R. (2017, October 13). Psychologists are facing consequences for helping with torture. It's not enough. *Washington Post*. https://www.washingtonpost.com/outlook/psychologists-are-facing-consequences-for-helping-with-torture-its-not-enough/2017/10/13/2756b734-ad14-11e7-9e58-e6288544af98_story.html

Faber, S. C., Khanna Roy, A., Michaels, T. I., & Williams, M. T. (2023). The weaponization of medicine: Early psychosis in the Black community and the need for racially informed mental healthcare. *Frontiers in Psychiatry*, *14,* 1098292. https://doi.org/10.3389/fpsyt.2023.109829

Fadus, M. C., Ginsburg, K. R., Sobowale, K., Halliday-Boykins, C. A., Bryant, B. E., Gray, K. M.,& Squeglia, L. M. (2020). Unconscious bias and the diagnosis of disruptive behavior disorders and ADHD in African American and Hispanic youth. *Academic Psychiatry, 44*(1), 95–102.

Fanon, F. (2020). The meeting between psychiatry and society. In J. Khalfa, & R. Young (Eds.), *Frantz Fanon: Alienation and freedom*. Bloomsbury Publishing.

Finn, J. L. (2021). *Just practice: A social justice approach to social work* (4th ed.). Oxford University Press.

Grande, S. M. (2003). Whitestream feminism and the colonialist project: A review of contemporary feminist pedagogy and praxis. *Educational Theory, 53*(3), 329–346. https://doi.org/10.1111/j.1741-5446.2003.00329.x

Gumbs, A. P. (2018). *M Archive: After the end of the world*. Duke University Press.

hooks, b. (1991). Theory as liberatory practice. *Yale Journal of Law and Feminism*, *4*(1), 1–12. https://hdl.handle.net/20.500.13051/7151

hooks, b. (1994). *Teaching to transgress*. Routledge.

Kelley, R. D. G. (2002). *Freedom dreams: The Black radical imagination*. Beacon Press.

Lorde, A. (2007). *Sister outsider: Essays and speeches*. Crossing Press.

Martín-Baró, I. (1994). *Writings for a liberation psychology* (A. Aron & S. Corne, Eds.). Harvard University Press.

Mayor, C., & Williams, B. (2024). Dreaming of an abolitionist drama therapy. *The Arts in Psychotherapy*, *90*, 102189. https://doi.org/10.1016/j.aip.2024.102189

Meerai, S., Abdillahi, I., & Poole, J. (2016). An introduction to anti-Black sanism. *Intersectionalities: A Global Journal of Social Work Analysis, Research, Polity, and Practice, 5*(3), 18–35. https://journals.library.mun.ca/ojs/index.php/IJ/article/view/1682

Metzl, J. (2009). *The protest psychosis: How schizophrenia became a Black disease*. Beacon Press.

Moore, N., Salter, A., Stanley, L., & Tamboukou, M. (2016). *The archive project: Archival research in the social sciences* (1st ed.). Routledge. https://doi.org/10.4324/9781315612577

Morrison, T. (1975, May 30). *Novelist Toni Morrison will speak on "A humanistic view."* [Keynote address]. Public Dialogue on the American Dream Theme, Portland State University.

Mullan, J. (2023). *Decolonizing therapy: Oppression, historical trauma, and politicizing your practice.* W. W. Norton.
Patel, L. (2021). *No study without struggle: Confronting settler colonialism in higher education.* Beacon Press.
Pilgrim, D. (2008). The eugenic legacy in psychology and psychiatry. *The International Journal of Social Psychiatry, 54*(3), 272–284. https://doi.org/10.1177/0020764008090282
Sale, M. (1992). Call and response as critical method: African-American oral traditions and beloved. *African American Review*, *26*(1), 41–50. https://doi.org/10.2307/3042075
Smith, B. (1983). *Home girls: A black feminist anthology* (1st ed.). Women of Color Press.
Tanksley, T. (2023). Towards a method of Black feminist archival bricolage: Memory-keeping within, beneath and beyond the archive. *a/b: Auto/Biography Studies*, *38*(2), 559–581, https://doi.org/10.1080/08989575.2023.2221951
Taylor, P. C. (2016). *Black is beautiful: A philosophy of Black aesthetics* (1st ed.). Wiley-Blackwell.
Toliver, S. R. (2021). *Recovering Black storytelling in qualitative research:* Endarkened *storywork.* Routledge.
Williams, B. (2021). Tracks on repeat. Voices*: A World Forum for Music Therapy*, *21*(1), 1–10. https://doi.org/10.15845/voices.v21i1.3227
Williams, B. (2023). Poetic awakenings: (Re)imagining epistemic justice and academic writing through a Black aesthetic lens. *Qualitative Studies, 8*(1), 58–86. https://doi.org/10.7146/qs.v8i1.136781
Williams, B. (2024) "The Black MAP project: A Black people's epistemology of healing" *CUNY Academic Works.* https://academicworks.cuny.edu/gc_etds/5632
Williams, B. (in press). Old couches and complicated stages: A literary quilt of drama therapy in the US. In M. Clarke, & A. Kshetrapal (Eds.), *Dramatherapy: International perspectives, paradigms, and pedagogies.* Methuen Drama.
Wilson, S. (2008). *Research is ceremony: Indigenous research methods*. Fernwood Publishing.
Yakushko O. (2019). Eugenics and its evolution in the history of western psychology: A critical archival review. *Psychotherapy Politics International, 17*, e1495. https://doi.org/10.1002/ppi.1495

10 "Al-Umm Bitlim"

A Life Source and Life Force Amid Grief, Loss, and Death

Hana R. Masud

The Arabic saying, "al-umm bitlim," translated into "the mother gathers" speaks to the way that mothers are imagined as an essential force that holds the family and wider social relations together. While Palestinian motherhood has been the subject of violence in the settler colony given our life-giving and sustaining qualities, the epistemic practices of motherhood in Palestine and its diasporas have been alternatively politicized and devalued by liberation movements. Amid continued rupture and loss, it is mothers who are often tasked with the life-sustaining labor of managing survival, rebuilding homes, and creating the paths of alternative futures for our future generations. In March, we celebrate Palestinian motherhood in all of its complexities. How does Palestinian motherhood disrupt the ongoing power of settler colonial violence and oppression? How do the diverse practices of Palestinian mothers—in Palestine and its diaspora—sustain communities, transmit cultural memory, and cultivate resilience in the face of ongoing dispossession and displacement? How do these practices, rooted in acknowledging and moving *with* pain, allow Palestinian mothers to fully engage with life's complexities? How do these practices challenge dominant narratives and assert Palestinian self-determination? How do we, as Palestinian mothers in diasporic spaces, navigate the complexities of raising children in contexts where our Palestinian identity is racialized, surveilled, and criminalized? How do we harness our collective power to create spaces of belonging, resistance, and healing for ourselves and our children? Finally, how can we center the generative and transformative power of Palestinian motherhood, recognizing its crucial role not only in enduring suffering but also in cultivating hope, fostering resilience, and envisioning a future free from colonial violence? This chapter delves into these questions through a deeply personal journey, exploring how the enduring strength of Palestinian motherhood, embodied in the Arabic saying "al-umm bitlim," offers a path toward healing and freedom even amidst profound loss.

Al-umm bitlim—"the mother gathers"—speaks to the vital role mothers play in holding families and communities together. Yet, for Palestinian mothers and daughters, this act of gathering, of nurturing and sustaining life, takes place against a backdrop of profound loss and ongoing oppression. The settler colonial project, with its relentless violence and dispossession, inflicts wounds that run deep, impacting not only individual lives but also the very fabric of Palestinian society. This pain is not abstract; it is etched into the bodies and souls of Palestinian women. It manifests as the chronic ache of displacement, the gnawing anxiety of living under constant threat, the gut-wrenching fear for their children's safety. It is the inherited trauma of dispossession, passed down through generations, a silent scream echoing through their DNA. The loss is tangible: the stolen land, the demolished homes, the vanished olive groves, the silenced stories. It is the constant struggle for basic human rights, the denial of freedom of movement, the humiliation of checkpoints, the ever-present specter of violence. And yet, amidst this pain, amidst the rubble and the tears, Palestinian mothers and daughters continue to gather. They rebuild homes, both physical and emotional. They cultivate gardens of hope in the barren landscape of occupation. They weave stories of resilience and resistance into the fabric of their

DOI: 10.4324/9781003492214-12

children's lives. They embody the spirit of *sumud*, steadfastness, a quiet defiance that refuses to be extinguished. Their love, a fierce and unwavering force, becomes a shield against despair, a beacon of hope for a future where their children can finally breathe free. This is the enduring strength of Palestinian motherhood, a testament to the power of love to transcend even the deepest wounds, a promise that even in the face of unimaginable loss, life, like the olive tree, will find a way to flourish again.

This journey delves into the raw, visceral reality of suffering—not merely the physical sensation of pain but the profound depths of anguish that reverberate through the human experience. It's a descent into my own unconscious, a confrontation with the genocidal horrors imprinted on my memory, and an overwhelming empathy for the mothers of Gaza who have known the unbearable grief of losing a child, and for the children who now navigate a world without their mothers. To truly understand suffering, we must move beyond the surface of pain. We must acknowledge the intricate web of emotions, thoughts, and memories that ensnare us. We struggle with fear, anger, and despair. We are haunted by the past and terrified of the future. We wrestle with intrusive thoughts, unwanted urges, and the crushing weight of our own mortality (Hayes & Smith, 2005). Even in the face of profound darkness, mothers demonstrate an extraordinary capacity for radical healing resilience. They confront fear with courage, offering boundless love and compassion amidst overwhelming loss. They find the strength to carry their pain and move forward, driven by an unwavering will to nurture, to hope, and to build meaning for their children and themselves, even in a world overshadowed by suffering. This chapter explores how, by acknowledging and moving *with* our pain, Palestinian mothers can truly engage with the fullness of life.

A Daughter's Journey through Grief: An Embodied Narrative

This exploration of grief emerges not from the detached pronouncements of textbooks but from the visceral depths of an embodied experience, cultivated within a meditative and intentional therapeutic space. Imagine a sanctuary where stillness cradles the raw vulnerability of the soul, where the echoes of generational trauma intertwine with the immediate pangs of personal loss. It is within this sacred container, far from the cacophony of the world, that I begin to untangle the intricate knots of pain, suffering, and the surprising resilience woven into the very fabric of my being. My body, a living archive, becomes the text through which these reflections are inscribed.

This embodied approach to understanding grief finds resonance in the work of scholars like Hortense Spillers (1987), who explores "the flesh" as a site of both profound vulnerability and enduring resilience, particularly within the context of Black women's experiences. Spillers' analysis of how trauma, particularly the trauma of enslavement, becomes inscribed upon the body offers a powerful lens through which to examine my own journey. While my personal history may differ, the concept of "flesh" as a living testament to experience resonates deeply. Like the narratives of countless women of color who have dared to challenge dominant discourses by centering their lived realities, I, too, seek to understand how my body holds the memory of trauma, both inherited and personally endured. This exploration acknowledges the wisdom embedded within physical sensations, emotions, and bodily experiences, recognizing them as vital sources of knowledge in the process of healing. By grounding my reflections in the embodied, I aim to disrupt traditional, often patriarchal, understandings of grief, offering instead a narrative that honors the profound connection between body, mind, and spirit.

I sought to understand what it takes to feel free from pain and truly embody freedom, not by waiting to win an internal struggle with my past, memories, fears, and sadness, but by accepting and moving beyond them. What I discovered was a process of death and dying, a continuous cycle of being and becoming. It was a raw and visceral encounter with life-making and creating, a reproduction of death in its own way.

The date is etched in my memory: Thursday, November 15th. It was then that I experienced my mother's passing in a way I could never have anticipated. I wasn't physically present, yet I felt her transition energetically. I found myself on my mother's deathbed, not in body, but in spirit. The slow, agonizing transition was filled with a deep, primal pain. I screamed for her to stay, to take me with her, but my voice was trapped, muffled, unable to escape the depths of my being. I felt her essence merging with mine, becoming a part of me. She was pulling away, slowly, and I was torn. A part of me yearned to surrender, to give up and die with her, while another part, a stubborn ember of determination, whispered that I had more life to live.[1]

Time lost all meaning. It felt like an eternity, each moment stretching into the next. The further she drifted, the more intense my muffled screams became, the more my emotions raged within. I was trapped, pinned down by an invisible force, unable to touch or reach her, yet I felt an undeniable connection. I was her, and she was me. Her life force pulsed within me, a testament to her enduring presence, and a clear sign that I needed to stay. I reached out, desperate for a hand to hold, but there was nothing. So I pulled my hand back, tracing my fingers across my chest, feeling for the reassurance of my own body, my own heartbeat. I needed to ground myself, to remember I was still here. But even in that surrender, I craved the comfort of touch. I reached out again, my fingers brushing against each other as if seeking the softness of a rose petal, a phantom limb yearning for connection in the vast emptiness. But there was only the reminder of all I had to let go.

I've kept reaching out for my fingers, making sure I feel a touch. When I regained a sense of control and awareness, I placed my hands on my heart, as if trying to preserve the sensation of pulling, replacing, or rebooting something before it came back together. I imagined holding my heart outside my chest, under the moonlight, before placing it back. I was terrified, so scared that I lost all my senses. I could not smell, taste, or hear anything. I kept reaching for anything to touch, as if I was under the rubble, under the aches. The image of holding a heart outside my body, exposed beneath the moon, is incredibly potent to cycles of death and rebirth, with its waxing and waning mirroring the rhythms of life. I was offering my heart to that cycle, seeking a kind of cleansing or transformation under its light. The fear, the loss of senses, speaks to the vulnerability of this process, in which it was the way true healing requires us to confront our deepest fears.

And then **Grief** was there, a presence both comforting and overwhelming. Grief held my hand, and I pulled it close, needing to feel its weight against my heart as if drawing the pain closer could somehow ease its burden. The hand felt like a lifeline, helping me push the muffled sounds out of my tight chest. It was a birthing of sorts, not through the channels of my womb, but through the very core of my being. **Grief,** the midwife, was guiding me to deliver a new self, or perhaps to finally release the pain that had been lodged there for far too long.

Trauma, both personal and generational, often manifests in symbolic and non-linear ways. As I grappled with the immense pain of my mother's passing, a powerful image emerged from the depths of my being: a V-shape, reminiscent of a woman's reproductive power, yet also echoing the losses and displacements etched into my family's history. This image became a lens through which I began to understand the intricate interplay of grief, resilience, and the enduring power of the feminine spirit. What follows is an exploration of this symbol and its profound connection to my lived experience.

Just as I felt myself surrendering to the pull of oblivion, an image materialized in the darkness—a V-shape, like a vagina, the intricate and multi-layered system of a woman's reproductive power. Each layer, delicate as a rose petal, held something that needed to be released, a secret too tightly guarded. It was then I understood: freedom wasn't about clinging to life, or even to her, but about surrendering to the intricate unfolding, petal by petal, of what needed to be released. This V-shape, this symbol of creation and birth, also echoed the losses etched into my family's history, the forced displacements, the stolen homelands. It spoke to the resilience of Palestinian women, who, like the earth itself, endure, nurture, and ultimately blossom anew, even in the face of unimaginable grief.

The experience shifted. Darkness enveloped me, thick and suffocating, yet eerily silent. Then came the sounds, piercing through the silence, each one a shard of glass driven straight into my heart. I was parched, my throat aching for relief, until I felt it—a single tear tracing a path down my cheek. But this was no ordinary tear. It was a torrent, a wellspring of grief erupting from within, cascading down my face in a wave of heat and sorrow. And yet, through it all, the sound remained constant—the steady, rhythmic rush of water, a symphony of release.

This was my journey into the heart of freedom—a raw, visceral, and ultimately transformative experience of death and rebirth, one that echoes the enduring spirit of Palestinian mothers across generations. I named him Grief (Grief, in this context, is personified as a supportive presence, a companion who facilitated my healing journey), this Grief that clung to me. Sometimes, he was a comforting weight, a heavy blanket on the coldest nights. In those moments, I'd let him pull me close, his presence a stark reminder that I was still here, still breathing, even if my world had shattered. We sat together in silence, Grief and I, two mourners united by a language only our broken hearts could speak. His rough edges, the ones that snagged on my insides and threatened to unravel me, felt strangely soothing then, a testament to the depth of my love, the immensity of my loss.

But then Grief would shift. The weight that felt grounding, a necessary anchor in the initial storm of loss, would morph into a suffocating pressure, his presence a leaden anchor dragging me down into a bottomless abyss. My breath would hitch; each inhale a shallow gasp as if the air itself had thinned, unable to penetrate the thickness of my sorrow. It was in these moments, paralyzed and breathless, that I yearned to peel him off, to set him outside of myself. I craved the distance, the space to examine the wreckage without being consumed by it. This duality of grief, its simultaneous comfort and suffocation, mirrored another tension within me: the urge to expand, to stretch and occupy space, clashed with the ingrained habit of shrinking, of making myself smaller in a world that often felt unsafe for a woman like me.

In the journey, I wanted to stretch, stretch, extend my parts, to take place to occupy space, to allow my cells to feel life from head to toe. But I also noticed that I may be or not in a safe place to feel, a place where a divided world of white, black, brown, and Latino, men, and women was disillusioned. The conflict between wanting to stretch, to take up space, and the learned need for self-preservation, spoke to the ways in which women, in particular, are often conditioned to shrink themselves, to prioritize modesty over their own need for expansion. This fact and this tension, made me acknowledge both the desire to stretch and the ingrained habits of self-concealment, recognizing the parallel between grief's fluctuating presence and my own internal struggle, became a powerful step in itself.

This journey, like all paths of healing and self-discovery, has been a profound teacher. It resembled a lotus flower—its roots submerged in mud, yet its blossom reaching for the light. My journey was a descent into the murky depths of pain, not to linger, but to draw strength and nourishment, rising above to bloom into a renewed state of being. Tapping into the unconscious was to be my water, allowing me to soften into the discomfort, to stop resisting the currents that threatened to pull me under.

The path wasn't clear, not at first. Twisted roots snagged at my ankles, branches clawed at my face, and the air hung heavy with an unfamiliar scent—the cloying sweetness of decay mingling with the sharp tang of fear. This was the landscape of my grief, a dark forest where every step forward felt like a battle against the encroaching shadows. The path ahead was shrouded in mist, the weight of sorrow heavy on my heart. Yet, even in the face of such immense darkness, something within me, perhaps an ancient instinct for survival, sought grounding and light.

What Pain Has Taught Me

Importance of Witnessing

Allowing ourselves to be seen in our vulnerability, and offering that same compassionate witnessing to others, is a powerful catalyst for healing and connection. True witnessing is not passive observation; it's an active, engaged practice rooted in empathy, accountability, and a commitment to justice. It's about recognizing the inherent dignity and humanity of the other, even in their suffering, and refusing to turn away from their pain. We can underscore the power of committed and accountable witnessing by the following.

Centering Empathy and Connection

Witnessing begins with deep listening and a genuine desire to understand the other's experience. It requires us to step outside our own perspectives and connect with the other's humanity.

Bearing Witness to Truth

Witnessing involves acknowledging and validating the other's reality, even when it's difficult or uncomfortable. It means speaking truth to power and challenging dominant narratives that perpetuate injustice. Fitzpatrick (2009) discusses the role of the spectator as witness in performances that depict traumatic events.

Taking Action in Solidarity

Witnessing is not a passive act; it demands action. This might involve advocating for policy changes, supporting community organizing efforts, or simply offering a compassionate presence to those who are suffering. Watkins (2015) mentions the concept of "accompaniment," which emphasizes active engagement and working together for liberation. Practicing Reciprocal Recognition: Witnessing is not a one-way street. It requires mutual recognition and respect, acknowledging the interconnectedness of our lives and experiences. Atallah and Dutta (2023) discuss the importance of understanding trauma within specific cultural and historical contexts, which is crucial for effective witnessing.

Cultivating Self-Awareness

To be effective witnesses, we must also examine our own biases and privileges. This involves acknowledging the ways in which we might be complicit in systems of oppression and actively working to dismantle them. Thambinathan and Kinsella (2021) discuss the importance of self-reflection and challenging colonial methodologies in research and education.

The Cyclical Nature of Growth

Healing isn't always linear. Sometimes we need to contract and retreat before we can fully expand and step into our power. Honoring those rhythms is essential.

The Power of Unconventional Perspectives

Beauty and meaning can be found in unexpected places. Embracing diverse perspectives, even those that challenge societal norms can deepen our understanding of ourselves and the world around us. Embracing pluriversality and multiple ways of seeing and being is central to this practice. It's about recognizing that there are many valid ways of understanding the world and that knowledge is not solely the domain of dominant cultures or institutions. This includes valuing indigenous knowledge systems, lived experiences, and perspectives that challenge conventional wisdom. Adams et al. (2015) discusses the limitations of Western-centric psychological science and the need to decolonize research practices. Akomolafe (2018) explores the concept of "sacred activisms," which challenges traditional notions of activism and encourages us to embrace unconventional approaches to social justice. By opening ourselves to these diverse perspectives, we can deepen our understanding of ourselves, the world around us, and the possibilities for transformative change.

The Value of Self-Compassion

Meeting ourselves with grace and understanding, especially during times of challenge and transformation, is crucial for navigating difficult emotions and fostering resilience.

Having borne witness to the profound suffering in Gaza, I felt compelled to turn inward, to explore the echoes of pain within my own heart. With each intentional breath and guided reflection, I delved deeper into the landscape of my own suffering. This time, I focused on living fully as a way to accept pain and move beyond suffering. I explored resolutions, aims, and pathways to love—seeking ways to live, love, and thrive, not just survive, beyond the echoes of my losses.

I decided to take a walk to the park, took my journaling book and walked mindfully. I walked and chose a tree carefully, sat directly on the dirt, and rested my back on the truck of the tree. I did breath work, and allowed my body to sit, to rest, to be in now with the earth, laid my hands, until my fingers and palms touched the dirt, and asked to release all the bad energy outwards, and laid my hands like the roots asking them to guide me to steadiness, strength, and connectedness. The grounding ritual is my yearning for a solid foundation from which to experience life more fully[2].

The cranberry trees stopped me in my tracks, a blaze of crimson against the muted landscape. The cranberry's journey from bog to air, hidden before reaching full ripeness… it mirrors so much of what I've been feeling, – the need to delve into the darkness, to embrace the tartness of my own experiences, before I can truly savor the sweetness of healing. Could the cranberries be a reminder to embrace transformation, to seek out hidden depths, or to connect with the life *force within and around you?* The cranberry's lifecycle links to the cycle of death and rebirth. The berries ripen in the fall, a time associated with decay and the end of the growing season. Yet, these berries are harvested and preserved, their essence carried through the winter months, a time of dormancy and waiting. When we consume them, we partake in a symbolic act of rebirth, incorporating the cranberry's life force into our own. This cycle reminds us that endings are not final, but rather opportunities for renewal and transformation.

I felt I was still seeing trees in my meditative and visualization journey, and inside of an orgasm cell, splitting, forming, and unfolding; I was trying so hard to focus, begging my inner mind to show me symbols, paths, anything to connect and reflect on, but I didn't get anything. I was not angry, in fact I asked my body to surrender and find more comfort as I come back from the trip.

This experience, from the depths of that therapeutic journey to the unexpected encounter with cranberry trees, has offered powerful lessons. **First, surrender is not defeat,** but a doorway to deeper healing. **Second, our subconscious speaks in a language of symbols and sensations,** whispering wisdom when we least expect it. And **finally, healing is not a destination,** but a winding path that unfolds in its own time. This connects directly to my experiences, for example, *healing is not a destination:* an ongoing process. I am constantly learning and evolving, refining my abilities and expanding my knowledge base. This continuous process of learning and growth mirrors the concept of healing as a journey, not a destination. Just as trees continue to grow and change throughout their lives, I am constantly evolving and adapting to new information and challenges. Similarly, in the context of activism, surrendering to the complexities of a situation, acknowledging the limitations of one's own perspective, and being open to collaboration and compromise can be powerful strategies for achieving meaningful change. It's not about giving up, but about adapting and evolving. As I continue on this journey, I will strive to listen to the whispers, to trust the process, and to find solace in the vibrant resilience of the natural world.

The clove necklace has been calling me for weeks, a quiet insistence from deep within. It's not just a beautiful adornment; it's a thread woven with memory and meaning. Back in my village, clove necklaces were more than just accessories. They were talismans, crafted with care by the women in our families, imbued with a legacy of love and tradition.

My first clove necklace, a gift from my mother, held a special kind of magic. The scent, warm and spicy, always evoked a sense of comfort and protection. When she passed, laying one of her own clove necklaces on her grave felt like a tangible way to honor her memory, to weave her presence into the fabric of my grief.

Cloves have always been woven into the tapestry of our lives. A natural remedy for toothaches, a source of fragrant oil for hair treatments, a protector against moths in our closets, a warming spice in our kitchens, and a comforting addition to our coffee and tea—their presence is both subtle and profound. Perhaps that's what this calling is about—a reminder of the simple yet powerful ways that tradition, healing, and love intertwine.

This encourages deeper reflection on the clove necklace's meaning: What aspects of my heritage and lineage do I feel most called to honor and embody at this time? How can I tap into these sensory experiences for grounding and comfort? How can I use the clove necklace as a focal point for my spiritual practice and exploration? What intentions do I want to set for this symbol? I do not know. What I know is that my intuition is guiding me toward a deeper understanding of its significance in my life. While the clove necklace holds symbolic meaning, it's also a tangible object with specific sensory qualities. For example, **scent:** the pungent aroma of cloves is likely the most immediate and evocative aspect of the necklace. When I wear the necklace, breathe in the scent, feel the texture against my skin, and notice the visual details. This mindful attention connects me to my mother and helps me stay present and grounded in my own body.

The pain and struggle force you to grapple with a profound question: who am I? The suffering can alter your destiny, the way you move in life. Unintentionally your sense of self starts going through a process of deconstruction or expansion, moving beyond the limitations of language and pre-defined identities.

Who am I? It's a question that has echoed through different chapters of my life, but it took on a new resonance in the heart of that deconstruction and expansion. It wasn't about seeking a concrete answer, a neat label to define the totality of my being. It was more about surrendering to the mystery, allowing myself to simply *feel* the weight of that question without the pressure of needing a response. What surfaced were sensations, emotions, and a kaleidoscope of images that defied easy categorization. It was unsettling, yes, to confront the vastness of my own being, to acknowledge the parts of myself that exist beyond language and definition. But within that surrender, there was also a profound sense of liberation. It's fascinating how this question, so closely tied to my younger years, reemerged with such force in my 30s. It's as if the grief created a bridge, allowing me to approach this fundamental inquiry with a newfound depth and maturity. And what emerged from that space was the undeniable truth of my womanhood, a realization that resonated through every fiber of my being. The realization of my womanhood isn't just an abstract concept; it's an embodied experience with potential practical implications in various aspects of life. For example, it deepened my understanding of womanhood and changed the way I interact with family and friends. I find myself seeking deeper connections with other women and setting healthier boundaries in relationships that don't align with my values. The process of integrating such a profound realization takes time. The "practical" doesn't always mean immediate action. It can also be a shift in perspective, a change in the internal landscape that gradually manifests in the external world.

My reflections on healing and empowerment led me to explore how physical objects can serve as tangible anchors for these processes. One piece in particular, a painting, seen in Figure 10.1, has become a powerful symbol of this connection.

The painting is a Palestinian peasant dress, hanging quietly in my closet, which holds more than just fabric and thread. It holds the weight of longing, a question whispered in the stillness: *will I ever feel joy, happiness, moments where I can wear it with pride again?* Grief, like the intricate patterns of tatreez, can be a shared experience, a tapestry woven with threads of sorrow, support, and resilience. Just as it takes a village to create those elaborate embroideries, sometimes it takes a community to mend a broken heart, to stitch together the fragments of loss and find wholeness again. The act of tatreez, with its rhythmic repetition and intricate designs, can be a meditative practice, a way to channel grief into something tangible and beautiful. Each stitch—a silent prayer, a testament to the enduring spirit that refuses to be silenced by sorrow. And in the shared language of symbols—the birds, trees, and flowers—there's a reminder that even in the darkest of times, hope and beauty persist. The description of the dress resonated deeply, even bringing tears to Jesica Fernandez's eyes, in the process of reviewing the writing. Her reaction underscores the potent connection we have with certain garments, those we often reserve for moments of joy and celebration. But what if, as Jesica wondered, we dared to wear these garments in times of despair and grief? Could they serve as a portal, transporting us to a place of solace, strength, or even defiance? Would wearing them be a transgression, a reclaiming of our bodies and emotions in the face of adversity? Could this act be a form of resistance, a refusal to let grief consume us? The ritual of adorning ourselves with these symbolic garments becomes a prayer, a process of refusing to hang our hopes, pain, and grief in the closet. It's a way of mothering ourselves, nurturing our spirits, and embodying the love that sustains us through life's challenges.

The woman in the painting radiates strength and resolve, standing tall and proud, deeply connected to the ancient traditions and heritage woven into every fiber. She embodies my mother, myself, and my unborn daughter—a daughter I deeply long to welcome into my life someday.

My mentors, sensing my struggle, suggested an unexpected balm for my grief: a visit to the Art Institute. A place where beauty and reflection intertwine, it became a catalyst for my own journey through grief. It was there, amidst the hushed galleries and evocative brushstrokes, that they gently guided me back to the raw vulnerability of those early days after my mother's passing. And it was there, in the quiet spaces between loss and healing, that a vision took root.

I saw a gathering, not of mourning, but of remembrance and renewal. A circle of loved ones, drawn together by a shared love for a woman who had touched each of our lives in profound ways. We would gather, not in a place of sorrow, but in the embrace of nature, where the cycle of life and death unfolds with quiet grace. At the heart of this gathering would stand a tree—a young sapling, symbolizing the promise of growth and resilience.

Each person would choose a tree that resonated with their own connection to my mother, a living embodiment of her spirit. With hands joined and hearts open, we would plant the sapling, whispering prayers and memories into the fertile earth. As the roots took hold, so too would our love for her find a new home, intertwined with the very essence of the tree.

In the years to come, as the tree grew taller, its branches reaching toward the heavens, it would become a living testament to her legacy. A place of quiet reflection, where we could gather to share stories, find solace in its shade, and remember the woman who had brought us together. For in the timeless cycle of nature, there is no true ending, only transformation. And in the rustling leaves and the whisper of the wind, we would hear her voice, reminding us that love, like the roots of a tree, runs deep and endures long after the physical form has passed.

In Closing

Perhaps these expressions—the metaphorical, the visionary, the literal—resist a neat weaving together. Perhaps the messiness itself is the point. The earth, after all, is not always orderly.

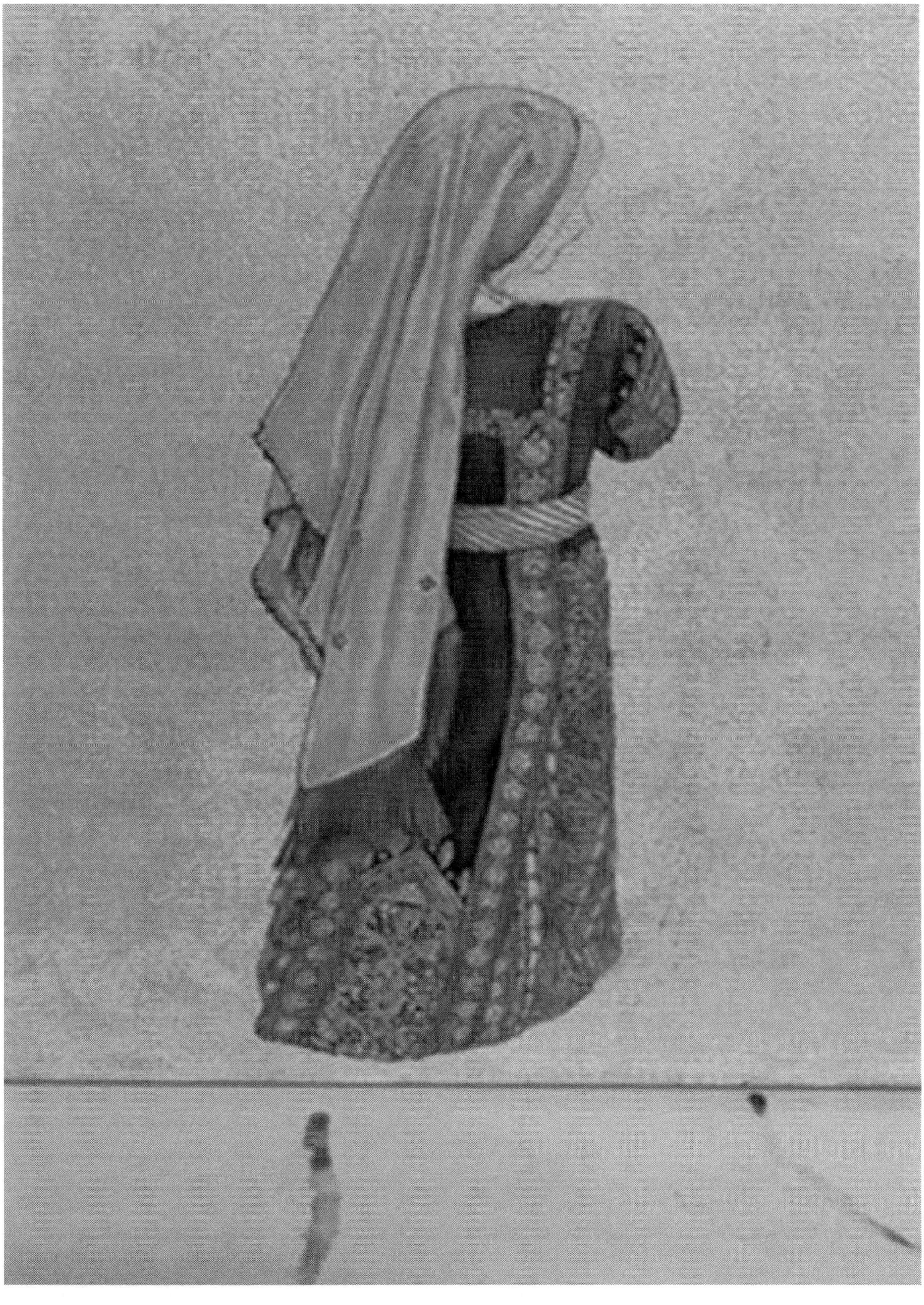

Figure 10.1 Painting Woven Heritage: Woman in Tatreez by Fatin Nassan, photograph by the author

It erupts, it floods, it decays, and yet it also blossoms, fruits, and sustains. Like the land, our grief, our visions, and our actions may seem chaotic, but they are part of a larger cycle of transformation. It is difficult to speak of hope when grief is so present, so tangible. Yet, like seeds scattered on the wind, they hold the potential for new life. The earth, our mother, teaches us that even in the harshest landscapes, life finds a way. These expressions, in their messy, untidy totality, are not about weaving a perfect tapestry of hope but about scattering seeds of possibility, trusting that in time, something new will emerge. This mothering—of ourselves, of others, of the land—born of grief and nurtured by the land, is a testament to the enduring power of love, even in the face of despair.

And so, on January 30, 2023, as represented in Figure 10.2, with hands in the earth and hearts turned toward the heavens, we wove together a tapestry of love and remembrance, honoring her memory with every root that takes hold, every leaf that unfurls, and every blossom that graces the sun.

Figure 10.2 Collective Remembrance: Replanting the Loss, photograph by the author

Notes

1 This dreamlike experience, while intensely real, could be interpreted through several lenses. The blurring of time and the visceral nature of the sensations suggest the possibility of a dream or vision, a powerful expression of unconscious emotions surfacing during a period of profound grief. Dreams, as we know, can offer profound insights into our inner world, often revealing what our conscious minds struggle to process. Simultaneously, this experience resonates with the concept of a trauma response. The intense grief of losing my mother could have manifested as a somatic or emotional flashback, where my body and spirit relived the trauma of her passing, even in the absence of a physical threat. This interpretation acknowledges the powerful impact of grief on our entire being, blurring the lines between the physical and the emotional, the real and the imagined.

2 The connection between ecofeminism and the healing power of mothers, particularly in the context of Palestinian motherhood as described in the opening, lies in the shared experience of nurturing and life-giving amidst exploitation and devaluation. Ecofeminism, as highlighted in (Anjum, 2020), points out how patriarchal systems devalue "feminine" traits like nurturing and caregiving. This devaluation mirrors the ways in which the labor of Palestinian mothers, as described in the opening, is often "politicized and devalued by liberation movements." Despite this devaluation, Palestinian mothers continue to perform the essential work of "managing survival, rebuilding homes, and creating paths of alternative futures." This resilience and commitment to life-sustaining labor directly challenge the forces of settler colonial violence and oppression.

References

Adams, G., Dobles, I., Gómez, L. H., Kurtiş, T., & Molina, L. E. (2015). Decolonizing psychological science: Introduction to the special thematic section. *Journal of Social and Political Psychology, 3*(1), 213–238. https://doi.org/10.5964/jspp.v3i1.564

Akomolafe, B. (2018, April 3). *Sacred activisms*. Bayo Akomolafe. https://www.bayoakomolafe.net/post/sacred-activisms.

Anjum, T. (2020). Ecofeminism: Exploitation of women and nature. *International Journal of English Literature and Social Sciences, 5*(4), 846–848. https://doi.org/10.22161/ijels.54.2

Atallah, D. G., & Dutta, U. (2023). Decolonization unnamed: Echoes of healing and refusal in the face of dehumanization and alienation. *Peace and Conflict: Journal of Peace Psychology, 29*(2), 77–81. https://doi.org/10.1037/pac0000686

Fitzpatrick, L. (2009). Ethics of spectatorship and the performance of violence on stage. In *Unknown host publication. Repertoires of violence: Multidisciplinary analyses of the representation of peace and conflict* (pp. 1–14). York St John University. https://pure.ulster.ac.uk/en/publications/ethics-of-spectatorship-and-the-performance-of-violence-on-stage-3

Hayes, S. C., & Smith, S. X. (2005). *Get out of your mind & into your life: The new acceptance & commitment therapy.* New Harbinger Publications.

Spillers, H. J. (1987). Mama's baby, papa's maybe: An American grammar book. *Diacritics, 17*(2), 64–81. https://doi.org/10.2307/464747

Thambinathan, V., & Kinsella, E. A. (2021). Decolonizing methodologies in qualitative research: Creating spaces for transformative praxis. *International Journal of Qualitative Methods, 20*, 1–9. https://doi.org/10.1177/16094069211014766

Watkins, M. (2015). Psychosocial accompaniment. *Journal of Social and Political Psychology, 3*(1), 324–341. https://doi.org/10.5964/jspp.v3i1.103

11 Interstitial Onto-Epistemologies in Liberatory Praxis and Clinical Practice

Zenobia Morrill

What does it take to construct selves and worlds differently? Transformation often is a project of imagination. We have to imagine other possible selves and worlds to transform into, often those that we hope to be more just and less brittle—less susceptible to the perversions of dehumanizing degradation and violent atrocities. In addition, we must conceive of pathways and methods for *how* we can pursue such transformation.

In this chapter, I describe a particular way of being and knowing that I believe offers us one such inroads, or methods, to open up decolonial possibilities, an *interstitial onto-epistemology*. An interstitial onto-epistemology is a way of knowing and being from the in-between. I use in-between to describe subjectivities, knowledge practices, and relational encounters that do not fit neatly within constructed binaries and defined categories that often are used to organize experiences, by psychology especially. Interstitial experiences and modes-of-being tend to be rendered unintelligible by dominant discourses and frameworks and are often flattened by traditional identity, cultural, or other instantiated labels. Although these labels may sometimes apply, they do not fully capture interstitial experiences. As such, interstitial onto-epistemologies are subjected to colonial violence and erasure when models of thought, practice, and constructions of reality imposed by Western modernity in a mainstream order (Mignolo, 2011; Quijano, 2000).

However, when reclaimed, interstitial onto-epistemologies represent alternatives to this violence by embodying epistemic, cultural, and political alternatives. Existing at the intersections or defying what is legible within a mainstream order, interstitial experiences are paradoxes that invariably perturb logics of modernity, such as global hierarchies and truth claims (Lugones, 2010). For this reason, it is important to identify and reclaim interstitial experiences, or specifically those ways of being, knowing, or relating that are deemed paradoxical or irreconcilable according to this colonial logic. Otherwise, it may be difficult to pierce through it because imagining more just or ethical alternatives is riddled with incommensurability (Atallah, 2022; Dutta, 2022). Doing so requires a shift outside of dominant structures and views, though we are necessarily constrained by and situated within them (Sharpe, 2016). Interstitial onto-epistemologies engage with this incommensurability directly because they are defined by existing between or across multiple social experiences without being fully defined by any of them.

Meaningful transformation therefore does not entail recreating another version of hegemony where one ontological, epistemological, or cultural stance exercises dominion over others, nor does it occur simply by denying irreconcilabilities across contextually situated models. Rather, a decolonial *praxis* (Freire, 1970) entails a cyclical process of reflection, theory, and action. Praxes are recursive processes, fueled by radical relationality and accountability. Crucial to transformative praxes also is the capacity to contend with the irreconcilabilities, the gaps in-between instantiated knowledges. Atallah (2022) writes that decolonial praxis "unfold[s] in the in-between spaces of intersections and crossings marked by the emergence of radical understandings and relationalities capable of shattering colonially-structured realities" (pp. 76–77).

DOI: 10.4324/9781003492214-13

In this way, a decolonial praxis is aided by radical ways of knowing and relating that are rooted in the in-between, beyond the edges and within the intersections of what is known. In this chapter, I draw from a practice of *testimonio* to describe the role of interstitial onto-epistemologies in constructing liberatory selves and worlds. Then, the triadic parts of an interstitial onto-epistemology are clarified as ways-of-being, -knowing, and -relating. Subsequently, this chapter is organized into three sections where an interstitial onto-epistemology is delineated into methods that correspond to the three cyclical parts of praxis: (1) reflecting, (2) theorizing, and (3) action, or encountering. In each section, the methods offered by interstitial onto-epistemology are described in terms of how it serves to contend with paradoxes and irreconcilabilities, bridge the gaps of (im)possibilities, and access novel forms of personhood, meaning, and worlds.

A *Testimonio* on Being and Knowing from the In-Between

The interstices represent alternative ways of being, knowing, and relating that risk being obscured by, or collapsed within, existing power structures. The purpose of my writing, however, is to prevent such an obfuscation and rather underscore how the in-between offers a break from order. My lived reality is grounded in this liminal way of being. I felt the obfuscation as hermeneutical injustices and alienation when my existence has not been clearly situated within established categories—unique from other marginalized positions because I am in-between, neither, and multiples that overlap and contradict.

I draw from the narrative liberation practice of *testimonio* (Cervantes, 2020; Forcinito, 2016), as I write bearing my own paradoxical tensions and irreconcilabilities. I, quite literally, was formed out of, and into, paradoxes as well as, you could say, my parents' dreams to destabilize a particular order of things (Foucault, 1975) that they had known. And if their union was contending with a paradox, then some alternative could be born from it. I live that hybridity with synthesis, fragmentation, *and* refusal—with contradiction.

My father, an 11th generation Anglo-Saxon American, was born into the California Church of the Nazarene as the son of cattle ranchers. A few decades ago, he gifted me a poem titled *The Naming of Zenobia*. In the last stanza, he breaks out of the third person for the first time and addresses my mother. My mother is a Pakistani woman and daughter of a military colonel. She was born just six years after Pakistan and India were fractured upon the destabilizing departure of the British Raj. They met at the US Embassy in Pakistan's capital, Islamabad. So, my father breaks out of the third person, in this poem about my name, and he speaks now to my mother directly:

> "You are the East; I am the West. We may need a link in between.
> Our second girl should bear the name of the Palmyrene Queen."

Perhaps you hear the imaginings—or hope—that some third possibility could form and bridge the two known ones—rein as Queen in the midst of an interregnum. In this case, link the East to the West. Indeed, that such a union might require a link like this, like *me*? But as described, this link invites a paradox, a reconciliation of dualities. I should share here that my parents are divorced. And ever since those years ago, they have more or less lived on opposite sides of the globe, resembling repelling magnets. You could say that I have inherited a crisis of meaning—or do I embody it? Am I the crisis of meaning? Nevertheless, here I am. In between. In between being White and Person of Color; Christian and Muslim; 12th and first-generation American; Pakistani and not; and having ancestral ties to Colonizer and Colonized.

This lived experience is contextualized by a dearth of resources to make sense of my being. My personal struggle mirrors a collective lack of available knowledge necessary to understand, interpret, and communicate my being—to engage in the type of meaning-making that permits *worlding*. Certainly, the world around me lacked models for these reconciliations. I could not turn there to link or even make sense of being in-between, I wasn't clear on my *self* when I seemed so clearly other, by account of the frameworks available to me. This inadequacy of collective interpretive resources (e.g., language, models, concepts) has implications for participation in social and political life, culminating in epistemic and hermeneutical injustices that perpetuate oppression (Fricker, 2007).

The remedy for this meaning crises was paradoxically sourced from within the imprints of my seemingly incompatible locations. I could understand these dual locations with perspicacity—because I inhabited them but also existed somewhat outside of them, rupturing them all the same. The order of things (Foucault, 1975) that labeled me, while also defining the politics of my belonging, became something I was particularly apt to observing, understanding, and perturbing. The taken-for-granted logics of dominant power relations were made more visible and analyzable to me from this interstitial position. It has been from here that I could contend with incommensurabilities and access novel possibilities.

Three Dimensions: Interstitial Being, Knowing, and Encountering

Importantly, I am not describing an experience unique to me, or distinctive of biracial or bicultural identities. Being in-between is a positionality that arises by the surrounding episteme and through its constructed hierarchies. Because interstitial experiences, as I describe them here, are those that defy, do not fit, or occur within the gaps of mainstream knowledge and systems, they are marginalized, misunderstood, and unaccounted for in a unique way. Unlike other marginalized standpoints that may be structurally recognized as an oppressed group, interstitial positions—such as being both queer and diasporic, or being agender—often go unrecognized and excluded from social justice movements.

I believe that disavowing and erasing liminality delimits how we understand humanity more broadly and conceive of alternative possibilities for being and knowing. One could argue that the human experience is constituted by paradoxes (Anzaldúa, 1987; Beauvoir, 1948). There are indeterminable parts of all of us that surface when we feel our experiences defy or transcend psychological models and categorization systems, such as any framework that is acontextual, reductive, or objectifying. Psychology's universalist paradigms, for instance, tend to categorize static essences that make up who we are and determine aspects of our lives, as though we somehow live lives separately from contexts. To think psychology otherwise (Bhatia et al., 2023) entails both a process of changing it, recovering historical memory, and envisioning what else it could be. Processes of transformation are alterations in the form, structure, and perspectives, including those that make up mainstream ideological value systems. Interstitial examples demonstrate another way to be, think, and relate.

An interstitial onto-epistemology is triadic. Three parts or dimensions are central to the notion of interstitial: (1) being, (2) knowing, and (3) encountering. First, interstitial ontologies refer to being in-between or of multiple identities, cultures, and ideologies or value systems (Morrill, 2023; Morrill et al., 2024). These interstitial onto-epistemologies, by defying dominant categories, exemplify modes-of-being outside of and beyond them. Second, interstitial epistemologies refer to the perspectives offered from this in-between vantage point, including perspectives that are not only made-up-of, but model methods to make sense of paradoxes, contradictions, and plurality (Morrill et al., 2024). And third, interstitial *encounters* are emphasized to specifically underscore that the interstices include *interactions* (in-)between persons and ideas that exemplify other ways of relating and dynamics for *doing* (Morrill, 2024; Sonn et al., 2024). For example, interstitial encounters may include relationship dynamics that upend power structures or ways to take up liminal experiences of transitioning between poles or mainstream constructs that tend to be dichotomized (e.g., becoming a parent, transitioning genders, migration, implementing systems, or policy change).

The three interstitial parts—being, knowing, and encountering—correspond to the cycles of reflection, theory, and action in a decolonial praxis. Accordingly, this chapter is organized into sections describing interstitial (a) ontologies to *reflect* upon states of ontological ambiguity and alienation experiences, (b) epistemologies to *theorize* its potential to advance liberation psychologies, and (c) encounters that *enact liberatory clinical practices.*

Reflection: Ontological Ambiguity & the Politics of Belonging

Existential thinkers have posited that simply on the basis of being human, we all contend with paradoxes. Interstitial ontologies are relevant in that sense that our very existence may be characterized by seeming dualities and the ambiguity that results when hegemonic categories are used to understand our being (Beauvoir, 1948). These limits and paradoxes require us to contend with the tensions and transitions between contradictory states or situations. I draw upon Simon de Beauvoir's *Ethics of Ambiguity* (1948) to suggest that existing includes navigating these interstitial components of being, such as reconciling subjectivity and objectivity, our freedom and the limits that constrain it, as well as additional paradoxical tensions outlined in this section.

For example, the interstitial experience of shuttling between *subjectivity and objectivity* is ubiquitous. We are all subjects in that we experience ourselves and interpret our world through our unique vantage point, but we are also objects in others' worlds, where we are externally understood, defined, and inevitably objectified. Similarly, individuals navigate tensions between *freedom and facticity*, a paradox closely tied to tensions between *individual freedom and collective freedom.* Existentialists highlight that individuals exercise a radical freedom to make choices and create meaning in life. However, these choices, meanings, and outcomes are beset by the constraints of reality. We are limited by physical, sociostructural, and historical conditions, including, of course, our own mortality. Beauvoir argues that freedom demands making ethical choices rather than denying this responsibility in bad faith or fleeing from honest accountability. Moreover, Beauvoir argues the interconnectedness of human freedoms, noting that true freedom is intertwined with the freedom of others. Freedom and wellbeing are interdependent.

These paradoxes carry implications for understanding the tensions between *oppression and liberation*. Sociopolitical oppression and dynamics of subjugation is a denial of freedom and accountability. How, then, can liberation be pursued within the constraining realities of our world and capacities? Rather than seeking a universal set of ethical principles purported to decolonize or resolve oppression, it is important to acknowledge situationality, so that authentic ethical decisions are made based upon the contingencies of unique situations and their contexts. We cannot undo these paradoxes or fully claim to resolve them. How then do we exist with their dual tensions and the pluralistic realities of their overlap? But we must contend with the ethics of living with them. If paradoxical tensions indeed define what it means to be human, then each person faces interstitial components of being and experiences of transitioning or existing between dualities and multiple overlapping situations. Identifying the role of an interstitial onto-epistemology also in transformation processes articulates how this positionality may provide inroads to ethical and liberatory action when these situations arise.

However, these interstitial experiences are often obscured and marginalized, deemed less real or meaningful when language, paradigms, and constructs fail to account for them. This presents forms of epistemological and hermeneutical injustices when the interstitial modes-of-being are dismissed or erased. A profound effect is exacted on one's ability to participate in personal, relational, social, and political forms of life. Moreover, the oversight of interstitial onto-epistemologies precludes access to self-determination, foments alienation, and glosses over the creative reconciliations and forms of resistance that already exist, thereby depriving collective humanity of these examples of ways and possibilities to be more ethical and just.

Theorizing Alternatives: Epistemological Possibilities

In what ways does an interstitial onto-epistemology contribute to more just alternatives? Lived experiences, transitions, and encounters in-between the gaps of categories can, though not always, provide incredibly insightful and shrewd understandings of the rules and taken-for-granted assumptions that characterize the cultures from which one has been othered, marginalized, or exiled. I argue that these experiences provide several pathways into *how to think and do* them differently.

First, an interstitial onto-epistemology renders the rules of power more visible and amenable to critique. Change first requires the perspicacity to pierce through hegemony's taken-for-granted logics and silences to identify its limitations and harms. When one exists outside of or at the intersection of their contradictions, it is easier to see where meaning systems clash, fail, do harm, and may be renegotiated. It is also a vantage point from which the taken-for-granted politics of power are visible, which is a precursor to demystifying and contesting damaging truth claims. For example, an interstitial standpoint can enable one to see the flawed logic underlying universalist assumptions, such as the Euro-colonial and Enlightenment-era assumption that nature is separate from humanity, and is an *object* to be controlled, mastered, exploited, and subordinated to human will. From within the gaps where meaning breaks down, power can be better understood. The invisible is made visible so that too, alternatives come to the fore.

Second, the interstices provide a method to contend with, rather than foreclose around, crises of meaning because interstitiality entails existing in the counter-site, or as counter example. It is only when clashes of meaning are acknowledged that they may be contended with in pursuit of ethical reconciliation and transformation. As transformation involves cycles of destruction, creation, and renewal, crises of meaning are necessary to reconsider, rethink, and reimagine. Contending with the failures of systems, theories, and practices can be disorienting, however. It may be tempting—and it may deceptively appear convenient or more efficient—to ignore the tensions and crises posed when mainstream approaches are not working, or worse, are unjust. However, evading these encounters means foreclosing upon status quo systems, theories, and practices that shore up hegemonic power and disavow alternatives.

Alternatively, the interstices, by definition, include ways-of-being that go beyond the edges of widely accepted meanings and values systems. Interstitial onto-epistemologies presuppose that some mainstream logic has already been defied or destroyed. For example, the logic that a person cannot be more than one gender is defied by the countless examples across cultures and time that contradict this universalist truth claim. As a result, those who experience being, knowing, and relating in ways that do not fit in binary gender system have lived epistemological insights about how social mores of gender are limiting, insufficient, or harmful. These interstitial standpoints carry vital critiques not only of a binary gender system and its erasure of queer or nonbinary ways of being but also of how gender has been a colonial tool used to structure social hierarchies and enforce religious and moral universalist truth claims (Lugones, 2010)—framed under the guise of science—about social roles, sexuality, and legal conduct. In the interstices, there does not exist the same privilege of collapsing into mainstream frameworks. Rather interstitial experiences occur from outside of them, so the tensions between dominant logics are pronounced and contended with to live differently.

Third, interstitial onto-epistemologies as grappling with paradox through duality. As counterexamples, they serve as other ways to make sense of liminal states as veritable positionalities in their own right. This position models how ambiguities, binaries, and the tensions that arise from meaning paradoxes can be weathered without resulting in the shattering of meaning altogether. Under the title "Of Our Spiritual Strivings" in the 1903 book *The Souls of Black Folk*, W. E. B. Du Bois and colleagues (2004) hold this duality, when he figured the term "double consciousness." He wrote here:

> It is a peculiar sensation, this *double consciousness*, this sense of always looking at oneself through the eyes of others, of measuring one's soul by the tape of a world that looks on in amused contempt and pity. One ever feels his two-ness, an American, a [Black]; two souls, two thoughts, two unreconciled strivings; two warring ideals in one dark body, whose dogged strength alone keeps it from being torn asunder.
>
> (p. 2)

This *double consciousness*, and the strength required to brave these tensions rather than shatter their distinct meanings altogether, demonstrates a holding of warring dualities from the interstices. As Du Bois (2004) goes onto describe, this in-between position is meant to avoid collapsing this two-ness into one state or another, nor does it seek to merely merge the two states in order to disappear the gaps between them.

> The history of the [Black American] is the history of this strife—this longing to attain self-conscious manhood, to merge his double self into a better and truer self. In this merging he wishes neither of the older selves to be lost. He does not wish to Africanize America, for America has too much to teach the world and Africa. He wouldn't bleach his [Black] blood in a flood of [White] Americanism, for he knows that [Black] blood has a message for the world. He simply wishes to make it possible for a man to be both [Black and American] without being cursed and spit upon....
>
> (p. 2–3)

In this way, interstitial epistemologies exemplify a type of strength and retainment of a position that is neither one nor the other and, at the same time, both overlapping in multiplicity. An interstitial onto-epistemology is not only well-positioned to critique mainstream binaries but also to exemplify two-ness and model an alternative to either/or with both/and.

Thirdness—or taking up the overlap of both and gaps of neither—is the fourth possibility outlined herein that interstitial onto-epistemologies can offer. In other words, this two-ness merges not into one or the other, but into another. Gloria Anzaldúa (1987) invokes a similar spatial metaphor to describe how two cultures merge in the borderlands to create a third culture, a *border culture*. The concept of being in a state of in-betweenness is vital to this third culture, and Anzaldúa gives this in-betweenness a name, *Nepantla*. She argues that *in-between spaces* are crucial to understanding the fluid and dynamic nature of identity formation in the borderlands. And she puts forward *Mestiza consciousness* a sort of hybrid identity of living without borders, reclaiming native languages, and creating novel decolonial pathways of resistance—by cultivating and enacting this third way as an alternative. Moreover, I believe thirdness and border culture can be used as to transcend hyperindividualist logics that structure mainstream societies through privatization and personal success. Thirdness is not merely about identity formation but pertains to interstitial ways-of-encountering that disrupt the notion that the world is made up of individual actors and isolated interests and experiences. Interstitial onto-epistemologies include the spaces in-between individuals and their overlaps in relationships, reclaiming how individuals live interdependently—within shared crises and freedom struggles, relational networks, and environmental ecosystems that demand more regenerative ways of relating.

The fifth possibility offered by interstitial onto-epistemologies includes that it embodies plurality, fluidity, and the transitional components of change and interactions. Beyond a third way, the interstices make available the spectrum between instantiated, well-formed ways of being, knowing, and encountering. Mary Watkins and Helene Shulman (2008) have described that liberation psychologies demand a capacity to "[work] in the pluralism" (p. x). They write

> our hope is that [this] work will be seen as dynamic, ongoing, never to be finally achieved and never capable of being taught from above. To work in the pluralism of liberation psychologies is to state our sense that we must always be involved in the seeing through of psychological theory.

Indeed, inhabiting the gaps and reclaiming the fluidity between, and beyond, apparent dualities expand the range of possibilities for alternatives. The liminality offered by the interstices provides also the malleability to contend with tensions, rupture concretized hegemonic hierarchies and categories and instead, honor the situational contingencies necessary for ethical being, knowing, and encountering. This type of inhabiting between and multiple undergirds capacities for adaptivity, creativity, flexibility, and empathy. Such capacities enrich relational encounters and the mentalization required to navigate multiple perspectives, realities, and connections. Creativity and reflection are vital in a praxis of iterative reflecting, theorizing, and acting.

Liberatory Praxis and Transformation in Psychology

These ruderal possibilities do not promise liberation. There is no guarantee we are freed from instantiated power relations just because one inhabits their counter-sites. But, for Foucault (1975), it is in the interstices where knowledge emerges *because* meaning and knowledge clash (p. 66). So, it is where the potential for new knowledges exists, if we choose to harness it. I humbly believe a type of *critical consciousness* within a liberatory praxis can take shape from/in the interstices.

"To create cultural alternatives," Watkins and Shulman (2008) write, "people have to break with taken for granted ways of thinking that prevent them psychologically from interrupting the status quo" (p. 2). Similarly, Homi Bhabha (1994) has attested that we need to do the work which "renews the past, refiguring it as a contingent in-between space, that innovates and interrupts the performance of the present" (p. 37). I believe these decolonial writers refer precisely to the type of figuring and refiguring that an interstitial onto-epistemology may enable us to do. Desi scholar Kakali Bhattacharya (2019) wrote about her decolonial "homecoming," when she reclaimed knowledge from parts of herself that were "fragmented along the way." She provided a method for decolonial change:

> De/colonizing represents both the continuous desire for and the imagination of a utopia wholly free from colonization, and the (im)possibilities of such a dream that keep us shuttling between oppressive and liberative ontoepistemic states of being and knowing.
>
> (p. 178)

Once more, imagination seems to hinge on understanding *and undoing* these ingrained power relations—and their constructed binaries—by taking up the liminal shuttling between them. Bhattacharya (2019) expressly shares her intent to unsettle fixed categories of meaning, such as by complicating the clear distinction between decoloniality, as some utopian realm wholly free of colonization, and coloniality, as the type of oppression that makes such a dream utterly impossible.

These iterative cycles, taken up in the interstices, are processes of complicating politics and transforming them, that we can emulate in praxis—research, clinical work, pedagogy, and they kindle imagination, and I believe a praxis conducive to liberatory hope (Luiggi-Hernández, 2023). In *Toward Psychologies of Liberation*, Watkins & Shulman (2008) write: "Learning to create conditions for social and personal regeneration, for an awakening of hope and imagination, is one of the central psychological tasks of our era."

Action: Interstitial Onto-Epistemology and Clinical Practice

If we are accountable to, for instance, liberation movements, then we must reconsider the ethics of those paradoxes—how are *self and other* reconciled by interdependence and collective liberation? And how do we construct different worlds, or practices, when we inhabit this world and its systems of power? This section highlights interstitial components used to develop a model for clinical psychological practice. Interstitial onto-epistemologies inform a type of clinical sensibility that aims to construct different relationships and forms of personhood that support liberation (Ingle & Morrill, in press). From this premise, a Critical-Liberation Psychotherapy model was stewarded in a project of *Nepantla* (Morrill & Comas-Díaz, 2024, in press). To counter the erasure of interstitial onto-epistemologies, I outline here the ways my reflection and theorizing from an interstitial position has provided me with methods to reimagine and rethink some of the taken-for-granted logics in mainstream psychotherapy. The following considerations map onto the five pathways outlined in this chapter about interstitial pathways for thinking and doing differently.

Analyzing and Critiquing Hegemonic Power in Psychotherapy

First, interstitial onto-epistemologies are well-positioned to analyze and critique power in psychotherapy. Truth claims about and maintained by psychotherapy, therefore, can be rethought. For example, rethinking taken-for-granted notions that psychotherapy is an objective and value-neutral technique that can be standardized and universally applied as a medical treatment. Alternatively, its implicit cultural situatedness, values, and assumptions can be made visible to question, what is the *function* of psychotherapy? Critical questions reveal how mainstream psychotherapy—and its rootedness in scientific objectivism and positivism—may unwittingly extend hegemonic cultural assumptions, such as taking individuals and suffering out of context, and placing them into dichotomous categories and classifications constructed implicitly shaped by modernity. In turn, clinical practices may support these systems in subtle ways, such as by carrying forward hyperindividualism and productivity through practices designed to increase clients' mastery and control over tasks, emotions, relationships, and their symptoms, deemed natural "kinds" of things (i.e., mastery over nature). Making these contexts and systems of power visible enables not only critique but also recentering alternatives and envisioning other possibilities, such as psychotherapy functioning to promote critical consciousness, interdependence, and regenerative modes-of-relating compatible with collective liberation movements.

Contending with Psychotherapy Ethical Dilemmas and Crises of Meaning

Second, this analysis of power brings to the fore important tensions between a type of hegemonic psychotherapy that is oppressive and harmful, and, in contrast, one that can be liberatory and healing. An interstitial position contends with this clash, and the crises of meaning surrounding this dilemma. For instance, how can psychotherapy support decolonial possibilities given its constraints in institutions, ideologies, and knowledge practices of modernity? A decolonial epistemic shift would be required to highlight psychotherapy's cultural- and value-laden rootedness in power and then, actively subvert it. For instance, rather than psychotherapy working in service to quash discomfort or pathologize deviations from culturally-specific norms, clients' health and problems can be understood in context, as occurring in relation to systems of power. Then, the mark of health would not necessarily be symptom reduction or increased conformity to, and productivity within, social hierarchies, but critical consciousness. This epistemic shift in psychotherapy opens up different practices, such as facilitating narrative *testimonio* and *phenomenological exploration* of clients' subjective lived realities in context. Rather than foreclosing to a one-size-fits-all psychotherapy rooted in power systems of modernity, aspects of clinical practice may be destroyed, created, and renewed—including the recentering of the diverse healing practices which have always existed.

Moreover, the importance of contending with tensions and paradoxes with an interstitial onto-epistemology not only includes reckoning with the institution of psychotherapy or between contradictions in clinical theory but also contending with clashes of meaning in the relational encounter of therapy. Rather than the therapist as a detached observer of suffering, and provider of knowledge and solutions, an interstitial sensibility supports the therapist in weathering clashes *with* the client, such as when a crisis of meaning occurs in the therapy relationship. When this is done with genuine presence to explore and contextualize—rather than avoid or solve—crises, therapists are engaging in mutual acompañamiento (Morrill & Comas-Diaz, in press). They can pursue a similar type of *homecoming* process that Bhattacharya (2019) described, or a reclamation of fragmented parts of self, ways of being, and ancestral wisdoms.

An interstitial onto-epistemology demystifies the complex dynamics of domination and subjugation that make this radical relating less possible in mainstream therapy. *A*compañamiento is a practice of recentering marginalized epistemology because it disrupts an expert-learner or savior-victim dynamic in therapy. Moreover, it disrupts the theoretical assumption that psychological theory is *the* authority on human health and healing when in-session practices are not focused on prescribing solutions or explanations.

Inhabiting and Rupturing Dualities

An interstitial onto-epistemology provides a model for inhabiting and rupturing constructed paradoxes and dualities. Many individuals who find themselves in the interstices of constructed cultural categories reckon with questions of inhabiting or ruptures, as I myself have referenced throughout—am I Pakistani if I don't speak Urdu? Am I "American" even though my mother is an immigrant? Psychotherapy theory, training, and practices tend to be shaped around dominant binaries too, such as notions of normal-abnormal, doctor-patient, right-wrong, oppressor-oppressed, and healthy-unhealthy. For example, therapists may find themselves in the role of determining whether a patient's thoughts, feelings, or behaviors are healthy or unhealthy. Does their way of grieving meet the threshold for a clinical diagnosis? Perhaps they are taught that certain in-session techniques are right, and others are wrong—self-disclosures should be avoided, but more silence is good.

These dichotomies not only obscure how things, persons, and relationships are multitudinous but also that they are dynamic and tend to change based upon situational contingencies. Silence in one therapy moment or relationship might convey disconnection or abandonment, while in another it expresses communion. It also may be the case that the same person, moment, or approach contains two contradictory elements or has contradictory effects. That a client is both suicidal *and* normal, or some action by the therapist is painful, but has a liberatory effect. A liberatory psychotherapy would depart from binary and situationally-independent modes of thinking, doing, and relating, which constrains the diverse range of human realities and possibilities.

Encountering and Co-Creating Othered Possibilities

In addition to being ontologically rooted in duality, interstitial onto-epistemologies transcend both and neither, embodying a third way of being, knowing, and relating that represents multiple influences and at the same time, can be coded as foreign to each of them. In psychotherapy, this concept of *thirdness* has been used (Benjamin, 2004) to describe the shared relational space between the client and therapist that transcends the binary dynamic between "self" and "other," or what she refers to as "doer" and "done-to" dynamics. Interstitial onto-epistemologies highlight how thirdness can be apt to understanding more than individual identity formation (Anzaldúa, 1987) and modes-of-relating (Benjamin, 2004). It also can be applied to liminal possibilities for thinking and doing (see, e.g., Sonn et al., 2024, participatory research methods) that tend to be shrouded and subsumed by binaries.

Moreover, the idea of the in-between as a relational space did not originate with Western psychotherapy. Rather, it has been deeply embedded in non-Western and Indigenous knowledge systems, including but not limited to Sufi mysticism (see e.g., Morrill & Comas-Díaz, in press), Taoism, and African Ubuntu philosophy, that emphasize interdependence with community, ancestors, and the natural world. For example, Indigenous and Afro-diasporic healing practices already enact "thirdness" and fluid ontologies. This could illuminate how, in many contexts, the "in-between" is not peripheral but central to communal frameworks of health, spirituality, and cultural continuity. Applying an interstitial onto-epistemology to liberatory clinical practices therefore includes applying thirdness and border culture to psychotherapy that not only conceptualizes the client, therapist, and their co-created relational dynamic but also that each of these parts also conjoins with various systems and discourses that are therefore also present in psychotherapy, forming a type of third cultural possibility. In other words, interstitial ways of thinking and doing in psychotherapy are inseparable from knowledge practices, methods, and cultural values that seem external to them, providing multiple possibilities to subvert or resist hegemony.

Ethical Plurality in Transformative Processes

These reconfigurings of psychotherapy in and of themselves make them sites of resistance that defy a particular order and embody another way. Through an interstitial sensibility, plurality is held, and this opens up possibilities for the creation of a decolonial dynamic of thinking, doing, and relating between client and therapist. When interdependence is embraced as a way of understanding selves (i.e., therapist and client) and ways of relating (i.e., in the therapist and client relationship), objectification and self/other mutilation are resisted. Individual and interpersonal processes of objectification tie into cultural discourses and structural hierarchies. For example, bell hooks (2004) described these intersecting aspects of violence when she wrote

> The first act of violence that patriarchy demands of males is not violence toward women. Instead, patriarchy demands of all males that they engage in acts of psychic self-mutilation, that they kill off the emotional parts of themselves. If an individual is not successful in emotionally crippling himself, he can count on patriarchal men to enact rituals of power that will assault his self-esteem.
>
> (p. 66)

In contrast to critical frameworks that may theorize a static oppressor-oppressed or colonizer-colonized binary, an interstitial onto-epistemology foregrounds the lived experience of simultaneously occupying and subverting both positions—challenging rigid demarcations and illuminating a dynamic, in-between space where decolonial possibility is continuously enacted rather than theoretically dismissed.

Working with the pluralism and resisting hegemonic assumptions about clinical practice ultimately means that there is no one liberatory practice that can be arrived at or standardized into a manual. However, clinical practices can replicate or undo dynamics of violence and subjugation. Subjugation is replicated when therapists deny the relationship their genuine presence, are overly defensive, teach skills prematurely or without exploration, use one-size-fits-all prescriptions, uphold reductive binaries and *doer and done-to* dynamics (Benjamin, 2004), obscure the relational political contexts of lived experiences, and recapitulate the social order that constructs status quo forms of personhood. Alternatively, there is a ripple effect when the client is changed, when the therapist is changed, when the client-therapist relationship subverts dynamics of subjugation, or when any moment recenters marginalized perspectives to destabilize the order of things, another way can be put into motion. It is this kind of transformative praxis—ways of reflecting and doing, that undergirds collective change and liberation from constrained roles of being and relating.

References

Anzaldúa, G. (1987). *Borderlands/La frontera: The new mestiza*. Aunt Lute Books.

Atallah, D. G. (2022). Reflections on radical love and rebellion: Towards decolonial solidarity in community psychology praxis. In S. Kessi, S. Suffla, & M. Seedat (Eds.), *Decolonial enactments in community psychology* (pp. 75–97). Springer. https://doi.org/10.1007/978-3-030-75201-9

Beauvoir, S. D. (1948). *The ethics of ambiguity* (B. Frechtman, Trans.). Philosophical Library. (Original work published 1947).

Benjamin, J. (2004). Beyond doer and done to: An intersubjective view of thirdness. *Psychoanalytic Quarterly*, *73*(1), 5–46. https://doi.org/10.1002/j.2167-4086.2004.tb00151.x

Bhabha, H. K. (1994). *The location of culture*. Routledge.

Bhatia, S., Long, W., Pickren, W., & Rutherford, A. (2023). Engaging with decoloniality, decolonization, and histories of psychology otherwise. In L. Comas-Díaz, H. Y. Adames, & N. Y. Chavez-Dueñas (Eds.), *Decolonial psychology: Toward anticolonial theories, research, training, and practice* (pp. 45–64). American Psychological Association.

Bhattacharya K. (2019). (Un)settling imagined lands: A Par/Des(i) approach to de/colonizing methodologies. In Leavy P. (Ed.), *The Oxford handbook of methods for public scholarship* (pp. 175–215). Oxford University Press.

Cervantes, A. (2020). Testimonios. In L. Comas-Díaz, & E. Torres Rivera (Eds.), *Liberation psychology: Theory, method, practice, and social justice* (pp. 133–147). American Psychological Association. https://doi.org/10.1037/0000198-008

Du Bois, W. E. B. (2004). Of our spiritual strivings. In C. Lemert, M. Marable, & C. T. Gilkes (Eds.), *The souls of black folk* (pp. 7–14). Routledge.

Dutta, U. (2022). Decentering "community" in community psychology: Towards radical relationality and resistance. In S. Kessi, S. Suffla, & M. Seedat (Eds.), *Decolonial enactments in community psychology* (pp. 53–72). Springer. https://doi.org/10.1007/978-3-030-75201-9

Forcinito, A. (2016). Testimonio: The witness, the truth, and the inaudible. In Y. Martínez-San Miguel, B. Sifuentes-Jáuregui, & M. Belausteguigoitia (Eds.), *Critical terms in Caribbean and Latin American thought: New directions in Latino American cultures* (pp. 239–251). Palgrave Macmillan. https://doi.org/10.1057/9781137547903_22

Foucault, M. (1975). *The order of things* (1st ed.). Routledge.

Freire, P. (1970). *Cultural action for freedom*. Harvard Educational Review.

Fricker, M. (2007). *Epistemic injustice: Power and the ethics of knowing*. Oxford University Press.

hooks, b. (2004). *The will to change: Men, masculinity, and love*. Atria Books.

Ingle, M., & Morrill, Z. (2025). Anti(Capitalist) therapeutics: Analyzing psychotherapy's role within capitalism and proposing a Critical-Liberation Psychotherapy alternative. In J. Hook, & F. Gruba-McCallister (Eds.), *The Revolutionary psychologist's guide to radical therapy*. Palgrave Macmillan.

Lugones, M. (2010). Toward a decolonial feminism. *Hypatia*, *25*(4), 742–759. https://doi.org/10.1111/j.1527-2001.2010.01137.x

Luiggi-Hernández, J. G. (2023). *Hoping as a transformational imperative in Puerto Rico: A phenomenological and grounded theory study within colonized space* [Doctoral dissertation, Duquesne University]. Duquesne University Collection. https://dsc.duq.edu/etd/2246/

Mignolo, W. (2011). *The darker side of Western modernity: Global futures, decolonial options*. Duke University Press.

Morrill, Z., & Comas-Díaz, L. (2024). Feminist liberation psychotherapy: Re-politicizing intersectionality toward socially just clinical practice. *Women & Therapy*, *47*(3), 331–347. https://doi.org/10.1080/02703149.2024.2386513

Morrill, Z., Guterres, K., Rietti, S., & Goodman, D. M. (2024). Making sense of being and transforming: Introduction to the psychology and the other special issue. *Studies in Gender and Sexuality*, *25*(2), 71–75. https://doi.org/10.1080/15240657.2024.2346451

Morrill, Z. (2023, April 22). Liberation and the psychological humanities [Invited address]. *Annual Conference for the Society for Theoretical and Philosophical Psychology, Division 24 of the American Psychological Association*, Boston College, Chestnut Hill, MA.

Morrill, Z. (2024, July 11). Interstitial onto-epistemology: On being and knowing from the in-between [Invited address]. *Psychology and the Other Conference*, London, England.

Quijano, A. (2000). Coloniality of power, Eurocentrism, and Latin America. *Nepantla: Views from South*, *1*(3), 533–580. https://muse.jhu.edu/article/23906

Sharpe, C. (2016). *In the wake: On blackness and being*. Duke University Press.

Sonn, C. C., Agung-Igusti, R. P., Komba, G., Ruach, R. N., & Deng, E. E. (2024). Freedom dreaming from the university-community nexus: Relational praxis as counterspace. *Social and Personality Psychology Compass*, *18*(7), e12990. https://doi.org/10.1111/spc3.12990

Watkins, M., & Shulman, H. (2008). *Toward psychologies of liberation*. Palgrave Macmillan.

12 wangii wadhan biyay – Baskets of Listening and Respect

Mary Goslett and Belle Selkirk

Introduction

There is a distinct and growing field of Indigenous psychology, both in Australia and globally. Indigenous psychology asserts the legitimacy of Indigenous knowledge systems and healing practices as central to the wellbeing and flourishing of Indigenous peoples and challenges the hegemony of Western psychology (American Psychological Association, 2010; Dudgeon & Bray, 2023). This chapter is situated within this context and aims to reinforce traditional wisdoms of wellbeing while creating new paradigms based on those knowledges and decolonise psychology by critically examining Eurocentric hegemony (Ciofalo et al., 2022).

Social and emotional wellbeing (SEWB) is the bedrock of good health for Indigenous Australians, more than merely the absence of illness. This holistic wellbeing encompasses attachment to Country and community; relational selfhood and physical, social, emotional, cultural and spiritual welfare (Dudgeon et al., 2024; Gee et al., 2014). While Western psychological services ostensibly aim for a biopsychosocial perspective, conceptions of mental ill-health are deeply impacted by psychiatric and biomedical diagnostic taxonomies, in which the individual's familial, cultural, social and political milieus receive negligible recognition. Treatment is arguably then reduced to deficit identification and symptom reduction versus a relational model that embeds connection, strength and prospect of recovery (Goslett, 2022). In addition, the partiality towards Euro-Western psychological theory and practice limits the training and skills necessary for working with Aboriginal and Torres Strait Islander peoples (; Darnett et al., 2024; Dudgeon et al., 2014; Geerlings et al., 2018; Mcconnochie et al., 2012; Mullins & Khawaja, 2018).

The presented *wangii wadhan biyay,* meaning baskets of listening and respect in Dhurga language, framework offers one understanding of Indigenous Australian mental health and wellbeing, and how it can intersect with Western psychological practices (Goslett & Selkirk, 2023). Indigenous Australians are diverse peoples with rich histories, perspectives and lived experiences. Indigenous ways of knowing, being and doing impart and receive knowledge through story and metaphor, building understanding and strengthening culture by way of ongoing yarns and ceremony. Similarly, in the ceremony of therapy, we have listened to the stories of our community, teachers and clients, and a bottom-up, practice-based evidence approach arose that can meet and add depth to top-down Western frameworks, aiming for a deepening exchange and process that Paddy Roe, a Nyikina leader, explained as *"*things must go both ways*"* (Morrissey, 2019, pp. 105–106).

We suggest that psychological praxis can be of benefit to many Indigenous Australians if they honour the deep-time knowledges articulated in *wangii wadhan biyay* (Goslett & Selkirk, 2023). This requires a strong willingness to acknowledge Indigenous ways of knowing, being and doing, a complex task when one acknowledges that Indigenous Australians' "beliefs, knowledge, and

DOI: 10.4324/9781003492214-14

Figure 12.1 wangii wadhan biyay – baskets of listening and respect (Goslett & Selkirk, 2023).

social rules are actualised rather than intellectualised" (Holmes & Jampijinpa, 2013, p. 18). If Western psychology embodies genuine relationships with Indigenous Australians, it can foster self-determination, healing and wellness. Furthermore, therapies that embrace Indigenous knowledges and holistic conceptualisations of the self as a unified, interconnected being with inherent sacredness have the potential to provide advantages for people from all backgrounds.

wangii wadhan biyay (Figure 12.1) as described here incorporates seven layers, each representing a body or basket of knowledge. However, we recognise the number of baskets as potentially limitless, given the rich and diverse knowledge systems and lived experiences of Indigenous Australians and the evolving and dynamic understandings of SEWB, and we hope that others will build on this model (Goslett & Selkirk, 2023). As a starting point, we present the following layers and will discuss each in turn:

1 Relational, Sacred Self
2 SEWB
3 Decolonisation
4 Relational Processes
5 Indigenous-Informed Care (Trauma- and Violence-Informed and Healing-Aware)
6 Indigenous Healing Practices
7 Deep Yarning

Relational, Sacred Self

The first basket is the crucial understanding that Indigenous Australian cultures hold autonomous individuality within relationalism and networks of belonging (Graham, 2023; Yunkaporta, 2019). Many Indigenous Australians embrace a selfhood that is inextricably linked to one's physical and social ecology, including family, kinship, community, ancestors, Country, spirit, and broader society (Dudgeon et al., 2022).Consistently, Indigenous Australian wisdoms teach an interdependence with and respect for all things, the need to consider human impact on other people, animals, beings and land. Interconnection and resultant belonging then provide a grounded, resourceful sense of being able to survive and flourish (Dudgeon et al., 2022). As the Gay'wu Group of Women write,

> For us, we balance as we care for Country, and it cares for us. But we are not separate from it. We are in kinship with it. This kinship, gurrutu, underpins who we are. It is between us Yolnu, with each other and the land and all its beings.
>
> (Gay'wu Group of Women, 2019, p. 79)

An example of this embedded selfhood is reflected in first-person pronouns that reference non-dual interpersonal relationship. The term *Ngal* from the Wik Mungkan language group is roughly interpreted as "us-two" (Yunkaporta, 2019). According to Yuin Elder Aunty Trish Ellis (personal communication, 2020), the Dhurga language contains a comparable term, *ngul*. Much more than "us", these pronouns encompass a synthesis of individuality that fosters a cooperative and unified sense of self, a unity that is then deeply intertwined with one's social and physical ecology.

Ethnocentric, psychocentric Euro-Western notions of the self, conversely, are largely recognised as individualistic and rationalist, perspectives that were and are influenced by prevailing, philosophical, cultural, religious, and socio-political systems (Kelaher et al., 2010; Shahjahan & Haverkos, 2011). Brigg and Graham (2020) trace Euro-Western self-conceptions back to the fall of Rome and spread of Christian ideologies. Philosophies of the European Enlightenment period then reinforced ideas of individualism, freedom and a preoccupation with one's inner self. Descartes' 17th-century proclamation, commonly translated as "I think, therefore I am", emphasised thought over emotion and cognitions over soul, creating a framework that some used to justify racial categorisations and hierarchies and colonial imperialism (Gergen, 1995; Mbembe, 2017). Concurrently, classical liberalism arose, promoting possessive individualism linked to capitalism, private property, and self-interest (Macpherson, 1962). It devalued societal obligations, fostered an identity centred around ownership and control, and generated essentialised knowledges that perpetuate stereotypes, racialisation and othering (Macpherson, 1962; Thomas-Olalde & Velho, 2011).

The legacies of Cartes and others continue to create divisions in Western framings of secular and sacred, and psychology has historically aligned with secularism and empiricism at the exclusion of diverse knowledge systems (Cunningham, 2015; Shahjahan & Haverkos, 2011). Moreover, modern psychology and religion were shaped by anthropological theories promoting biased views of human evolution from "primitive" to "civilized" peoples (Leahey, 2015; Reber, 2006; Shankar, 2020; Stolzenberg, 2010), assigning hierarchies of value on people and land, with all things evaluated on material or financial worth (Dudgeon et al., 2014; Tripcony, 2007).

Colonisers failed to comprehend the sophistication and depth of spirituality inherent in Indigenous Australian cultures, the deep reverence for all entities which allowed for a harmonious coexistence with Country in all its forms. Darwinian theories of "survival of the fittest" blinded them to the survival of the harmonious, whereby the assumption of stewardship responsibilities towards Country ensured peoples' sustainable survival for millennia. Colonial world views are ignorant of Indigenous Australian understandings of being which place generosity, interconnectedness and obligation above individual achievement and possessiveness. Indigenous Australians have long acknowledged interconnections with and between all beings, and revered land and Country, which encompasses all beings and forms. Everything is viewed as possessing vitality, living energy and spiritual significance, of having intrinsic sacred value (Redvers et al., 2020). As written by Gudanji Wakaja woman Debra Dank (2022), "I don't know how our mob knew about souls, just that they did, because our stories and our kujiga live inside each other, as well as out there across our country, and inside our bodies" (p. 10).

Despite the persistent harms caused by colonisation, Indigenous Australians have endured, maintained culture, connection and sacredness and are continually strengthening. Us-two persist in a synthesis of selfhood existing in relation to all that is, in a constant state of co-creation and co-becoming as a relational sacred self (Goslett, 2022). Further, there is an appreciation of the sentient, sacred essence of all: "…everyday things…are also sacred things, deep things, knowledgeable things, meaningful things. Sacred, yes, but not like a religion…Everything is sacred. We do not believe in this or that. We are those things" (Gay'wu Group of Women, 2019, p. 20). In profound contrast to "I think, therefore I am", Dr Mary Graham, Kombumerri and Wakka Wakka person and Adjunct Associate Professor in Political Science at the University of Queensland offers "I am located, therefore I am" (2014, 2023). Yuin woman and Indigenous Clinical Psychologist Mary Goslett offers: "Us-two are because everything is, and everything is sacred", a vital realisation essential to the healing of our people (Goslett, 2022).

Authors' Reflections on Relational, Sacred Self

Belle: I lived overseas for many years and when I returned to live on Country I was struck by an awakened felt-sense of belonging and place. This felt-sense was its strongest when I was on my own navigating coastal hiking trails. I noticed my body felt a sense of being taken care of and that I was in good company, like a welcome home hug from a family member. A warm reminder that my relationship to place remained intact even after many years of being away. When we welcome stories and expressions of interconnection/s, we are welcoming the relational-self, and all that it is connected to, to be an active participant in the therapeutic work.

Mary: When I work with Indigenous Australians in particular, I always want to understand how they feel about their connections to others, culture and Country. I know that there is very probably an intergenerational severing of belonging, and of the sense of relationality, as well as an experience of being positioned as less-than. So I listen for what gives their lives meaning, what helps them feel in relationship with others, and how these can be strengthened, because that is where they can start to feel the sacred again.

Social and Emotional Wellbeing

The concept of human wellbeing is a complex, multi-faceted construct very much determined by one's culture (Inglehart & Klingemann, 2000; Mathews, 2012). For many Indigenous Australians, it is a holistic concept whereby wellbeing is determined by interconnections of selfhood, ecology, kinship, spirituality, body, emotions, mind, community and culture; and, determined by social, historical and political contexts. This is reflected in the Social and Emotional Wellbeing framework (SWB), which is underpinned by the nine guiding principles from the formative *Ways Forward* (Swan & Raphael, 1995) report and developed by Indigenous psychologists. Culturally validated through national, grass-roots, community consultations, SEWB represents ancient knowledges and lived experiences of Indigenous Australians, emphasising empowerment and self-determination (Dudgeon et al., 2024; Gee et al., 2014). As stated by Yankunytjatjara Elder Uncle Bob Randall, "the interconnectedness of every living thing is not just an idea but a way of life" (2022). Wiradyuri cosmology speaks of interconnectedness of all things – animals, plants, people, skies and waters – and that without all things or Country we cannot exist, an ideology expressed in the word and construct of *yindyamarra* (personal communication, Leticia Harris, 2024). As with all the words and concepts we have introduced here, *yindyamarra* is "a word that is beyond just translation to English because it is not just a word; it is an idea, it is a philosophy, it is a way of living, it is a way of being…" (Grant as cited in Hall, 2023).

SEWB recognises that way of being and that wellbeing is Intrinsically linked domains which do not simply exist for an individual, but the self in relation to all that is. "It is always about being in relationship, intertwined and connected…" (Gay'wu Group of Women, 2019, p. 176). As articulated by Larrakia and Wadjigan woman and Indigenous psychologist Carmen Cubillo (2021), the SEWB model is an "attempt to harness the unharnessable. Everything is actually interconnected and flowing, and it is more something that you experience and feel rather than understand intellectually or comprehend with your mind. It is felt with the heart" (para. 18).

The seven identified domains reflect connection and belonging as vital to a positive sense of identity, health and wellbeing for Indigenous Australians (Dudgeon et al., 2022; Ridges et al., 2020). For many Indigenous Australians, they form the ground for social identity within a kinship group, mob or community, which facilitates engagement in cultural activities and practices that foster the growth of protective factors (Hunter et al., 2021). This relational and culturally embedded selfhood means family, kin and community are vital in an individual's healing, and in turn, healing and strength through belonging builds community cohesion (Dudgeon et al., 2022).

As discussed in Chapter 2 of this book, the seven domains of SEWB are:

- Body, recognising the significance of physical health and wellbeing.
- Mind and Emotions, acknowledging the importance of mental and emotional wellbeing, considering psychological aspects of wellness.
- Family and Kinship, highlighting the significance of familial relationships and connections to extended kinship networks.
- Community, emphasising the value of community relationships, belonging and social connections.
- Culture, acknowledging the central role of culture in promoting wellbeing and fostering a strong and positive Indigenous Australian identity.
- Country, recognising deep connections to Land and Country, emphasising the importance of the relationship with the natural environment and ecology.
- Spirituality and Ancestors, encompassing spiritual wellbeing and connections to ancestors, acknowledging the role of spirituality in the relational-self.

Bardi woman and Indigenous psychologist Professor Pat Dudgeon AM and colleagues note that "the experience and expression of the domains of SEWB can vary across the life span and between communities" (Dudgeon et al., 2017, p. 137), thereby allowing for each community's unique knowledge systems, histories and lived experiences (Dudgeon et al., 2024; Gee et al., 2014). It also reflects the understanding that issues in mental health often arise when there are imbalances in one or more interrelated domains, with wellness optimised when there is balance between them (Parker & Milroy, 2014a). Crucially, SEWB acknowledges the cumulative impact of social, political, cultural and historical determinants that shape health outcomes (Dudgeon et al., 2024; Gee et al., 2014), particularly colonisation. Colonisation is a traumatic, violent act that continues within Australian systems and processes, and Western psychologies, entrenched in dualistic power differentials, are embedded in such systems which shape a complex web of racism and oppression towards Indigenous Australians. Therefore, psychology must be decolonised at all levels.

Authors' Reflections on Social & Emotional Wellbeing

Belle: SEWB has been embodied by Indigenous Australians for thousands of years and continues to evolve in contemporary contexts. Each person, family and community has their place-based, self-determined and diverse expression/s of SEWB. Exploring the different dimensions collaboratively is a strength-based way to privilege culture, work relationally, strengthen empowerment and honour the lived experiences of Indigenous Australians.

Mary: I am constantly curious about clients' connections and disconnections, the places where their domains of connection are unbalanced. We work together to find balance, to see where their connections have been disrupted, to strengthen those we can and be curious about what wellbeing means for them and what they want for themselves.

Decolonisation

Colonisation, falsely legitimised through anthropological, religious and capitalist theories, reinforced hierarchical and value-laden evaluations of humanity and assumed superiority. Colonisers strategically enacted ethnocide and genocide against Indigenous Australians then forced survivors onto missions and reserves and kidnapped children under the façade of "civilising" those with light-enough skin to be seen as somewhat redeemable (Goslett, 2022). These children were subjected to all the horrors human beings have in their arsenal, and then involuntarily sent away as "indentured labour" (the wages for which were never received). The decimation to Indigenous Australian culture and belonging was significant, and the wounds for many Indigenous Australians are ongoing, reinforced by contemporary social and political structures (Parker & Milroy, 2014b).

Unquestioned ideas of supremacy have not only been subsumed into Australia's systems but also the collective unconscious. Paired with the unacknowledged privileges that come with power and the fear of possible threats to that power, attempting to examine our unconscious bias brings pain, defensiveness and denial (Goslett, 2022). It takes courage to face that pain, to begin to decolonise our individual and systemic ways of doing and being, to commence redressing the resultant inequities. Acknowledging and dismantling the "whitewashing" of Western psychologies takes willingness and determination. As Cubillo (2021) explains; "To grow, we need to walk together into the discomfort" (para. 11).

Decolonisation requires developing culturally responsive and culturally safe praxis by tolerating this discomfort and engaging in critical self-reflexivity and examination of our core values and unconscious internalised attitudes, together with understanding the impact these attitudes have on Indigenous Australians (Brockman & Dudgeon, 2020). As written by Smith et al. (2022), "Cultural responsiveness, within the spirit of the [APS] apology is about listening more and talking less and working collaboratively with clients" (p. 2). It is within this reflexive space that psychologists can begin to unmask and unlearn their internalised colonial attitudes that perpetuate harm, and then identify where colonisation continues to emerge within systems and organisations (Smith et al., 2022; Wilson, 2014). This must include centring culturally appropriate models that encompass holistic models such as SEWB (Dudgeon et al., 2024; Gee et al., 2014) and decentring Western models of research and praxis informed by biomedical paradigms and the medicalisation of mental health and distress (Moreton-Robinson, 2004).

Decolonisation, then, involves moving towards a holistic approach that considers communal resilience in the face of systemic inequalities; recognises the influence of social determinants of health and emphasises Indigenous, community-based interventions and support systems. Indigenous Australian knowledges, belief systems and relational processes offer culturally grounded ways of engaging in critical self-reflexivity and transformational change much needed in psychology. Further, decolonisation invites psychologists to move beyond what is traditionally seen as their scope of practice and incorporate healing which encompasses critical consciousness, radical hope, strength and resistance, cultural authenticity and self-knowledge, and collectivism (French et al., 2020) often traced to the work of Freire (1970).

Authors' Reflections on Decolonisation

Mary: Besides constantly being shocked at how much I need to decolonise myself and my assumptions, I include advocacy in my work with clients. I work with them to access basic resources such as housing and health services, but wherever possible work to help them find a voice and agency in issues that affect them so that I don't unconsciously colonise their capacity.

Belle: Decolonising practice to me means looking for any and all opportunities to decentre Whiteness, and centring cultural ways of knowing and being. For example, psychological language can be quite oppressive. I stay away from terms such as "case study" or "client formulation" that reinforce power differentials. I honour the sacredness of peoples stories and histories and prefer language like "lived experience" and "culturally informed understandings".

Relational Processes

There are many Indigenous Australian relational processes that can facilitate decolonised practice in clinical, therapeutic and research spaces. We identify four:

Ganma (Two-Way Knowledge Sharing)

Indigenous psychology holds the hope of "two-way learning", strengthening the meeting of Indigenous and non-Indigenous paths (Purdie et al., 2012). This meeting has been called *ganma* in Yolngu Matha languages in Arnhem Land. The word refers to a line of foam that results from the local confluence of a freshwater river and ocean saltwater. It has become a metaphor for the meeting of non-Indigenous and Indigenous ways of being and doing, and the benefits from the interactions between the two (Marika, 1992). As described by Sharmil and colleagues (2021) "Ganma [involves] each person being mindful of the other's individual and combined experiences, and their contribution to the collaboration" (p. 6). It is a process that requires respect and gentleness, just as the *ganma,* the foam, must be held lightly or it will evaporate. The knowledge-making in *ganma* retains the identities and memories of the individuals who contributed to its creation while generating new knowledge that is not owned by any one individual but shared and valued by all. Within the context of psychological practice, it requires Western-trained psychologists to hold their knowledge lightly and balance it with coexisting ancient truths.

Deep Listening

To enter *ganma*, one must practise deep listening. *Dadirri*, a word and concept of the Ngan'gikurunggkurr peoples of the Daly River region in the Northern Territory, means a state of inner, deep listening and quiet, still awareness (Ungunmerr-Baumann et al., 2022). *Dadirri* is a way of life, a spirituality and a practice of reflection and contemplation that can lead to a greater understanding of the natural world and one's place within it; a heart-based practice essential to respectful communication and the building of authentic relationships (Ungunmerr-Baumann et al., 2022).

Dadirri has counterparts in numerous Indigenous Australian cultures across the continent (Atkinson, 2002). *wangii* is a word from the Dhurga language of the Yuin (Yuwinj) Nation on Australia's mid- to south-east coast. Yuin Elder Patricia Ellis (personal communication, 2020) said it was used by her mother and Elders to refer to someone who was respectful and open to knowledge, with that respect and openness leading to being given more knowledge. It also means walking with half of you in the Spirit world, listening to Ancestors and Country (Goslett, 2022).

Winanga-li, as described by Kamilaroi man and Indigenous psychologist Dr Peter Smith, also goes beyond just hearing the words of others to suspending one's answers, creating a safe space where meaning can be jointly held. As Smith points out,

> One of the important micro-credentials of counselling is the ability to listen, and listening is fundamental to Aboriginal and Torres Strait Islander culture and part of our spirituality... Winanga-li means more than listening and hearing the words. It means that I sit with you and understand you.
>
> (University of New England, 2022, para. 5)

Moreover, it is an equalising stance that facilitates the practice of cultural humility and cultural safety, requiring practitioners to suspend their own conditioning and allowing the client their cultural and personal expertise. *Dadirri*, *wangii* and *winanga-li* are integral in developing reciprocal, respectful interactions with the potential for healing (Sharmil et al., 2021). If grounded in authenticity, they can influence behavioural change and mitigate trauma by promoting deep acceptance, reciprocity and connection.

Dadirri has informed a trauma recovery model and healing practice developed by Morris et al. (2022) in collaboration with Jiman/Bundjalung woman and Emeritus Professor Judy Atkinson, whereby deep listening facilitates effective therapeutic outcomes "attained through an individualistic or in a relational engagement context" (p. 1). It involves therapeutic phases akin to the foundational trauma model of Judith Herman (1992), with each stage including both individual and relational therapeutic elements.

It is vital to appreciate that deep listening, such as *Dadirri*, is a way of life and relating, rather than a technique or strategy that can simply be added to a Western psychological approach. It must be understood in terms of its cultural and historical context and include comprehension of the determinants affecting SEWB. To authentically engage in deep listening, there must be an appreciation of the relationalism of Indigenous Australian cultures, where everything and everyone has value, the possibility of continual renewal is inherent in all aspects of life, and healing can flow to all – individual, family, community and Country.

Yarning

Yarning, like deep listening, is a culturally grounded process of conversing and relating for many Indigenous Australians. Much more than a conversation, it is a structured sharing of stories and the development of knowledge according to strong cultural protocols and principles embodying respect, cooperation, honour and spirituality (Lin et al., 2016). Most importantly, yarning brings all parties into relationship and accountability, embedding reciprocal-expected outcomes and responsibilities (Fredericks et al., 2011; Walker et al., 2014). In the yarning process, important knowledge is embedded within the story being told, and the listener has a responsibility to hold the information being shared and to make meaning with integrity. As Tyson Yunkaporta (2019) from the Apalech Clan says, it is a deep engagement "encompassing mind, body, heart and spirit" (p. 156). Developed as a decolonising methodology that has significant research, clinical and therapeutic applications, yarning challenges Eurocentric notions of knowledge production, allowing Indigenous Australians to control their own narratives and promote self-determination (Lipscombe et al., 2021).

Clinical yarning is a culturally responsive framework that has been developed for health practice that marries cultural ways of communication with medical understandings of health (Lin et al., 2016), enabling the reclamation of autonomy lost through coloniality (Burke et al., 2022). It has three interrelated phases: social (building rapport and relational safety); diagnostic (reciprocal interchange of information and storytelling to formulate a co-created assessment and health care plan); and management (employs stories to increase understanding and participation recovery) (Burke et al., 2022).

Atkinson et al. (2021) break down yarning even further, additionally identifying family yarning and cross-cultural yarning. Family yarning is where relationality and connection regarding kinship, spirituality and land is established. Cross-cultural yarning involves the meeting of Indigenous Australian and non-Indigenous peoples in the co-creation of a third space. Together, these different forms of yarning align with Indigenous Australians' lived experiences and relational ontologies and are likely to enhance experiences of cultural safety and decolonising practices in research, health care and therapeutic spaces. As discussed later, *deep yarning* is also being articulated as a distinct culturally grounded therapeutic praxis (Goslett & Selkirk, 2023).

Respect (ngumbudhaa and yindyamarra)

ngumbudhaa from the Dhurga language is a word that refers to like, love and respect (Aunty Trish Ellis, personal communication, 2020). Similarly, Yindyamarra is a Wiradyuri word and construct that means respecting, be gentle, be polite, honour, do slowly (Grant & Rudder 2010; personal communication, Leticia Harris, 2024). It guides Wiradyuri peoples' "proper way" living. Wiradyuri man Stan Grant explains "Yindyamarra. Quietness, kindness, respect. Strength in that quietness strength in that kindness, and strength in that respect" (Grant cited in Hall, 2023).

Respect is inherent to *ganma*, deep listening and yarning, and is integral to many Indigenous Australians' ways of being and relating, Law and lore, spirituality and belonging, and is offered to all things as sentient and deserving of regard (Poelina et al., 2022). Lack of respect for land and Country has led to the anthropocene age, this time of mass extinctions of plant and animal species, pollution of land and oceans and catastrophic climate change. The continued dualisms between human and nature, the rights of some humans over others and the subjugation of knowledges by Western economistic empiricism have led to this crisis, and deep-time understandings of respectful, relational ontologies can alter this trajectory.

Authors' Reflections on Relational Processes

Belle: Participating in yarning circles has taught me that authentic truth-witnessing of peoples stories and lived experiences requires a listening from an integrated whole-self, including our senses, identities and own relational-self. It is a relational experience of listening from one's inner being. The shared understandings that comes from this listening is profoundly richer compared to a clinical stance of expert-subject.

Mary: The Australian Psychological Society's 2016 Apology to Aboriginal and Torres Strait Islander peoples included a commitment to "Listening more and talking less". This encapsulates relational processes for me, and the need to drop any expert stance and simply bring my beingness to meet those of my clients. It's not that I don't have expertise, but that is backgrounded, and the personhood and needs of my client are foregrounded. We then work towards the co-creation of a space of healing and connection.

Indigenous-Informed Care (Trauma- and Violence-Informed)

The trauma of colonisation has had cross-generational consequences and continues to cause profound hurt, resulting in "trauma trails" across Australia (Atkinson, 2002). As stated by Indigenous psychologists Graham Gee and colleagues (2014), "This often translates into complex client and family presentations that involve multiple stressors and issues" (p. 62) and requires Indigenous-informed responses intrinsically imbued with belief in possibilities of healing. Such responses must centre the wellbeing of Indigenous Australians within health systems; offer culturally safe and respectful relationships; understand the dynamics of trauma and its impacts and the ongoing violences of coloniality; deconstruct power dynamics and privilege; empower Indigenous Australians in every aspect of their wellness and healing journeys and ensure coordinated, holistic care for individuals, families and communities (Cubillo, 2021).

However, health and power inequities continue to be maintained, systematically oppressing and preventing many Indigenous Australians to maximise opportunities to grow and thrive. As said, Western psychologies, entrenched in dualistic power differentials and principles, are embedded in systems that shape a complex web of embedded racism that continues to traumatise. Deep colonising narratives and assumptions persist and continue to manifest in systemic inequities, violence, racism and intersecting assaults on identity in Australia. These narratives persist because of a "... discourse of tolerance [that] works to position white people as racially disembodied while simultaneously exercising their white race privilege" (Moreton-Robinson & Nicoll, 2006, p. 155). Racism permeates our institutions, structures, practices and policies, as well as manifesting in interpersonal interactions and intrapersonal internalisations (Ben et al., 2022; Jones, 2000). Persistent exposure to racism and racially based inequities has detrimental effects on physical, emotional, mental and social wellbeing, resulting in chronic illness, higher mortality rates and psychological distress (Kairuz et al., 2021).

The individualisation of trauma in Western psychology is a further manifestation of racism, perpetuating ongoing violence towards Indigenous Australian peoples. Burrage et al. (2022) explain, "To decolonise itself as a discipline and better serve Indigenous communities, the field of psychology must open up to understandings of trauma, loss, and healing that decentralise the individual" (p. 27). Western psychology largely only offers treatment for psychopathologies, fails to address social ecologies perpetuating injury and trauma, pathologises understandable responses to structural harm and disregards psychology's complicity in the maintenance of racist understandings. As written by Kabi Kabi and South Sea Islander women Dr Nicole Tujague and Kelleigh Ryan (2021), "Looking through a trauma lens means changing your focus from a deficit model of what's wrong with that person to a strengths-based model of what is the story of that person" (p. 46). Moreover, a strength-based perspective acknowledges and even celebrates ways in which many Indigenous Australians have also maintained a vision of growth and healing and continue to offer an understanding of the essential and equal humanity of all peoples, to strive for shared power and resources and social justice.

Holistic care requires psychologists to "...embark on the transformative process of opening one's heart to recognise [Indigenous] worldviews as genuine and valid" (Cubillo, 2021, para. 14). This transformation must be supported by critical self-reflection and systemic examination, decentring racial and psychocentric constructions and creating cultural safety by considering "sociocentric, ecocentric, and cosmocentric terms [that] place deep importance on healing through connection to family, culture, and community" (Burrage et al., 2022, p. 27). Vitally, Indigenous-informed care, by recognising relational constructs of selfhood and Indigenous Australians' ways of knowing, being and doing, rightfully positioning Indigenous Australians in their strength and wisdoms, not just viewing them through the lens of colonial deficits. To be culturally responsive and trauma-informed means to believe in the philosophy of *Dadirri*, in the "deep inner spring" of all peoples; in their dignity and wisdom; and in their wholeness and capacity to flourish and heal.

To practice from a stance that is Indigenous-informed, as well as trauma- and violence-informed, is therefore a multilayered and complex process that incorporates Indigenous knowledge, science-informed understandings of traumatic consequences and decolonising praxis. It is not a treatment protocol or adaptation of a manualised programme. Rather, it involves deep listening and heart-based care. Moreover, these ways of knowing, being and doing, developed over millennia, offer a sovereign remedy for the increasingly global, neoliberal, capitalist systems with fascist tendencies that embed particular forms of subjectification. In Indigenous Australian cultures, power and resources are shared rather than hoarded, and individual autonomy stands within relationalism, philosophies that could mitigate the increasing structures of power and control we are experiencing.

Authors' Reflections on Indigenous-Informed Care

Belle: A vital element of Indigenous-informed care is taking considerable time to connect with the histories and lived experiences of families, communities and places in which we are working. The historical and contemporary contexts that many Indigenous Australians navigate cannot be separated from individual experience. Great care must be taken to contextualise experiences within the broader ecological context of the determinants of health.

Mary: Heart-based practice is essential to me. In my language group, Dhurga, *ngara-din wangiii* means to "hear from your deep knowing" – hear with your heart and body as well as your mind. I try to both use and invite that, so that clients can learn to hear their own truths and needs and strengths beyond their trauma.

Indigenous Healing Practices

Within Australia, diverse regions, Countries and Nations possess unique place-based knowledges, healing traditions and practices. Understanding the significance of place is fundamental to Indigenous Australian wellbeing and healing. Place-based Indigenous healing practices and programmes have emerged from generations of wisdom and knowledge systems deeply specific to that community, culture, Country and ancestry. Further, all these factors emerge and are indivisible from spirituality and sacredness (Dudgeon & Bray, 2018). They cannot be manualised or replicated, are often unable to be generalised to other Indigenous Australian groups and most likely cannot be applied by non-Indigenous psychologists. Indigenous healing has been said to be the "most efficacious way to assist distressed First Nations individuals due to the inherent potency of these traditions achieved through long pre-contact histories of therapeutic refinement" (Gone, 2013, p. 697). Therefore, Indigenous healing practices must be treated with the utmost respect and sacredness.

Indigenous healing programmes can and should coexist with psychology. The *Gayaa Dhuwi (Proud Spirit) Declaration* encourages the "best of both worlds", whereby Indigenous and Western approaches can co-occur (National Aboriginal and Torres Strait Islander Leadership in Mental Health, 2015). Consistent with this, the integration of Indigenous healing practices and Western methodologies has been identified by the Healing Foundation as an essential component in effective healing programmes (McKendrick et al., 2017, p. 2).

One example is the *Ngangkari*, the traditional healers of the Ngaanyatjarra, Pitjantjatjara and Yankunytjatjara in the Western desert of Central Australia. The Ngangkari have supported individual and community physical and emotional wellness for thousands of years, and now provide healing practices in community, clinical and hospital settings (NPY Women's Council Aboriginal Corporation, 2013). Dudgeon and Walker (2015) explain; "[The] Ngangkari focus on both physical pain relief and mental wellbeing, putting the spirit 'in the right place' or restoring the spiritual balance of someone who is not well through massage, coaxing, and using special powerful sacred tools" (p. 290). Such sacred practices can only be held by traditional healers and knowledge keepers. Therefore, partnerships between traditional healers and health services are fundamental to Indigenous healing and decolonising practices.

It is our experience and understanding that all psychologists must be aware of the presence of place-based healing programmes and practices (though psychologists will likely not know the sacred details of the practices) and be willing to support Indigenous Australians to connect with these programmes if they have identified it would be helpful alongside therapeutic work (Goslett & Selkirk, 2023).

Authors' Reflections on Indigenous Healing Practices

Belle: Working relationally, from Indigenous-informed and holistic stance, means there are practices that facilitate healing that psychology is not able to provide, explain or quantify. Cultural respect and humility, foundational in culturally responsive practice, means prioritising culturally based conceptualisations and ways of engagement as determined by the people we work with. Culture and cultural practices are brought to the forefront of the relationship and engagement.

Mary: Whenever I can I access NGangkaris and encourage my clients to do so. I am also constantly updating myself on programmes and practice that Indigenous Australians are developing, to learn from them, and to make sure I haven't gone off on a singular, individualised path without cultural grounding.

Deep Yarning

The dehumanisation and dispossession inflicted by colonial society has resulted in many Indigenous Australian peoples experiencing a disconnected from culture and Country; fractured holistic conceptions of selfhood, identity and kinship systems; and, ruptured multi-dimensional attachments. As aptly stated by Deninu K'ue woman and scholar Nicole Redvers and colleagues (2022), "When a sense of reverence for ourselves and our community is lost, so is our sense of belonging" (p. e159). The fore-mentioned *Dadirri*-based phasic approach to the mitigation of trauma (Morris et al., 2022) offers renewed reverence in recognising the "bubbling spring" (Ungunmerr-Baumann et al., 2022) in all peoples that hold the potential for growth, healing and flourishing. We offer *Deep Yarning* (Goslett & Selkirk, 2023) as a newly articulated culturally grounded therapeutic praxis that can complement this model by co-creating a space that holds *wangii* and recognises the sacred beingness and relationality of the healing frame.

Deep Yarning is a relational pedagogy, a shift towards a grounded, experiential and embodied inquiry into the connections between individuals, communities and their ecology. It aims to promote a sense of connectedness and responsibility towards self, others and all beings by curious inquiry into "the richness of the present, which is inclusive of the past in knowledge, memories, repeated actions and habits, and constantly allows for the eventualities of the future" (Poelina et al., 2022, p. 4) through exploration with direct experiences, sensory awareness, emotional responses and personal reflection. This includes an understanding of historical and continuing injustices, acts of violence and oppression towards Indigenous Australians, gently holding knowledges and histories with respect and humility and practising *gamma* (Goslett & Selkirk, 2023).

Deep Yarning is a holistic, flexible approach that meets the unique needs and circumstances of each individual, family or community; it is not a standardised treatment protocol. Entering a deep, therapeutic, yarning space requires a non-judgemental and empathic environment, allowing others to explore their responses without feeling criticised or invalidated; a space where the psychologist is an integral part of the process, but not controlling it, bringing expertise but not holding the "expert" position. As stated by Jonathan Ferrier, "Indigenous people are very scientific – it's just that our science includes the heart" (cited in Funes, 2020, para. 14) and *Deep Yarning* is an approach arising from practice-based evidence and ancient and contemporary Indigenous knowledge systems. Its application may vary depending on the psychologist and their training and may draw from Cognitive Behavioural Therapy, Dialectical Behaviour Therapy, Schema Therapy, Narrative Therapy, mindfulness, expressive arts, psychodynamic, sensorimotor and somatic approaches. Consistent with this, Indigenous scholars and practitioners have suggested that Western psychological approaches can be applied if incorporated into a broader framework underpinned by Indigenous paradigms (Dudgeon & Kelly, 2014; O'Shea et al., 2024). The goal is to facilitate healing, integration and personal growth by working with culturally grounded, adaptive and resilient response repertoire based on their own innate sacred potential.

Authors' Reflections on Deep Yarning

Mary: Deep yarning for me means I have held space for the deep inner spring of the client and of myself, and the co-creation of a place of exploration and transformation. I get out of my own way and I listen for the truths that arise between us. I still bring my expertise, pairing it with a belief in the process and healing through relationship.

Belle: Deep yarning is the space where the baskets of listening and respect intersect, the layering of the embodied knowledges and approaches, by all peoples in the therapeutic dialogue. This embodiment comes together over time and through relationship, and together we move into a space where co-creation of knowledges and lived experiences foster flourishing, empowerment and self-determination.

Conclusion

In this chapter, we have offered our collective learnings and perspectives as Aboriginal women and practising clinical psychologists. Our hope is that the reader has developed a comprehension that psychological care with Indigenous Australians must be grounded in Indigenous ways of knowing, being and doing, and an understanding of the determinants that affect all. We present *wangii wadhan biyay* as a culturally grounded framework of how this can be understood and put into practice; a dynamic interplay of theory, praxis and constructs that if incorporated can lead to effective, culturally safe, psychological healing for Indigenous Australians (Goslett & Selkirk, 2023). In our experience, when all aspects of *wangii wadhan biyay* are embraced, Western psychological approaches can be successfully merged with Indigenous Australian perspectives in psychology (Goslett & Selkirk, 2023). This integration is most effective when rooted in Indigenous ways of understanding, existence and action, and when the Indigenous Australians we collaborate with are open to such methods for comprehending their personal experiences and addressing trauma. Therapies that integrate Indigenous Australian views of the self as an interconnected entity with innate sanctity can be beneficial for all peoples. We invite all psychologists to consider *ganma* in their own work. To question their own ways of knowing, being and doing. An ongoing process of decolonising and endeavour means engage and stay open to learning from other cultures and intersectionalities.

Acknowledgement of Country and Positionality

We acknowledge the Elders and Sovereign Custodians of the lands and waters upon which the authors humbly live, work and play, those of the Eora and the Noongar nations. We recognise the sustained connection that Aboriginal and Torres Strait Islander peoples (hereafter Indigenous

Australians) have to land, culture and spirit and recognise the strength, resilience and diversity of all our Nations. Within the relationalism of Indigenous Australian peoples, cultures and communities, we recognise the immense diversity of Indigenous Australian identities, place-based knowledges and sovereignty.

We are two Aboriginal women and clinical psychologists. The knowledges shared here are our learnings and experiences from our positionalities as Aboriginal women and practising psychologists in Australia. We are grateful for the dedication of knowledge holders that have informed our understanding, and to whose wisdoms we hope to add, and it is hoped other Indigenous peoples will add to this discussion and contribute to its evolution.

The title of this paper honours Dhurga language of the Yuin (Yuwinj) Nation, reflecting the teachings held by the first author. Our intention is to highlight the interconnection between language and knowledge systems. We respectfully and humbly recognise the diversity of Indigenous Australian languages and place-based knowledges, including the variations of meanings and embodiment of culture.

References

American Psychological Association. (2010). *Task force on Indigenous psychology*. Retrieved January 13, 2021, from https://www.indigenouspsych.org/

Atkinson, J. (2002). *Trauma trails, recreating song lines the transgenerational effects of trauma in Indigenous Australia*. Spinifex Press.

Atkinson, P., Baird, M., & Adams, K. (2021). Are you really using yarning research? Mapping social and family yarning to strengthen yarning research quality. *AlterNative: An International Journal of Indigenous Peoples*, *17*(2), 191–201. https://doi.org/10.1177/11771801211015442

Ben, J., Elias, A., Issaka, A., Truong, M., Dunn, K., Sharples, R., McGarty, C., Walton, J., Mansouri, F., & Denson, N. (2022). Racism in Australia: A protocol for a systematic review and meta-analysis. *Systematic Reviews*, *11*(1), 47. https://doi.org/10.1186/s13643-022-01919-2

Brigg, M., & Graham, M. (2020, July 20). The relevance of Aboriginal political concepts (3): Autonomous selfhood. *ABC Religion & Ethics*. https://www.abc.net.au/religion/aboriginal-political-concepts-autonomous-selfhood/12472310

Brockman, R., & Dudgeon, P. (2020). Indigenous clinical psychology in Australia: A decolonising social–emotional well-being approach. In P. Rhodes (Ed.), *Beyond the psychology industry* (pp. 83–93). Springer. https://doi.org/10.1007/978-3-030-33762-9_8

Burke, A. W., Welch, S., Power, T., Lucas, C., & Moles, R. J. (2022). Clinical yarning with Aboriginal and/or Torres Strait Islander peoples—A systematic scoping review of its use and impacts. *Systematic Reviews*, *11*(1), 129. https://doi.org/10.1186/s13643-022-02008-0

Burrage, R. L., Momper, S. L., & Gone, J. P. (2022). Beyond trauma: Decolonizing understandings of loss and healing in the Indian Residential School system of Canada. *Journal of Social Issues*, *78*, 27–52. https://doi.org/10.1111/josi.12455

Ciofalo, N., Dudgeon, P., & Nikora, L. W. (2022). Indigenous community psychologies, decolonization, and radical imagination within ecologies of knowledges. *American Journal of Community Psychology, 69*(3–4), 283–293. https://doi.org/10.1002/ajcp.12583

Cubillo, C. (2021). Trauma-informed care: Culturally responsive practice working with Aboriginal and Torres Strait Islander communities. *InPsych*, *43*(3). https://psychology.org.au/for-members/publications/inpsych/2021/august-special-issue-3/trauma-informed-care

Cunningham, P. (2015). Empirical rationalism and transpersonal empiricism: Bridging the two epistemic cultures of transpersonal psychology. *The Journal of Transpersonal Psychology*, *47*(1), 83–120.

Dank, D. (2022). *We come with this place*. Bonnier Echo.

Darnett, E., Peters, A., & Thielking, M. (2024). Psychologists' experiences towards culturally responsive practices to strengthen social and emotional wellbeing with Aboriginal and Torres Strait Islander clients. *Australian Journal of Psychology*, *76*(1), 1–20, https://doi.org/10.1080/00049530.2024.2356116

Dudgeon, P., & Bray, A. (2018). Indigenous healing practices in Australia. *Women & Therapy*, *41*(1–2), 97–113. https://doi.org/10.1080/02703149.2017.1324191

Dudgeon, P., & Bray, A. (2023). The indigenous turn: Epistemic justice, Indigenous knowledge systems, and social and emotional well-being. In J. Ravulo, K. Olcoń, T. Dune, A. Workman, & P. Liamputtong (Eds.), *Handbook of critical whiteness*. Springer. https://doi.org/10.1007/978-981-19-1612-0_31-1

Dudgeon, P., Bray, A., D'costa, B., & Walker, R. (2017). Decolonising psychology: Validating social and emotional wellbeing. *Australian Psychologist*, *52*(4), 316–325. https://doi.org/10.1111/ap.12294

Dudgeon, P., Derry, K., Mascall, C., & Ryder, A. (2022). Understanding Aboriginal models of selfhood: The national empowerment project's cultural, social, and emotional wellbeing program in Western Australia. *International Journal Environmental Research Public Health*, *19*(7), 1–17. https://doi.org/10.3390/ijerph19074078

Dudgeon, P., Gibson, C., Walker, R., Bray, A., Agung-Igusti, R., Derry, K., Gray, P., McPhee, R., Sutherland, S., & Gee, G. (2024). *Social and emotional wellbeing: A review*. Lowitja Institute. https://doi.org/10.48455/4f9e-3v29

Dudgeon, P., & Kelly, K. (2014). Contextual factors for research on psychological therapies for Aboriginal Australians. *Australian Psychologist*, *49*(1), 8–13. https://doi.org/10.1111/ap.12030

Dudgeon, P., Rickwood, D., Garvey, D., & Gridley, H. (2014). A history of Indigenous psychology. In P. Dudgeon, H. Milroy, & R. Walker (Eds.), *Working together: Aboriginal and Torres Strait Islander mental health and wellbeing principles and practice* (pp. 39–54). Commonwealth of Australia.

Dudgeon, P., & Walker, R. (2015). Decolonising Australian psychology: Discourses, strategies, and practice. *Journal of Social and Political Psychology*, *3*(1), 276–297. https://doi.org/10.5964/jspp.v3i1.126

Fredericks, B., Adams, K., Finlay, S. M., Fletcher, G., Andy, S., Briggs, L., Briggs, L., & Hall, R. (2011). Engaging the practice of yarning in action research. *ALAR: Action Learning and Action Research Journal*, *17*(2), 7–19. https://alarj.alarassociation.org/index.php/alarj/article/view/29

Freire, P. (1970). *Pedagogy of the oppressed*. Continuum.

French, B. H., Lewis, J. A., Mosley, D. V., Adames, H. Y., Chavez-Dueñas, N. Y., Chen, G. A., & Neville, H. A. (2020). Toward a psychological framework of radical healing in communities of color. *The Counseling Psychologist*, *48*(1), 14–46. https://doi.org/10.1177/0011000019843506

Funes, V. (2020). The land's first caretakers. *Atmos*. Retrieved May 9, 2025, from https://atmos.earth/jonathan-ferrier-indigenous-knowledge-public-lands-caretakers-the-frontline/

Gay'wu Group of Women. (2019). *Songspirals. Sharing women's wisdom of Country through songlines*. Allen & Unwin.

Gee, G., Dudgeon, P., Schultz, C., Hart, A., & Kelly, K. (2014). Aboriginal and Torres Strait Islander social and emotional wellbeing. In P. Dudgeon, H. Milroy, & R. Walker (Eds.), *Working together: Aboriginal and Torres Strait Islander mental health and wellbeing principles and practice* (pp. 55–68). Commonwealth of Australia.

Geerlings, L. R. C., Thompson, C. L., Bouma, R., & Hawkins, R. (2018). Cultural competence in clinical psychology training: A qualitative investigation of student and academic experiences. *Australian Psychologist*, *53*(2), 161–170. https://doi.org/10.1111/ap.12291

Gergen, M. (1995). Postmodern, post-Cartesian positionings on the subject of psychology. *Theory & Psychology*, *5*(3), 361–368. https://doi.org/10.1177/0959354395053003

Gone, J. P. (2013). Redressing First Nations historical trauma: Theorizing mechanisms for Indigenous culture as mental health treatment. *Transcultural Psychiatry*, *50*(5), 683–706. https://doi.org/10.1177/1363461513487669

Goslett, M. (2022, November 4). Shut up and listen [Conference Presentation]. *APS College of Clinical Neuropsychology*, Sydney, NSW.

Goslett, M., & Selkirk, B. (2023, September 11–15). *wangii wadhan biyay* (Baskets of listening and respect) [Conference Presentation]. *Healing Our Spirits Worldwide Conference*, Vancouver, British Columbia, Canada.

Graham, M. (2014). Aboriginal notions of relationality and positionalism: A reply to Weber. *Global Discourse*, *4*(1), 17–22. https://doi.org/10.1080/23269995.2014.895931

Graham, M. (2023). The law of obligation, aboriginal ethics: Australia becoming, Australia dreaming. *Parrhesia*, *37*, 1–21. https://parrhesiajournal.org/wp-content/uploads/2023/06/the-law-of-obligation-aboriginal-ethics-australia-becoming-australia-dreaming_mary-graham.pdf

Grant, S., & Rudder, J. (2010). *A new Wiradjuri dictionary.* Restoration House.

Hall, A. (2023, May 23). Stan grant referred to Yindyamarra while signing off from Q+A. *Wh*at does it mean? *SBS News*. https://www.sbs.com.au/news/article/stan-grant-referred-to-yindyamarra-while-signing-off-from-q-a-what-does-it-mean/ochuweq0x

Herman, J. (1992). *Trauma and recovery: The aftermath of violence – From domestic abuse to political terror*. Basic Books.

Holmes, C. C., & Jampijinpa, W. (2013). Law for country: The structure of Warlpiri ecological knowledge and its application to natural resource management and ecosystem stewardship. *Ecology and Society*, *18*(3). https://doi.org/10.5751/ES-05537-180319

Hunter, S.-A., Skouteris, H., & Morris, H. (2021). A conceptual model of protective factors within Aboriginal and Torres Strait Islander culture that build strength. *Journal of Cross-Cultural Psychology*, *52*(8–9), 726–751. https://doi.org/10.1177/00220221211046310

Inglehart, R., & Klingemann, H.-D. (2000). Genes, culture, democracy, and happiness. In E. Diener, & E. M. Suh (Eds.), *Culture and subjective well-being* (pp. 165–183). The MIT Press.

Jones, C. P. (2000). Levels of racism: A theoretic framework and a gardener's tale. *American Journal of Public Health*, *90*(8), 1212. https://doi.org/10.2105/ajph.90.8.1212

Kairuz, C. A., Casanelia, L. M., Bennett-Brook, K., Coombes, J., & Yadav, U. N. (2021). Impact of racism and discrimination on physical and mental health among Aboriginal and Torres Strait Islander peoples living in Australia: A systematic scoping review. *BMC Public Health*, *21*, 1–16. https://doi.org/10.1186/s12889-021-11363-x

Kelaher, M., Ferdinand, A., Paradies, Y., & Exeter, D. (2010). The role of racism in the health and wellbeing of Aboriginal and Torres Strait Islander people. *Australian Journal of Primary Health*, *16*(3), 159–166. https://doi.org/10.5694/mja13.10503

Leahey, T. H. (2015). *A history of psychology: From antiquity to modernity*. Routledge.

Leticia, Harris, (2024). Wiradjuri Nation, New South Wales, Australia. *Personal communication*, 1.

Lin, I., Green, C., & Bessarab, D. (2016). 'Yarn with me': Applying clinical yarning to improve clinician–patient communication in Aboriginal health care. *Australian Journal of Primary Health*, *22*, 377–382. https://doi.org/10.1071/PY16051

Lipscombe, T. A., Hendrick, A., Dzidic, P. L., Garvey, D. C., & Bishop, B. (2021). Directions for research practice in decolonising methodologies: Contending with paradox. *Methodological Innovations*, *14*(1), 1–11. https://doi.org/10.1177/20597991211006288

Macpherson, C. B. (1962). *The political theory of possessive individualism: Hobbes to Locke.* Oxford Handbooks.

Marika, R. (1992). Always together, Yaka Gana: Participatory research at Yirrkala as part of the development of a Yolngu education. *Convergence*, *25*(1), 23–39.

Mathews, G. (2012). Happiness, culture, and context. *International Journal of Wellbeing*, *2*(4), 299–312. https://doi.org/10.5502/ijw.v2.i4.2

Mbembe, A. (2017). *Critique of black reason*. Duke University Press.

McConnochie, K., Ranzijn, R., Hodgson, L., Nolan, W., & Samson, R. (2012). Working in Indigenous contexts: Self-reported experiences of non-indigenous Australian psychologists. *Australian Psychologist*, *47*(4), 204–212. https://doi.org/10.1111/j.1742-9544.2011.00042.x

McKendrick, J., Brooks, R., Hudson, J., Thorpe, M., & Bennett, P. (2017). *Aboriginal and Torres Strait Islander healing programs: A literature review*. Healing Foundation. https://healingfoundation.org.au//app/uploads/2017/02/Aboriginal-and-Torres-Strait-Islander-Healing-Programs-A-Literature-Review.pdf

Moreton-Robinson, A. (2004). Whiteness, epistemology and Indigenous representation. In A. Moreton-Robinson (Ed.), *Whitening race: Essays in social and cultural criticism.* (pp. 75–88). Aboriginal Studies Press.

Moreton-Robinson, A., & Nicoll, F. (2006). We shall fight them on the beaches: Protesting cultures of white possession. *Journal of Australian Studies*, *30*(89), 149–160. https://doi.org/10.1080/14443050609388100

Morris, G., Groom, R., Schuberg, E., Atkinson, J., Atkinson, C., & Ungunmerr-Baumann, M. R. (2022). Mitigating contemporary trauma impacts using ancient applications. *Frontiers in Psychology*, *13*, 1–7. https://doi.org/10.3389/fpsyg.2022.645397

Morrissey, P. (2019). The Muecke/Roe relationship as a model for Australian Indigenous studies. In P. Morrissey, & C. Healy (Eds.), *Reading the country: 30 Years on* (pp. 102–113). UTS ePRESS. https://doi.org/10.5130/978-0-6481242-8-3

Mullins, C., & Khawaja, N. G. (2018). Non-Indigenous psychologists working with Aboriginal and Torres Strait Islander people: Towards clinical and cultural competence. *Australian Psychologist, 53*(5), 394–404. https://doi.org/10.1111/ap.12338

National Aboriginal and Torres Strait Islander Leadership in Mental Health. (2015). *Gayaa Dhuwi (Proud Spirit) Declaration*. https://natsilmh.org.au/sites/default/files/gayaa_dhuwi_declaration_A4.pdf

NPY Women's Council Aboriginal Corporation. (2013). *Ngangkari – Traditional Healers*. NPY Women's Council.https://www.npywc.org.au/what-we-do/ngangkari-traditional-healers/

O'Shea, M., Klas, A., Hardy, T., Stone, J., Frangos, T., Jacobs, T., … Ryan, K. (2024). Weaving Wayapa and cognitive behaviour therapy: Applying research topic yarning to explore a cultural interface between Western and Indigenous psychology practice in Australia. *Australian Psychologist, 59*(3), 228–244. https://doi.org/10.1080/00050067.2024.2322710

Parker, R., & Milroy, H. (2014a). Aboriginal and Torres Strait Islander mental health: An overview. In P. Dudgeon, H. Milroy, & R. Walker (Eds.), *Working together: Aboriginal and Torres Strait Islander mental health and wellbeing principles and practice* (pp. 25–38). Commonwealth of Australia.

Parker, R., & Milroy, H. (2014b). Mental illness in Aboriginal and Torres Strait Islander peoples. In P. Dudgeon, H. Milroy, & R. Walker (Eds.), *Working together: Aboriginal and Torres Strait Islander mental health and wellbeing principles and practice* (pp. 113–124). Commonwealth of Australia.

Poelina, A., Wooltorton, S., Blaise, M., Aniere, C., Horwitz, P., White, P., & Muecke, S. (2022). Regeneration time: Ancient wisdom for planetary wellbeing. *Australian Journal of Environmental Education*, *38*(3–4), 397–414. https://doi.org/10.1017/aee.2021.34

Purdie, N., Milgate, G., & Bell, H. R. (2012). *Two way teaching and learning: Toward culturally reflective and relevant education*. Acer Press.

Randall, R. (2022). *The land owns us.* https://www.globalonenessproject.org/library/films/land-owns-us

Reber, J. S. (2006). Secular psychology: What's the problem? *Journal of Psychology and Theology*, *34*(3), 193–204.

Redvers, N., Celidwen, Y., Schultz, C., Horn, O., Githaiga, C., Vera, M., Perdrisat, M., Mad Plume, L., Kobei, D., Kain, M. C., Poelina, A., Rojas, J. N., & Blondin, B. (2022). The determinants of planetary health: An Indigenous consensus perspective. *Lancet Planet Health*, *6*(2), e156–e163. https://doi.org/10.1016/S2542-5196(21)00354-5

Redvers, N., Poelina, A., Schultz, C., Kobei, D. M., Githaiga, C., Perdrisat, M., Prince, D., & Blondin, B. (2020). Indigenous natural and first law in planetary health. *Challenges*, *11*(9), 1–12. https://doi.org/10.3390/challe11020029

Ridges, M., Kelly, M., Simpson, G., Leys, J., Booth, S., Friedel, M., & Country, N. (2020). Understanding how Aboriginal culture can contribute to the resilient future of rangelands—The importance of a Aboriginal core values. *The Rangeland Journal*, *42*(5), 247–251. https://doi.org/10.1071/RJ20031

Shahjahan, R., & Haverkos, K. (2011). Revealing the secular fence of knowledge: Towards reimagining spiritual ways of knowing and being in the academy. *Counterpoints*, *379*, 367–385. https://www.jstor.org/stable/42980908

Shankar, A. (2020). *Primitivism and race in ethnographic film: A decolonial re-visioning*. Oxford University Press.

Sharmil, H., Kelly, J., Bowden, M., Galletly, C., Cairney, I., Wilson C. Hahn, L., Liu, D., P., E., Else, J., Warrior, T., Wanganeen, T., Taylor, R., Wanganeen, F., Madrid, J., Warner, L., Brown, M., & de Crespigny, C. (2021). Participatory action research-Dadirri-Ganma, using Yarning: Methodology co-design with Aboriginal community members. *International Journal of Equity Health*, *20*(1), 160. https://doi.org/10.1186/s12939-021-01493-4.

Smith, P., Rice, K., Schutte, N., & Usher, K. (2022). Reflexivity: A model for teaching and learning cultural responsiveness in mental health. *Australian Psychologist, 57*(4), 209–214. https://doi.org/10.1080/00050067.2022.2078648

Stolzenberg, N. M. (2010). Theses on secularism. *San Diego Law Review*, *47*, 1041.

Swan, P., & Raphael, B. (1995). *Ways Forward: National consultancy report on Aboriginal and Torres Strait Islander mental health.* Commonwealth of Australia. https://library.bsl.org.au/jspui/bitstream/123456789/353/1/Ways%20forward_vol.1%20&%202%20_1995.pdf

Thomas-Olalde, O., & Velho, A. (2011). Othering and its effects—Exploring the concept. *Writing Postcolonial Histories of Intercultural Education*, *2*, 27–51.

Tripcony, P. (2007). Too obvious to see: Explaining the basis of Aboriginal spirituality. [Text of a Presentation to the Australian Association of Religious Educators Conference, Gold Coast, October 1996]. Indigenous Perspectives Reading, Queensland Studies Authority, Queensland Government.

Tujague, N. A., & Ryan, K. L. (2021). Ticking the box of 'cultural safety' is not enough: Why trauma-informed practice is critical to Indigenous healing. *Rural and Remote Health*, *21*(3), 1–5. https://doi.org/10.22605/RRH6411

Ungunmerr-Baumann, M.-R., Groom, R. A., Schuberg, E. L., Atkinson, J., Atkinson, C., Wallace, R., & Morris, G. (2022). Dadirri: An indigenous place-based research methodology. *AlterNative: An International Journal of Indigenous Peoples*, *18*(1), 94–103. https://doi.org/10.1177/11771801221085353

University of New England. (2022). *Ancient wisdom meets the modern world.* UNE Connect. https://www.une.edu.au/connect/news/2022/07/ancient-wisdom-meets-the-modern-world

Walker, M., Fredericks, B., Mills, K., & Anderson, D. (2014). "Yarning" as a method for community-based health research with Indigenous women: The Indigenous women's wellness research program. *Health Care for Women International*, *35*(10), 1216–1226. https://doi.org/10.1080/07399332.2013.815754

Wilson, A. (2014). Addressing uncomfortable issues: Reflexivity as a tool for culturally safe practice in Aboriginal and Torres Strait Islander Health. *The Australian Journal of Indigenous Education*, *43*(2), 218–230. https://doi.org/https://doi.org/10.1017/jie.2014.24

Yunkaporta, T. (2019). *Sand talk: How indigenous thinking can save the world.* Text Publishing.

Part 3

Disrupting Methods

Going beyond the University

13 The Intersections of Ethnicity, Exposure to Extreme Temperature and Mortality under a Decolonial Spotlight

Bridgette Masters-Awatere, Darelle Howard, Shaun Awatere, William (Bill) Cochrane and Kendon Bell

Introduction

As a discipline psychology has emerged from and continues to perpetuate colonial legacies. This is by no means restricted to psychology alone but thrives throughout academia and its processes (Sonn et al., 2024; Tuhiwai Smith, 2021). Although emerging scholarship and sub-disciplines (see for example Dudgeon et al., 2024; Masters-Awatere, et al., 2024; Sonn et al., 2024) hold the promise of a diverse future, the history and contemporary versions of individual disciplines and epistemological practices and processes of academia more broadly remain marred by a colonial violence (Tuhiwai Smith, 2021). It is not enough to see introductory psychology courses acknowledging that the history of the discipline was dominated by white men as though such experiences are relics of the past and no longer exist. Sadly, courses continue to teach the theories of those same white men without critically interrogating the socio-cultural or socio-political contexts of their work and the privileged assumptions afforded. As such, the investigation of mental processes and behaviour continues to reproduce and reinforce colonial doctrine. A transformative shift is necessary to see psychology and academia move beyond the acknowledgement of colonial epistemic violence and towards an approach that situates Indigenous and marginalised epistemologies alongside those that have emerged from the Global North.

Nsamenang argued that "every cultural community the world over has an Indigenous Psychology whether articulated or not. Thus, human psychological functioning predates psychology as an academic discipline" (Allwood & Berry, 2006, p. 257). Despite the accessibility of Indigenous Psychology descriptions from non-European countries across several continents (e.g., Africa/South Africa, Philippines, North and South America, Japan and others), the generalised history of psychology that continues to dominate teaching in universities across Aotearoa and Australia traces a loose path from the Greek philosophers, to German psychology, through structuralism and into the functionalism of the Americans, before emerging into behavioural psychology and finally into cognitive psychology (with offshoots along the way) (see Burton et al., 2024). The authority attributed to the accounts of psychology developed in Europe perpetuates psychology as "an outreach discipline of Europe's civilising mission" (Nsamenang in Allwood & Berry, 2006, p. 256).

Western positivist epistemology continues to underpin the discipline, prioritising one domain of practice and perpetuating academic histories that render Indigenous psychologies absent, or more egregiously, new to the discipline. The inclusion of two Indigenous Psychology chapters in the 6th edition Australasian psychology undergraduate textbook (Burton et al., 2024) is a late, but welcome, addition. This faulty timeline is attributable to the gendered and colonial violence of history upon Indigenous people, holding fast to the epistemologies of the colonial victors. That is, what is considered valuable and valid knowledge is premised on the use of methodologies contained to the narrow, albeit hugely dominant, worldview of Western empiricism – centring quantitative

DOI: 10.4324/9781003492214-16

positivist methods (Tuhiwai Smith, 2021). Articulation of the recent development of Indigenous Psychology only in response to "Western" psychology maintains an inferiority rhetoric while simultaneously presenting Western psychology as a universal science. Such tactics that position Indigenous Psychologies as one of the newest additions to the discipline function as tools contributing to the colonisation, control, oppression and assimilation of Indigenous peoples (Dudgeon & Pickett, 2000; Love, 2003).

To demonstrate the dominance and subsequent limitations of the Western episteme, this chapter centres a small case study about the impact of climate change on the rates of non-communicable diseases (NCDs) for Indigenous Māori and non-Māori (non-Indigenous) in Aotearoa New Zealand. This case study should be situated in the colonial history of Aotearoa which saw Māori violently and coercively dispossessed of land and resource and the emergence of deep institutional racism (Masters-Awatere et al., 2024). As land was forcibly and legislatively removed from Māori with the advent of a settler state, Māori were forced into alien capitalistic and individualist systems which have systemically failed Māori into the contemporary (Jackson, 2018; Mikaere, 2004; Mutu, 2019). Experiencing poorer outcomes across key socioeconomic indicators Māori have not only been resilient and adaptable but also actively strived for emancipation and decolonial visions of the future. Matike Mai is but one example of Māori envisioning a world of co-governance that honours Te Tiriti o Waitangi (the Treaty signed between Māori and the Crown in 1840 that is recognised as foundational) and its essence of self-determination and partnership.

Our case study is one example of ongoing health and climate inequity, c.f. health and climate coloniality (i.e. the inequities within health and climate settings as contemporary iterations/legacies of colonialism). Four authors of this chapter are Māori [BM-A, SA, BC, KB] and one is Pākehā [DH]. As a Pākehā (non-Māori) ally who recognises privileges afforded by the very system that continues to oppress Māori, they add their voice to a critical examination of potentially differentiated climate change impacts.

The World Health Organization identifies climate change "as one of the greatest health threats of the 21st century" (Campbell-Lendrum & Prüss-Ustün, 2019, p. 160). Research on the health impacts of climate change has largely focused on infectious and communicable diseases and deaths resulting from extreme weather events (Kjellstrom et al., 2010). Less focus has been directed towards increases in the rates of NCDs and NCD mortality and their connection to climate change. International literature on temperature exposure has highlighted the importance of investigating temperature variation and mortality rates (Benmarhnia et al., 2015; Carleton et al., 2022; Deschenes, 2018; Guo et al., 2014). There is evidence that the rates and prevalence of NCDs are increasing due to climate change and environmental risk factors (Demaio et al., 2013; Kjellstrom et al., 2010; Prüss-Ustün et al., 2019), which then intersect with existing socioeconomic factors to exacerbate NCDs for some groups (Benmarhnia et al., 2015; Campbell-Lendrum & Prüss-Ustün, 2019; Carleton et al., 2022; Deschenes, 2018; Guo et al., 2014). While the threat of climate change upon human existence has strengthened, research framing such studies tends to exclude an examination of the socio-cultural risks and how climate change impacts on people's lives (Tam et al., 2021).

NCDs are often understood as the chronic and acute exacerbations or complications of health conditions. The World Health Organization (2023) estimates that NCDs "kill 41 million people each year, equivalent to 74% of all deaths globally" (para. 1). As both the frequency and consequences of NCDs continue to grow, there is a call for NCDs "to be regarded as a global emergency" (Nugent & Fottrell, 2019 p. 622). The United Nation's Sustainable Development Goal 3.4 aims to "[r]educe by one third premature mortality from non-communicable diseases through prevention and treatment and promote mental health and well-being" (WHO, 2023, para. 1), signalling the importance of a concerted health response to NCD mortality prevention globally, and in Aotearoa.

It is widely acknowledged that the health impacts of climate change will not be borne equitably, with Indigenous peoples expected to endure more severe health impacts (Abate & Kronk, 2013; Campbell-Lendrum & Corvalán, 2007; Climate Change Adaptation Technical Working Group, 2018; Craighead & Yacelga, 2021; Ford, 2012; Ford et al., 2020; Jones, 2019; Jones et al., 2014, 2020; Masters-Awatere et al., 2022b; Neef et al., 2018; Nursey-Bray et al., 2020; Peters & Schneider, 2021; Watts et al., 2018). Despite recognition of the burden Indigenous peoples will experience, there remain only a few studies examining climate change health impacts on Māori, the Indigenous people of Aotearoa (Awatere et al., 2021; Jones et al., 2014, 2020; Lewis et al., 2020; Masters-Awatere et al., 2022b). Māori already face existing inequities within the health system in Aotearoa (Cormack et al., 2018; Graham & Masters-Awatere, 2020; Harris et al., 2012). For example, Māori experience a greater burden of disease (Jones, 2019) and have a lower average life expectancy than other New Zealanders (Walsh & Grey, 2019). Pertinently, Māori carry a heavy burden of rates of NCD in Aotearoa; experiencing greater prevalence of NCDs, including respiratory disease, cardiovascular disease and cancer compared to non-Māori (Ministry of Health, 2018a, 2018b, 2018c). Given the existing disparities, it is likely that the climate change risks associated with increased exposure to temperature extremes will disproportionately impact on Māori health; warranting a prioritisation of Māori health in Aotearoa's climate change responses (Masters-Awatere et al., 2022a).

Indigenous Epistemologies

Indigenous Psychology "promotes psychologies that are not imposed, that are influenced by the cultural contexts in which people live, which are developed from within the culture and result in locally relevant psychological knowledge" (Dudgeon et al., 2024, p. 85). Psychology and academia have been limited by the Global North – "Western," European and North American contexts (Dudgeon et al., 2024; Masters-Awatere et al., 2024). That is, Western psychology has dominated theory and practice (Dudgeon et al., 2024). The problem is not simply that Western psychology has dominated, but also the antithesis – that other psychologies have been subjugated (Dudgeon et al., 2024; Standing & Kahu, 2021). In this vein, Indigenous conceptualisations of health and wellbeing have been discredited and silenced (Dudgeon et al., 2024). As Dudgeon, Alexi, Derry and Selkirk (2024) point out,

> [i]n Australia, the Australian Psychological Society (APS) has formally acknowledged that the profession of psychology in Australia has been complicit in perpetuating poorer health outcomes for Aboriginal and Torres Strait Islander peoples by failing to recognise Australia's colonial history and the value of Aboriginal and Torres Strait Islander narratives and knowledge.
> (p. 86)

The assumed universality and superiority of Western science is challenged by Indigenous epistemologies (Masters-Awatere et al., 2024). For example, Kaupapa Māori Psychology emerges from a base position of being māori (normal/ordinary; Moewaka Barnes, 2000), asserting recognition, affirmation and validation of cultural world views as Māori (Pihama et al., 2019), enabling a culturally-defined theoretical space for Māori to explain their experiences (Tuhiwai Smith, 2021). As a challenge to Western domination in knowledge production, it is vital that Indigenous peoples see their cultural strengths reflected in psychology (Masters-Awatere et al., 2024, p. 159).

While mainstream or Western psychology continues the epistemological violence of the colonial project, Indigenous psychologies offer room to address racism and hold space for alternative views on knowledge, life and wellbeing (Masters-Awatere et al., 2024). Indigenous psychologies are met with resistance as the hegemonic power of Western empiricism defends itself with familiar claims about the inferiority and lack of validity of other knowledge forms and methods (Dudgeon et al., 2024; Masters-Awatere et al., 2024; Tuhiwai Smith, 2021). The presence and development of Indigenous psychologies within mainstream arenas (textbooks, courses, publications etc.) demonstrates the efforts of Indigenous scholars and allies to decolonise psychology and the academy. Indigenous psychologies and methods are valuable in our venture to understand the intersections of ethnicity, temperature exposure and mortality.

Our Case Study Findings

Mindful of arguments against "literature-only"-based studies that did not have "hard" (i.e. quantitative) evidence of disparate health impacts from climate change, we sought to conduct a small tightly focused study to explore the link between temperature exposure and NCD mortality for Māori and non-Māori in Aotearoa. This study developed from previous research and our identification of absent health data analyses of Indigenous factors as a risk to understanding differentiated risks between Māori and non-Māori. Because there is limited ability to capture hospital admissions data connecting NCDs to climate change, we chose to focus on the mortality rates from NCDs, namely, respiratory, and cardiovascular disease and cancer – each of which had data that could present a clearer connection to temperature exposure. Initiated as a follow-up study to a climate change research project (C01X1901)[1] where meaningful engagement with Māori in health policy was identified as absent (Masters-Awatere et al., 2023). This study, funded by the University of Waikato, explored differentiated risks of climate change to mortality with an intentional focus on Māori and non-Māori comparisons.

Using Statistics New Zealand's integrated data infrastructure (IDI) we analysed datasets sourced from the Ministry of Health. The IDI data was available at a fine spatial resolution of meshblock level (see Statistics New Zealand, 2016). Mortality rates were calculated based on counts of deaths by cause of death and by prioritised ethnicity. Base populations were estimated from annual national-level populations provided by the Ministry of Health and population distributions taken from the 2001, 2006, and 2013 census. Where meshblocks split boundaries over time, we created new meshblock identifiers in our dataset, essentially treating the original meshblock as a separate geographic unit from the new split meshblocks.

We combined the National Institute of Water and Atmospheric Research Virtual Climate Station Network data on historical local temperatures with the mortality data to estimate the causal effect of temperature fluctuations on mortality rates. Following Carleton et al. (2022), we used a fixed-effects approach that controls for unobservable local determinants of mortality rates that are fixed across time (e.g., spatial differences in age distribution) and unobservable determinants of mortality rates that are shared across the country within a year (e.g., a bad flu year). Both sets of controls are important as there are many such factors that could be incidentally correlated with temperature but are not related to the causal effect of temperature on health. We also used a quartic in daily temperature following the temperature aggregation method in Schlenker and Roberts (2009), which allows the model to estimate both the effects of extreme cold and hot temperatures.

From the perspective of Western positivist empiricism, the results of our case study looking at whether different temperatures over time predicted death for Māori might be deemed uninformative in that the results are unexpectedly statistically noisy and did not reveal statistical significance. We find that total deaths for "Māori" and total deaths for "other" does not reveal much about the impact of temperature exposure on mortality. When we focus on particular NCD mortality rates for Māori there is slightly more evidence that is consistent with other literature. For example, Māori respiratory deaths due to temperature exposure represent a closer pattern to what we would expect.

There is an effect on mortality in cold temperatures and somewhere from 20 to 25 degrees Celsius, the mortality rate starts to increase. In short, there is very slight statistical significance for Māori respiratory deaths driven by temperature exposure. However, other NCD mortality rates for cardiovascular disease and cancer failed to demonstrate the statistical significance we would expect. These findings were not at all convincing given the wider literature in this space (Benmarhnia et al., 2015; Carleton et al., 2022; Guo et al., 2014).

Our findings are both unexpected and unconvincing given the consensus argument evident in literature that climate change is driving increasing NCD mortality, and in particular, Māori health vulnerabilities in the NCD space. There is room to offer a critique of our methodology from within the Western empiricism paradigm. That is to say, we are not contesting the validity of Western positivist empiricism (Standing & Kahu, 2021). For example, to refine the findings of this study, it would be possible to carry out error reduction work, prioritising age standardisation. Beyond this, we analysed exposure to temperature in the year that people died. Looking at the temperature experienced in the last year of life, rather than the year of death would potentially make the results slightly more accurate, but we are unable to predict this with certainty. This would mitigate against instances where someone died early in the year, thereby reducing the data on temperature exposure. For example, if someone died in February, we would then only have January temperatures to predict mortality as opposed to the entire February-February calendar year.

We reflected on whether the causative impacts of temperature exposure on mortality using the fixed-effects regression approach was complicated by the small size of the population of focus. Previous studies that have shown similar time series analyses of heat have been able to draw upon much bigger population datasets (Benmarhnia et al., 2015; Carleton et al., 2022; Guo et al., 2014). Aotearoa's total population of five million, reduced to focusing specifically on Māori mortality in a given year (increasing from 4,002 in 2018 to 4,857 in 2022), resulted in a small population subset. Despite our number of observations being comparable to other studies, such as those mentioned above, they average over far more people which reduces the error in their models.

Other nations also have more extreme temperature changes than Aotearoa, However, research on heat waves within cooler climates such as Aotearoa highlights that relative shifts in temperatures (and not only absolute temperature levels) matter when there are at least three consecutive days exceeding a local epidemiological temperature threshold (Harrington, 2021; Harrington et al., 2018). Temperatures which may contribute to elevated cardiovascular events in Tairāwhiti (East coast region in North Island Aotearoa) will be much lower than temperatures which have an equivalent health effect in Northern Australia (Harrington & Frame, 2022). Beyond this, Deschenes (2018) argues that nations with cooler climates where high temperatures are infrequent will experience a larger increase in annual mortality rates. While potentially all valid avenues to investigate, rather than pursue a critique of our methodology and findings *within the Western episteme*, we argue that it is limitations with this very episteme that are hampering important findings and hence we bring in a decolonial lens and utilise Indigenous epistemology in place.

Using a Decolonial Lens

We argue that using an Indigenous lens/epistemology can offer an alternative insight into the results of our case study. Namely, we consider the significant finding of our study to be the limitations of Western positivist empiricism and its praxis in the health system of Aotearoa via the recording of health data. That is, rather than centring our focus on the results that did (or did not) emerge from a methodology abiding by Western empiricism and implicit guidelines about what constitutes valuable knowledge, we argue it offers an opportune moment to critique the very nature of Western empiricism as expressed in health data. By adopting Mi'kmaw elder Albert Marshall's (Bartlett et al., 2012) "two-eyed seeing approach," we posit that Western empiricism's inherent reductivism would discount this study as fruitless, which – by using an Indigenous epistemology – we argue is the very core of the problem. That in reducing people and phenomena to discrete, independent units the complexity and context is obfuscated, which in turn invisibilises and dismisses problems (Bartlett et al., 2012; Goduka, 2012; Mackay, 2022; Tuhiwai Smith, 2021). In this case, we suggest that an Indigenous epistemology is needed to argue that because our findings are statistically noisy and do not reveal the statistical significance one would expect we are revealing a problem with the recording of health data, couched in Western empiricism, that fails to account for the interdependent raft of socioeconomic conditions in which people experience relational and interconnected lives. This is symptomatic of wider approaches to recording health data. For example, a review of temperature change (heat waves) within medical literature reveals a mechanistic focus e.g., valve failure, blood flow risk (Balmain et al., 2017), with multinational studies paying minimal attention to Indigenous populations (Cui & Sinoway 2014) while maintaining Western Educated, Industrialised and Democratic perspectives (Semenza et al., 1996).

Our case study and the treatment of the findings demonstrate the failings of health data in Aotearoa and more broadly the approaches to people and bodies under Western empiricism. Significantly, these failings mean that the health crisis for Māori, that is clearly foreshadowed in the literature, is unable to be clearly articulated in a way that would be recognised as valid by those who hold power in research, knowledge and decision-making spaces. As such, this is both a theoretical and empirical challenge with real consequences for those vulnerable to climate change–driven NCDs. We argue that the application of an Indigenous perspective through Kaupapa Māori methodology is necessary to elucidate the problem to its full extent, to offer a critique of the dominant knowledge framework that holds fast to a narrow definition of valid and valuable knowledge, and to signpost direction to a solution.

Climate Change, NCDs and Indigenous Vulnerabilities

Climate change is causing an increase in the frequency of extreme heat episodes as well as an increase in average temperatures, both of which increase heat exposure with subsequent negative impacts on health (Campbell-Lendrum & Corvalán, 2007; Deschenes, 2018; Johnson et al., 2019; Kjellstrom et al., 2010; Li et al., 2012; McMichael et al., 2012; Peters & Schneider, 2021). The increase in global average temperatures along with an increased frequency, intensity and length of heat extremes is having the most direct impact on health (Watts et al., 2019). Factors will compound impacts on health while temperatures continue to rise (Li et al., 2012; Watts et al., 2018; 2019).

Acknowledgement of the impacts of climate change upon Indigenous peoples is widespread throughout literature (Abate & Kronk, 2013; Craighead & Yacelga, 2021; Ford, 2012; Ford et al., 2020; Jones et al., 2020; Neef et al., 2018; Parraguez-Vergara et al., 2016). The key argument is that the health impacts of climate change will not be borne equitably with Indigenous peoples expected to endure more severe health impacts (Abate & Kronk, 2013; Borg & Bi, 2021; Campbell-Lendrum & Corvalán, 2007; Jones et al., 2014; Jones, 2019; Jones et al., 2020; Masters-Awatere et al., 2022b, 2023; Nursey-Bray et al., 2020; Royal Society of New Zealand/Te Apārangi, 2017; Watts et al., 2018). Despite generally contributing relatively little to emissions, Indigenous peoples carry a disproportionate burden of health and other impacts from climate change (Abate & Kronk, 2013; Climate Change Adaptation Technical Working Group, 2018; Ford, 2012; Ford et al., 2020; Jones et al., 2014, 2020; Neef et al., 2018; Peters & Schneider, 2021; Royal Society of New Zealand/Te Apārangi, 2017). Common experiences among Indigenous people include an autonomous existence that was negatively impacted by colonising activities imposed by settler groups that continue to be perpetuated through constitutional systems that diminish Indigenous peoples' ability to enact relational values with the environment that are derived from generations of knowledge (Abate & Kronk, 2013; Freemantle et al., 2015; Lewis et al., 2020; Rout et al., 2021). Vulnerability to climate change is yet another legacy of the colonial harm experienced by Indigenous people (Ford, 2012; Green et al., 2009; Jones et al., 2014; Whyte, 2017). In fact, "[t]he World Health Organization's investigation into health determinants now recognizes European colonization as a common and fundamental underlying determinant of Indigenous health" (Freemantle, 2015, p. 644).

Māori continue to suffer the consequences of colonisation. Beyond already experiencing higher rates of NCDs and NCD mortality (Ministry of Health, 2018a, 2018b, 2018c), socioeconomic status, housing and geographical displacement, disruption of connection to the environment, employment in outdoor labour roles and other existing health disparities make Indigenous Māori populations particularly vulnerable to negative health impacts from climate change. Beyond this, existing Māori health disparities, which have their roots in historic and ongoing forms of colonisation, manifest as disproportionate risks to Māori public health from climate change. Major health inequities exist for Māori in Aotearoa (Bramley et al., 2004; Curtis et al., 2010; Masters-Awatere, 2017; Reid et al., 2019). As Curtis et al. (2010) summarise, Māori have a significantly higher rate of infant mortality, higher rates of

> 'all-cause mortality', and are more likely to die under the age of 65 in comparison to non-Māori, with life expectancy being approximately 8 years less than non-Māori. Māori health disparities are extensive and exist across a range of mortality and morbidity indicators including communicable disease, chronic disease, injuries, mental health and disability.
>
> (p. 316)

Throughout the colonial history of Aotearoa, health disparities between Māori and non-Māori have been apparent (Ellison-Loschmann & Pearce, 2006). The rates and prevalence of NCDs and NCD mortality are no less disparate.

Given the increase in NCDs and NCD mortality driven by climate change, it is necessary to bring to the forefront the existent disparities between Māori and non-Māori in this space; which is only set to be exacerbated under climate change. The prevalence of key NCDs (cardiovascular disease, respiratory disease and cancer) is far greater among Māori than non-Māori (Ministry of Health, 2018a, 2018b, 2018c; see Tables 13.1–13.3).

High temperatures have been linked to increased rates of cardiovascular mortality (Kjellstrom et al., 2010; Parsons, 2003; Peters & Schneider, 2021; Prüss-Ustün et al., 2019; Schwartz et al., 2004; Watts et al., 2019). The mortality generated by heat exposure is due in large part to the overloading of cardiovascular systems (Kjellstrom et al., 2010; Parsons, 2003; Prüss-Ustün et al., 2019). Increases in average and extreme temperatures cause heat waves and increases in air pollutants which both impact on cardiovascular disease (Peters & Schneider, 2021; Watts et al., 2018; Watts et al., 2019). Based on modelling, mortality rates caused by cardiovascular diseases that are linked to heat stress are expected to increase (Hussein & Chaudhary, 2008).

Cardiovascular disease is recognised as being a leading cause of death among Indigenous populations, specifically Māori in Aotearoa (Ministry of Health, 2018a; Tobias et al., 2009). There are notable disparities between Māori and non-Māori experiences of cardiovascular disease (Ministry of Health, 2018a; Tobias et al., 2009). This makes Māori particularly vulnerable to the recognised climate change–driven increases in rates of cardiovascular disease (Hussein & Chaudhary, 2008; Kjellstrom et al., 2010; Parsons, 2003; Peters & Schneider, 2021; Prüss-Ustün et al., 2019; Schwartz et al., 2004; Watts et al., 2018; Watts et al., 2019).

Table 13.1 Rates of Cardiovascular Disease among Māori and Non-Māori

Non-communicable disease (NCD)	*Māori*	*Non-Māori*
Cardiovascular disease – Total cardiovascular disease mortality, 35+ years, rate per 100,000, 2010–2012	346.9 (male) 232.3 (female)	168.2 (male) 99.2 (female)
Cardiovascular disease – Ischaemic heart disease mortality, 35+ years, rate per 100,000, 2012–2012	205.5 (male) 109.5 (female)	103.3 (male) 44.0 (female)

Note. Data sourced from Ministry of Health (2018a)

Table 13.2 Rates of Respiratory Disease among Māori and Non-Māori

Non-communicable disease (NCD)	*Māori*	*Non-Māori*
Respiratory disease – Asthma hospitalisation, 5–34 years, rate per 100,000, 2012–2014	193.7 (male) 247.9 (female)	112.6 (male) 113.3 (female)
Respiratory disease – Chronic obstructive pulmonary disease mortality, 45+ years, rate per 100,000, 2010–2012	106.9 (male) 110.6 (female)	43.7 (male) 32.1 (female)
Respiratory disease – Chronic obstructive pulmonary disease hospitalisation, 45+ years, rate per 100,000, 2012–2014	1157.0 (male) 1804.5 (female)	447.2 (male) 391.3 (female)

Note. Data sourced from Ministry of Health (2018b)

Table 13.3 Rates of Cancer among Māori and Non-Māori

Non-communicable disease (NCD)	*Māori*	*Non-Māori*
Cancer –Total cancer registrations, 25+ years, rate per 100,000, 2010–2012	455.5 (male) 552.5 (female)	419.2 (male) 394.7 (female)
Cancer –Total cancer mortality, 25+ years, rate per 100,000, 2010–2012	218.4 (male) 214.5 (female)	133.0 (male) 110.0 (female)

Note. Data sourced from Ministry of Health (2018c)

Respiratory diseases bronchitis and asthma are directly impacted by climate change through heat stress, higher ground-level ozone and air pollutants and increases in airborne pollens and spores (Alexis et al., 2004; D'Amato et al., 2005; Watts et al., 2019). Given the disparate rates of asthma between Māori and non-Māori, the burden of climate change–driven increases in asthma, and exacerbation of symptoms, will predominantly impact Māori. Alongside the overloading of cardiovascular systems, overloading respiratory systems contributes to heat-related mortality (Kjellstrom et al., 2010; Parsons, 2003; Prüss-Ustün et al., 2019). Based on modelling, mortality rates caused by respiratory diseases that are linked to heat stress are expected to increase (Hussein & Chaudhary, 2008).

Climate change increases exposure to risk factors of cancer and decreases access to treatment options (Nogueira et al., 2020). Given the disparate rates and experiences of cancer between Māori and non-Māori, climate change will exacerbate existing health inequities in this space.

In sum, Māori experience greater mortality from, and higher rates and prevalence of, NCDs, which have been shown to be increasing due to climate change. Given this, it is imperative that data on NCDs, like that presented by the Ministry of Health, be regularly updated and monitored. The Ministry of Health data on NCD prevalence and mortality between Māori and non-Māori is from 2018, indicating the need for greater emphasis on the maintenance of this data collection as a bare minimum, noting that we offer a critique of this data as a problem in and of itself below.

There is a growing recognition that Māori are particularly impacted by climate change and are already experiencing distinct challenges (Climate Change Adaptation Technical Working Group, 2018; King et al., 2010). Multiple factors intersect to create the present conjuncture that defines both Māori vulnerability and resilience (King et al., 2010). Different whānau, hapū and iwi have different capacities to respond to climate change impacts (King et al., 2010). However, some general factors help to paint the picture of the impact climate change will have on vulnerable Māori populations that will need to be considered alongside their distance to support services, cultural enablers or systemic barriers.

Māori are enduring specific vulnerabilities spanning most social structures in Aotearoa. Māori experience high rates of economic hardship, with just over half of Māori considered economically deprived (King et al., 2010; Walsh & Grey, 2019). Economic insecurity and deprivation substantially hinder capacities to respond to climate change impacts or seek health assistance (Ellison-Loschmann & Pearce, 2006; Lee & North, 2013). Thermal control of homes in extreme temperatures is an increasing concern for marginalised and Indigenous communities (O'Rourke & Nash, 2019). Inadequate facilities reduce the capacity to cope with heat stress and increase the vulnerability of Indigenous people to climate change (Green et al., 2009). Access to adequate housing for Indigenous people is typically more restricted than the access of non-Indigenous populations, complicated by historical, structural and cultural factors (Habibis, 2016); exacerbating susceptibility to climate change–driven health impacts (Ford, 2012). Access to adequate housing can be related to socioeconomic status but is also a separate issue driving vulnerability for Māori in the face of climate change. Māori experience decreased rates of home ownership compared to non-Māori (Goodyear, 2017; Houkamau & Sibley, 2015).

A large amount of Māori land is remote, and Māori experience restricted access to finance and tend to be located in areas with low investment in infrastructure, resulting in increased exposure to climate hazards (King et al., 2010; Kukutai, 2013). Māori have strong cultural, social and economic connections to the land and natural environment (King et al., 2010; Tassell-Matamua et al., 2021; Watene, 2016), creating a unique set of vulnerabilities as te taiao – the natural environment – comes under threat due to climate change.

Māori labour market participation also contributes to vulnerability to climate change impacts. Māori are overrepresented in low-skilled occupations, which includes labourers with outdoor work environments (Jones et al., 2014; Ministry of Business, Innovation and Employment (MBIE) Hikina Whakatutuki, 2017). That is, Māori are more likely to be employed in work environments with greater heat exposure and air pollution causing increased risk of NCDs and other illness (Borg & Bi, 2021; Jones et al., 2014).

Māori have a higher disability rate than non-Māori and are more likely to have unmet needs, and yet, disabled people experience heightened vulnerability to climate change (Bouchama et al., 2007). Finally, Māori experience a colonial health care system in Aotearoa; the neoliberal iteration of which continues to marginalise mātauranga Māori (Māori knowledge). Without a health care system that is culturally responsive to Māori needs, we see rampant health inequalities between Māori and non-Māori across a range of mortality and morbidity indicators, including NCDs, as has been explored above (Curtis et al., 2010).

These complex vulnerabilities experienced by Māori in Aotearoa intersect to create a multifaceted and enduring health crisis for Māori that will only be exacerbated by climate change. However, understanding that Indigenous people are more vulnerable to climate change should not imply passivity. Vulnerable communities demonstrate resilience and adaptation to the changing climate (Ford, 2012; Ford et al., 2020; Nursey-Bray et al., 2020). Beyond this, Māori have developed and adopted decolonial approaches to climate change embedded in mātauranga Māori and exemplifying visions of a transformed world. Māori are exercising their rights and interests to be part of Aotearoa's climate adaptation approach (Lawrence et al., 2024). Ensuring that these rights and interests are implemented in a manner consistent with the priorities of Māori is a challenge for institutions like civil defence and emergency management along with local authorities who for so long have assumed positions of authority over Māori (Rout et al., 2024). To address this challenge, Rout et al. (2024) developed a relational ontology that helped build the capability of civil institutions to better understand Indigenous perspectives on environmental management. It offers guidance for institutions to overcome barriers in implementing climate adaptation responses and empowering local communities.

Despite recognition of the burden Indigenous peoples will experience, there remain only a few studies examining climate change health impacts on Māori (Awatere et al., 2021; Jones et al., 2014, 2020; Lewis et al., 2020; Masters-Awatere et al., 2022b). Awatere et al. (2021) note the absence of Indigenous perspectives in government and assessment documents specific to climate change. In their systematic review of Indigenous inclusion in institutional responses to climate change, Masters-Awatere et al. (2022b) found that Indigenous people were included in design and data collection process, but less so in the translation into policy that would benefit the Indigenous people. Such a finding affirms earlier statements by Tuhiwa Smith (2021) that Indigenous knowledge continues to be regarded as local, anecdotal or non-scientific, and by Lewis et al. (2020) that scientific research is empirically based within a Western framework that tends to exclude all facets of Indigenous knowledge and delegitimises Indigenous cultural beliefs. A consequence of such lack of inclusions and consideration has resulted in Indigenous information being systematically excluded in climate change literature. This absence has implications for wider responses to climate change. Decolonising scientific research is needed to ensure the inclusion and valuing of Indigenous knowledge and associated records of changes in environment, climate and health spaces.

Discussion

When one steps outside of Western empiricism, fundamental problems with research systems (of collection and dissemination) come to the fore. In attempting to centre mortality rates, we discovered failings in health system data that hinder the ability to consider the double precarity crisis befalling Māori in the face of climate change and NCD burden. Firstly, we experienced difficulties coding deaths to the correct International Statistical Classification of Diseases and Related Health Problems codes (ICD) as a variety of ICD coding schemes were used. For death registration years 2000 to 2007 inclusive, the code table used is ICD-10-AM 2nd Edition. For death registration years between 2008 and 2013 inclusive, the clinical code table used is ICD-10_AM 6th Edition, while for death registration years between 2014 and 2018, the clinical code table used is ICD-10_AM 8th Edition. While this variation was addressed in our methodology using the Stata 17 coding tool and the Ministry of Health crosswalk tables (Te Whatu Ora, 2024), it did begin to raise flags about the recording of health data.

The ethnicity variable used in the Ministry of Health Mortality Collection was different from how ethnicity is reported in the census data. The Ministry of Health uses a prioritised ethnicity variable. Prioritisation is one of three methods of ethnic classification commonly used in Aotearoa, the others being total response and single/combination (Boven et al., 2020). With ethnic prioritisation, individuals are classified into one ethnic group, in a prioritised order as follows: Māori, Pacific Peoples, Asian, Middle Eastern/Latin American/African, Other, and European (Ministry of

Health, 2017). While prioritisation does some violence to the concept of ethnicity in that it makes the final categorisation on the basis of an algorithm rather than self-ascription, it has the advantage over other methodologies in that it focuses attention on the Māori population by prioritising that identification (Boven et al., 2020). This goes some way to rectifying the historical undercount of Māori in health statistics, reflecting the "importance of accurate counts for documenting inequities and enabling a Treaty of Waitangi "lens" on health outcomes" (Boven et al., 2020, p. 125). In any event, the mortality data provided to us was coded according to the Ministry of Health prioritisation methodology (Ministry of Health, 2017).

We also had to manage idiosyncrasies with the mortality data drawn from the Ministry of Health Mortality Collection. For example, the spatial frame changed a number of times; deaths are coded to meshblocks however, the meshblocks vary at random intervals throughout the period we considered from 2003 to 2018. The level of aggregation we used subsumed this variation in the ICD codes. Notably, utilising methodological manoeuvres to attempt to subsume variation in coded mortality speaks to inherent problems with the nature of health data and the underpinning epistemological approaches which we argue need to be subject to an Indigenous lens to consider failings.

This necessitates a wider critique of the Western approach to empiricism, predicated in the positivist paradigm, upon which the health system and health research in Aotearoa is largely centred. Our scoping study emphasised the limitations of a Western positivist approach to empiricism, namely its reductionism. The Western positivist approach to empiricism tends to reduce phenomena into discrete, de-contextualised, measurable units (Goduka, 2012; Mackay, 2022; Tuhiwai Smith, 2021). For example, the recording of mortality data in the health system attributes mortality to a single code which invisibilises co-morbidities. In striving to pursue universal laws or a presumed objective truth, Western positivist empiricism disregards contexts in which phenomena emerge. Data is not produced in a vacuum but rather emerges from rich socio-cultural environments. This context is particularly important in the conjunction of climate and health crises where mortality from temperature needs to be considered in the context of housing, geographical local, access to services and treatment within those services. A single mortality code fails to consider the context within which mortality occurs at the intersection of identity, resource and power. The dominance of the Western positivist paradigm within climate and health spaces limits our ability to gather knowledge and understand these social problems, highlighting the need for a shift from Western positivist to Indigenous-based empiricism (Goduka, 2012; Mackay, 2022; Tuhiwai Smith, 2021).

Kaupapa Māori epistemologies provide a lens through which to advocate for context sensitive, relational and holistic forms of health data recording that enables researchers to see the problem and in turn address it (McLachlan et al., 2021). Without employing such methodologies and epistemologies, we risk losing sight of the problem altogether. As such, we argue there is a clear need to centre Indigenous empiricism (Lutz, 2018). When applied to our case study, while Western positivist epistemology would dismiss the findings as noisy and statistically insignificant (attributing fault solely to researchers/methods used), Indigenous epistemologies provide room to challenge the approach to recording health data in the first place and offer a pathway to dissemination to demonstrate the need for this research. Real-world significance is emphasised over statistical significance. That is, while the dominant epistemology would have this study discarded, Indigenous epistemologies allow us as researchers to consider the context of death, ethnicity and climate vulnerability and realise that an absence of statistical significance does not imply the absence of a problem. Results that are statistically insignificant are not considered valid or valuable knowledge under the dominant epistemology. Taking an Indigenous epistemological approach, we emphasise the need to consider the wider context, to consider the practical impacts of not finding something.

That our research provided statistically noisy results and is thus deemed as less valid knowledge under Western positivist empiricism demonstrates the limitations of this episteme. As Tuhiwai Smith (2021) articulates, if we accept the Western position

> the ways we try to understand the world are reduced to issues of measurement, the focus of understanding becomes more concerned with procedural problems. The challenge then for understanding the social world becomes one of developing operational definitions of phenomena which are reliable and valid.
>
> (p. 49)

In centring measurement, procedure and statistical significance, the ways of understanding the world, and in our case, the complex intersection of ethnicity and climate change, are limited. As an aside, it must be noted that the decision about what data is collected and methods for collection are not made by Indigenous people to serve Indigenous agendas, but rather a colonial agenda that generates statistics "as 'evidence' for population monitoring and policy interventions" (Lovett et al., 2019, p. 26).

Our study demonstrates the difficulties centring Indigenous vulnerabilities in a world made to measure white bodies. That is, "[u]nderstanding is viewed as being akin to measuring" (Tuhiwai Smith, 2021, p. 49). Indigenous epistemologies urge us to consider that understanding should entail more than this. The Western treatment of data and bodies as discrete and independent entities fails to realise the inherently relational human experience. People are not skin sacks of data; we exist and experience the world in complex ways that impact that single mortality figure. An Indigenous epistemological approach allows us to consider co-morbidities. That is, that beyond the coded cause of death, a person may be experiencing other illness which is not captured in a Western approach to data but can be seen in a relational Indigenous approach. Even outside of the body, an Indigenous epistemology encourages us to consider the person in context; the socioeconomic conditions of experience, housing conditions, access to resources and treatment, geographical placement etc. The Indigenous epistemology urges us to consider heat exposure and death as relational, contextual and holistic. These factors are stripped away from a single ICD code (which is itself subject to change over time). As Sonn et al. (2024) suggest in seeking to decolonise psychology, we are seeking a rehumanisation of theory and practice. Indigenous epistemology allows us to understand the world beyond statistical principles and significance and recognise knowledge beyond these forms as equally valuable and valid. This speaks to a wider historical suppression of Indigenous epistemologies that have been marginalised by colonial frameworks that favour Eurocentric approaches to knowledge production.

An absence of clear results that align with wider literature speaks to the difficulties highlighting the Indigenous experience, *not that there is no problem to begin with*. Addressing the problem becomes a utopian venture if one cannot even present the problem due to reductivism tendencies in recorded health data and a dominance of Western positivist empiricism in the production and dissemination of knowledge. That is,

> Indigenous knowledge systems are still not allowed to stand on their own merits or explored in their own unique frameworks to reveal and answer new, and old, and questions. Rather, they are relegated to a secondary status within discussions and analyses. Recognizing Indigenous knowledge isn't simply about recognizing the knowledge as valid, it is about fully integrating that knowledge.
>
> (Mackay, 2022, p. 2)

As such, in venturing to present the differentiated risks of climate change to mortality and the particular vulnerabilities for Māori, the dominant frameworks available to us also inherently limit us. Both the nature of the recorded data we worked with and the methodologies given highest status in knowledge production and dissemination force us into colonial conformism. Rejecting this conformism becomes an enduring challenge. However, the very act of presenting such critiques resists the coloniality of academia. While "decoloniality is the breach in the wall of coloniality that opens the way to new worlds" (Sonn et al., 2024, p. 3) doing so requires constant effort and energy to push the boundaries of academia.

The attribution of validity and in turn considerations of what constitutes valuable knowledge is reserved for the very types of data that inherently restricted our ability to present a case for the abundantly apparent intersections of temperature exposure, climate change, NCD and Māori vulnerability. As Tuhiwai Smith (2021) articulates "[k]nowledge and the power to define what counts as real knowledge lie at the heart of the epistemic core of colonialism" (p. xii). Our research highlights the challenge Tuhiwai Smith (2021) lays before researchers, namely "to simultaneously work with colonial and Indigenous concepts of knowledge, decentring one while centring the other" (p. xii). The issue before us is that despite the apparent consensus argument in the literature which shows a clear, albeit not simple, relationship between climate change–driven increases in NCD and NCD mortality and Māori health vulnerabilities, the dominant episteme makes it difficult to present this in a format that is consistent with a colonial version of valid knowledge.

Nevertheless, in decolonising methodologies, it is important to recognise that Western paradigms and epistemologies should not be "disavowed, ignored, or otherwise repressed—that is a Westernized essentialist notion [...] which is in direct opposition to the plurality of thought and being that Indigenous traditions advocate for" (Mackay, 2022, p. 2). This is a caveat that perhaps need not be foregrounded due to the continued dominance of Western positivist empiricism which remains elevated above Indigenous empiricism. However, to adopt the pluralist Indigenous philosophy that comes from the Mi'kmaq, Etuaptmumk – two-eyed seeing (Bartlett et al., 2012; Mackay, 2022), we argue that the reductivism and de-contextualisation evident in the recording of mortality data limits our understanding of a complex reality. In turn, the knowledge that can be produced utilising this data is inherently constrained within an episteme that only recognises significance within the narrow confines of statistical margins; failing to see how the absence of a story is a particular problem in and of itself that holds value and warrants consideration. Herein lies the contradiction of attempting decoloniality with colonial tools (Lorde, 1983); of highlighting the Indigenous experience with colonial measures. While the reductivism of Western positivism applies whether the bodies being reduced, de-contextualised and measured are white or people of colour, the failing is particularly damaging for Indigenous people and the vulnerabilities they experience due to the ongoing fight for recognition of Indigenous rights and needs.

Conclusion

The dominance of Western epistemology throughout psychology and academia more broadly has led to a historical and contemporary subjugation of alternative epistemologies that emerge from Indigenous peoples and the Global South. Western epistemology is predicated on positivist empiricism and prioritises observable, measurable data as the key to understanding the world. In an attempt to produce data that would be recognised as valid and valuable in the dominant epistemology, we undertook a case study mobilising a typically quantitative methodology that utilised existing health data. Recognising the clear need to firstly, acknowledge and secondly, address the inequitable burden Māori will face due to climate change–driven increases in NCD, our case study explored the link between temperature exposure and NCD mortality for Māori and non-Māori in Aotearoa. We chose to focus on the mortality rates from NCDs that would likely present a clearer connection to temperature exposure, namely, respiratory and cardiovascular disease and cancer. The consensus narrative in the literature tells a simplistic tale of a complex reality in which Māori will be disproportionately affected by climate change–driven increases in the rates and prevalence of NCDs and subsequent NCD mortality. Climate change will impact on the prevalence of key NCDs and mortality rates (Demaio et al., 2013; Kjellstrom et al., 2010; Peters & Schneider, 2021; Prüss-Ustün et al., 2019). Māori have disproportionately higher rates of NCDs and mortality compared to non-Māori (Ministry of Health, 2018a, 2018b, 2018c) and thus will bear the brunt of the climate change–driven increase in NCD complications.

The argument presented here is that the dominance of Western positivist empiricism and the subsequent nature of the health data recorded is where the failings begin. The reductivism inherent in ICD mortality coding minimises a complex reality that must be recognised to make visible co-morbidities, and beyond this, experiences of the complex conjuncture of climate change–driven health impacts intersecting with identity, place and power. Our small scoping study highlights complications with mortality data working with small Indigenous population groups, and more broadly, the need for a two-eyed seeing approach to bring in alternative perspectives about the nature of data and what constitutes valuable knowledge. If the data we are working with is inherently limited the scope of the problem is obfuscated, which in turn pushes remedy even further from reach.

It is imperative to substantially delve into the realities of climate change–driven increases in the rates of NCD and NCD mortality. The lack of serious consideration of the current health burden Māori experience generates further risk in the face of climate change. Recognising that Māori disproportionately experience commonly identified NCDs – cardiovascular disease, respiratory disease, and cancer – and that climate change is driving an increase in the rates and prevalence of, and subsequent mortality from, NCDs, compounded by a range of social, cultural and economic factors, demonstrates that a foreseeable health crisis for Māori is evident. Lacking statistical significance Western epistemology would discount the study and relegate the problem to a dust-lined draw. Indigenous psychologies and epistemologies provide the tools to critique the nature of discrete, measurable, de-contextualised data and recontextualise data as *people in context* to highlight issues where statistical analysis may find none.

Note

1 https://deepsouthchallenge.co.nz/research-project/haumanu-hauora-health-responses-for-maori/.

References

Abate, R. S., & Kronk, E. A. (2013). Commonality among unique indigenous communities: An introduction to climate change and its impacts on indigenous peoples. *Tulane Environmental Law Journal, 26*(2), 179–195. https://www.jstor.org/stable/24673665

Alexis, N., Barnes, C., Bernstein, I. L., Nel, A., Peden, D., Diaz-Sanchez, D., Tarlo, S. M., Williams, P. B., & Bernstein, J. A. (2004). Health effects of air pollution (J. A. Bernstein Ed.). Health effects of air pollution. *The Journal of Allergy and Clinical Immunology, 114*(5), 1116–1123. https://doi.org/10.1016/j.jaci.2004.08.030

Allwood, C. M., & Berry, J. W. (Eds.). (2006). Origins and development of Indigenous psychologies: An international analysis. *International Journal of Psychology, 41*(4), 243–268. https://doi.org/10.1080/00207590544000013

Awatere, S., King, D. N., Reid, J., Williams, L., Masters-Awatere, B., Harris, P., Tassel-Matamua, N., Jones, R., Eastwood, K., Pirker, J., & Jackson, A. M. (2021). *He huringa āhuatanga, he huringa ao: A changing climate, a changing world.* Ngā Pae o te Māramatanga, Manaaki Whenua Landcare Research. https://www.landcareresearch.co.nz/assets/researchpubs/He-huringa-ahuarangi-he-huringa-ao-a-changing-climate-a-changing-world.pdf

Balmain, B. N., Sabapathy, S., Jay, O., Adsett, J., Stewart, G. M., Jayasinghe, R., & Morris, N. R. (2017). Heart failure and thermoregulatory control: Can patients with heart failure handle the heat?. *Journal of Cardiac Failure, 23*(8), 621–627. https://doi.org/10.1016/j.cardfail.2017.04.003

Barnes, M. H. (2000). Kaupapa maori: Explaining the ordinary. *Pacific health dialog*, *7*(1), 13–16. https://pubmed.ncbi.nlm.nih.gov/11709875/

Bartlett, C., Marshall, M., & Marshall, A. (2012). Two-eyed seeing and other lessons learned within a co-learning journey of bringing together Indigenous and mainstream knowledges and ways of knowing. *Journal of Environmental Studies and Sciences*, *2*(4), 331–340. https://doi.org/10.1007/s13412-012-0086-8

Benmarhnia, T., Deguen, S., Kaufman, J. S., & Smargiassi, A. (2015). Vulnerability to heat-related mortality: A systematic review, meta-analysis, and meta-regression analysis. *Epidemiology*, *26*(6), 781–93. https://doi.org/10.1097/ede.0000000000000375

Borg, M. A. & Bi, P. (2021). The impact of climate change on kidney health. *Nat Rev Nephrol 17*, 294–295. https://doi.org/10.1038/s41581-020-00365-4

Bouchama, A., Dehbi, M., Mohamed, G., Matthies, F., Shoukri, M., & Menne, B. (2007). Prognostic factors in heat wave–related deaths: A meta-analysis. *Arch. Intern. Med.*, *167*, 2170–2176. https://doi.org/10.1001/archinte.167.20.ira70009

Boven, N., Exeter, D., Sporle, A., & Shackleton, N. (2020). The implications of different ethnicity categorisation methods for under-standing outcomes and developing policy in New Zealand. *Kōtuitui: New Zealand Journal of Social Sciences Online*, *15*, 123–139. https://doi.org/10.1080/1177083X.2019.1657912

Bramley, D., Hebert, P., Jackson, R., & Chassin, M. (2004). Indigenous disparities in disease-specific mortality, a cross-country comparison: New Zealand, Australia, Canada, and the United States. *The New Zealand Medical Journal*, *117*(1207), 1–16.

Burton, L. J., Westen, D., & Kowalski, R. (Eds.). (2024). *Psychology: Sixth Australian and New Zealand edition*. John Wiley & Sons.

Campbell-Lendrum, D., & Corvalán, C. (2007). Climate change and developing-country cities: Implications for environmental health and equity. *Journal of Urban Health*, *84*, 109–117. https://doi.org/10.1007/s11524-007-9170-x

Campbell-Lendrum, D., & Prüss-Ustün, A. (2019). Climate change, air pollution and noncommunicable diseases. *Bulletin World Health Organisation*, *97*(2), 160–161. https://doi.org/10.2471/blt.18.224295

Carleton, T., Jina, A., Delgado, M., Greenstone, M., Houser, T., Hsiang, S., Hultgren, A., Koop, R. E., McCusker, K. E., Nath, I., Rising, J., Rode, A., Kwon Seo, H., Viaene, A., Yuan, J., & Tianbo Zhang, A. (2022). Valuing the global mortality consequences of climate change accounting for adaptation costs and benefits. *The Quarterly Journal of Economics*, *137*(4), 2037–2105. https://doi.org/10.1093/qje/qjac020

Climate Change Adaptation Technical Working Group. (2018). *Adapting to Climate Change in New Zealand: Recommendations from the Climate Change Adaptation Technical Working Group*. Ministry for the Environment, New Zealand.

Cormack, D., Stanley, J., & Harris, R. (2018). Multiple forms of discrimination and relationships with health and wellbeing: findings from national cross-sectional surveys in Aotearoa/New Zealand. *International Journal for Equity in Health*, *17*(1), 26–26. https://doi.org/10.1186/s12939-018-0735-y

Craighead, K. A., & Yacelga, M. (2021). Indigenous peoples' displacement and jaguar survival in a warming planet. *Global Sustainability, 4*(7). https://doi.org/10.1017/sus.2021.6

Cui, J., & Sinoway, L. I. (2014). Cardiovascular responses to heat stress in chronic heart failure. *Current Heart Failure Reports, 11*(2), 139–45. https://doi.org/10.1007/s11897-014-0191-y

Curtis, E., Harwood, M., Riddell, T., Robson, B., Harris, R., Mills, C., & Reid, P. (2010). Access and society as determinants of ischaemic heart disease in indigenous populations. *Heart, Lung and Circulation, 19*(5), 316–324. https://doi.org/10.1016/j.hlc.2010.04.129

D'Amato, G., Liccardi, G., D'amato, M., & Holgate, S. (2005). Environmental risk factors and allergic bronchial asthma. *Clinical & Experimental Allergy, 35*(9), 1113–1124. https://doi.org/10.1111/j.1365-2222.2005.02328.x

Demaio, A., Jamieson, J., Horn, R., de Courten, M., & Tellier, S. (2013). Non-communicable diseases in emergencies: A call to action. *PLoS Currents, 5*. https://doi.org/10.1371/currents.dis.53e08b951d59ff913ab8b9bb51c4d0de

Deschenes, O. (2018). Temperature variability and mortality: Evidence from 16 Asian countries. *Asian Development Review, 35*(2), 1–30. https://doi.org/10.1162/adev_a_00112

Dudgeon, P., & Pickett, H. (2000). Psychology and reconciliation: Australian perspectives. *Australian Psychologist, 35*(2), 82–87. https://doi.org/10.1080/00050060008260328

Dudgeon, P., Alexi, J., Derry, K., & Selkirk, B. (2024). Indigenous psychology in Australia. In L. Burton, D. Westen, & R. Kowalski (Eds.), *Psychology: Sixth Australian and New Zealand edition* (pp. 85–135). John Wiley & Sons.

Ellison-Loschmann, L., & Pearce, N. (2006). Improving access to health care among New Zealand's Maori population. *American Journal of Public Health (1971), 96*(4), 612–617. https://doi.org/10.2105/AJPH.2005.070680

Ford, J., King, N., Galappaththi, E., Pearce, T., McDowell, G., & Harper, S. (2020). The resilience of Indigenous people to environmental change. *One Earth, 2*(6), 532–543. https://doi.org/10.1016/j.oneear.2020.05.014

Ford, J. D. (2012). Indigenous health and climate change. *American Journal of Public Health, 102*(7), 1260–1266. https://doi.org/10.2105/AJPH.2012.300752

Freemantle, J., Ring, I., Solomon, T., Gachpin, F., Smylie, J., Cutler, T., & Waldon, J. (2015). Indigenous mortality (revealed): The invisible illuminated. *American Journal of Public Health, 105*(4), 644–652. https://doi.org/10.2105/ajph.2014.301994

Goduka, N. (2012). From positivism to indigenous science: A reflection on world views, paradigms and philosophical assumptions. *Africa Insight, 41*(4), 123–138.

Goodyear, R. (2017). A place to call home? Declining home-ownership rates for Māori and Pacific peoples in New Zealand. *New Zealand Population Review, 43*, 3–34. https://www.proquest.com/scholarly-journals/place-call-home-declining-ownership-rates-māori/docview/2052764120/se-2

Graham, R., & Masters-Awatere, B. (2020). Experiences of Māori of Aotearoa New Zealand's public health system: A systematic review of two decades of published qualitative research. *Australian and New Zealand Journal of Public Health, 44*(3), 193–200. https://doi.org/10.1111/1753-6405.12971

Green, D., King, U., & Morrison, J. (2009). Disproportionate burdens: The multidimensional impacts of climate change on the health of indigenous Australians. *Medical Journal of Australia, 190*(1), 4–5. https://doi.org/10.5694/j.1326-5377.2009.tb02250.x

Guo, Y., Gasparrini, A., Armstrong, B., Li, S., Tawatsupa, B., Tobias, A., Lavigne, E., de Sousa, M., Coelho, Z., Leone, M., Pan, X., Tong, S., Tian, L., Kim, H., Hasizume, M., Honda, Y., Guo, L., Wu, C., Punnasiri, K., Yi, S., Michelozzi, P., Saldiva, P., & Williams, G. (2014). Global variation in the effects of ambient temperature on mortality: A systemic evaluation. *Epidemiology, 25*(6), 781–789. https://doi.org/10.1097/ede.0000000000000165

Habibis, D. (2016). Indigenous housing. In R. Dufty-Jones, & D. Rogers (Eds.), *Housing in 21st-century Australia: People, practices and policies* (pp. 73–87). Routledge. https://doi.org/10.4324/9781315587110

Harrington, L. J. (2021). Rethinking extreme heat in a cool climate: A New Zealand case study. *Environmental Research Letters, 16*(3), 034030. https://doi.org/10.1088/1748-9326/abbd61

Harrington, L. J., & Frame, D. (2022). Extreme heat in New Zealand: A synthesis. *Climatic Change, 174*(2), 1–16. https://doi.org/10.1007/s10584-022-03427-7

Harrington, L. J., Frame, D., King, D., & Otto, F. (2018). How uneven are changes to impact to impact-relevant climate hazards in a 1.5C world and beyond? *Geographical Research Letters, 45*(13), 6672–6680. https://doi.org/10.1029/2018GL078888

Harris, R., Cormack, D., Tobias, M., Yeh, L.-C., Talamaivao, N., Minster, J., & Timutimu, R. (2012). The pervasive effects of racism: Experiences of racial discrimination in New Zealand over time and associations with multiple health domains. *Social Science & Medicine, 74*(3), 408–415. https://doi.org/10.1016/j.socscimed.2011.11.004

Houkamau, C. A., & Sibley, C. G. (2015). Looking Māori predicts decreased rates of home ownership: Institutional racism in housing based on perceived appearance. *PLoS One, 10*(3), 1–14. https://doi.org/10.1371/journal.pone.0118540

Hussein, T., & Chaudhary, J. R. (2008). Human health risk assessment due to global warming—A case study of the Gulf countries. *Int J Environ Res Public Health, 5*, 204–212. https://doi.org/10.3390/ijerph5040204

Jackson, M. (2018). Colonization as myth-making: A case study in Aotearoa. In N. Greymorning (Ed.), *Being indigenous* (pp. 89–101). Routledge.

Johnson, R. J., Sánchez-Lozada, L. G., Newman, L. S., Lanaspa, M. A, Diaz, H. F., Lemery, J., Rodriguez-Iturbe, B., Tolan, D. R., Butler-Dawson, J., Sato, Y., Garcia, G., Hernando, A. A., & Roncal-Jimenez, C. A. (2019). Climate change and the kidney. *Annals of Nutrition and Metabolism, 74*(suppl 3), 38–44. https://doi.org/10.1159/000500344

Jones, R., Bennett, H., Keating, G., & Blaiklock, A. (2014). Climate change and the right to health for Māori in Aotearoa/New Zealand. *Health and Human Rights Journal, 16*(1), 54–68.

Jones, R., Macmillan, A., & Reid, P. (2020). Climate change mitigation policies and co-impacts on Indigenous health: A scoping review. *International Journal of Environmental Research and Public Health, 17*(23), 9063. https://doi.org/10.3390/ijerph17239063

Jones, R. (2019). Climate change and indigenous health promotion. *Glob Health Promot, 26*(3),73–81. https://doi.org/10.1177/1757975919829713

King, D. N., Penny, G., & Severne, C. (2010). The climate change matrix facing Māori society. In R. A. C. Nottage, D. S. Wratt, J. F. Bornman, & K. Jones (Eds.). *Climate change adaptation in New Zealand: Future scenarios and some sectoral perspectives* (pp. 100–111). New Zealand Climate Change Centre.

Kjellstrom, T., Butler, A. J., Lucas, R. M., & Bonita, R. (2010). Public health impact of global heating due to climate change: Potential effects on chronic non-communicable diseases. *International Journal Public Health, 55*(97), 97–103. https://doi.org/10.1007/s00038-009-0090-2

Kukutai, T. (2013). The structure of urban Māori identities. In E. Peters, & C. Anderson (Eds.), *Indigenous in the city: Contemporary identities and cultural innovation* (pp. 311–333). UBC Press.

Lawrence, J., Wreford, A., Blackett, P., Hall, D., Woodward, A., Awatere, S., … & Milfont, T. L. (2024). Climate change adaptation through an integrative lens in Aotearoa New Zealand. *Journal of the Royal Society of New Zealand, 54*(4), 491–522. https://doi.org/10.1080/03036758.2023.2236033

Lee, R., & North, N. (2013). Barriers to Māori sole mothers' primary health care access. *Journal of Primary Health Care, 5*(4), 315–21.

Lewis, D., Williams, L., & Jones, R. (2020). A radical revision of the public health response to environmental crisis in a warming world: Contributions of indigenous knowledges and INDIGENOUS feminist perspectives. *Canadian Journal of Public Health, 111*(6), 897–900. https://doi.org/10.17269/s41997-020-00388-1

Li, B., Sain, S., O'Mearns, L., Anderson, H., Kovats, S., Ebi, K. L., Bekkedal, M. Y. V., Kanarek, M. S., & Patz, J. A. (2012). The impact of extreme heat on morbidity in Milwaukee, Wisconsin. *Climatic Change, 110*, 959–976. https://doi.org/10.1007/s10584-011-0120-y

Lorde, A. (1983). The master's tools will never dismantle the master's house. In C. Moraga, & G. Anzaldua (Eds.), *This bridge called my back: Writings by radical women of color* (pp. 90–101). Kitchen Table Press.

Love, C. (2003). Keynote Address. In L. Nikora, M. Levy, B. Masters, M. Waitoki, N. Te Awekotuku, & R. Etheredge (Eds.), *The Proceedings of the National Māori Psychology Graduates' Symposium 2002: Making a Difference*. Māori and Psychology Research Unit, Department of Psychology, University of Waikato.

Lovett, R., Lee, V., Kukutai, T., Cormack, D., Rainie, S. C., & Walker, J. (2019). Good data practices for Indigenous data sovereignty and governance. In A. Daly, S. K. Devitt, & M. Mann (Eds.), *Good data* (pp. 26–36). Institute of Network Cultures.

Lutz, H. (2018). "They Talk, We Listen": Indigenous knowledges and western discourse. *Zeitschrift für Kanada-Studien, 38*(1), 66–88.

Mackay, R. E. (2022). An Indigenous critique: Expanding sociology and recognizing unique Indigenous knowledge. *Frontiers in Sociology, 7*, 1–15. https://doi.org/10.3389/fsoc.2022.1047812

Masters-Awatere, B., Howard, D., & Young, P. (2023). Haumanu Hauora: refining public health institution policy to include Māori and climate change. *Climatic Change*, *176*(58), 1–15. https://doi.org/10.1007/s10584-023-03534-z.

Masters-Awatere, B., Waitoki, W., & McLachlan, A. (2024). Māori and psychology: Indigenous psychology in Aotearoa New Zealand. In L. Burton, D. Westen, & R. Kowalski (Eds.), *Psychology: Sixth Australian and New Zealand edition* (pp. 85–135). John Wiley & Sons.

Masters-Awatere, B., Young, P., Graham, R. (2022a). State agencies and researchers engaging with Indigenous communities on climate change adaptation planning: A systematic review. *MAI Journal, 11*(1), 294–308

Masters-Awatere, B., Young, T., Howard, D., Powell, E., Ranginui Charlton, A., Graham, R., & Dixon, R. (2022b). *Haumanu hauora: Strengthening health institution responsiveness to climate change.* Technical report prepared for Deep South National Science Challenge. Māori and Psychology Research Unit (MPRU), University of Waikato.

Masters-Awatere, B. (2017). A game of slides and ladders: Māori providers and funders. In S. Groot, C. Van Ommen, B. Masters-Awatere, & N. Tassell-Matamua (Eds.), *Precarity: Uncertain, insecure and unequal lives in Aotearoa New Zealand* (pp. 146–161). Massey University Press.

McLachlan, A., Waitoki, W., Harris, P., & Jones, H. (2021). Whiti Te Rā: A guide to connecting Māori to traditional wellbeing pathways. *Journal of Indigenous Wellbeing*, *6*(1), 78–97.

McMichael, T., Montgomery, H., & Costello, A. (2012). Health risks, present and future, from global climate change. *BMJ*, *344,* e1359. https://doi.org/10.1136/bmj.e1359

Mikaere, A. (2004). Are we all New Zealanders now? A Māori response to the Pākehā quest for Indigeneity. *Red and Green*, *4*, 33–45.

Ministry of Business, Innovation and Employment (MBIE) Hikina Whakatutuki. (2017). *Māori in the Labour Market*. MBIE. https://www.mbie.govt.nz/dmsdocument/1041-2017-monitoring-report-maori-in-the-labour-market-pdf

Ministry of Health. (2017). *HISO 10001:2017 ethnicity data protocols*. Ministry of Health.

Ministry of Health. (2018a). *Cardiovascular disease*. https://www.health.govt.nz/our-work/populations/maori-health/tatau-kahukura-maori-health-statistics/nga-mana-hauora-tutohu-health-status-indicators/cardiovascular-disease

Ministry of Health. (2018b). *Respiratory disease*. Manatu Hauora, Minister of Health. https://www.health.govt.nz/our-work/populations/maori-health/tatau-kahukura-maori-health-statistics/nga-mana-hauora-tutohu-health-status-indicators/respiratory-disease

Ministry of Health. (2018c). *Cancer.* Manatu Hauora, Minister of Health. https://www.health.govt.nz/our-work/populations/maori-health/tatau-kahukura-maori-health-statistics/nga-mana-hauora-tutohu-health-status-indicators/cancer

Mutu, M. (2019). 'To honour the treaty, we must first settle colonisation' (Moana Jackson 2015): The long road from colonial devastation to balance, peace and harmony. *Journal of the Royal Society of New Zealand*, *49*(sup1), 4–18. https://doi.org/10.1080/03036758.2019.1669670

Neef, A., Benge, L., Boruff, B., Pauli, N., Weber, E., & Varea, R. (2018). Climate adaptation strategies in Fiji: The role of social norms and cultural values. *WordDevelopment*, *107*, 125–137. https://doi.org/10.1016/j.worlddev.2018.02.029

Nogueira, L. M., Yabroff, K. R., & Bernstein, A. (2020). Climate change and cancer. *CA: A Cancer Journal for Clinicians*, *70*(4), 239–244. https://doi.org/10.3322/caac.21610

Nugent, R., & Fottrell, E. (2019). Non-communicable diseases and climate change: Linked global emergencies. *Lancet*, *394*(10199), 622–623.

Nursey-Bray, M., Palmer, R., Stuart, A., Arbon, V., & Rigney, L.I. (2020). Scale, colonisation and adapting to climate change: Insights from the Arabana people, South Australia. *Geoforum*, *114*, 138–150. https://doi.org/10.1016/j.geoforum.2020.05.021

O'Rourke, T., & Nash, D. (2019). Aboriginal yards in remote Australia: Adapting landscapes for Indigenous housing. *Landscape and Urban Planning*, *182*, 124–132. https://doi.org/10.1016/j.landurbplan.2018.10.013

Parraguez-Vergara, E., Barton, J. R., & Raposo-Quintana, G. (2016). Impacts of climate change in the Andean foothills of Chile: Economic and cultural vulnerability of indigenous Mapuche livelihoods. *Journal of Development and Social Sciences*, *32*(4), 454–483. https://doi.org/10.1177/0169796X16667874

Parsons, K. (2003). *Human thermal environment. The effects of hot, moderate and cold temperatures on human health, comfort and performance* (2nd ed). CRC Press.

Peters,A.,&Schneider,A.(2021).Cardiovascularrisksofclimatechange.*NatureReviewsCardiology*,*18*(1),1–2. https://doi.org/10.1038/s41569-020-00473-5

Pihama, L., Tuhiwai Smith, L., Simmonds, N., Seed-Pihama, J., & Gabel, K. (Eds.). (2019). *Mana Wahine reader: A collection of writings 1999–2019 Volume II.* Te Kotahi Research Institute.

Prüss-Ustün, A., van Deventer, E., Mudu, P., Campbell-Lendrum, D., Vickers, C., Ivanov, I., Forastiere, F., Gumy, S., Dora, C., Adair-Rohani, H., & Neira, M. (2019). Environmental risks and non-communicable diseases. *BMJ*, *365*, 17–19. https://doi.org/10.1136/bmj.l265

Reid, P., Cormack, D., & Paine, S. J. (2019). Colonial histories, racism and health—The experience of Māori and indigenous peoples. *Public Health*, *172*, 119–124. https://doi.org/10.1016/j.puhe.2019.03.027

Rout, M., Awatere, S., Mika, J. P., Reid, J., & Roskruge, M. (2021). A Māori approach to environmental economics: Te ao tūroa, te ao hurihuri, te ao mārama—The old world, a changing world, a world of light. In *Oxford research encyclopedia of environmental science*. https://doi.org/10.1093/acrefore/9780199389414.013.715.

Rout, M., Awatere, S., Reid, J., Campbell, E., Huang, A., & Warmenhoven, T. (2024). A 'te ao Māori' disaster risk reduction framework. *Disasters*, *48*(3), e12622. https://doi.org/10.1111/disa.12622

Royal Society of New Zealand/Te Apārangi. (2017). *Human health impacts of climate change for New Zealand: Evidence summary*. Royal Society Te Apārangi. https://www.royalsociety.org.nz/assets/documents/Report-Human-Health-Impacts-of-Climate-Change-for-New-Zealand-Oct-2017.pdf

Schlenker, W., & Roberts, M. J. (2009). Nonlinear temperature effects indicate severe damages to U.S. crop yields under climate change. *Agricultural Sciences*, *106*(37), 15594–15598. https://doi.org/10.1073/pnas.0906865106

Schwartz, J., Samet, J., & Patz, J. (2004). Hospital admissions for heart disease: The effects of Temperature and Humidity. *Epidemiology*,*15*(6), 755–761. https://www.jstor.org/stable/20485985

Semenza, J. C., Rubin, C. H., Falter, K. H., Selanikio, J. D., Flanders, W. D., Howe, H. L., & Wilhelm, J. L. (1996). Heat-related deaths during the July 1995 heat wave in Chicago. *New England Journal of Medicine*, *335*(2), 84–90. https://doi.org/10.1056/nejm199607113350203

Sonn, C. C., Fernández, J. S., Moura, J. F., Madyaningrum, M. E., & Malherbe, N. (2024). Decolonisation in and beyond community psychologies: A transnational plurilogue. In C. C. Sonn, J. S. Fernández, J. F. Moura Jr., M. E. Madyaningrum, & N. Malherbe (Eds.), *Handbook of decolonial Community Psychology* (pp. 1–22). Springer Nature Switzerland. https://doi.org/10.1007/978-3-031-67035-0_1

Standing, M., & Kahu, E. R. (2021). Story, myth, and purakau: An exploration of the use of narrative in the therapeutic setting in Aotearoa New Zealand. *New Zealand Journal of Psychology (Online)*, *50*(3), 29–38.

Statistics New Zealand. (2016). *Statistical standard for meshblock*. New Zealnd Government. https://www.stats.govt.nz/assets/Uploads/Retirement-of-archive-website-project-files/Methods/Statistical-standard-for-meshblock/stats-stnd-meshblock.pdf.

Tam, C. L., Chew, S., Carvalho, A., & Doyle, J. (2021). Climate change totems and discursive hegemony over the Arctic. *Frontiers in Communication, 6*, 518759. https://doi.org/10.3389/fcomm.2021.518759

Tassell-Matamua, N., Lindsay, N., Bennett, A., & Masters-Awatere, B. (2021). Māori cultural identity linked to greater regard for nature: Attitudes and (less so) behavior. *Ecopsychology, 13*(1), 9–18. https://doi.org/10.1089/eco.2020.0027

Te Whatu Ora. (2024). *Mapping tables*. Health New Zealand Te Whatu Ora. https://www.tewhatuora.govt.nz/for-health-professionals/data-and-statistics/nz-health-statistics/data-references/mapping-tables

Tobias, M., Yeh, L. C., Wright, C., Riddell, T., Chan, W. C., Jackson, R., & Mann, S. (2009). The burden of coronary heart disease in Māori: Population-based estimates for 2000–2002. *Australian and New Zealand Journal of Public Health, 33*(4), 384–387. https://doi.org/10.1111/j.1753-6405.2009.00412.x

Tuhiwai Smith, L. (2021). *Decolonizing methodologies: Research and indigenous peoples* (3rd ed.). Zed Books.

Walsh, M., & Grey, C. (2019). The contribution of avoidable mortality to the life expectancy gap in Maori and Pacific populations in New Zealand—A decomposition analysis. *New Zealand Medical Journal*, *132*(1492), 46–60.

Watene, K. (2016). Valuing nature: Māori philosophy and the capability approach. *Oxford Development Studies, 44*(3), 287–296. https://doi.org/10.1080/13600818.2015.1124077

Watts, N., Amann, M., Arnell, N., Ayeb-Karlsson, S., Belesova, K., Berry, H., Bouley, T., Boykoff, M., Byass, P., Cai, W., Campbell-Lendrum, D., Chambers, J., Daly, M., Dasandi, N., Davies, M., Depoux, A., Dominguez-Salas, P., Drummond, P., Ebi, K. L.,… & Costello, A. (2018). The 2018 report of the Lancet countdown on health and climate change: Shaping the health of nations for centuries to come. *The Lancet, 392*(10163), 2479–2514. https://doi.org/10.1016/S0140-6736(18)32594-7

Watts, N., Amann, M., Arnell, N., Ayeb-Karlsson, S., Belesova, K., Boykoff, M., Byass, P., Cai, W., Campbell-Lendrum, D., Capstick, S., Chambers, J., Dalin, C., Daly, M., Dasandi, N., Davies, M., Drummond, P., Dubrow, R., Ebi, K. L., Eckelman, M.,… & Montgomery, H. (2019). The 2019 report of the Lancet countdown on health and climate change: Ensuring that the health of a child born today is not defined by a changing climate. *The Lancet*, *394*(10211), 1836–1878. https://doi.org/10.1016/S0140-6736(19)32596-6

Whyte, K. (2017). Indigenous climate change studies: Indigenizing futures, decolonizing the Anthropocene. *English Language Notes*, *55*(1), 153–162. https://doi.org/10.1215/00138282-55.1-2.153

World Health Organization (WHO). (2023). *SDG Target 3.4 non-communicable diseases and mental health*. World Health Organization. https://www.who.int/data/gho/data/themes/topics/sdg-target-3_4-noncommunicable-diseases-and-mental-health

14 Centring Land in Decolonising Iterations of Psychology

Making the Case from South Africa

Nick Malherbe, Shahnaaz Suffla and Mohamed Seedat

Introduction

To control land is to control the populations living on and with the land (Bulhan, 2015). All over the world, colonial powers were consolidated on a global scale by dispossessing indigenous peoples from their land (Wolfe, 2006), while, at the same time, violently remoulding their relations with the land in the image of capital accumulation (Rosales, 2023; weNkosi, 2023). Today, this expropriative colonial order continues via the enormous siphoning of raw materials, energy, land, and under-compensated labour from the Global South to the Global North (Hickel et al., 2022).

It is because the project of settler colonialism was driven by the expropriation, dispossession, domination, and control of land – a project that is far from over, as evidenced in Palestine (e.g., Brathwaite et al., 2024; Shalhoub-Kervokian & Sheehi, 2023) – that land-based struggles must take centre stage in processes of decolonisation (Singh, 2019). Certainly, anticolonial rhetoric in the mid-20th century focused in large part on removing colonising powers and colonial capital relations from indigenous lands (Bulhan, 2015); those confronting today's enduring mechanisms of colonialism – known as coloniality (Ndlovu-Gatsheni, 2018) – must, similarly, take seriously the issue of land. The decolonial struggle for land is effectively a struggle over land as a system of reciprocal relations and obligations, and specifically what these relations and obligations can teach us about living with one another and the natural world in a manner that is free from exploitation and domination (Coulthard, 2014).

The material devastation that colonial powers have wrought on indigenous lands is incontestable. However, with knowledges, cultures, languages, relationships, human potentialities, and ways-of-being all tied in with land (see Ndlovu-Gatsheni, 2018; Ngcukaitobi, 2021; Readsura Decolonial Collective, 2022), decolonial struggles for land are psychological in as much as they are political. Identities, personhood, and communities are formed in relation to place, and therefore land, and the reclamation of land is then a reaffirmation of sovereignty and the self in relation to others and the world around us. The discipline of psychology has been slow to address the psycho-political constitution of land as a decolonial imperative. Brathwaite et al. (2024, p. 296) speak of "psychology's long-standing ignorance of land as a core nutrient of the soul, a people, a culture, and the desire to reclaim land and sovereignty as a refusal of alienation". Psychology tends to view the self, individuals, as well as communities or collectives as devoid of place, and therefore land. More often than not, psychology has been wielded in accordance with the individualising, pathologising, and regulating mandates of coloniality (see Seedat & Suffla, 2017). Nonetheless, and inspired in large part by the revolutionary psychological work of thinkers like Frantz Fanon (e.g., Fanon, 1963) as well as Hussein Bulhan (1985), some psychological practitioners have embraced the "decolonial turn" within their discipline, wherein efforts are made to pry psychology from the colonial episteme through which it was founded, and to put psychology to work for the

DOI: 10.4324/9781003492214-17

project of decolonisation (see Maldonado-Torres, 2017). Within this work, land is emerging as an increasingly central foundation for understanding, theorising, and enacting decolonial psychological praxis (see, e.g., Barnwell et al., 2021; Bryant & Sonn, 2022; Rai, 2022; Readsura Decolonial Collective, 2022; Rosales, 2023; Williams, 2019). Work of this kind understands psychology as context-based and thus land-situated, offering images and fragments of psychological praxis that take seriously the thefts, annexations, settlements, expulsions, struggles, returns, and cultivations of land in relation to decoloniality (see Brathwaite et al., 2024).

In this chapter, we are guided by the question of how psychological practice might be decolonised when it is led by ongoing land-based struggle. It is with land-based struggle, we argue, that both the material and the affective components of decolonisation are surfaced (for illuminating accounts of the role that place and coloniality have in research and place-based knowledges; see Abushama, 2024; Tuck & McKenzie, 2014). In this, we attempt to guard against decolonisation collapsing into mere metaphor (Tuck & Yang, 2012). To support our argument – and to pursue our guiding question – we draw from our community-oriented psychological work with land activists in South Africa. We demonstrate that work of this kind is far from universal; it is uneven and faces considerable setbacks and disappointments. Moreover, it compels us to abandon psychology's disciplinary dictates and imperialist impulses as related to the individualisation, management, adaptation, erasure, and/or pathologisation of collectives struggling for land, as well as the dehumanising, Eurocentric, ahistorical, and essentialising epistemes through which much of psychology is conducted (Readsura Decolonial Collective, 2022; Seedat & Suffla, 2017). Decolonising psychology, in short, calls on us to act in accordance with the imperatives of decolonial liberation – imperatives that are grounded in knowing, being, relating, and acting outside of the dehumanising dictates of coloniality (Ndlovu-Gatsheni, 2018).

Coloniality in South Africa: The Centrality of Land

All over the world, colonial authorities used land to control or destroy indigenous societies, while simultaneously consolidating new and existing colonial societies (Wolfe, 2006). This was certainly the case in South Africa. When European settlers arrived in the country in the mid-17th century, the land was inhabited, but it was not owned in an exclusive or privatised sense – which is to say, land did not constitute a colonial capitalist enterprise (Ngcukaitobi, 2021). It was in the colonial encounter that white ownership was violently exerted over Black subjects and the land.[1] Colonial authorities transformed indigenous lands and lives into racialised commodities that were plundered and destroyed as per the will of colonial capital (weNkosi, 2023). Colonial modernity was thus able to fix racialised categories into a hierarchy, endowing whiteness with humanity so that Blackness was denied ontological density, or a humanistic essence (Ndlovu-Gatsheni, 2013). In other words, colonial powers sought to hold Blackness apart from considerations of the human, denying Black populations the kinds of life and dignity afforded by land (see Wynter, 2003).

Scholars like Ngcukaitobi (2021) recount how legislation implemented in colonial-era South Africa focused to a large degree on land, and in particular on reconfiguring land and land taxes on a privatised basis (examples of such legislation included the 1894 Glen Grey Act; the 1902 Native Reserve Location Act; the 1936 Native Trust and Land Act; and the 1937 Black (Native) Laws Amendment Act). Legislation of this kind ensured that the best, most ideally situated land was reserved for white settlers, and that subsistence farming was replaced with commodity farming. An especially foundational piece of such legislation was the 1913 Natives Land Act, which appropriated 90% of the land surface in the country for white settlers, while confining indigenous populations to "reserves" on the remaining portions of the land (Hall & Ntsebeza, 2007). The formation of reserves functioned not only as a colonial strategy of divide and conquer but also as a means through which to reinforce the colonial project piece by piece, iteration by iteration, in transgenerational and geopolitical ways. Later, these reserves were slightly reconfigured (attributing 13% of South African land to 80% of the population) for the purpose of establishing a hyper-exploited Black migrant labour force (Turok, 2015).

The apartheid regime, founded in 1948, further consolidated colonialism's land-based legislation. Racialised land grabbing and segregation were enshrined in apartheid legislation, as were the violent dispossession, exploitation, and control of the country's Black population (Ngcukaitobi, 2021). In 1950, the Group Areas Act was passed. This, along with other "separate development" legislation, saw to the forced relocation of about 3.5 million Black people between the years 1960 and 1985 (Mamdani, 2020). Mass dispossession instated enormous psychic and material damage, as well as generational disenfranchisement and spatial apartheid (Manganyi, 1973/2019). As Bulhan (2015, p. 243) proclaims,

> After occupation of the land, control of the population followed to acquire not only cheap or free labor and market for manufactured goods, but also gradual erosion in the world of meaning … Lasting occupation of land, exploitation of human and material resources, and quelling resistance required the erosion of social bonding, indigenous beliefs, values, identities, and indigenous knowledge.

Although apartheid was officially dismantled in 1994, communities in South Africa remain, for the most part, racially segregated. The majority of Black communities in South Africa continue to experience marginalisation as a result of, among other deplorable injustices, impoverished or limited access to basic municipal services (e.g., water, housing, sanitation, electricity, adequate food, and healthcare); low pay and poor working conditions; and a lack of economic reform (Turok, 2015). These communities are, in other words, materially poor by design (Manganyi, 1973/2019). As was the case during apartheid, they are often intensely policed and managed, or they go ignored by the State (Turok, 2015). Moreover, although the post-1994 government has built millions of houses, these houses tend to be of poor quality, too small, and they are often less than ideally located within the country's town planning framework (Hendricks & Pithouse, 2013). The inadequacy of these housing projects reflects ongoing challenges in providing equitable and sustainable living conditions. Additionally, State-driven forced removals are increasingly common in the post-1994 era, exacerbating the struggles of vulnerable communities (Cornell et al., 2020; Hendricks et al., 2013). In each of these instances, we see how coloniality outlives colonisation and colonialism.

Although land reform appears to be a progressive value in the Constitution of South Africa (ratified in 1996), such reform has lagged in practice (Ngcukaitobi, 2021). Under South Africa's racial capitalist order, profitability rather than community interests, drives land use (Turok, 2015). Indeed, in contemporary South Africa, a powerful land-owning elite decides what land is to be sold, how it is to be sold, to whom it is sold, and how it will be used (Ngcukaitobi, 2021). Land reform tends to be confined to the logic of property rights (Hall & Ntsebeza, 2007). As weNkosi (2023) demonstrates, this logic conceals the systemic violence that reifies, maintains, and protects systems of coloniality in and beyond South Africa.

The South African State has neglected the land question. In addition to the lack of meaningful land reparation, legislation, or reform in South Africa, there has been little acknowledgement of the material and the psychic damages and losses instituted by colonialism's land-based project (see Ngũgĩ wa Thiong'o, 1986). Within this context, the urgency of insisting on the ontological density that is negated, refused, and eroded by coloniality – which is to say, the urgency of decoloniality – cannot be understated. There have always been grassroots movements that have responded to this urgency with a clear and politically committed vision that connects liberation and well-being to the psycho-politics of personhood, community, and land. These struggles insist that South Africa's colonial past will continue to structure the present if land-based structural inequalities are not addressed on a meaningful and systematic scale.

Decolonisation as a Psycho-Political Struggle for Land

Rather than a singular or linear formation, collective struggles over land in South Africa manifest differentially, as a pluriversal "reaction and a method of refutation" (weNkosi, 2023, p. 100). We see examples of these struggles in the actions taken by Durban's Industrial and Commercial Workers' Union in the 1920s and 1930s; the 1940s' land occupations in Johannesburg; the 1956 women's march and struggles against land evictions in Durban; mass land occupations and squats that took place throughout the country in the 1970s and 1980s; and in today's road blockades, occupations, strikes, and marches (Hendricks & Pithouse, 2013). Although post-1994 struggles over land have taken place through constitutionally protected forms of resistance (e.g., protest), such struggles have, as Desai (2002) demonstrates, also occurred at the legislative level (e.g., contesting land evictions in court), and through extra-legal measures (e.g., illegally connecting to the national electricity and water grids). Across South Africa, we continue to see community-led land occupations, collectives that defend indigenous land against corporate enclosures, and attempts to preserve the knowledges, spiritual capacities, and health practices deeply tied to land[2] (see Greco, 2013; Hart, 2002; Mahlatsi, 2018).

If not completely ignored by the South African State, post-1994 struggles are oftentimes met with disproportionate levels of violence from the South African Police Service. Relatedly, many individuals engaged in struggles for land have been criminalised by South Africa's political and media classes (Hendricks & Pithouse, 2013; Malherbe et al., 2021). As such, throughout the country, communities have mobilised to defend land-based struggles (Desai, 2002).

We can clearly see the structural and material manifestations of coloniality within different struggles for land in South Africa, with activists, movement facilitators, and State actors commonly referring to these struggles as "service delivery protests" (see Duncan, 2016). However, as noted above, to conceptualise struggles for land as solely material struggles is to miss the psychological character of these struggles, which is to say, how these struggles are made in and against different psychological registers, such as rage, mourning, affection, love, frustration, despair, disappointment, and joy. Struggles for land are, as they have always been, highly affective precisely because they are concerned with the work of (re)humanisation, relational ontologies, reckoning with colonial trauma and wounding, and the restoration of Black ontological density in the face of ongoing colonial violence (see Ndlovu-Gatsheni, 2018; Ngcukaitobi, 2021). To struggle for land is to attempt to wrest the locus of dignity and well-being from the violent, hierarchical impositions of coloniality.

With respect to the psycho-political constitution of land-based struggle in South Africa, we can understand land as forming part of what Erasmus (2017) calls "humaning". Seedat et al. (2021) note that humaning refers to ongoing processes of creating life in cooperation with others and in ways that move beyond coloniality's impositional racialisation. Humaning is contextually and socially rooted and speaks directly to those activist efforts that seek to undo the colonial coordinates of racialised space-making. It seeks to envision new futures that transcend coloniality, white supremacy, and regressive nationalism. With land being so central to the colonial project of dehumanisation, we can understand land reform as part of decolonial humaning efforts to restore the ontological density of colonised subjects.

Land, and indeed the decolonial struggle over land, is not merely an issue of commodities, nor is it only an issue of property rights. It is a process of refusing the logics of coloniality, and of remaking desire outside of colonial recognition (Coulthard, 2014), all while establishing new political communities forged through historical consciousness (Foley & Anderson, 2006; Mamdani, 2020). Here, decoloniality pushes us to understand land reform as a process of reimagining being in the world (Ngcukaitobi, 2021). The decolonial struggle for land is a struggle to restore and heal our very conception of the human (see Rosales, 2023); to disentangle subjective expression from colonial logics and to honour the knowledges, memories, identities, cultures, bodies, and relations connected to the land (e.g., Readsura Decolonial Collective, 2022). Decoloniality thus moves us beyond redistributing land, and towards engaging with how land is used, what knowledges and meanings are encompassed within land, how identities are forged through land, and in what ways land connects to health, well-being, spirituality, sustenance, and history. The connected practices and experiential knowledges inhered within land can inform ethical engagements between humans and nature over time, what Coulthard (2014) refers to as grounded normativity.

It is imperative that those wishing to embrace the decolonial turn within their psychological work make central the psycho-political character of land-based struggle. There is, of course, a relatively small body of important work that has been undertaken in this area. Bulhan (2015), for instance, has long stressed the importance of studying the psychological consequences of colonial occupation of indigenous land, while Fanon (1963/2004) and Manganyi (1973/2019) have emphasised the psychic processes involved in struggling for land, as well as being dispossessed of one's land. In more recent years, psychologists embracing the decolonial turn have engaged with the psycho-politics of land struggles in India (Rai, 2022), the United States (Rosales, 2023), Latin America (Ciofalo, 2019), Palestine (Makkawi, 2017), Australia (Bryant & Sonn, 2022), and South Africa (Cornell et al., 2020). It is within this tradition of work that we offer below a reflection of our community-oriented psychological work with land activists in Thembelihle, a historically marginalised South African community.

Our relationship with these activists is a long-standing one. The University of South Africa's Institute for Social and Health Sciences, the research institute in which each of us works, has partnered with residents of Thembelihle on a range of community projects for almost 40 years. These projects, underpinned by a collaborative and participatory paradigm, vary in their scope and duration. Broadly though, they are concerned with consolidating political coalitions; advocating for energy, educational, gender, and social justice; lobbying for service delivery; fostering community cohesion; and centring local knowledges and privileging epistemic justice.

Our long-standing collaborative partnership with Thembelihle has taken many forms, and its intensity has ebbed and flowed in accordance with the broader political climate in South Africa, as well as tensions within the community itself. Like all university-community partnerships, ours is structured by inherent unequal power differentials. Acknowledging that such power inequities cannot be definitively resolved, we focus on continuously negotiating our relations with the Thembelihle community through a reflexive and openly communicative ethic that has developed over the decades. The collaboration that we describe in this chapter emerged out of discussions with community partners around the need to address and engage with the various struggles in Thembelihle, with land being central to these struggles.

As researchers, each of us enters into community partnerships with particular histories, standpoints, complicities, and identities – all of which are shaped by coloniality as well as resistance to coloniality. Despite our long-standing engagements with and in Thembelihle, each of us is a community outsider. As individuals, we are of different ages, races, and genders. Thus, the "we" to which we refer to ourselves in the following reflections does not – because it cannot – capture the variability of our positionalities. As Choi (2021, p. 68) writes, we are "variously situated, and are at times beneficiaries, at times losers, but collectively, we lose, we harm, we sustain imperialism". Therefore, the "we" under which we write speaks to a shared political commitment to advancing decoloniality with community members – engaging with struggles for land as well as the effects of land dispossession. This commitment is complex. It strives, unevenly and at times in faltering ways, to consolidate decolonial struggles within and across different communities.

Case Example: Solidarity, Affect, and the Psycho-Political Struggle for Land in South Africa

Established in the mid-1980s, Thembelihle is a socioeconomically marginalised community located in the south-west of Johannesburg, South Africa. Since 2001, the community has been engaged in intensive struggles over land (Ngwane, 2021). Although these struggles have been led primarily by the Thembelihle Crisis Committee (TCC), an activist movement in the community, there are also smaller, informal organisations that engage in struggles over land and life in the community (see, e.g., Day et al., 2024). With most of Thembelihle's residents living in shack settlements, and with the community remaining chronically under-serviced (electricity, sewage, and paved roads are largely absent in the community), residents engaged in struggles over land have done so through protests, campaigns, marches, pickets, blockades, demonstrations, illegal electricity connections, and even electoral politics (Segodi, 2018).

The South African State's response to land activism in Thembelihle has been varied. In some instances, the State has taken seriously the demands of protesters (e.g., partially electrifying the catchment area in 2016). However, more often, the State has either ignored activists from Thembelihle or it has responded with force (Duncan, 2016; Poplak, 2015). The State has also forcibly relocated many Thembelihle residents to surrounding communities. These relocations were based on the results of a geotechnical study which found that Thembelihle is not fit for in situ development due to the community's location on dolomite, a porous rock type that causes sinkholes (Tselapedi & Dugard, 2013). Initially, the relocations relied on the illegal demolition of shacks in Thembelihle (Segodi, 2018), and although some people moved willingly to the surrounding communities, many waited for over a decade to be allocated new housing in these communities. Others were made to relocate through threats and intimidation by the State (Cornell et al., 2020). The TCC consistently resisted the forced relocations, and in 2004, it commissioned its own independent geological assessment which found that land in Thembelihle was fit for development. Such development would, however, come at a higher cost to the State due to precautionary measures required to develop on dolomitic land (Segodi, 2018).

Land-based struggles in Thembelihle are not unique to the community. In many respects, these struggles are indicative of the struggles that face South Africa more broadly. Although other land-based community struggles differ from those in Thembelihle, such as struggles against mining conglomerates (see, e.g., Barnwell et al., 2021), these struggles nonetheless form part of a broader movement to resist the totalising structures of coloniality. The TCC and other movements in Thembelihle have played an important role in connecting and, through these connections, strengthening seemingly disparate land-based struggles in South Africa.

Following on from the call to circulate the knowledges and voices of those engaged in decolonial struggles for land (see, e.g., Hendricks et al., 2013), we established a collaborative relationship with several land activists in Thembelihle. Some of us collaborated with these activists to produce and screen digital stories capturing their struggles (Lau & Seedat, 2015; Lau et al., 2017). Several of the activists involved in co-producing these digital stories noted the need for the struggles and histories of Thembelihle to be told in a nuanced, long-form manner. In dialogue with these activities, we collectively decided to co-produce a documentary film about Thembelihle, one that told stories of the community from the perspectives of those who live and work there.

In what follows, we reflect on this participatory documentary film project. The documentary film, titled by the community partners as *Thembelihle: Place of Hope*,[3] depicts the history of Thembelihle's psycho-political struggles over land, as well as how people live on and with the land in their daily lives. Due to space constraints, we cannot outline the particular stories which comprise the documentary. Instead, in returning to our guiding question – how we might decolonise psychology by centring community-led struggles for land – we reflect on how the documentary has been used to advance land struggles in and beyond Thembelihle, with a particular focus on various public screening events and the role that psychological practitioners might play here. Specifically, we consider below how the documentary has been used by land activists in Thembelihle for purposes of solidarity-building and affective connection.

Documentary film, we should be clear, is not an inherently decolonising method. However, because documentary film has shown to be an especially visceral mode through which to interrogate dominant narratives while strengthening community relations (see Canella, 2017), we argue that it can be mobilised to engage the psycho-political facets of organising collective decolonising struggle. Therefore, in what follows, we attempt to make clear how participatory documentary filmmaking is able to open space for consolidating land-based struggle by interrogating the political, affective, and historical facets of this struggle (see Tuck & McKenzie, 2014).

Solidarity-Building

To decolonise how we understand and make use of the land is, therefore, to de-link land redistribution and reform from capitalistic imperatives while, at the same time, rebuilding the kinds of equitable human-nature relations that have been disallowed by colonial capital. Contemporary South Africa is structured by a colonial logic, which is to say, it functions as a commodity; one that is to be competed for and whose exchange value is measured against other commodities in the marketplace (Ngcukaitobi, 2021; weNkosi, 2023). As such, actioning such a necessarily audacious vision of decolonisation in South Africa requires consolidating collective grassroots power, that is, the solidarity relations among those fighting for decolonisation must be made tantamount to today's land-based struggles.

The solidarity relation is neither static nor is it free from tension. It is built through value-based engagements that take up the dual task of consciousness-raising and forging political commitments across regions and struggles (see Sonn et al., 2022). In the case of *Thembelihle: Place of Hope*, community members were clear that merely screening the documentary was not sufficient for building solidarity. Rather, the documentary screenings would allow for dialogue and engagement around Thembelihle's various land-based struggles. It was in these audiencing spaces that people were able to connect their seemingly disparate activist interventions to broader emancipatory visions, or what we might think of as the decolonial imaginary (see Pérez, 1999).

Part of the effort to expand the solidarity relation was to connect land struggles in Thembelihle to a project of (re)humanisation, one that counters the relentless dehumanising apparatuses of coloniality that deny people the psychic and material conditions for dignity. During post-screening discussions, audiences made it clear that the TCC was not struggling for land as a commodity. Instead, it was struggling over an altogether new conception of land, one that was attuned to the humanity of colonised populations that has for so long been denied. As one audience member summarised these struggles: "we of Thembelihle, we are citizens of South Africa, we are human beings, we are here".

At several screening events hosted in Thembelihle, audiences made connections between their political struggles and quotidian life in Thembelihle. In responding to the documentary's depiction of a subsistence farmer, one activist in the audience of a screening event that we attended noted that "there's this brother … that's doing a garden … he did encourage me … As people, we have to care for each other". Several other audience members also expressed that the TCC's struggles for land and life appeared to be represented by this farmer who, although not an avowed activist, worked the land to ensure that those in Thembelihle were eating well (the farmer was engaged in community education initiatives on agriculture and did not charge people who could not afford his produce). Through his land-based activity, then, the farmer prefiguratively enacted a decolonising logic that guided the TCC's struggles for land. By connecting the quotidian with the political in this manner, audiences were able to build an expansive kind of solidarity that extended beyond organised grassroots activist politics. Such an expansive practice of solidarity serves as a mode of rehumanisation precisely because it insists on the human-nature entanglements that coloniality has worked to sever and disaggregate.

Residents of Thembelihle also hosted documentary screening events with other community activist groups. At these events, audiences forged connections between differently located political struggles – most of which oriented around land and living with dignity on the land. As community psychologists, we were not always invited to these screening events, demonstrating not only community ownership of the documentary but also the point at which psychology was not of use – and may have even served as a hindrance – to building the solidarity relation. Even at the screening events to which we were invited, it was important that the most pressing political concerns (e.g., organising demonstrations; arranging community assemblies; facilitating transportation for comrades) were foregrounded and given space over any institutional priorities that we may have had. If, indeed, psychologists are invited to participate in these spaces as psychological workers (they may well participate equally as activists), then the role that they play must be determined by the psycho-political requirements of the collective. This may involve, for instance, addressing debilitating intergroup tensions within the collective; co-facilitating dialogical spaces where comrades can confront one another and constructively navigate difference, divergence, and discomfort; co-creating spaces where members of the collective can mourn or sit in the hardships and that decolonial struggle so often entails; and supporting community-led healing practices. It is in these ways that psychological practice can be shaped and led by land-based struggle.

Expanding the solidarity relation also saw the documentary being screened in communities that were not engaged in land-based struggles. For example, the documentary was screened at a community campaign event that took place in the wider Johannesburg area; at an event in the Central Business District; and in two of Johannesburg's wealthiest suburbs. At the various screening events, residents of Thembelihle articulated and historicised their struggles over land in ways that countered the individualising, dehumanising media depictions of these struggles (see Malherbe et al., 2021). Moreover, it was at these events that residents of Thembelihle were able to build solidarities across geographies, and with people who were not always aware of Thembelihle's history of land-based struggle.

As was to be expected, at the screening events in the wealthier communities, residents from these communities were resistant to the documentary being screened and, in one instance, authorities were summoned with instructions for us to cease screening the documentary. Nonetheless, within these wealthier areas, activists from Thembelihle connected and built solidarity with low-wage workers who were facing similar struggles. They did this by engaging in discussions, either in small groups or on a one-to-one basis, about the particularities of their respective struggles as well as potential connections between these struggles (e.g., a common adversary or a shared political goal). Although the pressure that was being applied in some instances by state authorities meant that these interactions were often brief, plans were made among the different social actors to stay in contact with one another, to attend other documentary screenings, and to continue fostering solidarity across communities. These efforts highlighted the importance of collective action and mutual support in the face of the challenges posed by external forces.

It should be noted that the post-screening discussions that we have described here are not, in and of themselves, solidarity. These discussions do not in every instance lead to solidarity action. It is more accurate to understand these discussions as a component of building the kinds of bonds and communicative relations that are necessary for actioning solidarity. The post-screening discussions, which were led by community-led activists and facilitated by us, saw activists working through tension, confronting intergroup tensions, discussing where to meet before a protest event, outlining which resistance tactics work and which do not, bringing people's attention to new or unforeseen struggles, making connections between struggles, and allowing people the space to reflect on why struggle is important and, indeed, what struggle means to them, especially in moments of defeat that might feel hopeless. In allowing space for people to engage collectively with the various psycho-political components of building solidarity – which are not, in and of themselves solidarity – psychology can play a part in consolidating decolonial struggles for land.

The solidarity relation is not fixed. It twists and turns in accordance with the political milieu in which it is situated. Although the documentary does not transcend the historical moment in which it was produced, it nonetheless remains a representation of struggle and history in Thembelihle as told by specific actors. At the different screening events, all of which are led and co-facilitated by residents of Thembelihle, audiences drew from this representation to undertake the combative work required to build the solidarity relation robustly and openly. This is ongoing work. As one audience member declared at a screening event in Thembelihle: "the struggle for a better Thembelihle continues". The documentary thus serves as a tool for building, strengthening, and expanding solidarity with this struggle.

Centring Affect

Affect can be understood as the complex, intersubjective feelings of bodily intensity (Rutherford, 2016). The documentary screenings served as a means by which to take seriously the affective dimensions of the struggles over land in Thembelihle. In this, the psycho-political character of struggles for land was engaged explicitly and in ways that did not seek to fit neatly within the schemas made available by the discipline of psychology on affect.

In some respects, the documentary screenings functioned as spaces in which audiences could articulate feelings of melancholy, rage, bitterness, and burnout in relation to land dispossession and struggles over land. One audience member recounted that he was "emotionally triggered" after being presented with Thembelihle's histories of land-based struggle, while others expressed feeling a mixture of pride and despair after watching the struggle and fortitude of the activists in the documentary. The documentary film, one audience member noted, appeared to grapple with "the water and the mud" that constituted Thembelihle's land struggles. Although these are undoubtedly difficult affective states, the articulation of difficult affect can serve as a conscientising mode of externalising the internalisation of coloniality (Coulthard, 2014). Or, as Anzaldúa (2002) points out, in these moments of unease, there lies an opportunity for *conocimiento*, a form of interconnectedness that bridges solidarities in action with political intention and values forged in struggle. Indeed, it was through difficult affect that people in Thembelihle connected emotionally with one another and to ongoing struggles for decolonisation and, by extension, humanisation.

Centring affect also meant sitting with the sorts of disagreements and agitations that mark collective struggle. The successes and failures of struggle are always perceived in different ways, and people are differentially invested in different aspects of struggle. Indeed, at several screening events, audience members disagreed with one another regarding representation in the documentary.

Although most audience members expressed approval over how community members in the documentary represented Thembelihle and its struggles for land, some argued that these community members were attributing to Thembelihle an essentialised experience of struggle; a "face of poverty" as one audience member described it. At other moments, audience members wrangled over what it meant to accept the State's relocations, and why some in the community chose to resist these relocations (see Cornell et al., 2020 for more on these tensions). There were also screening events where audiences, in assessing TCC's land-based activism, debated the different strategies and tactics that would be most effective. Much of this audience discussion was centred on whether the TCC should work with or against the South African State, with many audience members becoming visibly emotional when discussing State violence. It was not intended that such tension would be resolved and entirely worked through, as is the wont of much mainstream psychology. Rather, the screening spaces were intended to allow people a space to speak openly, while acknowledging and holding the tensions inherent to struggle that so often go unarticulated and unnamed.

The intensive affective connections observed at the different documentary screenings were, of course, momentary; they appeared to have been experienced most acutely in the very moments at which they arose. However, these affective connections could be reactivated at different moments (see, e.g., Day et al., 2024). For example, despite in-person political organising being tremendously challenging during South Africa's COVID-19 lockdown period in 2020, activists in Thembelihle continued to push the State to provide services, food parcels, and healthcare. It was through an already established affective intensity – built over many years of struggle – that people in the community remained committed to ongoing struggles for dignity during this time. The documentary screenings served as spaces in which to further consolidate such affective connections.

Psychologists embracing the decolonial turn are challenged to work with affect in ways that are not predetermined or foreclosed by mainstream psychological theory. In this, psychological theory and methodologies should be drawn on only insofar as they assist people in articulating, strengthening, and drawing out the affective character of struggle. It is in this manner that psychologists can contribute to understanding and consolidating psycho-political currents within land-based struggle that seeks to defend against coloniality's attack on the epistemological, health-related, cultural, spiritual, relational, livelihood, environmental, and historical practices that are tied in with the land.

Conclusion

Through its Eurocentric epistemological frameworks, as well as its individualising and pathologising impulses, psychology has by and large functioned as a kind of management apparatus rather than praxis attuned to the psycho-political currents of liberation (Seedat & Suffla, 2017). The discipline of psychology has more often than not aligned with coloniality (Maldonado-Torres, 2017; Manganyi, 1973/2019; Readsura Decolonial Collective, 2022; Seedat & Suffla, 2017). However, the decolonial turn within psychology has pointed towards a different sort of psychological work, wherein differently wounded subjects work with one another to rupture and move beyond the coloniality of knowledge, power, and being. In focusing on our work, undertaken in collaboration with residents of Thembelihle, we have argued in this chapter that decolonising psychological work must attune itself to land as central to psycho-political mobilisation and humanisation.

Struggles over land, it should be emphasised, do not need psychology. For psychology to be of use to these struggles, it must shed itself of its disciplinary and epistemological hubris, giving way to the demands of decolonial struggle. The demands of this struggle are particular, in that they connect with indigenous values as well as the histories, knowledges, and relational practices tied in with place (see, e.g., Anzaldúa, 2002; Ciofalo, 2019; Coulthard, 2014; Foley & Anderson, 2006;

Nabulsi, 2023; Okoth-Ogendo, 2008), but it is also internationalist – connecting global struggles that are actively resisting coloniality's global purview (see, e.g., Brathwaite et al., 2024; Mamdani, 2020). It is those engaged in land-based struggles who are to determine what use, if any, psychology is to their struggles. It is in this respect that we must both take up and abandon psychology in accordance with what decolonising visions of life, dignity, well-being, and liberation require. The realisation of these visions necessitates that we do not lose sight of coloniality as a land-based project of domination and dispossession.

We must, of course, avoid temporally, geographically, and politically flattening decolonial struggles for land. In South Africa, for instance, the struggles for land in the era of classical colonialism were not the same as those carried out during the apartheid era, just as they are not the same as those undertaken today. Each of these struggles is, in some respects, bound to a particular geo-temporal and political location. Nonetheless, each is bound by a common refusal of colonial capitalism whose operations depend upon land dispossession. At the level of geography, the struggles for land in South Africa are not identical to the indigenous struggles for land in what are currently known as Australia and Canada, nor are they identical to the displacements and genocidal erasures faced by Palestinians. Again though, there is an underlying refusal of colonial occupation and the systemic violence of dispossession, erasure, and exploitation in each of these instances, and committing to decoloniality requires aligning with these different struggles, and recognising and consolidating the linkages between them.

It is precisely because land is fundamental to coloniality that today's decolonial struggles must centralise issues of land. In this chapter, we have attempted to show that, although most of psychology understands individual subjects as devoid of place or land, there is nonetheless a decolonising tradition of psychological practice – albeit modest – that takes seriously belonging, history, place, commitment, tension, identity, place, dignity, and humanisation in relation to land-based struggle. We believe that it is more productive not to prescribe specific actions for aligning psychology with decolonial struggles for land. Instead, we insist that psychology should be led by the psycho-political imperatives of these struggles.

Notes

1 We do not use race or racial categories in this chapter to uncritically refer to biological essences. Instead, we understand race as a socialisation process, one that is rooted in the structures of coloniality. Thus, 'race', socially constructed as it is, continues to have material and psychological consequences. 'Race' is the basis of racist oppression, but it has also been a modality through which to organise decolonial resistance.

2 There are many land-based movements in South Africa. To catalogue each of these is beyond the scope of this chapter. Nonetheless, it is worth mentioning Abahlali baseMjondolo, the largest shack-dwellers movement in the country. Though not beyond criticism, Abahlali has consistently fought to de-link from the South African State's control over land while, at the same time, holding the State accountable and making demands of it.

3 Community members who co-produced the documentary film requested that it not be shared on publicly available online platforms so that they could lead on the post-screening discussions. The quotations that we draw on in this chapter are from these discussions.

References

Abushama, H. (2024). Mapping and countermapping dispossession in Palestine. *Transactions of the Institute of British Geographers*, *50*(1), e12708. https://doi.org/10.1111/tran.12708

Anzaldúa, G. (2002). (Un)natural bridges, (un)safe spaces. In G. Anzaldúa, & A. Keating (Eds.), *This bridge we call home: Radical visions for transformation* (pp. 15–19). Routledge.

Barnwell, G., Makaulule, M., Stroud, L., Watson, M., & Dima, M. (2021). The lived experiences of place severing and decolonial resurgence in Vhembe District, South Africa. *Awry: Journal of Critical Psychology*, *2*(1), 49–68. https://www.awryjcp.com/index.php/awry/article/view/39

Brathwaite, B., Abi-Ghannam, G., & Fine, M. (2024). Refusing necropolitics in St. John and in Palestine: Unearthing stories of land dispossession, desire and the will to live. In C. C. Sonn, J. S. Fernández, J. F. Moura Jr., M. E. Madyaningrum, & N. Malherbe (Eds.), *Handbook of decolonial community psychology* (pp. 295–318). Springer.

Bryant, E. K., & Sonn, C. C. (2022). Country and climate: Journeys toward the decolonial option among non-indigenous climate activists. *Psychology in Society*, *63*, 52–82. https://www.scielo.org.za/scielo.php?script=sci_arttext&pid=S1015-60462022000100004

Bulhan, H. A. (1985). *Frantz Fanon and the psychology of oppression*. Plenum Press.

Bulhan, H. A. (2015) Stages of colonialism in Africa: From occupation of land to occupation of being. *Journal of Social and Political Psychology, 3*(1), 239–256. https://doi.org/10.5964/jspp.v3i1.143

Canella, G. (2017). Social movement documentary practices: Digital storytelling, social media and organizing. *Digital Creativity*, *28*(1), 24–37. https://doi.org/10.1080/14626268.2017.1289227

Choi, S. (2021). Everyday peace in critical feminist theory. In T. Väyrynen, S. Parashar, É Féron, & C. C. Confortini (Eds.), *Routledge handbook of feminist peace research* (pp. 60–69). Routledge.

Ciofalo, N. (Ed.). (2019). *Indigenous psychologies in an era of decolonization*. Springer.

Cornell, J., Seedat, M., Malherbe, N., & Suffla, S. (2020). Splintered politics of memory and community resistance. *Journal of Community Psychology*, *48*(5), 1677–1695. https://doi.org/10.1002/jcop.22394

Coulthard, G. S. (2014). *Red skin, white masks: Rejecting the colonial politics of recognition*. University of Minnesota Press.

Day, S., Malherbe, N., Suffla, S., & Seedat, M. (2024). Building decolonial peace into the everyday: A feminist intervention. *Journal of Intervention and Statebuilding, 18*(4), 436–452. https://doi.org/10.1080/17502977.2023.2241754

Desai, A. (2002). *We are the poors: Community struggles in post-apartheid South Africa*. NYU Press.

Duncan, J. (2016). *Protest nation: The right to protest in South Africa*. University of KwaZulu-Natal Press.

Erasmus, Z. (2017). *Race otherwise: Forging a new humanism for South Africa*. Wits University Press.

Fanon, F. (1963/2004). *The wretched of the earth*. Grove Press.

Foley, G., & Anderson, T. (2006). Land rights and Aboriginal voices. *Australian Journal of Human Rights, 12*(1), 83–108. https://doi.org/10.1080/1323238X.2006.11910814

Greco, E. (2013). Struggles and resistance against land dispossession in Africa. In T. Allan, M. Keulertz, S. Soujamo, & J. Warner (Eds.), *Handbook of land and water grabs in Africa* (pp. 456–468). Routledge

Hall, R., & Ntsebeza, L. (2007). Introduction. In L. Ntsebeza, & R. Hall (Eds.), *The land question in South Africa: The challenge of transformation and redistribution* (pp.1–24). HSRC Press.

Hart, G. (2002). Linking land, labour and livelihood struggles. *South African Labour Bulletin, 26*(6), 26–29.

Hendricks, F., Ntsebeza, L., & Helliker, K. (2013). Land questions in South Africa. In F. Hendricks, L. Ntsebeza, & K. Helliker (Eds.), *The promise of land: Undoing a century of dispossession in South Africa* (pp. 1–23). Jacana.

Hendricks, F., & Pithouse, R. (2013). Urban land question in contemporary South Africa: The case of Cape Town. In F. Hendricks, L. Ntsebeza, & K. Helliker (Eds.), *The promise of land: Undoing a century of dispossession in South Africa* (pp. 103–129). Jacana.

Hickel, J., Dorninger, C., Wieland, H., & Suwandi, I. (2022). Imperialist appropriation in the world economy: Drain from the global South through unequal exchange, 1990–2015. *Global Environmental Change*, *73*, 102467. https://doi.org/10.1016/j.gloenvcha.2022.102467

Lau, U., & Seedat, M. (2015). The community story, relationality and process: Bridging tools for researching local knowledge in a peri-urban township. *Journal of Community & Applied Social Psychology, 25*(5), 369–383. https://psycnet.apa.org/doi/10.1002/casp.2219

Lau, U., Suffla, S., & Kgatitswe, L. B. (2017). Catalysing transformation through stories: Building peace in recognition, struggle and dialogue. In M. Seedat, S. Suffla, & D. J. Christie, (Eds.), *Emancipatory and participatory methodologies in peace, critical, and community psychology* (pp. 147–164). Springer

Mahlatsi, M. L. (2018). The peasants revolt: Analysing the role of the democratic state in the struggle for land and environmental justice in Xolobeni, Eastern Cape, South Africa. *Journal of Public Administration, 53*(2–1), 615–631. https://hdl.handle.net/10520/EJC-1486887507

Makkawi, I. (2017). The rise and fall of academic community psychology in Palestine and the way forward. *South African Journal of Psychology*, *47*(4), 482–492. https://doi.org/10.1177/0081246317737945

Maldonado-Torres, N. (2017). Frantz Fanon and the decolonial turn in psychology: From modern/colonial methods to the decolonial attitude. *South African Journal of Psychology*, *47*(4), 432–441. https://doi.org/10.1177/0081246317737918

Malherbe, N., Seedat, M., & Suffla, S. (2021). Analyzing discursive constructions of community in newspaper articles. *American Journal of Community Psychology*, *67*(3–4), 433–446. https://doi.org/10.1002/ajcp.12477

Mamdani, M. (2020). *Neither settler nor native: The making and unmaking of permanent minorities*. Harvard University Press.

Manganyi, N. C. (1973/2019). *Being-black-in-the-world*. Wits University Press.

Nabulsi, J. (2023). Reclaiming Palestinian indigenous sovereignty. *Journal of Palestine Studies, 52*(2), 24–42. https://doi.org/10.1080/0377919X.2023.2203830

Ndlovu-Gatsheni, S. (2018). *Epistemic freedom in Africa: Deprovincialization and decolonization*. Routledge.

Ndlovu-Gatsheni, S. J. (2013). Perhaps decoloniality is the answer? Critical reflections on development from a decolonial epistemic perspective. *Africanus, 43*(2), 1–11. https://hdl.handle.net/10520/EJC142701

Ngcukaitobi, T. (2021). *Land matters: South Africa's failed land reforms and the road ahead.* Random House.

Ngũgĩ wa Thiong'o. (1986). *Decolonising the mind: The politics of language in African literature*. J. Currey.

Ngwane, T. (2021). *Amakomiti: Grassroots democracy in South African shack settlements*. Pluto Press.

Okoth-Ogendo, H. (2008). The nature of land rights under Indigenous law in Africa. In A. Claassens, & B. Cousins (Eds.), *Land, power and custom: Controversies generated by South Africa's Communal Land Rights Act* (pp. 95–108). University of Cape Town Press with the Legal Resources Centre.

Pérez, E. (1999). *The decolonial imaginary: Writing Chicanas into history*. Indiana University Press.

Poplak, R. (2015, May 5). The army vs. Thembelihle: Where the truth lies. *Daily Maverick*. https://www.dailymaverick.co.za/article/2015-05-05-the-army-vs-thembelihle-where-the-truth-lies

Rai, A. (2022). Chasing the ghosts: Stories of people left behind on the frontline of climate and ecological crisis. *South African Journal of Psychology*, *52*(4), 460–471. https://doi.org/10.1177/00812463221130902

Readsura Decolonial Collective (in random order: Glenn Adams, Kopano Ratele, Shahnaaz Suffla, & Geetha Reddy). (2022). Psychology as a site for decolonial intervention. *Journal of Social Issues, 78*(2), 255–277. https://doi.org/10.1111/josi.12524

Rosales, C. E. (2023). Finding a community in plants: Reexamining the decolonial project of rehumanization with our nonhuman relatives. *Peace and Conflict: Journal of Peace Psychology*, *29*(1), 52–59. https://psycnet.apa.org/doi/10.1037/pac0000628

Rutherford, D. (2016). Affect theory and the empirical. *Annual Review of Anthropology*, *45*, 285–300. https://doi.org/10.1146/annurev-anthro-102215-095843

Seedat, M., & Suffla, S. (2017). Community psychology and its (dis)contents, archival legacies and decolonisation. *South African Journal of Psychology*, *47*(4), 421–431. https://doi.org/10.1177/0081246317741423

Seedat, M., Suffla, S., & Ndlovu-Gatsheni, S. (2021). Mbeki's 'I am an African' speech: Mobilising psychopolitical resources for political reconstitution of post-apartheid South Africa. *African Studies, 80*(3–4), 451–465. https://doi.org/10.1080/00020184.2021.2012754

Segodi, S. (2018, March 13). The never-ending housing challenge – reflection on Thembelihle. *Daily Maverick*. https://www.dailymaverick.co.za/article/2018-03-13-op-ed-the-never-ending-housing-challenge-reflection-on-thembelihle/

Shalhoub-Kevorkian, N., & Sheehi, S. (2023). Abolitionism, settler colonialism and state crime. *State Crime Journal*, *12*(2), 132–145. https://www.jstor.org/stable/48774400

Singh, J. (2019). Decolonizing radical democracy. *Contemporary Political Theory*, *18*, 331–356. https://doi.org/10.1057/s41296-018-0277-5

Sonn, C. C., Fox, R., Keast, S., & Rua, M. (2022). Fostering and sustaining transnational solidarities for transformative social change: Advancing community psychology research and action. *American Journal of Community Psychology, 69*(3–4), 269–282. https://doi.org/10.1002/ajcp.12602

Tselapedi, T., & Dugard, J. (2013). Reclaiming power: A case study of the Thembelihle Crisis Committee. *Good Governance Learning Network*. Retrieved from https://ggln.org.za/images/solg_reports/SoLG_2013.pdf#page=58

Tuck, E., & McKenzie, M. (2014). *Place in research: Theory, methodology, and methods*. Routledge.

Tuck, E., & Yang, W. (2012). Decolonization is not a metaphor. *Decolonization: Indigeneity, Education & Society, 1*(1), 1–40.

Turok, I. (2015). The dual economy and spatial inequalities in South Africa. In B. Turok (Ed.), *Changing the colour of capital: Essays in politics and economics* (pp. 87–97). David Philip Publishers.

weNkosi, M. (2023). *These potatoes look like humans: The contested future of land, home and death in South Africa*. Wits University Press.

Williams, L. (2019). Reshaping colonial subjectivities through the language of the land. *Ecopsychology, 11*(3), 174–181. https://doi.org/10.1089/eco.2018.0077

Wolfe, P. (2006). Settler colonialism and the elimination of the native. *Journal of Genocide Research, 8*(4), 387–409. https://doi.org/10.1080/14623520601056240

Wynter, S. (2003). Unsettling the coloniality of being/power/truth/freedom: Towards the human, after man, its overrepresentation—An argument. *CR: The New Centennial Review, 3*(3), 257–337. https://doi.org/10.1353/ncr.2004.0015

15 Narratives of Young People in Lahore Navigating Multiple Belongings, Expectations, and Aspirations in the Process of 'Becoming'

Irum Maqbool

Introduction

In 2021, I interviewed students, between ages 16 and 18 years, studying in secondary schools in Lahore, Pakistan. These interviews were for a research project aiming to explore everyday experiences of a diverse group of school students within important spheres of their lifeworld: school, family, and friends. Among other factors, these students were from a range of schools which varied on a spectrum of socioeconomic demographic of target population, curriculum offered, and other material factors such as school building and learning resources. These many interesting conversations on a variety of topics inspired thinking about how young people navigated their choices and aspirations for constructing identity in a postcolonial context. Based on Reflexive Thematic Analysis of narratives of four participants, I draw on discussions of consumption choices, higher education aspirations, and peer relations to illustrate these navigations. The following chapter draws on the interdisciplinary field of Global South Youth Studies and relates it to writings in Decolonial Psychology to understand narratives highlighting processes of identity construction. I first discuss the idea of lifeworld followed by an account of the research context. I then discuss the three themes highlighted in the narratives of these young people before pondering on the possible alternatives foregrounding the constitutive and relational aspects of identity in ways that foreground a decolonial understanding of voices often missing in mainstream Psychology.

Defining Lifeworld

Lifeworld, Schutz (1970) writes, is the 'total sphere of experiences of an individual which is circumscribed by the objects, persons, and events encountered in the pursuit of the pragmatic objectives of living' (p. 320).

The concept of lifeworld is anchored in a tradition of writings about reality and consciousness. Schutz (1970), focusing on everyday life, discusses lifeworld as the social and material world with its own knowledge systems or meaning which is often taken-for-granted. This material and social world is the *'here'* in which individuals orient themselves and is encountered in a particular space and time (Schutz & Luckmann, 1973). Individuals who share a spatiotemporal context often share an understanding of the meanings underpinning social and material interactions resulting in a taken-for-granted lifeworld or the world of everyday life. Therefore, lifeworld has a history, a spatial-material context, norms, or practices and underpins a way of being.

Social relations are an essential part of this lifeworld, as Schutz writes, 'the social world into which [an individual] is born and within which [they] have to find [their] bearings is experienced by [them] as a tight knit web of social relationships… of institutionalised forms of social organisations…' (1970, p. 80). These social relationships share a common communicative environment

DOI: 10.4324/9781003492214-18

which includes shared signs, symbols, and meanings. Fine (2012) argues that social relationships and interactions in the small group bridge local reality and other relevant social institutions. Together, these underpin the lifeworld and support in understanding culture and culture change. In my research with secondary school students, I found Phelan et al. (1991, 1994) writing instrumental in reflecting on the small groups that I needed to take into account when focusing on the lifeworld of young people in my research. Phelan et al. (1991, 1994) focus on three significant communities of secondary school students in their research. These include the school, friends, and family. Everyday experiences within these spheres of lifeworld offer a nuanced understanding valuable for research into identity construction, among other ideas. Importantly, the spatiotemporal lifeworld is underpinned by knowledge that is not only taken-for-granted by individuals but is also remnant of historical influences.

Schutz (1970) refers to this as 'ways of life'. 'Everywhere, too, we find an accepted way of life, that is, how to come to terms with things and [others], with nature and the supernatural' (p. 79). This accepted way of life, he states, is the taken-for-granted knowledge or understanding that enables and underpins everyday experiences with social relations in the lifeworld. Schutz (1970) calls this the 'folkways of the ingroup' which form the 'social heritage' knowledge that enables individuals to function smoothly in their everyday experiences with their groups, communities, and the wider society. This includes cultural patterns that '*carries evidence in itself*' and it includes 'trustworthy recipes for interpreting the social world and for handling things and [people] in order to obtain the best results in every situation with a minimum effort by avoiding undesirable consequences' (Schutz, 1970, p. 81). Social heritage knowledge often forms the foundation of one's understanding and usually underwrites experiences involving other social relations in one's lifeworld. Nevertheless, people are not merely limited by social heritage knowledge as experiences contribute to knowledge (Wiencke, 2008).

In the context of my research, this concept of lifeworld enables in explaining everyday experiences of secondary school students' and the knowledge that seems to underwrite these experiences thereby contributing to processes of identity construction. Knowledge and power are intricately tied (Foucault, 1980). The interwoven nature of power and knowledge is, for instance, reflected in what kind of knowledge is valued, where it is produced, and the role it plays in the maintenance of social structures and individuals' relative position to these. Therefore, in my research, Schutz's lifeworld lends vocabulary to the contextual colonial influences that not only shape the geographical landscape but also the ways of life that individuals navigate and often take-for-granted.

This vocabulary is enriched by writings discussing coloniality and cosmopolitanisation, thereby enabling reflection on everyday experiences in the Global South. Arguably, social heritage knowledge is embedded in a long history of colonial influence on every aspect of life (Bhambra & Santos, 2017). This colonial influence erases or privileges certain ways of life. Moreover, in Global South contexts, this colonial influence has continued in patterns of neoliberal capitalism which often objectifies culture and privileges individualism (Mignolo, 2018; Nandy, 1989). These patterns are evident in the local-global hierarchies navigated by young people in the face of neoliberal globalisation (Bulhan, 2015). Beck (2016) in his discussions of globalisation and young people uses the term 'cosmopolitanisation of the lifeworld'. 'Cosmopolitanisation means that the key questions of a way of life, such as nourishment, production, identity, fear, memory, pleasure, fate, can no longer be located nationally or locally, but only globally or glocally' (Beck, 2002, pp. 29–30). This conceptual understanding of lifeworld and its cosmopolitanisation informs my research into everyday experiences of secondary school students. Analysing these experiences through the lens of lifeworld and its navigation helps appreciate identity construction as a process open to a decolonial reading.

Contextualising the Study

As mentioned earlier, I interviewed students in secondary schools. In this chapter, I draw on narratives of a few students who attend somewhat similar schools. School is one of the three spheres of lifeworld discussed by Phelan et al. (1991, 1994) in their model. Schools have been discussed as sites where neoliberal practices and globalisation are performed (Kenway, 2018; Klees, 2008; Robertson et al., 2007). These often lead to and are indicative of social disparities (ibid). In the context of education in Pakistan and the cosmopolitanisation of young people's lifeworld, education can be appreciated as one of the flows shaping everyday life (Urry, 2000), schools are part of this flow.

In thinking about the place of school and the everyday experiences of young people that inform discussions illustrating identity construction, I find it useful to situate the schools attended by my participants in the broader literature on school education in Pakistan. Schools often highlight the socioeconomic and cultural disparities in Pakistan's megacities (Burki et al., 2005). The education system in Pakistan has a colonial legacy often interwoven in factors such as language of instruction and curriculum taught in schools. Public or private ownership further highlight the socioeconomic disparities accelerated and deepened by neoliberal economic development prerogatives (ibid). Language, especially the teaching or learning of English, has a colonial legacy in Pakistan and continues to be an important factor stratifying the education system (Coleman & Capstick, 2012; Tamim, 2014, 2017). Rahman (2005) labels schools as 'elite' vs 'non-elite' with the former being those schools that use English as language of instruction, use the Cambridge International Curriculum, have high fee, and offer pathways to acquiring or maintaining cultural capital associated with power and privilege in the sociocultural context of Pakistan. Non-elite schools use Urdu as language of instruction, even if the curriculum is in English, teach local curriculum, and have lower fees in comparison. A neat categorisation of elite vs non-elite schools may not be possible due to a growing number of schools for the new middle class, the changing nature of cultural capital, the limited nature of public provision for education and the diversity of resources and capital in urban centres (Burki et al., 2005; Maqsood, 2017). Nevertheless, schools exist along a spectrum of elite and capture the socioeconomic diversity alongside aspirational trajectories of young people growing up in Pakistan.

The four participants, henceforth young people, on whose narratives this chapter is based were studying in same-sex schools which would be on the high end of the elite spectrum discussed above. These schools are seemingly 'cosmopolitan enclaves' (Chen, 2015, 2018; Rey et al., 2021) in a sociocultural tapestry of disenfranchisement and socioeconomic and material disparities (Cooper et al., 2021). All four of these young people, two boys (18 and 17 years) and two girls (18 and 17 years), lived in a nuclear family setting. Following is a brief introduction before a discussion of their narratives.

Ahmed (18 years) was the youngest of three siblings. His older sisters had studied in international universities in the Global North. His parents were associated with the medical profession and his father worked abroad. Basit (17 years) was the eldest of three siblings. His mother was a homemaker and his father held a corporate job. Basit was the only one in his extended family attending an international school. Nazli (18 years) was the youngest of three siblings. Her sister was married and her brother worked abroad. She lived with her parents. Her father held an administrative position in an organisation while her mother was affiliated with a caring profession. Anika (17 years) had an older and a younger brother. Her father was a doctor and her mother was a homemaker. During interviews with these four young people, I discussed their aspirations and everyday choices. Together, these reflect the way in which the spheres of lifeworld (Phelan et al., 1991, 1994) are navigated in a process of identity construction in everyday experiences of growing up in a Global South urban context.

Identity Construction and Young People's Narratives

'People's knowledge, views, understandings, interpretations, experiences, and interactions are meaningful properties' (Mason, 1996, p. 39). Narratives of everyday experiences offer a subjective and valuable insight into the lifeworld. This means of and for knowing experiences, organised in retrospect, illustrate the symbolic, constitutive, and interpretive function of culture (Bruner, 1990). In analysing narratives of these young people, I engaged in Reflexive Thematic Analysis (Braun & Clarke, 2019, 2023; Terry & Hayfield, 2020). This is an inductive approach to analysis which is subjective and grounded in the researchers' conceptual or theoretical leanings (ibid). Furthermore, the themes I expand on below and which illustrate a process of identity construction are grounded in thinking about identity as fluid, relational, and socioculturally constituted (Bhatia, 2017; Bulhan, 2015). I use identity construction to think about experiences reflecting an 'articulation' (Bhatia, 2017). This articulation illustrates the way young people engaged in an active process of navigating social and symbolic boundaries, some of which are (re)shaped as lifeworld cosmopolitanises. Social boundaries are related to 'objectified forms of social difference' and symbolic boundaries are related to 'conceptual distinctions' which lead 'individuals and groups [to] struggle over and come to agree upon definitions of reality' (Lamont & Molnár, 2002, p. 168). Viewed through the lens of navigation, identity construction, and everyday experiences that illustrate these processes offer a vantage point for a decolonial understanding of developmental psychology.

Narratives of Higher Education Aspirations

These young people were in the final year of school and were considering options for higher education. Ahmed and Nazli wished to study in Higher Education Institutions (HEI) in Lahore, whereas Basit and Anika aspired to study abroad. Universities in the US were preferred due to likelihood of getting a full scholarship, without which such aspirations could not be met. Alongside high grades, the credentials often needed to secure these scholarships were associated with participation in extracurricular activities (Maqbool & Cremin, 2023). These include a range of debating, sports, entrepreneurship, and similar activities which are often evidenced in testimonials and personal statements. Moreover, interschool competitions of extracurricular activities were spaces for meeting peers from similar schools and were mixed gender spaces in an otherwise predominantly same-sex school education system.

Two of the participants, Ahmed and Nazli, aspired to attend HEI in Pakistan. Their aspirations were embedded in personal ambitions and family commitments. Ahmed wished to become a doctor and attend a local medical college.

> My father had to take on a loan to pay for my sisters fee when they studied abroad … I don't want to put the same pressure on him…I know the standard of Education here is not as good … but at the end of the day this is where my heart is.

Nazli wanted to explore Architecture or related disciplines.

> I don't want to go abroad. I want to live here, I feel like my parents need me because my sister is married and brother lives abroad so I would want to live close to my parents that is why I am looking for options over here.

Ahmed and Nazli's HEI aspirations illustrate the intertwined nature of identity construction in this context which may often be relational. Family appears to play a vital role in informing one's agency and aspirations which are related to a fluid construction of identity (Aitken, 2018). In this regard, the social boundaries of family alongside the shaping of one's aspirations based on the choices made by others indicate that elements illustrating identity construction are often embedded in the lifeworld young people navigate (Mughal, 2021).

On the other hand, Basit and Anika wished to study in the US. They shared the following regarding their aspirations. Basit:

> I am applying to summer schools in US universities to improve my profile. I am taking a lot of extracurricular activities so I can study [for undergrad] in the US. My aim with [extracurriculars] is that these will support me in my personal statement. I want the admissions committee to admire me for all my activities. You have to stand out, I want them to get to know me. I am doing film, art, music and debates… My parents aren't convinced yet, but I hope they will be if I get a scholarship because they said they'd think about it then… I participate in a lot of extracurricular competitions. My parents have started being comfortable with it because they see that I can manage my grades too, so my parents trust me a little more…Actually what I want is that I want to live away from home … For most of the time, for example, my life is dictated, I cannot do the things I really want to do. So, for instance, if I have to go with friends I can't, so I guess if I have my own peace of mind [I will do] what I actually want

Anika shared the following:

> I want to study abroad, in the US and I want to participate in extracurricular activities because that's how you can have the experience needed. But convincing parents to participate in anything is so difficult. They don't see the point. They don't agree with going abroad. My father used to but I don't know if he does anymore. He wants me to become a doctor and obviously it is better here and shorter, abroad it is expensive and way longer. I don't know what I am doing with my life… I just don't like Pakistan's environment … I think it is very suffocating especially for girls.. I feel like even my friends are allowed to do stuff… like going out with friends, so I'm just like I don't want to deal with this for the rest of my life. I'm just tired of it… my mother is like I won't let you go but my dad is like if you get a scholarship I will let you go, so my main goal is getting a scholarship. I haven't shared it with [parents] …I just have a communication gap with everyone …

Narratives from Anika and Basit illustrate the fluid and iterative process of identity construction in cosmopolitanising and globalising contexts (Arnett, 2002; Nilan & Feixa, 2006). Education is one of the flows that offers scripts for imagination in these contexts (Urry, 2000). Real and imaginary mobilities interweave in this process of identity construction (Beck, 2011; Beck & Beck-Gernsheim, 2009). Furthermore, the above two narratives illustrate the navigation of parental expectations, social heritage knowledge regarding norms, and one's own interests informed by a view of education and related pathways. These young people appear to resist, rework, and reimagine social and symbolic boundaries (Lamont & Aksartova, 2002) in their everyday experiences such that desired mobilities and associated identities are acquired. This navigation of cosmopolitanising lifeworld appears to be embedded in obedience and deference, also highlighted by Kapadia (2017) in her work with students in India. Extracurricular engagement and the identity construction in relation to these can be read as either a continued form of 'colonialism' that privileges certain ways of being (Bulhan, 2015) or it could be interpreted as a pathway enabling young people to construct plural identities that transcend geographies and reflect a time and place that young urban people in similar contexts navigate (Bhatia, 2020; Waldron, 1992). Nevertheless, HEI aspirations inform an attitude to difference and shape the boundary work that goes into constructing identities that bring together the many influences navigated by young people in their lifeworld (Beck, 2002, 2003; Hannigan, 2002; Levander & Mignolo, 2011).

Narratives of Consumption Choices

I found discussions of young people regarding their social media usage or buying practices to reflect the process of constructing identity or exploring individuality. Similar to HEI, these narratives illustrated a process of navigating choices in the spatiotemporal and intersubjective lifeworld. Ahmed:

> Social media has affected everything, most people are very success driven now. I see that in my friends. Everything that is portrayed in a way is seen to be good. I have social media accounts and I follow sports, politics, and musicians etc… I try to learn as much about local politics as possible but I try not to get into arguments [online] … And I think when you go out you represent your values and what you learn from your family. My parents have always helped other people, that's the profession they are in too, so that is what I want to do… My opinion has been shaped by my gratefulness to Allah and I do think a lot that I could have been a guy on the street but I have been given the opportunity for a reason. I want to try and make the most of it because I have been blessed with a comfortable living and I want to try and make a difference for others as well. I know I go to a good school and I try not to take it for granted…The school maintains discipline and has strict rules on uniform and hairstyles and I understand that. But sometimes it can be demotivating and very harsh too… I wear what I think is good and don't really focus on what others are saying although I do like the approval of my sisters and mother, my sisters are pretty stiff on this point, they do give me fashion advice and stuff. I like to wear what I think is good, not what's going on.

Nazli also shared:

> I like watching home videos on social media and making transition videos. I used to have a food channel but now I have paused it since I have school work… My parents are okay with my social media usage. They know me… I meet friends and I go to events in schools but I don't stay out late. I know my parents will worry.

These narratives illustrate how identity is constructed in a cosmopolitanising context such that young people have '"roots" and "wings" at the same time' (Beck, 2002, p. 19). These offer individuals a dialogic imagination underpinned by and shaped by knowledge that shapes the fluid and relational formation of identities (Beck, 2002). This 'dialogic imagination … explores and exploits the creative contradictions of cultures' (Beck, 2002, p. 35) including 'the clash of cultures and rationalities within one's own life' (Beck, 2002, p. 18).

The above everyday experiences of consumption choices highlight the glocal context of young people and the way in which they navigate the possibilities in their lifeworld. These experiences reflect a process of constructing identity that is grounded in young people navigating their agency and choices alongside taken-for-granted parental expectations. Rao et al. (2013), writing about young people navigating identity construction in the context of India, discuss the process of 'remixing'. This remixing, they write, is the process of young people bringing together different cultural flows and intertwining these with tradition to construct fluid and relational identities in context. The above narratives similarly indicate a remixing and a balancing act in which both Ahmed and Nazli engage in processes of identity construction that enmesh consumption choices underwritten by a deference and obedience observed in other contexts as well (Kapadia, 2017; Rao et al., 2013). Basit:

> I spend a lot, my parents are actually sick of me at this point. I attend school extracurricular competitions and we have themes for dressing up… I follow university pages, celebrities etc. I have my family and friends on social media. I don't post much. I don't like the scrutiny… You can't judge me and my parents at the same time. I like trendy fashion and what ever is cool. My father doesn't approve. He wants me to dress up like a decent good boy. He sometimes makes me change if I have to go with him somewhere… I need a new iPhone too but my father doesn't think that there is anything wrong with the one I have… I used to have long hair but he made me cut it short… I play guitar and my parents are cool with it. They appreciate that there is someone creative in the family at least. I can play guitar as long as my studies are not affected. My family used to say, don't become a 'marasi'… My dad dislikes some things that I do in terms of fashion and spending. I used to resist, now I don't…

Anika mentions:

> Girls who wear crop-tops in school are penalised it shouldn't be anyone's problem… I know what is socially acceptable and what isn't, [I get comments] not like from teachers but like from my parents. Anything I wear like they will be go change … even though I don't wear such stuff, I know my values, I'm like OK if I am going in a boy gathering I am not supposed to wear such clothes … so even if I wear like a jeans or a shirt and if it doesn't cover my hips and then they'll not let me wear it. And they'll ask me to put a dupatta (scarf) on my hair, and that's something that is suffocating for me, it's my own choice, like it should come to me naturally, if you are forcing it on me it would just take away its beauty from me… Sometimes my brother has to take me to places and he comments and that would piss me off because I am old enough to know what I am supposed to wear and it is not like I don't dress modestly, I do.

These narratives illustrate that remixing identities involved boundary work. While resisting and reworking may be possible for some young people in some instances, accepting or appearing to accept the predominant ways of being may be the only option. This knowledge in the lifeworld, which appears to come through different flows as contexts cosmopolitanise and globalise, can offer new imaginaries for identity construction (Beck, 2016; Urry, 2000). Nevertheless, these also seem to produce certain resistance as can be inferred from these two accounts. The integration of different or plural ways of being in order to construct identities on the confluence of glocalising binaries and imaginaries paves the way for an attitude towards difference which underpins relational, fluid, and discursive identity construction (Alam & Marston, 2023; Rao et al., 2013). Furthermore, Anika's and Basit's comment on the implication of their parents' feedback on their consumption choices illustrate the role of gendered expectations and religion in the process of identity construction. Khoja-Moolji's 2017, 2021) discussion is important in understanding this. She notes that gender as a sociocultural script underwrites a discursive production. In terms of identity construction, therefore, this discursive production of gender plays a vital role. In the context of Pakistan, masculinity is often anchored in ideas of power intertwined with thinking about nation-state, maintenance of status-quo, and historical forms of violence (ibid). Girls, similarly, are offered sociocultural scripts that categorise individuals along a good girl–bad girl binary. Religion is interwoven in this binary with markers of chastity and submission to authority being privileged as the right ways of being (Khoja-Moolji, 2017). Consumption choices reflect a process of identity construction in the cosmopolitanising lifeworld of young people where one's own and others' expectations are underwritten by forms of knowledge and associated imaginaries.

Narratives of Peer Relations

The lifeworld of secondary school students includes friends. Young people's narratives of their peer relations offered interesting insight into processes of identity construction and their navigation of social and symbolic boundaries. In line with the above discussion on gender and religion, these narratives illustrate the expectations or accepted ways of being that underpin these interactions. Young people were in gender segregated schools; however, extracurricular competitions were spaces shared by boys and girls. Ahmed:

> I am lucky that I have good friends and I am close to them. My parents have met most of them and it is important for me that they do. My mom knows who I meet. Boys in my school became disruptive in [High School] so that was annoying, they were disrespectful towards teachers. Some of the boys in my school also started getting involved with girls so I guess at this age [that I am in] you have to be careful about who you hang out with… deciding between good and bad is very important and it shapes your life… I always remember my parents' sacrifice and their hard work which has allowed me to go to this school and also the luxury that they have given me …if I do turn to other things and habits I will be throwing it away and I do not want to do that so that is why I try to keep it cool…

Nazli expressed the following:

> Our generation is very confident and I like that about us… I have friends who are closer to boys than I am and I am fine with it, for me the most important thing is that my parents should know who my friends are and I take their trust very seriously… My mom knows all of my friends and I know my values…Some of my friends have started vaping and their grades have deteriorated because of the friends they have… I sometimes take a break from people if it starts annoying me but I am fine with their choices as long as it doesn't affect me… I know my limits and if I think my friends are doing something that my parents won't approve of, I don't get involved in it.

Basit also shares:

> I was scared of finding friends and especially being comfortable with being friends with girls but I am more confident now, I have a very good group of friends… my parents were concerned about who I become friends with... they just want to know what is going on… They tell me where the limit is and I know that. I know it won't be tolerated if I went beyond that. They have made the margins clear to me… I am more reserved at home than I am with my friends, but I guess that is how all of us are, my friends and I…My mom sometimes compares me to her friend's son who scores higher and I show her his social media posts, that look, he smokes. I don't do that… I keep my life private, I don't post much on social media. My parents know what I do but I don't want to be the centre of gossip of my [extended] family because that used to happen. They would judge me based on my friend group.

Lastly, Anika mentions:

> It was my decision, I didn't want to use social media and everyone in class had it. So it was difficult to make friends but then people added me to their social groups and it all worked out. I

> am closer to a few girls now… And not just that, also girls who wear crop-tops to school events because our teachers are the same as like non-liberal parents, there are a few teachers wo are like OK with it... but most of the teachers like they do look down upon you if you are someone who doesn't fit their criteria of how girls should be. I prefer being friends with girls who are not involved with boys. I care about how people see me…I think most of the girls in my school are very judgmental and I don't have a sister. I wish I had a sister, my brothers are close to each other and I feel like I have no one.

Peer relations play an important role in the process of identity construction as young people navigate glocal contexts (Rao et al., 2013). These relations are, however, underpinned by predominant ways of being that may often prefer deference to elders and scrutiny of peer relations out of concerns for detrimental behaviours (Kapadia, 2017; Sucharita, 2014). Such narratives, however, call on one to think about the interaction of spheres of family and friends in contexts that prioritise a relational understanding of self and in which young people appear to perform boundary work which includes navigating cosmopolitanisation and multiple relational belongings.

The above narratives of peer relations highlight the kinds of boundary work these young people perform. Ahmed's and Nazli's narrative illustrate the reworking of boundaries such that deference is prioritised. Mughal (2021) writing in the context of rural Pakistan argues that these symbolic boundaries of age, gender, and related ideas of obedience or deference are learnt by individuals and organise social life. Hashmi & Fayyaz (2022) in their research with young people in Karachi also opine that parents and teachers see themselves as elders who wish to guide adolescents in the best possible manner. This guidance and learnt deference interweaves with processes of identity construction that bring together knowledge in the lifeworld and navigation of social and symbolic boundaries in innovative and contextualised ways (Lamont & Aksartova, 2002).

The above narratives echo the perspective on gender and religion. Additionally, conversations on others' judgements and the discomfort these appear to cause illustrate the process of identity construction and navigation that involves gender and religion as symbolic boundaries. Donlic's (2023) research with young Muslims in the Alps-Adriatic similarly highlights that young people inhabiting a cosmopolitanising lifeworld exercise diverse choices and their idea of being a Muslim may be different to what their parents had resulting in a discursive production of plural Muslim youth identities.

Religion seems to underpin the judgmentalism young people's peers may face and informs the choices young people make in navigating boundaries. Religion, therefore, informed the ongoing discursive construction of identity (Donlic, 2023; Dunne & Crossouard, 2020). In these relational and contextualised identity construction processes, religion and related practices are 'differentiated internally into a number of, in principle, negotiable detailed commitments' (Bilgrami, 2019, p. 27).

Conclusion

Young people's narratives of higher education aspirations, consumption choices, and peer relations support in understanding relational and contextual aspects of identity construction. These aspects are often either overlooked or considered to be homogenising factors (Ahmed, 2016; Donlic, 2023), particularly in research focusing on young people's development in Global South contexts (ibid). This leads to discourses that portray certain young people and youth identities as embedded in deficit and social othering (Crossouard & Dunne, 2020; Durrani & Dunne, 2010). Alternatively, as this chapter highlights, an analysis grounded in lifeworld and navigation of social and symbolic boundaries offers a broader understanding of the relational and discursive process of identity construction. Thinking about the constitution of identity and its performance or embodiment from such a stand-point supports in taking a nuanced and holistic view which situates narratives in a decolonial and reparative understanding of the constitutive process of youth identity formation (Bhatia, 2017).

Young people draw on different knowledge systems for navigating conceptualisations of youth identity in a context with its particular history and sociocultural understanding (Rao et al., 2013). This navigation includes trespassing, resisting, and reproducing boundaries of local-global or individual-relational. In transitioning through these boundaries of local and global, personal and relational new forms of identity are constituted on the confluence of multiple belongings and identifications (Beck, 2011; Beck & Beck-Gernsheim, 2009). Nevertheless, the emotional cost of this constitutive process is often paid by the young people, especially if their chosen pathways are not in line with those preferred by the adults they defer to. Decolonial approaches to Psychology that situate identity construction in context offer an alternative to pathologising or critiquing the individual for this emotional cost alongside offering a holistic and empowering understanding that does not reify global-local hierarchies (Bhambra, 2014; Sugarman, 2015).

To conclude, a decolonial understanding of Psychology privileges plural ways of being which inform the constitutive process of identity construction, a process that is fluid and discursive. In contexts with colonial histories (Mignolo, 2010), globalised influences of constructing a neoliberal self (Sugarman, 2015), and cosmopolitan Muslim understandings (Donlic, 2023), this constitutive process can yield hyphenated identities (Fine & Sirin, 2007). These hyphenated identities when viewed through a lens of everyday lifeworld can be appreciated for their potential of not only reimagining identity construction but also for reimagining the layered process of identity development and ways of understanding it (Bhatia, 2017; Lamont & Aksartova, 2002). Such an approach to understanding identity that takes into account young peoples' narratives of multiple belongings and navigation of boundaries offers a nuanced and holistic perspective. This understanding takes into account the structures that enable or discourage ways of conceptualising self, trajectories privileged by certain structures, and the ideal youth identities promoted in a globalising world. Once these are accounted for, there is scope for holistic understanding that does not commit the epistemic fallacy of attributing to individuals' ideas that are structural (Furlong & Cartmel, 2001). Moreover, such an understanding helps understand the negotiations that play a role in constituting identity processes. These negotiations or navigations are relational and underpinned by an often taken-for-granted understanding which can be erased by neoliberal privileging of certain forms of identity. However, identity if understood as a constitutive process with reference to contextual and relational aspects of one's lifeworld stands to add valuable insight that helps appreciate multiple ways of being in a plural world (Datta, 2012; Khan, 2010; Mignolo, 2010). Such an understanding celebrates a kaleidoscope of youth identity processes that do not privilege characteristics entrenched in an individual understanding of self on which much of identity formation discourse rests. A relational self and contextualised consciousness become the baseline from which navigation of differences or similarities in the process of identity formation is understood. Such a decolonial understanding, anchored in youth narratives, would offer representative conceptualisations that offer inclusive and plural scripts for understanding identity.

References

Ahmed, S. H. (2016). A decade of Muslim youth: Global trends in research. *Journal of Muslim Mental Health*, *10*(1). https://doi.org/10.3998/jmmh.10381607.0010.104

Aitken, S. C. (2018). Children's geographies: Tracing the evolution and involution of a concept. *Geographical Review*, *108*(1), 3–23. https://doi.org/10.1111/gere.12289

Alam, P., & Marston, C. (2023). "People are having lots of other kinds of sex": Exploring sexual lifeworlds of LGBTQ+ young people in Bangladesh. *Cogent Social Sciences*, *9*(1), 2185305. https://doi.org/10.1080/23311886.2023.2185305

Arnett, J. J. (2002). The psychology of globalization. *American Psychologist*, *57*(10), 774–783. https://doi.org/10.1037/0003-066X.57.10.774

Beck, U., & Beck-Gernsheim, E. (2009). Global generations and the trap of methodological nationalism for a cosmopolitan turn in the sociology of youth and generation. *European Sociological Review*, *25*(1), 25–36. https://doi.org/10.1093/esr/jcn032

Beck, U. (2002). The cosmopolitan society and its enemies. *Theory, Culture & Society*, *19*(1–2), 17–44. https://doi.org/10.1177/026327640201900101

Beck, U. (2011). Multiculturalism or cosmopolitanism: How can we describe and understand the diversity of the world? *Social Sciences in China*, *32*(4), 52–58. https://doi.org/10.1080/02529203.2011.625169

Beck, U. (2016). Varieties of second modernity and the cosmopolitan vision. *Theory, Culture & Society*, *33*(7–8), 257–270. https://doi.org/10.1177/0263276416671585

Bhambra, G. K., & Santos, B. de S. (2017). Introduction: Global challenges for sociology. *Sociology*, *51*(1), 3–10. https://doi.org/10.1177/0038038516674665

Bhambra, G. K. (2014). Postcolonial and decolonial dialogues. *Postcolonial Studies*, *17*(2), 115–121. https://doi.org/10.1080/13688790.2014.966414

Bhatia, S. (2017). *Decolonizing psychology: Globalization, social justice, and Indian youth identities*. Oxford University Press.

Bhatia, S. (2020). Decolonization and coloniality in human development: Neoliberalism, globalization and narratives of Indian youth. *Human Development*, *64*(4–6), 207–221. https://doi.org/10.1159/000513084

Bilgrami, A. (2019). What is a Muslim? Fundamental commitment and cultural identity. *Journal of Human Rights*, *14*(2), 23–48. https://doi.org/10.22096/hr.2020.121448.1193

Braun, V., & Clarke, V. (2019). Reflecting on reflexive thematic analysis. *Qualitative Research in Sport, Exercise and Health*, *11*(4), 589–597. https://doi.org/10.1080/2159676X.2019.1628806

Braun, V., & Clarke, V. (2023). Toward good practice in thematic analysis: Avoiding common problems and be(com)ing a knowing researcher. *International Journal of Transgender Health*, *24*(1), 1–6. https://doi.org/10.1080/26895269.2022.2129597

Bruner, J. (1990). *Acts of meaning* (pp. xvii, 179). Harvard University Press.

Bulhan, H. A. (2015). Stages of colonialism in Africa: From occupation of land to occupation of being. *Journal of Social and Political Psychology*, *3*(1), 1. https://doi.org/10.5964/jspp.v3i1.143

Burki, S. J., Hathaway, R. M., & Woodrow Wilson International Center for Scholars (Eds.). (2005). *Education reform in Pakistan: Building for the future*. Woodrow Wilson International Center for Scholars.

Chen, M. Z. (2015). Constructions of cosmopolitanism in teenage citizenship in Singapore. *Children's Geographies*, *13*(5), 537–555. https://doi.org/10.1080/14733285.2014.900986

Chen, W.-F. (2018). The perceived cosmopolitan consumption of globally mobile, young consumers from China. *Young Consumers*, *19*(4), 450–464. https://doi.org/10.1108/YC-01-2018-00769

Coleman, H., & Capstick, T. (2012). *Language in education in Pakistan: Recommendations for policy and practice*. Islamabad: British Council.

Cooper, A., Swartz, S., & Ramphalile, M. (2021). Youth of the global south and why they are worth studying. In S. Swartz, A. Cooper, C. M. Batan, & L. Kropff Causa (Eds.), *The Oxford handbook of global south youth studies* (pp. 33–54). Oxford University Press. https://doi.org/10.1093/oxfordhb/9780190930028.013.3

Crossouard, B., & Dunne, M. (2020). Muslim youth as global citizens. *Social Identities*, *26*(3), 298–313. https://doi.org/10.1080/13504630.2020.1765760

Datta, A. (2012). "Mongrel City": Cosmopolitan neighbourliness in a Delhi squatter settlement. *Antipode*, *44*(3), 745–763. https://doi.org/10.1111/j.1467-8330.2011.00928.x

Donlic, J. (2023). New Muslim generations: Shaping self-image, reshaping religion: A theoretical and empirical study of inter-religiosity with Muslim youth in the alps-adriatic region. *Religions*, *14*(8), 8. https://doi.org/10.3390/rel14080993

Dunne, M., & Crossouard, B. (2020). Introduction: Pluralising Muslim youth identities: intersections of nation, religion and gender. *Social Identities*, *26*(3), 287–297. https://doi.org/10.1080/13504630.2020.1765759

Durrani, N., & Dunne, M. (2010). Curriculum and national identity: Exploring the links between religion and nation in Pakistan. *Journal of Curriculum Studies*, *42*(2), 215–240. https://doi.org/10.1080/00220270903312208

Fine, G. A. (2012). *Tiny publics: A theory of group action and culture*. Russell Sage Foundation. https://www.jstor.org/stable/10.7758/9781610447744

Fine, M., & Sirin, S. R. (2007). Theorizing hyphenated selves: Researching youth development in and across contentious political contexts. *Social and Personality Psychology Compass*, *1*(1), 16–38. https://doi.org/10.1111/j.1751-9004.2007.00032.x

Foucault, M. (1980). *Power/knowledge: Selected interviews and other writings, 1972–1977*. Random House USA Inc.

Furlong, A., & Cartmel, F. (2001). *Young people and social change: Individualization and risk in late modernity*. Open University Press.

Hannigan, J. (2002). Culture, globalization, and social cohesion: Toward a de-territorialized, global fluids model. *Canadian Journal of Communication*, *27*(2/3), 277–287. https://doi.org/10.22230/cjc.2002v27n2a1301

Hashmi, K., & Fayyaz, H. N. (2022). Adolescence and academic well-being: Parents, teachers, and students' perceptions. *Journal of Education and Educational Development*, *9*(1), 27–47. https://doi.org/10.22555/joeed.v9i1.475

Kapadia, S. (2017). Uncertainties, insecurities, and worries: The bane of globalization. In S. Kapadia (Ed.), *Adolescence in urban India: Cultural construction in a society in transition* (pp. 115–137). Springer India. https://doi.org/10.1007/978-81-322-3733-4_5

Kenway, J. (2018). The work of desire: Elite schools' multi-scalar markets. In C. Maxwell, U. Deppe, H.- H. Krüger, & W. Helsper (Eds.), *Elite education and internationalisation: From the early years to higher education* (pp. 93–110). Springer International Publishing. https://doi.org/10.1007/978-3-319-59966-3_6

Khan, T. (2010). *Emerging Muslim identity in India's globalized and mediated society: An ethnographic investigation of the halting modernities of the Muslim youth of Jamia Enclave, New Delhi* [Doctoral dissertation, Ohio University]. OhioLINK. https://rave.ohiolink.edu/etdc/view?acc_num=ohiou1239996089

Khoja-Moolji, S. (2017). *Forging the ideal educated girl the production of desirable subjects in Muslim South Asia / Shenila Khoja-Moolji.* University of California Press.

Khoja-Moolji, S. (2021). *Sovereign attachments: Masculinity, muslimness, and affective politics in Pakistan*. University of California Press. https://ezp.lib.cam.ac.uk/login?url=https://search.ebscohost.com/login.aspx?direct=true&db=nlebk&AN=2905410&site=ehost-live&scope=site

Klees, S. J. (2008). A quarter century of neoliberal thinking in education: Misleading analyses and failed policies. *Globalisation, Societies and Education*, *6*(4), 311–348. https://doi.org/10.1080/14767720802506672

Lamont, M., & Aksartova, S. (2002). Ordinary cosmopolitanisms: Strategies for bridging racial boundaries among working-class men. *Theory, Culture & Society*, *19*(4), 1–25. https://doi.org/10.1177/0263276402019004001

Lamont, M., & Molnár, V. (2002). The study of boundaries in the social sciences. *Annual Review of Sociology*, *28*, 167–195. https://doi.org/10.1146/annurev.soc.28.110601.141107

Levander, C., & Mignolo, W. (2011). Introduction: The global south and world dis/order. *The Global South*, *5*(1), 1–11. https://doi.org/10.2979/globalsouth.5.1.1

Maqbool, I., & Cremin, H. (2023). Students' experiences of extracurricular activities in elite secondary schools in Lahore. *Compare: A Journal of Comparative and International Education*, *54*(8), 1253–1270. https://doi.org/10.1080/03057925.2023.2195048

Maqsood, A. (2017). *The new Pakistani middle class / Ammara Maqsood.* Harvard University Press.

Mason, J. (1996). *Qualitative researching / Jennifer Mason.* SAGE, Sage.

Mignolo, W. (2010). Cosmopolitanism and the de-colonial option. *Studies in Philosophy and Education*, *29*(2), 111–127. https://doi.org/10.1007/s11217-009-9163-1

Mignolo, W. D. (2018). *Forward: On pluriversality and multipolarity*. In B. Reiter (Ed.), *Constructing the pluriverse: The geopolitics of knowledge* (pp. iv–xvi). Duke University Press. https://read.dukeupress.edu/books/book/2479/chapter/1191552/ForwardOn-Pluriversality-and-Multipolarity

Mughal, M. A. Z. (2021). Children's perception of social boundaries: The intersectionality of age and social group affiliation in rural Pakistan. *Children & Society*, *35*(2), 213–228. https://doi.org/10.1111/chso.12417

Nandy, A. (1989). Shamans, savages and the wilderness: On the audibility of dissent and the future of civilizations. *Alternatives: Global, Local, Political*, *14*(3), 263–277. https://doi.org/10.1177/030437548901400301

Nilan, P., & Feixa, C. (2006). *Global Youth?: Hybrid identities, plural worlds*. Routledge.

Phelan, P., Davidson, A. L., & Cao, H. T. (1991). Students' multiple worlds: Negotiating the boundaries of family, peer, and school cultures. *Anthropology & Education Quarterly*, *22*(3), 224–250. https://www.jstor.org/stable/3195764

Phelan, P., Yu, H. C., & Davidson, A. L. (1994). Navigating the psychosocial pressures of adolescence: The voices and experiences of high school youth. *American Educational Research Journal*, *31*(2), 415–447. https://doi.org/10.3102/00028312031002415

Rahman, T. (2005). Passports to privilege: The english-medium schools in Pakistan. *Peace and Democracy in South Asia*, *1*(1), 24–44.

Rao, M. A., Berry, R., Gonsalves, A., Hastak, Y., Shah, M., & Roeser, R. W. (2013). Globalization and the identity remix among urban adolescents in India. *Journal of Research on Adolescence*, *23*(1), 9–24. https://doi.org/10.1111/jora.12002

Rey, J., Bolay, M., & Gez, Y. N. (2021). Cosmopolitan enclaves: An introduction. *Critique of Anthropology*, *41*(4), 331–344. https://doi.org/10.1177/0308275X211059659

Robertson, S., Novelli, M., Dale, R., Tikly, L., Dachi, H., Alphonce, N., Robertson, S., Novelli, M., Dale, R., Tikly, L., Dachi, H., Alphonce, N., Robertson, S., Novelli, M., Dale, R., Tikly, L., Dachi, H., & Alphonce, N. (2007). *Globalisation, education and development: Ideas, actors and dynamics*. DFID

Schutz, A., & Luckmann, T. (1973). *Structures of the life-world: Vol 1* (R. M. Zaner & J. T. E. Jr, Trans.). Northwestern University Press.

Schutz, A. (1970). *On phenomenology and social relations: Selected writings / edited and with an introduction by Helmut R. Wagner.* University of Chicago Press.

Sucharita, V. (2014). Negotiating between family, peers and school: Understanding the world of government school and private school students. *Compare: A Journal of Comparative and International Education*, *44*(3), 379–393. https://doi.org/10.1080/03057925.2013.792671

Sugarman, J. (2015). Neoliberalism and psychological ethics. *Journal of Theoretical and Philosophical Psychology*, *35*(2), 103–116. https://doi.org/10.1037/a0038960

Tamim, T. (2014). The politics of languages in education: Issues of access, social participation and inequality in the multilingual context of Pakistan. *British Educational Research Journal*, *40*(2), 280–299. https://doi.org/10.1002/berj.3041

Tamim, T. (2017). Languages, symbolic power and multidimensional poverty in the context of Pakistan. *European Journal of Language and Literature*, *9*(1), 70. https://doi.org/10.26417/ejls.v9i1.p70-79

Terry, G., & Hayfield, N. (2020). Reflexive thematic analysis. In M. Ward, & S. Delamont (Eds.), *Handbook of qualitative research in education* (2nd ed., pp. 430–441). Edward Elgar Publishing.

Urry, J. (2000). Global flows and global citizenship 1. In E. Isin (Ed.), *Democracy, Citizenship and the Global City*. New York: Routledge.

Waldron, J. (1992). Minority cultures and the cosmopolitan alternative. *University of Michigan Journal of Law Reform*, *25*(3), 751–793.

Wiencke, M. (2008). Theoretical reflections on the life world of Tanzanian street children. *Anthropology Matters*, *10*(2). https://doi.org/10.22582/am.v10i2.35

16 The Forgotten Ones

On Memorialising the Life of Nokukhanya Luthuli

Puleng Segalo and Tinyiko Chauke

Introduction

At a poignant commemoration event in September 2023, South African storyteller and author Gcina Mhlophe invited us to pause and reflect on the remarkable life of Nokukhanya Luthuli. With an encouraging challenge, "Forget her if you can!" – she reminded us of the enduring importance of keeping Nokukhanya's memory alive. In a moment echoing through history, Nelson Mandela once urged people to cast aside their weapons and embrace peace. He presented a gift to the crowd in the form of Nokukhanya Luthuli herself, asking everyone to shout her name "Nokukhanya!" three times. The stadium erupted with admiration, and in her bright white dress, she stood tall and proud, radiating the respect and love of her people. This occasion served as a profound tribute to her pivotal role in the life of the renowned global figure, Albert Luthuli (Mandela, 1996). Her name, meaning "mother of light," embodied her parents' dreams that she would illuminate the lives of South Africans through education and faith (Rule et al., 1993).

Yet, amidst the rich history of South Africa's movements, countless stories, especially those of remarkable women like Nokukhanya, often remain hidden in the shadows, eclipsed by the more prominent narratives of their male counterparts. However, as we delve deeper into this biographical exploration, drawing inspiration from scholars such as Hughes (2012), a significant truth unfolds before us; a thorough understanding of African nationalism requires acknowledging the indispensable contributions of these women. In her compelling work, "Lives and Wives," Hughes (2012) emphasises that to truly grasp the dynamics of the national movement, we must recognise women not just as supporters but as formidable architects of resistance. Their sacrifices and struggles are important chapters in our history that often go unnoticed. This thinking bodes well with our mission to shed light on Nokukhanya's legacy, not merely as Inkosi Luthuli's wife, but as a powerful force for change and a catalyst in the wider struggle for liberation. Her story, rich with resilience and courage, deserves to be celebrated and remembered by all of us. Moreover, the partnership between Nokukhanya and Inkosi Luthuli embodies a revolutionary model of activism, one that possesses the potential to reshape the political landscape and challenge entrenched gender roles. Together, they forged a union that stood firmly against the limitations imposed by their time, displaying the strength that arises from collaboration. By embracing this holistic understanding of their partnership, we allow Nokukhanya's narrative to ascend from the margins, transforming her life into a poignant testament to the history of tangled experiences of African men and women unwavering in their quest for liberation and equality.

Women involved in the liberation struggle experienced great difficulty in retelling their stories independently of their interactions with men. Vahed (2015) argues that the media and public discourse often perpetuate women's subordinate positions, making it difficult for women to recount their narratives and construct their identities independently of those of men. Our reading of and

DOI: 10.4324/9781003492214-19

engagement with the silencing of women's voices take place through the lenses of African feminism (Ahikire, 2014; Chilisa & Ntseane, 2014) and decolonial feminism (Lugones, 2010), which challenge the linear and often ahistorical Western hegemony in grappling with and understanding gender injustice. We acknowledge the role played by colonialism in disrupting African cultures and how African people generally understand and conceptualise gender relations. Through these analytical lenses, we can better comprehend the roles of African women in the struggle for liberation against colonialism and apartheid in South Africa.

We recognise and confront the erasure and marginalisation of women's contributions to South Africa's liberation movements, which serves as a metaphor for a more extensive pattern in epistemology where marginalised voices are often overlooked within historical narratives. For a long time, psychology has shied away from gendered theorising, thereby rendering women's experiences to the periphery. Amplifying lives of women such as Nokukhanya's not only memorialises their lives and serves as decolonial praxes but also deconstructs the heteronormative, male-dominated narratives that have historically overshadowed women's roles in societal transformations.

It becomes increasingly clear that, despite the prevalence of male figures in historical discourse, the contributions of women remain critical yet frequently concealed and subsequently erased. Our project boldly advocates for the recovery of these hidden stories, asserting that Nokukhanya deserves to be honoured in her own right, not merely as a footnote to her husband's legacy but as one of the key figures in the ornate fabric of South Africa's liberation movement. In doing so, we hope to inspire a richer, more inclusive, and fair understanding of our liberation history. This analytical perspective positions women as critical contributors to social justice, recognising them as pivotal architects of liberation significantly redefining socio-political and historical narratives while reshaping communities and their histories. In this context, the importance of acknowledging the stories of marginalised communities in South Africa is powerfully illustrated by the work of the Apartheid Archive Project, spearheaded by Stevens, Duncan, and Sonn (2010). This initiative not only seeks to document often-overlooked narratives but also emphasises the critical need to prioritise these voices in discussions regarding dismantling the dominant patriarchal discourses.

The Apartheid Archive may be perceived as part of the decolonial project as it seeks to centre the often-silenced narratives. This is in line with the decolonial turn within psychology. Decolonising psychology necessitates a departure from the Eurocentric and universal ways of understanding the world that have long influenced the discipline. This transformation requires an embrace of multiple perspectives, particularly those of women who have confronted the consequences of oppressive systems. By valuing and amplifying these experiences, we not only honour the legacies of figures such as Nokukhanya but also create a pathway towards a more balanced and fair understanding of our history.

In the spirit of decolonisation and acknowledging indigenous peoples varied identities and realities, it is important to note that, for the rest of the chapter, we will use Nokukhanya and MaBhengu interchangeably to honour not only her as an individual (Nokukhanya) but also the clan (the Bhengus) and community she comes from.

The Heart of a Lioness Has Ceased [Continues] to Beat

Nokukhanya! "intombi kaMaphitha, oyisokanqangi lika Ndlokolo kaNkungu kaMepho kaNgwanekaLamula" (Ilanga lase Natal, 1957)

As the project embraces the significance of inclusivity in historiography, it challenges the deafening silences that have shrouded African women's struggles. Much like Kelly (2024), it advocates for a balanced portrayal that acknowledges the multifaceted realities of those who were pivotal in the fight for freedom. By centring women's experiences, this initiative not only confronts the traditionally male-centric narratives but also enriches our understanding of history, revealing a complex interplay of voices that have long been relegated to the margins. Thus, through this project, we highlight the need to illuminate the urgency of reassessing the legacies of women whose contributions have invariably been minimised.

In the same vein, Magadla's (2023) work, *Guerrillas and Combative Mothers: Women and the Armed Struggle in South Africa*, emerges as a vital thread, illuminating the profound impact of women during the fight against apartheid. Magadla's research reveals that these women were not mere bystanders; they were fierce warriors and nurturing caregivers, deftly navigating the often-conflicting demands placed upon them within the liberation movement.

This narrative aligns closely with our project, which aims to amplify the often-silenced voices of women in the context of South Africa's history. At the heart of our work, alongside that of Kelly (2024), Hughes (2012), and Magadla (2023), is a passionate commitment to enhancing the visibility and recognition of women. We seek to shift the focus of historical narratives from the periphery to the forefront, illuminating the vital contributions of African women. By centring our attention on Nokukhanya Luthuli, we aim to highlight a significant figure whose role in the liberation struggle has been largely overlooked. Through our initiative, we construct a nurturing space for black women from all walks of life, acknowledging and addressing the layered challenges they constantly navigate. Our aim is to confront the prevailing male-centric narratives that have long dominated historical scholarship. Further, our oral history project yearns to illuminate the lives and contributions of women, pushing back against the long-standing neglect and, in line with Magadla's (2023) critique of "HIStory," advocating to reclaim "HERstory." This journey is not merely academic; it is a reclamation of identity, belonging, and honour in a history that belongs to women as much as it does to anyone else. Our project therefore contributes to the archive and commemoration of women's contributions in the making and shaping of freedom and liberation. Moreover, incorporating these narratives into the broader discourse significantly enhances our understanding of community-building. It nurtures a sense of belonging that is crucial within the context of decolonial psychology. Women like Nokukhanya not only represent their individual journeys but also symbolise the collective struggles and triumphs that unite marginalised communities through a shared identity.

The Visual Commemoration of Women, or Persistent Patriarchy?

We shift our focus briefly from MaBhengu specifically to a broader reflection on the extent to which women's participation in the struggle for democracy is represented, remembered, and in many cases forgotten, in contemporary South African visual culture, including commemorative sites. For this reflection, we shall confine our analysis to the representations of women's contributions through monuments at the Union Buildings and Freedom Park, respectively. We find the monuments useful as guides to feminist researchers and the South African public in interpreting the way in which public memory practices regulate gender and the implications of this for women's contributions and roles in political struggles during apartheid and post-apartheid politics in South Africa.

Since its reveal, there has been debate concerning the women's monument located at the Union Buildings in Pretoria, South Africa. The monument incorporates various visual and audio components, including written text, spoken words, sculpture, and lighting. It is politically important to the nation, making women's political efforts and achievements visible. The work's primary sculptural element is an *imbokodo*, a large grinding stone used primarily by rural women for grinding maize, on a base consisting of two flat reflective bronze plates (see Figure 16.1). The location of the work is significant, as the late President Nelson Mandela stood and took his inaugural oath of office at the Union Buildings in 1994 (Marschall, 2011).

Figure 16.1 South African women's memorial (photo taken from Segalo, 2013)

On 9 August 1956, 20,000 women marched to the Union Buildings in protest against the law requiring black people to carry passes. They elected not to engage in violent protest, but rather to protest through written, spoken, and sung texts (Marschall, 2011). Their freedom song, written specifically for this mass demonstration, framed women's strength: "You strike a woman, you strike a rock." Implicit, however, is the notion of rock as weapon, to be used under provocation; the underlying warning to the then Prime Minister was that women were a force to be reckoned with.

However, it is our contention, together with that of Marschall (2011) and Segalo (2013), that the monument to the women of South Africa and its location are very much out of the public eye. Whereas the monument is intended to acknowledge women's political contributions, by its hidden away nature, it does the opposite, rendering them invisible. Thus, it visually represents the silencing of women's histories, their political erasure, and exclusion from post-apartheid historical commemorative sites and discourses. This assessment invites a deeper exploration of the perceived visibility of the monument, situated in a palace of political power, the Union Buildings, often overshadowing the monument's presence due to the significance of its location. Being a symbol of male political dominance, the Union Buildings serve as the centrepiece of historically male-oriented narratives, which renders this tribute to women somewhat invisible. While the monument exists as a physical structure, the cultural and historical weight of the site creates a disconnection that diminishes its intended impact. Therefore, it stands not only as a tribute to women's contributions to democracy but also as a poignant reminder of their ongoing marginalisation within the broader socio-historical and political context of South Africa.

Marschall's (2011) observation regarding the 2006 *Sunday Times* newspaper heritage project is helpful in our reflection as we journey towards excavating women's hidden histories. The objective of this heritage project was to construct street memorials across South Africa to commemorate critical figures who contributed to building the South Africa we see today. The advertisement read "a trail of memorials to some of the remarkable people and events that made our news century" (Marschall, 2011, p. 7). However, Marschall (2011) draws our attention to the distressing fact that of the 40 planned sites for commemoration, only two were dedicated to prominent female figures in the liberation struggle: Lilian Ngoyi and Cissie Gool. These two sites are reported to be in obscure locations and go unnoticed by the residents of those areas and the global community. This is consistent with South Africa's persistent patriarchy, which continues to erase and invisibilise women and their contributions to the history of our country (Marschall, 2011).

Liberation Struggle Heroines and Post-Apartheid Visual Culture and Memory: The Curious Case of South Africa's Amnesic Museums

In light of the above, it is noteworthy that the invisibilisation of women's memory in sites purported to be visibilising women's achievements and contributions to the struggle is a recurring motif. The Freedom Park Heritage Site epitomises South Africa's attempt at memorialisation. Through the works and the artefacts displayed, the organisation's mission and vision are evident – namely being inclusive, addressing historical gaps, and, finally, healing and reconciling South Africans (Miller, 2011). However, as Miller (2011) observes, this inclusivity does not extend to women or translate into equality in gender representation. We see this in the wall panels, which represent primarily the masculine, with only a few images of women among the men. Women's heroic contributions and sacrifices continue to be minimally recognised, and the women themselves not acknowledged. The narratives of a few selected feminine figures are deemed worthy of display and accepted as a sort of blanket representation of all the women who participated in the liberation struggle. This, and the erasure of women's leadership, is evident in an introductory video on leadership that can be viewed at the museum. As Miller (2011) observes, this video focuses exclusively on heroic South African masculine figures who made remarkable contributions and sacrifices in South Africa and beyond.

Other memorial structures and sites in addition to the Union Buildings and Freedom Park that commemorate heroic male figures and celebrate masculine narratives include the Hector Pieterson Memorial and Museum, the Apartheid Museum, the Nelson Mandela Museum (situated in three different locations), and memorials dedicated to Sol Plaatje, Steve Biko, Nelson Mandela, Walter Sisulu, the Craddock Four, Bram Fisher, the Guguletu Seven, and the four Nobel Peace Prize winners (Miller, 2011). As mentioned earlier, the house that Albert Luthuli shared with his wife, MaBhengu, was also transformed into a museum – yet, even though the street near the house has been named after her, she appears as nothing more than a footnote in the museum that was once her home. Her home reads as a tribute to a heroic masculine figure, not a collaboration between two liberation heroes and leaders who strove for a socially just South Africa. Unterhalter (2000) writes that, in South African liberation historiography, women are constructed as a homogeneous group, lacking autonomy and diversity of political interests because their views are interpreted and expressed by men; Unterhalter's assertion is borne out by what we observed. There is a sad irony in the fact that viewing these sites of memory through gender and feminist lenses in fact reveals them to be an *erasure* of women's political agency and a denigration of the immense contributions made by women to South Africa's ever-changing socio-political landscape.

That women are overlooked in the historical memory of this country may perhaps be traced to the fact that women appeared to be absent from the political institutions. However, Ginwala (1990) cautions that this apparent absence should not be understood to mean that women were missing from the political domain; women chose rather to focus on issues that affected their everyday lives. This made it easier to garner support from other women to mobilise and set up campaigns. Prime examples of this mobilisation against the injustices of oppressive states are the 1913 anti-pass campaign and the widely recognised 1956 women's march to the Union Buildings. These are just two of many examples of situations in which women took on the roles of freedom fighters and intellectuals. Worthy of note is the fact that some of the women's liberation struggle heroines used the imposed mission education of the day to their advantage in fighting the oppressive regime at the time. MaBhengu was a woman who did precisely that, utilising the colonial and mission education she had received – and which was designed to brainwash and subsequently oppress the black nation – to advance her community.

A Brief Background on Nokukhanya (MaBhengu) Luthuli: Mother of Light

Nokukhanya Bhengu was born at the Umngeni American Board (Congregationalist) Mission on 3 March 1904. Her paternal grandfather, Ndlokolo Bhengu, was the chief of the Ngcolosi people. Her father, Bhengu, was one of the early converts of the Umngeni Congregationalist Mission and a farmer. This led to her learning how to work in the fields from an early age. Nokukhanya began her schooling at the Ohlange Institute in Inanda in 1913, where she performed very well academically. One of the teachers at Inanda Seminary recommended her to Adams College for a teacher's training course. During this time in South Africa, there were very few opportunities for black people to develop their skills, with teaching, nursing, and clerical opportunities being among the few popular career options available to black women. It was at Adams College that she met Albert Luthuli. After her marriage to Albert Luthuli, MaBhengu's life went through some significant changes. Adams College's regulations meant she had to stop teaching, as married women were prohibited from being employed in a salaried position. Instead, she focused on creating a comfortable and welcoming home for her family in a town called Groutville in what is now KwaZulu-Natal province. Upon her marriage, because of the oppressive system of the day, which treated women as second-class citizens, she also lost her legal autonomy. Despite the struggles faced by black people at the national level and within her community, MaBhengu remained resilient and unwavering in her mission to free her people. She continued to serve the needs of her family and community, seemingly unperturbed by external forces.

A Description of the Luthuli Museum

In 2021, we had the opportunity to visit the Luthuli Museum, an important cultural and historical landmark nestled in Groutville, South Africa. This museum is dedicated to honouring the Luthuli family's enduring legacy and is located within their historic home. Inside, it boasts a fascinating collection of personal artefacts, photographs, and documents that tell the story of the family's significant role in the struggle for liberation in South Africa. As you enter the museum's doors, you are greeted by exhibits that thoughtfully illustrate Inkosi Luthuli's political activism, alongside the family's steadfast commitment to social justice. The displayed artefacts not only chronicle their resistance against apartheid but also highlight the Luthuli couple's influence as national leaders, community leaders, and activists. Furthermore, the museum serves as a critical resource for community engagement and education, hosting various programmes that celebrate the Luthuli family's contributions while encouraging discussions on critical issues relevant to South Africa, such as land rights, identity, and Luthuli's critical role in the liberation movement.

One poignant element of the museum's story is the overlooked contribution of Nokukhanya Luthuli. Despite her significant role in both her family's life and South Africa, her impact was absent from the exhibitions. This is particularly disheartening, especially considering her monumental work in organising community gatherings and leading the community in finding solutions to the structural challenges that arose in Groutville during apartheid. The omission speaks to a broader issue regarding the neglect and erasure of women's contributions in history, highlighting the urgent need for a more inclusive narrative that acknowledges the diverse voices woven into South Africa's liberation story. Amidst the beautifully tended gardens surrounding the museum, visitors discover a peaceful space that encourages deeper reflection on the intricate history of the

Luthuli family. Local community members share their oral histories of Groutville, adding richness to the area's narrative. Despite the many narratives on her husband's legacy, there exists a profound opportunity to fully illuminate Nokukhanya's remarkable story in the house that they both shared. Her unwavering spirit not only sustained a household amid the tumult of apartheid but also created a nurturing sanctuary for individuals from diverse backgrounds. Nokukhanya's exceptional talents as a homemaker transformed the Luthuli residence into a beacon of resilience and warmth, embodying a deep sense of community and care even in the darkest of times. This enduring legacy is palpable today, resonating with visitors who pass through the gates of her home, where the echoes of her love and strength continue to inspire and uplift visitors.

Exploring the Shadows: Our Encounter with Nokukhanya

Our oral history project also included archival materials relating to MaBhengu, and for this purpose we visited the Luthuli Museum, which is situated in the home of the Luthuli family, in Groutville. This carries great significance, as it is the repository of the history and significance of who the Luthuli family was and continues to be. Upon exploring the museum for the purpose of the oral history project, we found several omissions that have contributed to the erasure of MaBhengu from history. First, we noted the absence in the collection of tangible items belonging to MaBhengu, while many items belonging to the late Albert Luthuli were on display. Second, despite our inquiries, the museum could not at the time provide us with photographic images of MaBhengu. Third, we were presented with only two newspaper articles about her, and these contained brief and derogatory references to MaBhengu, such as "Luthuli's wheelchair widow." Fourth, the museum possessed only two video home system (VHS) recordings, of which only one was playable. The Mayibuye iAfrika documentary DVD, which was said to contain some information about MaBhengu, proved non-functional, a fact the museum only became aware of following our inquiry. The second video was just a 15-minute-long recording and featured Dr Albertina Luthuli, the eldest daughter of MaBhengu. She was asked to speak about her mother towards the end of the video, but her contribution lasted a mere five minutes. We were greatly concerned by this, as individuals or children who visit the museum searching for information on the Luthulis will find no (or very limited) information about MaBhengu. Such an omission diminishes the perception of women's contributions to the struggle and teaches children and other museum visitors that it is acceptable to disregard the efforts of women.

Given our experiences as described above, we align ourselves with Zungu et al. (2014) who argue that history is not an accurate representation of what occurred but is instead relayed based on the interpretations of men. This is exacerbated by social constructions of the power imbalance between men and women, giving HIStory precedence over HERstory (Zungu et al., 2014). Our oral history project therefore hopes to contribute towards highlighting these imbalances and re-visibilise lives of some of the overlooked women such as MaBhengu. Her contribution continues to be in the periphery despite the significant role she played in her community and South Africa broadly. Goettsche's statement about remembering the past becomes relevant here. Goettsche (2001) makes the observation that when we neglect our past and do not recognise the work done by those who came before us, we fail to truly appreciate our freedom and the price paid to attain it. This makes history vital, and the collection and preservation of ordinary people's narratives, particularly in a country such as South Africa, with its contested history, aids our understanding of the past, and counters the so-called official narratives (Zungu et al., 2014). In this regard, Miller (2011) proposes that constructing sites of memory serves to prevent forgetting.

Like that of many other South African struggle heroines, MaBhengu's life story remains relegated to the periphery and is not accorded a place at the centre of our history; her life journey continues to be omitted from the official historical accounts of black women in the liberation movement. Furthermore, many young people do not know the history of black women who were part of the struggle, as the materials available and knowledge produced tend to be skewed towards centring men at the expense of the women who fought alongside them. Pető (2021) argues that women have been excluded from formal historical inquiries and, as a result, excluded from being viewed as "scientific" subjects. To this end, we consciously use MaBhengu as a scientific subject – drawing from her life and contributions she made to the South African liberation struggle to assist us to understand the importance of memorialisation and historical preservation. In the rest of the chapter, we present a brief overview of our oral history project through offering some reflections of our engagements with those who knew and lived with MaBhengu, and examples of the contributions she made to her community.

The Narrators' Enchanting Encounters with Nokukhanya

As part of our quest to excavate the hidden narrative of struggle heroines such as Nokukhanya Luthuli, we embarked on an oral history project to explore her life. People we spoke to included Mrs Veli Luthuli (her daughter-in-law), the Ndaba family (neighbours and close family friends), Mrs Guma (a neighbour), Albertina Luthuli (her daughter), and Mrs Mngadi (her friend and helper). All the people we spoke to emphasised the importance of land in MaBhengu's life and how she used it for the economic survival of her family. This bears out MaBhengu's own words, as captured in her biography: "the soil was our only means of living"; she further describes how the soil became her friend because it allowed her to earn extra income (Rule et al., 1993, pp. 59–61). MaBhengu also recalls how she used the agricultural lessons she learned as a child to build her success (Rule et al., 1993). Mrs Veli Luthuli recalls how MaBhengu started with two plots of vegetables near the Umvoti River and gradually built up enough capital to invest in the thriving sugar cane industry on the Coast. Mrs Luthuli also mentions how MaBhengu experimented with rice during the Second World War and cotton at the encouragement of the then Native Affairs Department. Mrs Luthuli fondly remembers how her mother-in-law expressed her love for her family by providing them and her extended family with fresh produce, often delivering it herself to those who lived kilometres away. Similarly, the Ndaba family reminisced about MaBhengu's ability to bring her family together through the simple tradition of family dinners despite their busy schedules. They explained that this was a rare occurrence in African households of that time, as parents seldom partook of meals with their children or inquired about their daily encounters at the dinner table.

The Fields Are Calling Us, Nokukhanya! Leading through Service

The words above come from a song that South African storyteller, author, and praise poet, Gcina Mhlophe, often sings as part of her praise poetry to capture MaBhengu's dedication and determination to working hard. MaBhengu's exemplary agricultural accomplishments are a testament to her unwavering fortitude and hard work despite the oppressive apartheid laws that sought to keep African women in subordinate positions, denying them the opportunity to realise their full potential and accomplishments. She understood the importance of the land to her family's livelihood and used her knowledge and resources to establish a thriving business. Her meticulous cultivation techniques and diverse crop selection ensured long-term sustainability, even during times of hardship such as the Second World War (Rule et al., 1993). MaBhengu's story is a powerful reminder of African people's strong connection to the land. This connection and being attuned to the land was perceived as a threat by the colonial and apartheid regimes, which thwarted any hope for land ownership for many African people. The effects of these oppressive regimes continue to reverberate even today.

MaBhengu was widely recognised by her family and neighbours for both her exceptional abilities and strong work ethic in the fields. Despite her family having hired help to tend their cattle, MaBhengu would still harness the oxen to till the fields. According to the people we spoke to and as reflected in her biography, MaBhengu's morning departure for the fields was so punctual that her neighbours would set their clocks by it, often remarking, "There goes MaBhengu. The fields are calling us." Mrs Veli Luthuli attested to how MaBhengu created employment opportunities in her community, allowing families to provide for their children and fostering independence among the most vulnerable members of any community, namely women.

In 1935, Albert Luthuli was urged to run for chief of Groutville, following in the footsteps of his grandfather and uncle. This made MaBhengu's work within her family and community even more important. Although Luthuli could now live full time with his family, his income as chief (as opposed to being a teacher – a position he had to forego when he accepted chieftaincy) in 1936 was significantly reduced. MaBhengu felt it was their responsibility to serve, and she became the primary breadwinner. In a letter to the government requesting an increase in remuneration, Luthuli expressed his concern about his wife's strenuous workload. He was grateful that she bore it all without complaint, as he could not afford to pay helpers (Luthuli 1940, cited in Rule et al., 1993).

In addition to her agricultural and domestic work, MaBhengu was highly regarded as an excellent host. The Ndaba family remembers how the Luthuli family frequently welcomed guests, including foreign dignitaries, presidents, members of the Zulu royal family, politicians, and activists in the liberation movement, such as His Excellency Prince Buthelezi and Nelson Mandela. Luthuli was considered a mentor to many of these individuals. When a procession of large black cars arrived in Groutville, the neighbours would know that these were Luthuli's guests. MaBhengu remained humble in response to the attention and did not discuss it with neighbours or family friends. Moreover, MaBhengu transitioned effortlessly from being a host to guests in her home to actively participating in discussions with them about national politics. During an interview about Luthuli's political position, when asked about her relationship with politicians, she explained that she was used to being in their company, since her father was a community leader (Rule et al., 1993).

By Way of Conclusion: Oral History as Praxis

This chapter draws attention to the persistent silencing and *invisibilisation* of women's contributions in the making and shaping of South Africa's democracy. By focusing on the life of Nokukhanya (MaBhengu) Luthuli, we aimed to illuminate not only her individual journey but also the broader narrative on women's roles in the South African liberation struggle. As indicated early in the chapter, this exploration is grounded in a wider oral history project that emphasises the importance of community participation, highlighting collaborative storytelling as a significant method of decolonial practices. Our objective is not only to produce accessible narratives that amplify community voices but also to foster a richer understanding of our intertwined histories. Central to this endeavour is the embroidered Nokukhanya Quilt (produced in collaboration with the Intuthuko community women's collective as part of the oral history project) which depicts her journey to freedom and the freedom of her people, currently showcased at the Luthuli Museum. Further, we have hosted two Nokukhanya theatre productions, which were recorded and are available on YouTube, further extending our reach and impact with diverse groups and communities. Through these manifold efforts, we aspire to create a welcoming space where African women's stories are shared and celebrated, fostering a sense of belonging and connection among different communities in South Africa, including the academic community.

In conclusion, we advocate for the urgent need to create spaces that excavate women's hidden histories and contributions, emphasising the importance of centring HERstory in our collective narrative. In this way, we not only honour their legacies but also enrich our understanding of the diverse experiences that have shaped our nation.

References

Ahikire, J. (2014). African feminism in context: Reflections on the legitimation battles, victories and reversals. *Feminist Africa*, (19), 7–23. https://www.jstor.org/stable/48725801

Chilisa, B., & Ntseane, G. (2014). Resisting dominant discourses: Implications of Indigenous, African feminist theory and methods for gender and education research. In B. Chilisa, & G. Ntseane (Eds.), *Rethinking gendered regulations and resistances in education* (pp. 23–38). Routledge.

Ginwala, F. (1990). Women and the African national congress: 1912–1943. *Agenda, 6*(8), 77–93. https://doi.org/10.1080/10130950.1990.9676171

Goettsche, B. (2001). *The importance of the past*. Retrieved November 23, 2011, from https://www.unionchurch.com/archive/071501.html

Hughes, H. (2012). Lives and wives: Understanding African nationalism in South Africa through a biographical approach. *History Compass*, *10*(8), 562–573. https://doi.org/10.1111/j.1478-0542.2012.00869.x

Kelly, J. E. (2024, August 21). Nokukhanya Luthuli. *Oxford Research Encyclopedia of African History*. Retrieved 10 May. 2025, from https://doi.org/10.1093/acrefore/9780190277734.013.1442

Lugones, M. (2010). Toward a decolonial feminism. *Hypatia*, *25*(4), 742–759. https://www.jstor.org/stable/40928654

Magadla, S. (2023). *Guerrillas and combative mothers: Women and the armed struggle in South Africa*. Taylor & Francis.

Mandela, N. R. (1996). Speech by president Mandela at the funeral of Nokukhanya Luthuli, 22 December 1996, Groutville. *South African History Online*. Retrieved June 29, 2024, from https://www.sahistory.org.za/archive/speech-president-mandela-funeral-nokukhanya-luthuli-22-december-1996-groutville

Marschall, S. (2011). The Sunday Times heritage project: Heritage, the media and the formation of national consciousness. *Social Dynamics*, *37*(3), 409–423. https://doi.org/10.1080/02533952.2011.656430

Miller, K. (2011). Selective silence and the shaping of memory in post-apartheid visual culture: The case of the monument to the women of South Africa. *South African Historical Journal*, *63*(2), 295–317. https://doi.org/10.1080/02582473.2011.554851

Pető, A. (2021). Far-right expectations of women in Central-Eastern Europe. In K. Fabian, J. E. Johnson, & M. Lazda (Eds.), *The routledge handbook of gender in Central-Eastern Europe and Eurasia* (pp. 207–215). Routledge.

Rule, P., Aitken, M., & Van Dyk, J. (1993). *Nokukhanya, mother of light*. Grail.

Segalo, P. J. (2013). *In our own voices: Black women's narratives of conflict and post-conflict experiences*. City University of New York.

Stevens, G., Duncan, N., & Sonn, C. (2010). The apartheid archive: Memory, voice and narrative as liberatory praxis. *Psychology in Society*, *40*, 8–28.

Unterhalter, E. (2000). The work of the nation: Heroic masculinity in South African autobiographical writing of the anti-apartheid struggle. *The European Journal of Development Research*, *12*, 157–178. https://doi.org/10.1080/09578810008426770

Vahed, G. (2015). Women and national liberation in South Africa: an oral history perspective. *South Asian Diaspora*, *7*(2), 129–147. https://doi.org/10.1080/19438192.2015.1007635

Zungu, M., Manqele, N., de Vries, C., Molefe, T., & Hadebe, M. (2014). HERstory: Writing women into South African history. *Agenda*, *28*(1), 7–17. https://doi.org/10.1080/10130950.2014.871459

17 Archiving Lebanese Women in Diaspora

The Necessity of Decolonial Frameworks

Janan Akram Shouhayib

To archive is to testify. Whether against erasure, loss and repression of memory, historical revision, or stereotypes crafted to dehumanize, the power of archives is garnered through a bearing of witness, through documentation, often existing against odds. By connecting us to the past, present, and future, archives pause and immortalize histories, asserting existence and belonging. Because of this, they hold a powerful role in challenging injustice and erasure.

Archives can also take many forms. They can be governed by the state, such as the United States National Archives, which holds documents such as the country's Constitution, but they can also be housed in universities or exist as their own entity, such as the South Asian American Digital Archive (SAADA).

However, not all voices are captured, or captured correctly, within an archive. This is because archives reflect the realities from the perspective of the archivers, in what Ketelaar (2001) calls "tacit narratives." Jarenski (2018) echoes this observation:

> The material available in archives often dictates whose stories are told and how; and even when an archive does have material that reflects the voice of a historically underrepresented population, the way that material is labeled and catalogued effects how this material is accessed and interpreted.
>
> (p. 31)

This necessitates the question: if the victor is he who writes the history, what about the histories of those whose countries were invaded, colonized, and stolen? What about the histories that are purposefully buried or neglected? What about those on the margins, whose lives are trod upon by nationalism?

Critical archivist and co-founder of SAADA Michelle Caswell asks directly, "what does it mean to be omitted from history textbooks?" (Caswell, 2014, p. 26). These omissions have been circumvented and resisted through the creation of grassroots archives. For example, the Ramallah Preservation Project, a community-built archive nested in diaspora, aims to preserve the city's historical and ancestral heritage. Descendants of Ramallah, scattered across the globe, collectively document its history through the collection of photographs, documents, oral histories, and other archival materials, histories unhoused by mainstream sources.

In this way, archives help us construct, witness, and preserve the past, but as noted by Fabian (2022), archives also "provide evidence, justify, explain, educate, entertain, support research, help protect human rights, confirm identity, invoke imagination, manipulate, seduce, and lie" (para. 1).

In this chapter, I outline the ways archives have been used to further colonial agendas but also subverted to decolonize knowledge and history. In particular, I use the example of researching Lebanese women in diaspora to show the necessity of adopting decolonial frameworks when

DOI: 10.4324/9781003492214-20

researching and archiving postcolonial groups. Legacies of colonialism affect individuals of previously colonized nations due to the pervasive effects imperialist supremacy has on multiple aspects of society. Therefore, I argue that research on Lebanese women, both in Lebanon and abroad, should adopt a decolonial framework.

Counter-Archiving

Archives can be inclusionary or exclusionary, depending on their construction (Belmonte & Opotow, 2017). To mitigate this imbalance, many have turned to *counter*-archives to reclaim authority and rewrite historical narratives.

The creation of counter-archives can help to disrupt the hegemonic nature of archives. However, as noted by Conroy (2021), "counter-archiving is more than a process of diversifying conventional archives. This means it is not simply about adding previously erased or hidden histories to an archive, but a method of interrogating the logic of archives" (para. 7). Not only do counter-archives document marginalized voices, they also provide opportunity to think and document *contrapuntally*, comparing discrepant narratives together (Said, 1993). This framework allows us to examine both dominant histories and marginalized perspectives simultaneously.

An excellent portrayal of counter-archives is the pioneering work of W. E. B. Dubois in his data portraits (Dubois, 1900). First presented in 1900 at the Paris Exposition, Dubois' accessible, imaginative, and critically interrogative portraits depict social science data displayed in colorful, creative charts. The portraits included demographic data of the Black American population, such as literacy rates, postbellum migration journeys, valuation of Black-owned properties, and other statistical information about descendants of enslaved people, all of which were published at the height of the Segregation Era (Battle-Baptiste & Rusert, 2018). His work can be considered a counter-archive, as he self-documented essential information that recorded various experiences of his marginalized community.

The work of Alixa Naff (1985), a Lebanese immigrant and historian, represents a similar moxie. Unable to discover primary materials of her Arab American community, Naff spent the 1960s traveling across the U.S. and Canada with her tape recorder, interviewing community elders and collecting artifacts of the time, slowly creating a rich archive of oral histories of early Arab immigrants that is now publicly accessible and housed at the Arab American National Museum, established in 2005. As anti-Arab sentiment has only grown and institutionalized in recent years, Naff's self-guided research stands as a pillar against these forces.

Additionally, the Lesbian Herstory Archives, founded in the 1970s, assert how the gathering and preserving of lesbian *herstories* "serves to uncover and document our herstory previously denied to us by patriarchal historians in the interest of the culture that they served" (2019, para. 1). In this way, the archive not only works toward historical preservation of lesbians, but it also corrects the dominant discourse that refused its existence.

I also invite us to broaden our imagination of what an archive, and counter-archive, can be. For example, a family's personal collection of family heirlooms; a digital folder of old photographs; my grandmother smuggling fig tree seeds from Lebanon and re-planting them in her American yard; and journalists live-tweeting news violently absent from mainstream media.

Women's lives are also notably absent from archives and historical narratives in general (Perkins, 2012). Women of color, in particular, are denied both presence and agency in representations of history and collective memory, an absence that subsequently affects senses of belonging, political engagement, and the movement toward gender liberation (McEwan, 2003).

As theorized by Hill Collins (1994), the voices, experiences, and spirit of marginalized communities, such as women of color, are often so misrepresented in dominant discourse that communities resort to resources and platforms outside of research and academia, including "personal narratives, autobiographical statements, poetry, fiction, and other personalized statements" (p. 174). Although these avenues are incredibly rich sources of knowledge and testimony, it is essential to ensure and protect communities' right to self-determine their own means of knowledge and creation and preservation.

Archives, as time capsules, help us to address such absences of knowledge. By recasting histories and filling gaps of omission and erasure, community archives also resist traditional forms of knowledge and history. Noted by Caswell (2014), "the creation of community archives can be seen as a form of political protest in that it is an attempt to seize the means by which history is written and to correct or amend dominant stories about the past" (p. 32).

This delineation between dominant stories and community-based stories illustrates how the archiving of histories can either reinstate or challenge the status quo. We can see these processes clearly when examining how archives are manipulated in colonial contexts, and then subverted by those aiming to decolonize archival knowledge.

Archives Manipulated by Colonial Powers

Archives have been utilized to wield power, becoming "the backbone of the nation-state" (Desai & Shahwan, 2022, p. 477). Archives play a particularly important role in colonial and decolonial thought, used by both colonizer and colonized to assert a right to existence.

Often, the archive is propagandized by colonial entities that rely on the complete suppression—physical, spiritual, psychological, and epistemological—of the Indigenous peoples within their colony. Summarized succinctly by Liebert (2019), "Coloniality is dependent on a hierarchy of Knowing, Knowers, Knowledge" (p. 78). This hierarchy subsequently strips the colonized of epistemic privileges (Mignolo, 2007).

Emphasizing the critical role of constructing knowledge, decolonial theorist Fanon (1961) argues that

> colonialism is not satisfied merely with holding a people in its grip and emptying the native's brain of all form and content. By a kind of perverse logic, it turns to the past of the oppressed people, and distorts it, disfigures and destroys it.
>
> (pp. 210–211)

The critically perceptive work of Rayan (2021) outlines how imperial nations assert sovereignty over colonies by constructing representations that support their colonial agenda. Depicting Indigenous inhabitants as inferior, they do this to show how a native population is so barbaric and in need of guidance that colonizing their land is actually *beneficial*. These stereotypes are promoted within the media and news circuits, but also in literature, film, visual art, and in our language, eventually seeping into the social zeitgeist and reinforcing support for colonial policies, such as "justifying" land grabs. In this way, coloniality is maintained and reproduced.

Beyond stereotypes, another colonial tactic is to strip Indigenous people of their indigeneity, often, settler states manipulate archives to bolster such logics. For example, in the state archives of Canada, "Indigenous peoples are often either absent, depicted as ciphers of the real individuals they are meant to represent, or presented as always already disappearing from the landscape" (Hunt, 2016, p. 26).

Building upon Said's (1978) theories, Genovese (2016) notes that "imperial powers were able to secure and maintain power by controlling the information that was recorded, essentially deliberately creating an archival gap by omitting—either explicitly or implicitly—the ideas of the conquered" (p. 34). Luker (2017) also reminds us that this lack of archival evidence makes it difficult to make legal claims for reparations and compensations for Indigenous groups.

In order to fulfill their epistemological hegemony, many colonial powers also commit epistemicide, seeking the full annihilation of Indigenous knowledge and records as a way to seize the narrative and push dissenting voices deeper into the ground.

Epistemicide and Theft of Records

Whoever stands until the end will tell the story. We did what we could. Remember us.

—Dr. Mahmoud Abu Nujaila

As mentioned, colonial nations actively target Indigenous knowledge and records, classified by Rayan (2021) as a "colonization of information" and by Liebert (2019) as "the epistemological empire" (p. 10). The supremacy is often exercised through the destruction of historical records, knowledge centers, attacks on personnel working within both, as well as efforts to prevent their revivals. This destruction of culture represents an attack on both native history and memory upon the colonized land, aiming to erase evidence of existence and indigeneity prior to the colonial regime (Desai & Shahwan, 2022).

Mowases (2024) defines *epistemicide* as "the destruction of knowledge systems and the knowledge that they generate" (para. 4). Therefore, it contains both the destruction of physical centers of knowledge, such as universities, libraries, and archives, as well as the potential for knowledge created within those centers. Epistemicide remains a tool of hegemony, erasure, and genocide and is also reinforced by its counterpart: the privileging of Western knowledge above Indigenous knowledge (Grosfoguel, 2013).

Examples of epistemicide include the destruction of Indigenous education systems, the loss of native languages, and the demolition of universities, archives, and libraries. The destruction of the Sikh Reference Library in 1984 by the Indian government is an example of epistemicide (Tatla, 2020). The library, which previously housed over 500 years of Sikh literature and heritage, has since been revived. Of such targeted destruction, Isabella Hammad (2024) discerns how the destruction of knowledge is used to both invisibilize history and threaten potential futures.

The imperialist goal to destroy Indigenous knowledge and memory renders the work of documenting even more important. Colonial logics require a suppression of knowledge as much as an occupation of land; it is because of this threat of epistemicide that we must constantly work toward preservation.

Archives as Decolonial Praxis

Just as archives are manipulated to dominate, they can also be used to subvert, resist erasure, and decolonize. Māori decolonial scholar Linda Tuhiwai Smith (2012) reminds us how "imperialism frames the Indigenous experience" (p. 19). This framing, often embraced within academic research, involves erasing the indigeneity of the colonized group, a cog of what Desai and Shahwan (2022) call "archival violence," that reinforces colonizer hegemony. By silencing colonized groups, the colonizer seizes control over the knowledge, narratives, and framing of Indigenous peoples. With colonialism wielding power over epistemology, history, and Indigenous will to live, the preservation of Indigenous livelihood is crucial to efforts to decolonize.

Because the grip of colonialism involves the manipulation of archives and the attempt to obliterate knowledge and records, preserving and reconstructing Indigenous histories allows us to resist colonialism and its legacies. This, in turn, reinstitutes Indigenous people the control over how people interpret public history.

The power of archives lies in its ability to preserve, which, in colonial contexts, supports the self-determination of Indigenous groups. This self-determination includes critiquing how Indigenous people have been Otherized, represented, and excluded (Tuhiwai Smith, 2012) as well as honoring surviving Indigenous knowledges. Smith asserts that Indigenous people "want to tell our own stories, write our own versions, in our own ways, for our own purposes" (p. 28).

This mirrors the work of Kathy Travis, a First Nations' historian in Australia of Arrernte origin. Travis and her siblings, mother, and grandmother were all forcibly removed from each other to be enslaved and institutionalized in anti-Indigenous policies. Travis's work (2023) has worked to co-construct the "her-stories" of her family to "re-author, re-tell, and re-matriate a new family narrative back to family and country" (p. 111). This re-authoring is a decolonial practice that retrieves family and community histories intentionally lost, reframing and preserving history. This practice, which relies largely on archival materials in the absence of intergenerational family stories, reconstructs history, centering the experiences of Indigenous peoples.

In the words of Maldonaldo-Torres (2016), decoloniality necessitates "the production of counter-discourses, counter-knowledges, counter-creative acts, and counter-practices that seek to dismantle coloniality and to open up multiple other forms of being in the world" (p. 10). These are also referred to as "resurgent histories" by Simpson (2014) and "archival reclamation" by Desai and Shahwan (2022). Such practices help subvert colonial-based representations that exist within archives (Sela, 2016).

An example of a decolonial counter-archive is the Memories Museum, housed at the Beirut's Shatila Palestinian refugee camp. The museum was created in 2005 by Muhammad al-Khatib, displaced to Lebanon during the Nakba, and contains old objects that other Nakba survivors brought to Lebanon, providing evidence and testimony against attempts of erasure by gathering community-based counter-histories (Edwards, 2023).

As outlined, to decolonize knowledge includes analyzing how Euro-American knowledge is privileged and centering the experiences and voices of Indigenous or non-Western knowledges; however, this shift in epistemic power is not nearly an exchange of perspective but involves an interrogation of how imperialism privileged Euro-American knowledge and power and inserted them into non-Western spheres (Bhatia, 2017). This practice also "involves understanding how power shapes intersecting spaces, stories, identities, subjectivities, histories, languages, and resistances" (p. 238). Mignolo (2010) also reminds us that decoloniality entails an analysis of how a Euro-American-centered knowledge is seen as universally applicable.

To decolonize archives, subsequently, requires an acknowledgment and resistance of colonial history and legacy while actively remembering and centering Indigenous counter-narratives. Within the context of decolonial archives, it is also imperative to emphasize land and sovereignty (Desai & Shahwan, 2022) and to note that these counter-archives often rely on local knowledges and resources such as oral histories, particularly in the absence of other records (Hunt, 2016; Desai & Shahwan, 2022).

In the following section, I argue that studying the lives of Lebanese individuals, whether in Lebanon or diaspora, requires a holistic interrogation of coloniality through the use of decolonial methods. I outline similar tactics to utilize archival methods through a decolonial framework, exemplified through research on Lebanese women in diaspora. These tactics include examining histories and legacies of colonialism, embracing multiple forms of knowledge and centering embodied experiences, emphasizing questions of land, sovereignty, and repatriation, and consolidating efforts with other archives to centralize knowledge.

Employing Decolonial Archival Methods to Research Lebanese Women in Diaspora

On January 26, 2025, a woman native to the town of Maroun El Ras in southern Lebanon defiantly stood ground against a tank invading the town in violation of the newly-agreed ceasefire. The woman, later identified as Zahraa al-Kobeisi, unarmed and arms spread open, shouted to the occupying soldiers: "Qawwes, hay ardena" (Shoot, this is our land). Within hours, I had been forwarded the video on multiple WhatsApp groups and stumbled across it across social media websites, spreading quickly across Lebanese and Arab communities globally.

The Lebanese diaspora is one of the largest existing despite the country's small area, spread out across all regions of the world. Many Lebanese abroad maintain a strong connection to their homeland, even those generations removed, a relationship reinforced through economic remittance, nostalgia, artistic expression, and regular visits back home.

Like many regions of the world, the Middle East has continuously been choked by colonizers and their legacies. Beginning in the 13th century, Lebanon has endured waves of invasions that have shaped its history, culture, and society, beginning with Ottoman Turks and handed off to French colonizers between 1920 and 1943. More recently, growing American involvement in Lebanon since the 1980s and the continual Western-financed annexation of Lebanese lands represent new waves of colonial presence within the country.

Lebanon's colonial legacy seeps into many aspects of everyday life, including language and education, architecture, collective memory, and identity formation. It is also deeply entwined with the preservation of records and archives.

For example, rather than a central data, genealogy records are kept at the local level, able to be requested by municipality officials called *makhatir*, a position that was established in 1861 by the Ottoman administration and later adapted by French authorities (Family Search, 2023; Stel, 2015). Additionally, censuses conducted by both the Ottoman and French empires are still housed at the Turkish Ministry of Interior. Lebanon also maintains a citizenship law that provides male citizens, but not female citizens, the ability to pass their nationality to their wives and children, a law that was first codified in 1920 during the French Mandate (Abou-Habib, 2024). Additionally, Mikdashi (2022) highlights how Lebanese archives are regularly threatened: "The Middle East is a space where are archives and documents are routinely damaged and targeted by war and occupation practices" (p. 59). These structures work alongside domestic patriarchal laws that keep Lebanese women's histories particularly difficult to uncover, decipher, and preserve.

Lebanese women, both at home and in diaspora, are subjected to the layered, colonial-borne mechanisms of erasure and subjugation that are reinforced by Orientalism[1]. Therefore, archiving Lebanese women's histories necessitates a feminist decolonial framework. In laying out an argument for a decolonial feminism, Maria Lugones (2010) states that the coloniality of knowledge is gendered and that any discussion of coloniality of power, knowledge, and identity must include discussion of how the coloniality of gender is also constructed.

My work with Lebanese mothers and daughters pre- and post-emigration has exposed the ways that Lebanese women face and resist colonial legacies that challenge how their histories are preserved, even across generations. Therefore, to properly archive the experiences of Lebanese women, a feminist decolonial framework is imperative.

Decolonizing Lebanese women's archival work involves many tactics. First, it is vital to acknowledge and link the histories of colonialism to Lebanese women's everyday lives. This past year and a half have witnessed particularly dreadful catastrophes across the Arab World and its diaspora; Lebanese women in diaspora are subjected to, and affected by, both the attacks on their homelands as well as xenophobic, Islamophobic, and sexist policies and attitudes against them in their host countries. To name these multiple challenges, and the ways that they resist them, offers a necessary critical and authentic perspective of these multifaceted lives that analyzes at both structural and individual scales (Weis & Fine, 2012).

Second, since Arab women's lives are constantly commodified, fetishized, and flattened by colonial Orientalist stereotypes, it is also crucial to honor the complexity, contradictions, and heterogeneity of their experiences. Due to the lack of centralized records on Lebanese women both in Lebanon and diaspora, researchers should embrace additional forms of knowledge, including oral histories and storytelling (Sonn et al., 2013), visual arts, films, photographs, and activist testimonials. To create more authentic knowledge, it is also vital to center the voices of Lebanese women, while challenging Western dominant, decontextualized histories that seek to define their narratives on their behalf (Fine, 2016). This includes the full participation and leadership of Lebanese women archivists. Researchers and archivists should also center the ways Lebanese women, contrary to Orientalist claims of a weak victim, regularly resist, protect, desire, and dream of liberatory futures.

Furthermore, in creating a decolonial archive, land is a key factor in understanding the relationship Lebanese women have to their culture, whether in Lebanon or abroad. Land plays a vital role in Lebanese life and culture. Notably, many Lebanese live off their land, but land is also inextricable from Lebanese culture, identity, and sense of belonging. Most Lebanese families have been living in Lebanon for centuries and can trace family roots to their respective towns, reinforcing senses of attachment, belonging, and community within the land. Resisting repeated invaders, rebuilding after wars, and remaining on the same land as our ancestors have also deepened this connection, and the Lebanese exercise a strong commitment to their land, even in times of war. Amid incessant attacks on southern Lebanon in April 2024, Wael Taleb (2024) reported that during Eid al-Fitr, Lebanese families from villages in the war-ridden south returned to their ancestral homes near the border. Their powerful images of return have shown the devotion of the Lebanese people to their land, especially when under attack by colonial forces.

In diaspora, this devotion persists. Lebanese outside of Lebanon are deeply affected while following the news of the country being invaded and attacked, such as this past year. This physical separation from Lebanon may also evoke feelings of sorrow, alienation, and longing for homeland that affects daily life. Many Lebanese in diaspora retain their connections to their land through foods such as spices, jams, nuts, and olive oil brought from Lebanon to enjoy abroad, continuing to be sustained by and connected to their homeland. Many also visit regularly, maintain family properties and own land, stay connected to local communities, and work to retire back home.

Overall, land is tightly woven into the Lebanese sense of identity, community, and belonging, persisting in diaspora. This relationship is deeply informed by the country's colonial legacy and need to protect its land against colonizers. Questions of decoloniality thus cannot be properly addressed without the acknowledgment and centering of questions of land and land sovereignty.

Lastly, despite the repression threatening knowledge about Lebanese people, many community-based archives work to piece together these histories, including the Lebanese Memory Archive and the Khayrallah Center for Lebanese Diaspora Studies. Feminist archives such as Al Warsha's Knowledge Workshop also bridge the gap of Lebanese women's histories by deliberately focusing upon the narratives of Lebanese women and their histories. Because the documented experiences of Lebanese women are fragmented and insufficiently archived, efforts should also be made to collaborate across groups to utilize whatever recorded history is available, expand knowledge accessibility, create alliance across communities, and build toward a pluralistic history. In recent years, many cities and villages across Lebanon have also created Facebook pages to publish family photographs, connect with family globally, and centralize knowledge about the area, exemplifying the powerful role of social media and digital technologies to bolster preservation work and expand access (Sonn et al., 2013). Efforts to collaborate with such community-created digital archives are also essential.

All in all, Lebanese women in diaspora migrate with their histories, often remaining connected to their homeland and its society. Because of this, despite living in diaspora, a holistic account of Lebanese women's histories both at home and abroad is necessary. This includes interrogating Lebanon's colonial past and how it continues to affect Lebanese people globally, and how Western academic discourse has Otherized and demeaned the lives of Arab women. By adopting a decolonial framework, inextricable from questions of land, and working within a pluralistic archival network, we can slowly piece together an authentic account of Lebanese women's lives abroad, constructed from our own experiences.

Conclusion

Colonial legacy is ubiquitous and palpable across the world, whether in the land of colonizers of the colonized. Though too often decontextualized and seen as a concluded historical phase, the immense effects of colonization of the Global South by the Global North is still highly active today. Hickel et al. (2024) found that the Global South labor force provides 90% of the labor in the world economy, while receiving only 21% of income. These statistics exemplify the financial effects of colonial legacy not always presented by scientists. These financial gains enjoyed by colonizers were reinvested into their state's infrastructure, development, education, and record-keeping, further widening a parasitic gap between colonizer and colonized.

In the realm of knowledge, the legacy of colonialism "has been perpetuated through the ways in which knowledge about Indigenous peoples was collected, classified, and then represented in various ways back to the West, back to those who have been colonized". This hegemonic relationship creates hierarchies of knowledge that privilege Euro-American knowledges, records, and narratives above colonized and Indigenous peoples' histories, such as in the construction and destruction of archives.

Within this chapter, I discussed the way archives are utilized as decolonial praxis, contextualized in the study of diasporic Lebanese women. I argued that to critically study Lebanese women requires a deep inquiry into legacies of colonialism, even in diaspora.

In this context, a decolonial archival praxis requires four central tenets. First, researchers should acknowledge the history of colonialism and how it affects Lebanese lives in diaspora and at home, also highlighting the circumvention of these challenges. Second, researchers should actively challenge minimizing, Orientalist stereotypes by including Lebanese women in the archiving process and containing multiple forms of knowledge, records, and data. Researchers should also contextualize their work in the history of how Lebanese/Arab women have historically been framed in a Western, Orientalized lens. Third, inquiries of coloniality should center land, including issues of archival possession, land and resource repatriation, and active resistance against colonizers. Finally, researchers should also prioritize collaborating with other archives and community groups to centralize collected knowledge and expand access.

Lebanese women in Lebanon and abroad face multiple barriers to accessing, preserving, and controlling their own histories, yet they confront and resist these barriers constantly. Due to the impact of Lebanon's colonial history on its current records, archives, and public history, understanding Lebanese relationship to their histories, homeland, and culture globally requires a decolonial inquiry. To acknowledge and interrogate these legacies of colonialism is to unravel them, to reclaim control and re-author, to move toward a liberated future.

Note

1 Orientalism, theorized by Said (1978), refers to the hegemonic relationship between the West and the "Middle East" that depict Arabs as inferior and dominate Western policy, media, academia, and other domains.

References

Abou-Habib, L. (2024, April 8). *When citizenship is denied: The case of gendered citizenship in Lebanon.* Asfari Institute for Civil Society & Citizenship, American University of Beirut. https://asfariinstitute.org/2024/04/08/ggco-oped-4/.

Battle-Baptiste, W., & Rusert, B. (2018). *W.E.B. Du Bois's data portraits: Visualizing black America.* Princeton Architectural Press.

Belmonte, K., & Opotow, S. (2017). Archivists on archives and social justice. *Qualitative Psychology, 4*(1), 58–72. https://doi.org/10.1037/qup0000055

Bhatia, S. (2017). *Decolonizing psychology: Globalization, social justice, and Indian youth identities.* Oxford University Press.

Caswell, M. (2014). Seeing yourself in history: Community archives and the fight against symbolic annihilation. *The Public Historian*, 36(4), 26–37. https://doi.org/10.1525/tph.2014.36.4.26

Collins, P. H. (1994). Shifting the center: Race, class, and feminist theorizing about motherhood. In L. Forcey, G. Chang, & E. N. Glenn, (Eds.), *Mothering* (pp. 45–65). Routledge.

Conroy, B. (Host). (2021, January 27). Walking as counter-archiving (No. 3) [Audio podcast episode]. In *Walking lab.* https://walkinglab.org/walkinglab-podcast/

Desai, C., & Shahwan, R. (2022). Preserving Palestine: Visual archives, erased curriculum, and counter-archiving amid archival violence in the post-Oslo period. *Curriculum Inquiry*, *52*(4), 469–489. https://doi.org/10.1080/03626784.2022.2114778

Dubois, W. E. B. (1900). *Charts and graphs showing the condition of African Americans at the turn of the century exhibited at the Paris Exposition Universelle in 1900.* Prints and photographs online catalog (PPOC). Library of Congress. https://www.loc.gov/pictures/item/2005679642/

Edwards, M. (2023, 13 May). Hidden in a Shatila alleyway, a one-room museum preserves Palestinian history. *L'Orient Today.* https://today.lorientlejour.com/article/1337297/hidden-in-a-shatila-alleyway-a-one-room-museum-preserves-palestinian-history.html

Fabian, L. (2022). *Critical archiving, tacit narrativses and participatory knowledge production: The social and political history of archiving.* Narcotic City Archive. https://narcotic-archive.org/s/archive/page/the-social-and-political-history-of-archiving

Family Search. (2023, July 25). *Overcoming challenges of connecting with your Middle Eastern roots* [Video]. YouTube. https://www.youtube.com/watch?v=SXeqRH11mF4

Fanon, F. (1961). *The wretched of the earth.* François Maspero.

Fine, M. (2016). Just methods in revolting times. *Qualitative Research in Psychology*, *13*(4), 347–365. https://doi.org/10.1080/14780887.2016.1219800

Genovese, T. R. (2016). Decolonizing archival methodology: Combating hegemony and moving towards a collaborative archival environment. *AlterNative: An International Journal of Indigenous Peoples*, *12*(1), 32–42. https://doi.org/10.20507/AlterNative.2016.12.1

Grosfoguel, R. (2013). The structure of knowledge in Westernized universities: Epistemic racism/sexism and the four genocides/epistemicides of the long 16th century. *Human Architecture: Journal of the Sociology of Self-Knowledge*, *11*(1), 73–90. https://scholarworks.umb.edu/humanarchitecture/vol11/iss1/8

Hammad, I. (2024). *Recognizing the stranger: On Palestine and narrative.* Grove Atlantic.

Hickel, J., Hanbury Lemos, M., & Barbour, F. (2024), Unequal exchange of labour in the world economy. *Nature Communications*, *15*(1), 6298. https://doi.org/10.1038/s41467-024-49687-y

Hunt, D. (2016). Nikîkîwân: Contesting settler colonial archives through Indigenous oral history. *Canadian Literature*, *230*(1), 25–42. https://doi.org/10.14288/cl.v0i230-1.187955

Jarenski, S. (2018). Ghost towns and ghost-ed riders: Nature as a radical archive in the African American experience. *Resilience, 6*(1), 27–60. https://doi.org/10.5250/resilience.6.1.0027

Ketelaar, E. (2001). Tacit narratives: The meanings of archives. *Archival Science, 1*, 131–141. https://doi.org/10.1007/BF02435644

Lesbian Herstory Archives. (2019). Why we exist. *Lesbian Herstory Archives*. Retrieved 11 May 2025, from https://lesbianherstoryarchives.org/about/

Liebert, R. J. (2019). *Psycurity: Colonialism paranoia, and the war on imagination*. Routledge.

Lugones, M. (2010). Toward a decolonial feminism. *Hypatia, 25*(4), 742–759. https://doi.org/10.1111/j.1527-2001.2010.01137.x

Luker, T. (2017). Decolonising archives: Indigenous challenges to record keeping in 'reconciling' settler colonial states. *Australian Feminist Studies*, (32), 91–92, 108–125. https://doi.org/10.1080/08164649.2017.1357011

Maldonado-Torres, N. (2016). *Outline of ten theses on colonially and decoloniality*. The Frantz Fanon Foundation. https://fondation-frantzfanon.com/wp-content/uploads/2018/10/maldonado-torres_outline_of_ten_theses-10.23.16.pdf

McEwan, C. (2003). Building a postcolonial archive? Gender, collective memory and citizenship in post-Apartheid South Africa. *Journal of Southern African Studies, 29*(3), 739–757. https://www.jstor.org/stable/3557440

Mignolo, W. (2007). Delinking: The rhetoric of modernity, the logic of coloniality and the grammar of de-coloniality. *Cultural Studies, 21*(2–3), 449–514. https://doi.org/10.1080/09502380601162647

Mignolo, W. (2010). Introduction: Coloniality of power and de-colonial thinking. In W. Mignolo, & A. Escobar (Eds.), *Globalisation and the decolonial option* (pp. 1–21). Routledge.

Mikdashi, M. (2022). The archive is burning: Law, unknowability, and the curation of history. In L. Deeb, T. Nalbantian, & N. Sbaiti (Eds.), *Practicing sectarianism: Archival and ethnographic interventions in Lebanon* (pp. 52–80). Stanford University Press. https://doi.org/10.1515/9781503633872-006

Mowases, A. (2024, February 2). The epistemicide of the Palestinians: Israel destroys pillars of knowledge. *Institute for Palestine Studies*. https://www.palestine-studies.org/en/node/1655161

Naff, A. (1985). *Becoming American: The early Arab immigrant experience*. Southern Illinois University Press.

Perkins, Y. (2012, September 3). Women and archival silences. *Stumbling through the Past*. https://stumblingpast.com/2012/03/09/women-and-archival-silences/

Rayan, T. N. (2021). Archival imperialism: Examining Israel's Six Day War files in the era of "decolonization". *Across the Disciplines, 18*(1/2), 108–121. https://doi.org/10.37514/ATD-J.2021.18.1-2.09

Said, E. (1978). *Orientalism*. Pantheon Books.

Said, E. (1993). *Culture and imperialism*. Knopf.

Sela, R. (2016). The hump of colonialism, or the archive as a site of resistance. In L'Internationale Online, & R. Ištok (Eds.), *Decolonising Archives* (pp. 50–57). L'Internationale. https://internationaleonline.org/publications/decolonising-archives/

Simpson, A. (2014). *Mohawk interruptus: Political life across the borders of settler states*. Duke University Press.

Smith L. T. (2012). Decolonizing methodologies: research and Indigenous peoples. Zed Books.

Sonn, C. C., Stevens, G., & Duncan, N. (2013). Decolonisation, critical methodologies and why stories matter. In G. Stevens, N. Duncan, & D. Hook (Eds.), *Race, memory and the Apartheid Archive: Towards a transformative psychosocial praxis* (pp. 295–314). Palgrave Macmillan.

Stel, N. (2015, December 4). Mukhtars in the middle: Connecting state, citizens, and refugees, *Jadaliyya*. https://www.jadaliyya.com/Details/32751

Taleb, W. (2024, April 10). Lebanese with southern roots head to home villages for Eid despite war. *L'Orient Today*. Today.lorientlejour.com/article/1409886/lebanese-with-southern-roots-head-to-home-villages-for-eid-despite-war.html?utm_source=olj&utm_medium=email&utm_campaign=alertot.

Tatla, D. S. (2020). The loss of Sikh heritage: The missing manuscripts of Sikh Reference Library since June 1984. *Sikh Formations*, *16*(4), 385–409. https://doi.org/10.1080/17448727.2020.1804200

Travis, K. A. P. (2023). A her-storical biography and finding family history through the archives, *Australian Journal of Politics and History*, 69(1), 110–121. https://doi.org/10.1111/ajph.12871

Weis, L., & Fine, M. (2012). Critical bifocality and circuits of privilege: Expanding critical ethnographic theory and design. *Harvard Educational Review, 82*(2), 173–201. https://psycnet.apa.org/doi/10.17763/haer.82.2.v1jx34n441532242

18 (Mis)recognition, (De)coloniality and Climate Psychology

Implications for Marginalised Youth Climate Activism

Brendon R. Barnes

Introduction

There is a growing body of psychological literature on the climate emergency (Steg, 2023). A small group of critical psychologists, hereafter referred to as critical climate psychologists, have attempted to address the climate emergency by drawing on concepts such as justice, coloniality and decoloniality. However, some justice scholars from outside of psychology point out that these liberatory concepts, if uncritically applied, may run the risk of reinforcing climate injustices (explained below). How can we strengthen justice and decoloniality in critical climate psychology particularly as they may apply to marginalised youth activist groups in the global South? I consider marginalised groups as those politically and ideologically underrepresented or excluded in mainstream Western and white-dominated youth climate activism based on their race, gender, sexuality, ability, location, religion, ethnicity and/or class. Around the world, marginalised youth are mobilising to draw attention to justice, human rights and the climate crisis. These formations have developed around indigeneity (e.g., First Nation youth), race (black youth), geopolitics (e.g., Africa), sexuality (e.g., queer activism), ability and the intersections thereof, and a multitude of activist and advocacy networks now exist. At their core, these activist formations bring different perspectives such as systemic justice, Indigenous knowledge and human rights, which many popular white and Western youth movements overlook. My work is rooted in racism and youth climate activism in Africa but extends to the exclusion of black women activists worldwide. Before proceeding, it is important to discuss climate change and youth activism.

The world is experiencing unprecedented global heating with adverse weather events such as heatwaves, floods and hurricanes (Intergovernmental Panel on Climate Change, 2022). Global heating is also associated with negative impacts on biodiversity, animal migration and ecosystem and human health (Pfenning-Butterworth et al., 2024). Global heating is also associated with increased geo-environmental conflict and climate-associated migration. Global heating intersects with social asymmetries such as class, race, gender and ability informing the rallying call that those least responsible for global heating experience the worst impacts (Wretched of the Earth, 2019). First Nation, Indigenous and other marginalised groups are disproportionately affected by global heating (Williams, 2012). Global climate change treaties, programmes and interventions have made little impact on curbing global heating. In addition, there has been very little progress in addressing reparations for historical and contemporary injustices (Chapman & Ahmed, 2021).

Young people are mobilising against government and large industry inaction by highlighting, in particular, the intergenerational impacts of global heating (O'Brien et al., 2018). Youth activism has taken the form of large-scale formalised global movements such as Fridays for Future (through school strikes) and smaller, more fluid, grassroots configurations focusing on localised issues with specific intended targets (Fisher & Nasrin, 2021). Activists have also come together in coalitions

DOI: 10.4324/9781003492214-21

to focus on specific issues and have used varying tactics including disruptive, performative and sometimes violent protests. A growing body of academic scholarship has focused on youth climate activism and asked important questions about the nature of youth activism, why youth participate in climate activism, how media and society view the impact of youth activism and the impact of activism on the youth activism themselves (Neas et al., 2022).

However, youth from marginalised groups have reported feeling excluded from mainstream (white and Western) youth activist groups and organised events (Grosse & Mark, 2020). In addition, some marginalised activists have disagreed with the priorities and tactics of climate activist groups. For example, disruptive transport strikes by Extinction Rebellion, for example, while serving to highlight the climate emergency, negatively impacted marginalised groups' ability to get around (Bell & Bevan, 2021). Perhaps the most salient example of exclusion was when Vanessa Nakate, a Ugandan climate activist, was deliberately cropped out of a photo following an engagement at a World Economic Forum meeting (Rafaely & Barnes, 2020). Only the four other white activists, including Greta Thunberg, were included in the photo despite Vanessa having participated in all the events. The 'cropping-out' incident drew much-needed attention to racism and climate action. Marginalised youth activists report hostile digital activism responses (Tanksley & Hunter, 2024) and hold the additional psychological burden of having to represent the interests of their communities (Yarde, 2021). Similarly, a chapter of the School Strike 4 Climate in New Zealand was disbanded because of allegations of racism and failure to recognise black, Indigenous and Pasifika issues (Cardwell, 2021). Tonny Nowshin drew attention to how exclusion in the reporting of marginalised reflected a lack of recognition of black people's interests in climate change discourses (Barnes, 2024). Beyond publicised examples of exclusion, marginalised climate activist groups mobilise to be recognised in the climate youth activist space. Before proceeding, it is important to briefly summarise recent moves to incorporate climate justice and decoloniality into climate psychology.

Climate Psychology and Climate Justice

Since climate change was brought to the fore in the first American Psychological Association report on climate change in 2011 (Swim et al., 2011), psychologists have been developing theories, research and practice to understand the roles of cognitions, emotions, behaviours and social factors on climate change mitigation and adaptation. Various fields of psychology (for example, health, social, critical and political) have attempted to strengthen concepts to understand the impacts of climate change on mental health (see, for example, Palinkas & Wong, 2020), to develop strategies for adaptation and mitigation (see, for example, Nielsen et al., 2021), and to support individual and social activism (see, for example, Vestergren et al., 2024). Some work has used existing psychological concepts for climate action while some work has focused on developing 'new' concepts such as climate anxiety (Crandon et al., 2022).

Psychologists' responses to the climate emergency have been criticised by critical psychologists for several reasons (See Adams (2021) for a useful overview of critical psychology and climate change). The focus on individuals, or by the very least groups of individuals, overlooks the structural determinants of climate change (Barnes et al, 2022). Citizens are not the primary cause of climate change (large companies, extractive industries and governments are) and the focus on individuals obfuscates larger structural sources and possible solutions to the climate emergency. A second criticism is that psychologists have also overlooked (in)justice, particularly the disproportionate impacts of global heating on the resource-poor and other marginalised groups (Trott et al., 2022). The neglect of justice in climate psychology may be partly explained by the dominance of global North scholarship based on WEIRD (Western Industrialised, Educated, Rich and

Democratic) settings (Trott et al., 2022). The neglect, I believe, is also driven by a deeper epistemic disrespect for knowledge from marginalised groups. Third, climate psychology has ignored the devastating impacts of imperialism, colonisation and coloniality on climate injustices.

As a response to these criticisms, some critical climate psychologists have been advocating for climate *justice* and *decoloniality* as a useful framing to address the climate and environmental emergency (Trott et al., 2022). Examples of critical climate psychology work include several special issues (for example, in the *South African Journal of Psychology*, *Psychology in Society* and the *Journal of Community Psychology in Global Context*, *Italian Journal*) (see, for example, Fernandes-Jesus et al., 2020, Barnes et al., 2022, Barnwell et al., 2022, Fedi, 2023), sections of books (for example, the Handbook of Community Psychology) and organised events such as the symposium for Community, Psychology and Justice held in Johannesburg in 2023.

How have critical climate psychologists used climate justice in their framings? Psychologists have commonly drawn on *distributive justice* to bolster their arguments for climate justice. Distributive injustice refers to the disproportionate distribution of environmental harms and goods (but mostly harms) on marginalised groups (Walker, 2012). The starting point is that resource-poor and other marginalised groups are disproportionately impacted by climate and environmental events. For example, in addition to historically being dislocated from their lands through segregationist policies, resource-poor communities often live in industrialised and heavily polluted neighbourhoods with devastating impacts on health and mental health. Importantly, marginalised groups often receive less protection from the State following natural disasters than their wealthier counterparts (Bullard & Wright, 2012). Some scholars take this further and argue that marginalised groups are often blamed for their (environmental) trauma. For example, some conservative commentators blamed the LGBTIQ community for Hurricane Katrina in the United States because of their 'moral degeneration' that led to divine punishment (Richards, 2010).

A second common conceptualisation of climate justice is *procedural justice*. Procedural justice focuses on the extent to which the voices of marginalised people are incorporated into decisions that affect their lives (Bell & Carrick, 2017). Procedural injustice occurs when decisions are made without meaningful consultation with communities whose lives will be impacted by those decisions. Where consultation does happen, it is often to 'educate' communities about the proposed project. Sometimes community consultation takes place in an atmosphere of intimidation including people from outside of the community are brought in to support problematic projects. In some contexts, public participation is written into policies but these often do not offer meaningful chances to say *no* to the problematic projects. Occasionally, disinformation is meant to coerce communities into supporting problematic projects. For example, communities are promised jobs, economic development and other social protections if they agree to extractive projects (see Healy, 2022, Mbuthuma, 2022 for an interesting case example).

In addition, there have also been calls for *decoloniality* as a framing for critical climate psychology. A small body of psychology and climate justice literature has started explicitly framing their work as *decolonial*. For example, Bryant and Sonn (2022) explored how non-Indigenous activists in Australia conceptualised decoloniality. The study found that activists highlighted, among others, the development of positional awareness, learning and unlearning, fostering a decolonial imagination and disrupting hegemonic colonial systems. Lies et al. (2022) used decoloniality to explore environmental scepticism in a United States park. Climate change scepticism was higher among white participants compared to participants of colour. Many participants viewed the wilderness as areas for individual gain and consumption and ignored historical, colonial and imperial systems of domination and extraction, which may run counter to decoloniality. Importantly, the authors draw attention to the historical roots of scepticism, colonial domination and 'progress' that are evident in the contemporary conceptualisation of the park. Similarly, Suffla et al. (2023) suggested several manifestations of coloniality including the extracting of knowledge from Africa, for example, imposing knowledge from the global North and applying it as 'universal' in the global South, using this knowledge to position the global South as inferior and the omission of colonialism in conceptualising the human-nature relationship.

Critical climate psychologists have made important strides in strengthening critical thinking, particularly in relation to justice and decoloniality. However, this literature is still small, draws heavily on distributive and procedural justice and may run the risk of unintentionally reinforcing inequities in climate activism. How can we strengthen justice and decolonial concepts in critical climate psychology particularly as they may apply to marginalised youth climate activists? I argue for two things: to strengthen (mis)recognition as an important starting point for justice and decolonial work and to focus on (mis)recognition of coloniality as a particularly important tool in decolonial work.

On (Mis)Recognition and Justice

Calls for decolonial climate justice stem, in part, from critiques of Western conceptualisations of distributive and procedural justice. Here, we must recognise the plurality of conceptualisations of equity and justice and that scholars have drawn on a range of conceptualisations (Walker et al., 2024; Newell et al., 2021). However, some scholars have highlighted that distributive and procedural justice may be another form of Western colonialism (Alvarez & Coolsaet, 2020). Distributive justice was popularised in the United States where African-American populations were, and continue to be, disproportionately affected by environmental harms compared to white populations. However, the idea of the equal distribution of climate harms and goods may not 'travel well' to other contexts for several reasons. Distributive justice focuses on the equal distribution of harms rather than reducing those harms in the first place thereby leaving the colonial underpinnings of the climate crisis (for example, extractivism, industrialisation and racial capitalism) largely untouched (Alvarez & Coolsaet, 2020). In addition, the State, often in collaboration with large industry, governs the parameters of engagement and marginalised groups become assimilated into the decision-making of the State as opposed to marginalised groups' own decision-making processes. Procedural justice is often limited to the (legal and procedural) parameters defined by the State, for example, public participation consultations that serve as tick-the-box exercises to endorse decisions that may already have been made (Bell & Carrick, 2017).

In addition, Western conceptualisations of distributive and procedural justice are premised on Western 'modes of life' that include dualism, consumption and extractivism (Whyte, 2011). In this conceptualisation, nature can be separated from humans, objectified, measured and distributed. On the contrary, many people in the global South believe that people and nature are inherently connected, relational and reciprocal (Martin et al., 2016). Moreover, it is important to acknowledge that countries in the global North owe much of their 'development' to countries in the global South through imperialism, colonisation, extractive violence and unequal trade which are the causes of the climate crisis (Sultana, 2022). Western models of justice have largely focused on issues within countries in the global North and largely ignored the calls for loss and damage reparations for the damage inflicted by the global North on the global South. In addition, Western models of justice largely ignore the contemporary neo-colonial power imbalances between the global North and South in global climate change treaties, meetings and discourses (Grosse & Mark, 2020).

In response, recognition justice refers to the legal, structural, political and discursive recognition of culture, language, race, class, gender and language of marginalised people in climate struggles (Whyte, 2017). In addition to distributive and procedural justice, recognition justice may be useful for critical climate psychologists working with marginalised youth climate activists.

Recognition justice is often used in the emancipatory struggles of Indigenous and First Nation groups for self-determination, sovereignty and autonomy but can also be applied to other marginalised groups. Recognition justice is difficult to define but is fundamentally about respecting, understanding and acknowledging *local* issues as they relate to marginalised groups. Recognition justice includes acknowledging *difference*s within marginalised groups (for example, two First Nation groups can have very different sociopolitical and political dynamics) and between those groups and dominant, for example, WEIRD groups (where WEIRD groups do not acknowledge that First Nation groups may have different understandings of the earth and ways of protecting it) (Whyte, 2017). While distributive justice seeks equality of climate harms and goods and equal treatment in how these are addressed, recognition justice views a failure to recognise *difference* as a source of injustice (Massarella et al., 2020).

A very important tool for recognition justice is to identify *misrecognition* (Benjaminsen et al., 2022). There is an overlap between recognition justice and procedural justice mentioned earlier, for example, when scholars and practitioners misrecognise *local* dynamics and *differences* that may influence participation. Marginalised youth climate activists are often blatantly excluded or silenced in discussions of climate justice, as is the case of black youth activists mentioned earlier (Barnes, 2024). However, scholars and practitioners may overlook more complicated local dynamics that may influence participation. For example, participation may be influenced by the lack of respect for traditional structures and processes of decision-making (Parsons et al., 2021). In some instances, misrecognition can occur through failure to appreciate the language of the marginalised group, e.g., advertisements for public participation only in English or published in media outlets that are inaccessible to local people (Edge et al., 2020). Scholars and practitioners may also misrecognise local conflicts and disagreements that may include who claims to represent communities. Climate struggles are also sometimes characterised by violent intimidation (including murder) (Menton & Le Billon, 2021). Many marginalised youth activists experience violence and intimidation acutely (see more than 2,100 defenders killed between 2012 and 2023 | Global Witness for examples of the extent of the violence). In other cases, activists are subjected to, or by the very least fear, strategic litigation against publication participation where resource-poor activists are sued for exorbitant sums of money to stop them from continuing their work. The local atmospheres of intimidation, disagreements and conflict are difficult to prove and often overlooked in conventional Western accounts of procedural justice that are framed as a regulatory exercise and requirement.

In addition, Indigenous justice scholars are quick to point out that not only is it important to recognise the complexity of marginalisation and indigeneity but it is also important to recognise that traditional structures and leadership do not always have their constituents' best interests at heart (Mbuthuma, 2022; Whyte, 2017). Traditional leaders are sometimes complicit in extractive development based on political and financial self-interest, and it is crucial to recognise that. It is important, therefore, to also hold traditional structures accountable.

Misrecognition includes overlooking the *natural world* in justice efforts (Martin et al., 2016). 'Justice' is often human-centred and nature exists to 'serve' humans. Sometimes nature needs to be protected over people, particularly resource-poor communities. Sometimes laws and programmes are introduced in the name of conservation and protection that may have negative impacts on marginalised groups. For example, the Great Green Wall of Africa, which aims to reforest a large part of the Sahara Desert across the width of the continent, has displaced local people who traditionally relied on that land (Benjaminsen et al., 2022). In South Africa, a law aimed at protecting small-scale fishing may have had the unintended consequence of criminalising marginalised groups who (responsibly) relied on those stocks for their livelihoods (see Mbhele, 2024). Recognition justice, therefore, involves appreciating that for many marginalised people and activists, nature is inherently co-constituted with being and that ancestral, spiritual and intergenerational dimensions are not easily disconnected.

Misrecognition can be blatant and obvious but can also be subtle and *discursive*. Often there are assumptions about marginalised groups that shape what can be said, by whom and under what conditions. It is very important to reveal those assumptions, contexts and actors and how they serve to reinforce power imbalances. Benjaminsen et al. (2022), for example, focus on the discourse about how climate change magnified the longstanding conflict in Syria. The discourse was taken up by many famous political and climate leaders to reinforce the point that climate change is having a profound impact. While this may seem like the discourse reinforced climate change messaging, it obfuscated the complex history of the conflict. Interviews with Syrians revealed that they were dissatisfied with the assumptions that climate change was responsible for the conflict and that the climate change-conflict narrative served to veil the real causes of the conflict.

Similarly, linking back to youth climate activism, following Vanessa Nakate's allegation of racism after she was cropped out of the photograph, journalists and online commentators subtly undermined her allegations in several ways (Barnes, 2024). For example, some commentators indicated that she was overly emotional because she was young and female. She should know that being in the limelight as an activist requires resilience. Journalists, mostly African journalists, also questioned that she had a right to comment on global climate change because she should stick to local Ugandan issues. She should first prove herself in Africa and in Uganda in particular before she qualified to comment on global issues. African journalists also suggested that she was not as famous as the white activists and she should have expected this for 'sticking her neck out'. Interestingly, much of the undermining emanated from African commentators. I will return to the point about coloniality below.

Recognition justice moves us in an important direction by expanding our conceptualisations of justice through foregrounding injustices among marginalised youth activist groups, including First Nation, Indigenous and other marginalised groups. It does so by acknowledging that marginalised youth activist groups may have different priorities and needs (for example, a climate justice orientation). It also encourages us to acknowledge that injustices occur through misrecognising local contexts, nature and the discursive nature of climate injustices. Importantly, scholars and practitioners often misrecognise coloniality.

On (De)Coloniality and Justice

While recognition justice is important, some scholars view decolonisation as an important framing for the climate justice struggles of marginalised groups. Importantly, they argue that we should reveal the various ways that 'coloniality' affects the climate emergency and marginalised groups' responses. Decolonial scholars make an important distinction between colonisation and coloniality. Colonisation refers to the historical process of colonisation that was propped up by imperialism, racist capitalism and patriarchy. In a neo-colonial era, coloniality refers to the discourses, ideas and processes that have become institutionalised in climate change discourse that continue after colonisation ended. Decolonial justice theorists highlight three areas of coloniality, namely, coloniality of **power** (economic and political), **epistemic** (knowledge) and importantly for a discussion of psychology and coloniality of **being** (sometimes referred to as subjective or cognitive justice) (Alvarez & Coolsaet, 2020)

Climate coloniality is a powerful feature of modernity and refers to a set of structures, systems, ideas, rights, privileges and practices that drive extractivism, violence, geographies, exclusion and planetary ill-health (Rodriguez, 2020; Pulido & De Lara, 2018). There are several implications for understanding climate justice through the lens of coloniality. Coloniality transcends time, structure and place. This means that coloniality continued even after 'formal' political colonisation ended, for example, after colonial powers left Africa. However, the assumptions, structures, systems and practices left by colonisation, albeit in the neo-colonial era, have remained.

At the level of power, climate coloniality is constituted through globalisation, racial capitalism, patriarchy and extractivism (Sultana, 2022). Climate coloniality is written into governance, structures and systems that continue to privilege WEIRD societies. Climate coloniality can also be seen in global treaties, and trade agreements that not only sideline marginalised groups but also allow global North nations to continue emitting greenhouse gasses at excessive levels while marginalised groups experience the brunt of those emissions. Climate coloniality is also visible in the idea that the answer to the climate crisis lies in Western science, a 'green' (nonetheless capitalist) economy, technological innovation and that nature is to be *used* as a commodity for human benefit and economic development. Put differently, governments, political ideologies, and economic policies may change, but the structural and subjective correlates of climate coloniality have remained.

Coloniality is also characterised by epistemic violence or, at the very least, the epistemic neglect of the knowledge(s) from marginalised groups informing climate action (Rodríguez & Inturias, 2018). Indigenous, First Nation and other marginalised groups have a wealth of knowledge about their environments and how the environment is constituted *with* spiritual, physical and relational being. Arguably, these knowledges make for healthier relationships with the planet. However, Indigenous and traditional knowledge is rarely valued and integrated into impactful climate action. Even when knowledge systems are included, they tend to be about how those in the global South can adapt to a heating world. The source of global heating is left untouched.

The call to integrate traditional knowledge, and by implication, traditional peoples' rights and entitlements, into climate action may resemble calls for recognition justice mentioned earlier. Indeed, the two are linked. However, decolonial scholars would extend the call for recognition by arguing that traditional knowledge, cultures and languages were *deliberately* decimated through imperialism, colonisation and white supremacy (Suffla et al, 2023). Epistemic violence was not arbitrary nor was it an artefact of a 'natural' economic and cultural development. Historically, traditional languages, structures and relations were deliberately excluded through settler colonial educational policies, enslavement, indenture, language policies, land appropriation and economic interventions to prop up racial capitalism and industrialisation. Often, colonisation was framed as for the good-of-the-poor. Importantly, the epistemic violence was framed by powerful moral civilising discourses of how traditional people should 'develop' in pursuit of whiteness and Western-ness. Importantly, coloniality through epistemic violence was often internalised by traditional people (I will return to this point below). It is important, therefore, to identify the links between colonisation and contemporary coloniality.

In terms of the *coloniality of being*, colonisation and coloniality have had a profound impact on the 'psychology' of marginalised groups through a racialised, classed and gendered hierarchy (Bulhan, 2015). Marginalised people were positioned in servitude and racialised labour through land, economic, epistemic and political dispossession, often with devastating psychological impacts. Climate coloniality continues to have psychological impacts including ongoing trauma, anxiety, dislocation, loss and distrust. Coloniality also manifests in dehumanisation, stigmatisation and disconnection between people and between people and nature. However, communities are resisting coloniality by reclaiming power and revisiting climate extractivism (Cantzler & Huynh, 2016; Fernandes-Jesus et al., 2020).

Coloniality of being can be subtle. For example, climate coloniality frames how society views climate activism, including how marginalised youth should voice their concerns as 'responsible' citizens. When, for example, a group of black youth activists through human faeces in public spaces to protest the injustices of living in squalor with no flush sanitation in informal settlements in Cape Town, they were labelled uncivilised and un-citizen-like for not raising their concerns through proper 'democratically elected' channels (the dangers of a State-controlled procedural justice mentioned earlier) (Barnes, 2018). The youths' involvement in the disruptive protest, for many conservative commentators, merely reinforced the reason that they find themselves living in squalor in the first place, that is, they are lazy, uncivilised and entitled. Often, the undermining of marginalised activists focuses on the individual psychological traits, ideas, emotions and behaviours. For example, youth activists are positioned as naïve, ignorant, emotional, irrational, uncivilised, selfish, self-interested, having ulterior motives (e.g., having political office aspirations) and so forth. Of course, these traits all form part of a moralising discourse of what constitutes a 'good' planetary subject.

Oppressed people may also internalise coloniality (through, for example, internalised oppression) and continue to perpetuate coloniality. Drawing on an example from earlier, Vanessa Nakate's claim of racism was met with hostile responses from black African interviewers who delegitimised her claims of racism who, among other claims, questioned her 'sticking her neck out' on global climate change issues (she should be focusing on environmental issues in her own country) with legitimate white activists (she was just there as a token African). We also see how coloniality works to divide marginalised communities with many conflicts revolving around the politics of 'development', for example, those for and against extractivist economic development.

Importantly, the coloniality of being can not only be found *both* in the governance, systems and structures but also in the *everyday* interactions in media interviews, comment sections, radio interviews and podcasts (see Rafaely [2021] for an example of how the racism allegation by Vanessa Nakate unfolded in the 'everyday'). They can be found in the ways that climate racism allegations are made and responses to those. From a theoretical and methodological view, climate coloniality is not necessarily seen as a product of fixed opinions, attitudes and beliefs but, in itself, produces and reproduces those ideas through interactions. Thankfully, there exists a rich theoretical and methodological literature on the study of interaction in racism, gender and class and the intersections thereof that can be drawn on to understand climate coloniality in this way. There also exists a rich decolonial scholarship in psychology that could be useful to decoloniality and climate psychology.

It is important to acknowledge that decolonisation can mean different things to different activists. For some, decolonisation seeks to remedy the epistemic exclusion of marginalised peoples, and for marginalised people to realise their rights. Others push this further in a quest for self-determination and autonomy separate from the State. Some environmental justice scholars, for example, have explored alternative modes of development based on traditional forms of relationality often, but not exclusively, with the aim of promoting autonomy and self-determination. It is also important to understand how epistemic neglect and violence manifest in climate struggles. Importantly for climate psychology, we need to understand how the subjective and psychological dimensions of climate coloniality manifest. Climate coloniality does not need to be in the present. We can (and should) understand the historical underpinnings of coloniality to inform efforts at decoloniality and its links with the past.

Implications for Marginalised Youth Climate Activism Scholarship and Praxis

Critical climate psychologists and activists often draw on justice (particularly distributive and procedural justice) and increasingly decoloniality to strengthen their work. We often hear scholars mentioning that those least responsible for climate change experience the brunt of those impacts. Similarly, we often hear how marginalised voices are silenced in climate movements and that decolonisation is the remedy to climate justice. While this may true, it is important to be mindful that Western conceptualisations of justice are premised on the distribution of toxic environments and do not address the root causes of the climate crisis. It is also premised on Western modes of life (for example, dualism between nature and humans) that may not be applicable to all contexts. Importantly, distributive and procedural still include assimilation with the State, regulatory and legal systems that are themselves associated with repression. Do not get me wrong, distributive and procedural justice are essential, but other conceptualisations of justice exist and may be particularly useful for marginalised youth climate activism.

Marginalised youth activist groups often seek recognition when drawing attention to climate (in)justices. Yet, recognition of justice is probably the most overlooked dimension of marginalised youth climate activism. Calls for recognition also occur when there are contestations, usually around racism, within youth activist organisations or between marginalised youth activists and media. For example, Vanessa Nakate, after being erased from a media photograph, implicitly made a plea for recognition when she stated, 'You did not erase me, you erased a continent'. In doing so, she asked for *recognition* of Africa as a continent and she asked for recognition that her personal experiences of racism reflected structural racism. Put differently, both Africa and structural racism were misrecognised in the cropping-out incident and the aftermath, for example, in the apology. Greta Thunberg and Vanessa Nakate facilitated a press conference showcasing African science and activism, to correct the misrecognition of African climate action. Not only were the journalists there because of Greta Thunberg (she kept having to ask journalists not to focus on her) but it inadvertently sent the message that African climate scientists and activists needed white and global North activists and platforms to have their voices heard. Another perhaps unintended consequence was that African youth climate activists are the same.

Recognition justice also encourages us to appreciate differences within marginalised youth activist groups. Marginalised youth activism varies considerably in its focal areas and local dynamics. Some may focus on specific local issues while others on broader regional and global issues. Activists may also adopt different racial, gender and geopolitical identities. For example, a German youth activist who also alleged racism because she was excluded from images, self-identified as 'non-white', a term that many black people around the world would find demeaning. We should be careful, therefore, not to assume that all marginalised activists share the same identities, aspirations, cultures and histories. Sometimes the stereotypes associated with marginalised youth activists as in need of special help or who are different may serve to undermine their activism. Recognition justice implores us to appreciate differences, even within marginalised activist groups, and to focus on local issues and dynamics. Labelling and drawing on the insights from recognition justice may help us to strengthen calls for justice and equity in marginalised youth activist groups.

Developing a language and methodology to identify *misrecognition* may be particularly useful for work with marginalised youth activists. While recognition is a common theme, youth activists' grievances often centre on allegations of misrecognition. For example, many of the publicised incidents of marginalised youth exclusion alleged that mainstream white, Western youth activists and media misrecognise the role of (structural) racism, coloniality, Indigenous knowledge and structural barriers to participation. More research and praxis could focus on identifying the many and varied ways misrecognition manifests in youth climate activism. Identifying misrecognition may be useful in developing possible strategic responses by marginalised youth climate activists.

It is crucial for scholars to identify and address the coloniality of the climate emergency as well as how climate coloniality may shape activism. These include structures, systems, epistemic coloniality and the coloniality of being. Informed by decolonial, psychologists have started writing about climate coloniality drawing inspiration from a broader literature on decolonial psychology. In addition to the multiple and compounding impacts of the climate crisis on the marginalised (what some environmental justice scholars call cognitive injustices), it is equally important to focus on identifying how the ideas underpinning coloniality continue to harm the planet and people. For example, that marginalised youth activists need special attention; that youth are naïve and ignorant of how the world works; that resource-poor people need to change their behaviours to progress in life; that the environment exists for the benefit of people; that marginalised activists can only speak about localised issues and so forth. These ideas transcend race, gender, class and geography and explain how coloniality operates even in politically 'emancipated' contexts. It is also important to identify the features of internalised oppression.

Decolonial scholarship also encourages us to interrogate the relationship between marginalised groups and the State. In many contexts, decoloniality would support efforts at holding the State to account and promote marginalised groups' efforts at self-determination and autonomy. However, it is virtually impossible to operate completely out of the State's ambit but there are examples of pluriverse governance structures that integrate local and traditional structures and processes. Digital activism is one potentially interesting area. Youth activists are active in the digital space, for example, social media. Digital activism allows activists to connect globally, extend their messaging reach and potentially provide relative physical protection for activists. However, we must acknowledge that activists suffer immense online abuse and trolling. Online activism does not mean complete protection from harm nor complete separation from the State. In some extreme contexts, States can be equally oppressive through digital surveillance, banning platforms and internet blackouts. Nonetheless, digital and online activism is an important space for decolonial youth activist praxis and scholarship.

There is an urgent need for critical climate scholars to work *with* youth climate activists, to understand their needs and to support their efforts for just climate action. There is also a need to support efforts for global solidarity among marginalised youth activists from around the world. Critical climate psychology scholars have an important role in supporting marginalised youth climate activism. A small (psychology) literature has started to focus on marginalised youth activism, highlighting in particular how youth's voices can be supported in their fight against climate change. Importantly, this work does not only focus on the (many) obstacles that marginalised youth activists endure, but also how they deploy their agency in their activism. The critical climate psychology literature has also pointed to the necessity of critically oriented research methodologies such as participatory, visual and other creative methodologies (Peters, 2022). A key lesson from this work is to foreground methodologies that focus on communities' power, working *with* marginalised communities to reclaim power and change in positionality from expert to accompaniment and stewardship.

Limitations

It might be tempting, based on what I have stated above, to think that one needs recognition justice to develop decolonial justice. I would urge caution here because both forms of justice are useful without drawing on each other. In fact, scholars have been writing about them separately for decades. I have suggested that misrecognition of coloniality may be a way to bring recognition and decolonial justice together, but this too is a tentative argument. It is feasible to frame youth activism work as *both* recognition *and* decolonial justice.

I have referred to marginalised youth as one category, in part, because of common experiences of exclusion from mainstream, white-dominated youth climate activism. In doing so, I risk simplifying and flattening the differences and experiences between marginalised groups. While it may be politically expedient to view commonalities between marginalised groups, acknowledging differences is one of the main points of recognition justice. We need to be cautious, therefore, not to oversimplify the experiences and priorities of 'marginalised' groups.

While recognition and decolonial justice offer us an additional set of theoretical resources to foreground marginalised youth climate activism, these resources are still primarily written from the global North in an academic language of justice that may be exclusionary. Like criticisms of distributive and procedural justice above, we need to be mindful that there may be other ways to formulate justice and youth climate activism that may be more accessible and appropriate. I have also not paid attention to the growing interest in generational justice by critical climate psychologists.

It could be argued that it might be difficult to reconcile psychology with climate justice. However, as mentioned earlier, there is a group of critical psychologists who are actively integrating climate justice into their work. This work adds to the critiques of some of the assumptions of mainstream psychology. I also believe that work in decolonial psychology can be useful to decolonial justice scholars who sometimes conceptualise the link between psychology and decolonisation in superficial ways.

Conclusion

I have attempted to strengthen climate justice and marginalised youth activism in critical community psychology. I have argued that recognition justice and decoloniality can be taken further in our conceptualisations of climate justice. Critical climate psychologists, including those with a decolonial leaning, have an important role to play. It is hoped that this chapter may stimulate more interest in theorising justice and decoloniality to support marginalised youth climate activism.

References

Adams, M. (2021). Critical psychologies and climate change. *Current Opinion in Psychology*, *42*, 13–18. https://doi.org/10.1016/j.copsyc.2021.01.007

Álvarez, L., & Coolsaet, B. (2020). Decolonizing environmental justice studies: A Latin American perspective. *Capitalism Nature Socialism*, *31*(2), 50–69. https://doi.org/10.1080/10455752.2018.1558272

Barnes, B. (2024). Racism and youth climate activism: what can we learn from racism allegations about the image exclusions of black women activists?. In J. Conner (Ed.), *Handbook on Youth Activism* (pp. 196–209). Edward Elgar Publishing. https://doi.org/10.4337/9781803923222.00026

Barnes, B. R. (2018). Politics and activism in the water and sanitation wars in South Africa. *Journal of Social and Political Psychology*, *6*(2), 543–555. https://doi.org/10.5964/jspp.v6i2.917

Barnes, B. R., Barnwell, G., & Hendricks, L. (2022). Psychology, environment and climate change: foregrounding justice (part one). *Psychology in Society*, *63*(1), 1–5. https://doi.org/10.57157/pins2022Vol63iss1a5438

Barnwell, G., Barnes, B., & Hendricks, L. (2022). Psychology and the climate emergency. *South African Journal of Psychology*, *52*(4), 419–422. https://doi.org/10.1177/00812463221130900

Bell, D., & Carrick, J. (2017). Procedural environmental justice. In R. Holifield, J. Chakraborty, & G. Walker (Eds.), *The Routledge handbook of environmental justice* (pp. 101–112). Routledge.

Bell, K., & Bevan, G. (2021). Beyond inclusion? Perceptions of the extent to which Extinction Rebellion speaks to, and for, Black, Asian and Minority Ethnic (BAME) and working-class communities. *Local Environment*, *26*(10), 1205–1220. https://doi.org/10.1080/13549839.2021.1970728

Benjaminsen, T. A., Svarstad, H., & Shaw of Tordarroch, I. (2022). Recognising recognition in climate justice. *IDS Bulletin*, *53*(4), 13–30. https://doi.org/10.19088/1968-2022.136

Bryant, E. K., & Sonn, C. C. (2022). Country and climate: Journeys toward the decolonial option among non-indigenous climate activists. *Psychology in Society*, *63*(1), 52–82. https://doi.org/10.57157/pins2022Vol63iss1a5441

Bulhan, H. A. (2015). Stages of colonialism in Africa: From occupation of land to occupation of being. *Journal of Social and Political psychology*, *3*(1). https://doi.org/10.5964/jspp.v3i1.143

Bullard Walker, G. (2012). *Environmental justice: Concepts, evidence and politics*. Routledge.

Bullard, R. D., & Wright, B. (2012). *The wrong complexion for protection: How the government response to disaster endangers African American communities*. NYU Press.

Cantzler, J. M., & Huynh, M. (2016). Native American environmental justice as decolonization. *American Behavioral Scientist*, *60*(2), 203–223. https://doi.org/10.1177/0002764215607578

Cardwell, H. (2021, June 15). School Strike 4 Climate Auckland declares itself racist and disbands. RNZ. Retrieved March 1 2024, from School Strike 4 Climate Auckland declares itself racist and disbands | RNZ News.

Chapman, A. R., & Ahmed, A. K. (2021). Climate justice, human rights, and the case for reparations. *Health and Human Rights*, *23*(2), 81.

Crandon, T. J., Scott, J. G., Charlson, F. J., & Thomas, H. J. (2022). A social–ecological perspective on climate anxiety in children and adolescents. *Nature Climate Change*, *12*(2), 123–131. https://doi.org/10.1038/s41558-021-01251-y

Edge, S., Brown, E. L., Ghosh, S., & Murnaghan, A. M. (2020). Procedural environmental (in) justice at multiple scales: Examining immigrant advocacy for improved living conditions. *Local Environment*, *25*(9), 666–680. https://doi.org/10.1080/13549839.2020.1812554

Fedi, A. (2023). Introduction. Community Psychology in the face of the climate crisis: What contributions? *Psicologia di Comunita*, (1). https://doi.org/10.3280/PSC2023-001001

Fernandes-Jesus, M., Barnes, B. R., & Diniz, R. F. (2020). Communities reclaiming power and social justice in the face of climate change. *Community Psychology in Global Perspective*, *6*(2/2), 1–21. https://doi.org/10.1285/i24212113v6i2-2p1

Fisher, D. R., & Nasrin, S. (2021). Shifting coalitions within the youth climate movement in the US. *Politics and Governance, 9*(2), 112–123. https://doi.org/10.17645/pag.v9i2.3801

Grosse, C., & Mark, B. (2020). A colonized COP: Indigenous exclusion and youth climate justice activism at the United Nations climate change negotiations. In B. Richardson (Ed.), *From student strikes to the Extinction Rebellion* (pp. 146–170). Edward Elgar Publishing. https://doi.org/10.4337/jhre.2020.03.07

Healy, H. (2022). Struggle for the sands of Xolobeni–From post-colonial environmental injustice to crisis of democracy. *Geoforum*, *133*, 128–139. https://doi.org/10.1016/j.geoforum.2022.05.002

Intergovernmental Panel on Climate Change. (2022). *Climate change 2022: Impacts, adaptation, and vulnerability* (H.-O. Pörtner, D. C. Roberts, M. Tignor, E. S. Poloczanska, K. Mintenbeck, A. Algeria, M. Craig, S. Langsdorf, S. Löschke, V. Möller, A. Okem, & B. Rama, Eds.). Cambridge University Press. https://www.ipcc.ch/report/ar6/wg2/

Lies, T. S., Adams, G., & Santangelo, B. (2022). Decolonial considerations of environmentalism: Observations from a (US) State Park. *Psychology in Society*, (64), 21–43. https://doi.org/10.57157/pins2022Vol64iss1a5453

Martin, A., Coolsaet, B., Corbera, E., Dawson, N. M., Fraser, J. A., Lehmann, I., & Rodriguez, I. (2016). Justice and conservation: The need to incorporate recognition. *Biological Conservation*, *197*, 254–261. https://doi.org/10.1016/j.biocon.2016.03.021

Massarella, K., Sallu, S. M., & Ensor, J. E. (2020). Reproducing injustice: Why recognition matters in conservation project evaluation. *Global Environmental Change*, *65*, 102181. https://doi.org/10.1016/j.gloenvcha.2020.102181

Mbhele, S. (2024, October 17). *Local fishing communities struggle against exclusion and ocean industrialization.* Female and Guardian. https://mg.co.za/thought-leader/2024-10-17-local-fishing-communities-struggle-against-exclusion-and-ocean-industrialisation/

Mbuthuma, N. (2022). Resisting extractivist development. *New Agenda: South African Journal of Social and Economic Policy*, *2022*(83), 90–94.

Menton, M., & Le Billon, P. (Eds.). (2021). *Environmental defenders: Deadly struggles for life and territory.* Routledge. https://doi.org/10.4324/9781003127222

Neas, S., Ward, A., & Bowman, B. (2022). Young people's climate activism: A review of the literature. *Frontiers in Political Science*, *4*, 940876. https://doi.org/10.3389/fpos.2022.940876

Newell, P., Srivastava, S., Naess, L. O., Torres Contreras, G. A., & Price, R. (2021). Toward transformative climate justice: An emerging research agenda. *Wiley Interdisciplinary Reviews: Climate Change*, *12*(6), e733. https://doi.org/10.1002/wcc.733

Nielsen, K. S., Clayton, S., Stern, P. C., Dietz, T., Capstick, S., & Whitmarsh, L. (2021). How psychology can help limit climate change. *American Psychologist*, *76*(1), 130. https://doi.org/10.1037/amp0000624

O'Brien, K., Selboe, E., & Hayward, B. M. (2018). Exploring youth activism on climate change: dutiful, disruptive, and dangerous dissent. *Ecology and Society, 23*(3), 42. https://doi.org/10.5751/ES-10287-230342

Palinkas, L. A., & Wong, M. (2020). Global climate change and mental health. *Current Opinion in Psychology, 32*, 12–16. https://doi.org/10.1016/j.copsyc.2019.06.023

Parsons, M., Fisher, K., Crease, R. P. (2021). Environmental justice and indigenous environmental justice. In M Parson, K. Fisher, & R. Crease (Eds.), *Decolonising blue spaces in the Anthropocene: Freshwater management in Aotearoa New Zealand* (pp. 39–73). Palgrave Macmillan.

Peters, F. (2022). The role of critical methodologies in climate psychology scholarship: Themes, gaps, and futures. *South African Journal of Psychology, 52*(4), 510–521. https://doi.org/10.1177/00812463221130158

Pfenning-Butterworth, A., Buckley, L. B., Drake, J. M., Farner, J. E., Farrell, M. J., Gehman, A. L. M., … & Davies, T. J. (2024). Interconnecting global threats: climate change, biodiversity loss, and infectious diseases. *The Lancet Planetary Health, 8*(4), e270–e283. https://doi.org/10.1016/S2542-5196(24)00021-4

Pulido, L., & De Lara, J. (2018). Reimagining 'justice' in environmental justice: Radical ecologies, decolonial thought, and the Black Radical Tradition. *Environment and Planning E: Nature and Space, 1*(1–2), 76–98. https://doi.org/10.1177/2514848618770363

Rafaely, D. (2021). 'Cropped out': The collaborative production of an accusation of racism. *Discourse Studies, 23*(3), 324–338. https://doi.org/10.1177/1461445620982096

Rafaely, D., & Barnes, B. (2020). African climate activism, media and the denial of racism: The tacit silencing of Vanessa Nakate. *Community Psychology in Global Perspective, 6*(2/2), 71–86. https://doi.org/10.1285/i24212113v6i2-2p71

Richards, G. (2010). Queering Katrina: Gay discourses of the disaster in New Orleans. *Journal of American Studies, 44*(3), 519–534. https://doi.org/10.1017/S0021875810001210

Rodriguez, I. (2020). Latin American decolonial environmental justice. In B. Coolsaet (Eds.), *Environmental Justice* (pp. 78–93). Routledge.

Rodríguez, I., & Inturias, M. L. (2018). Conflict transformation in indigenous peoples' territories: Doing environmental justice with a 'decolonial turn'. *Development Studies Research, 5*(1), 90–105. https://doi.org/10.1080/21665095.2018.1486220

Steg, L. (2023). Psychology of climate change. *Annual Review of Psychology, 74*, 391–421. https://doi.org/10.1146/annurev-psych-032720-042905

Suffla, S., Ratele, K., Adams, G., Reddy, G., & Malherbe, N. (2023). Toward a decolonial Africa-centering ecological and social psychology. *Current Research in Ecological and Social Psychology, 5*, 100156. https://psycnet.apa.org/doi/10.1016/j.cresp.2023.100156

Sultana, F. (2022). Critical climate justice. *The Geographical Journal, 188*(1), 118–124. https://doi.org/10.1111/geoj.12417

Swim, J. K., Stern, P. C., Doherty, T. J., Clayton, S., Reser, J. P., Weber, E. U., … & Howard, G. S. (2011). Psychology's contributions to understanding and addressing global climate change. *American Psychologist, 66*(4), 241. https://doi.org/10.1037/a0023220

Tanksley, T., & Hunter, A. E. (2024). Black youth, digital activism, and racial battle fatigue: How Black youth enact hope, humor, and healing online. In J. Conner (Ed.), *Handbook on Youth Activism* (pp. 272–289). Edward Elgar Publishing. https://doi.org/10.4337/9781803923222.00032

Trott, C. D., Reimer-Watts, K., & Riemer, M. (2022). Climate justice: In pursuit of a practical utopia: Transitioning towards climate justice. In C. Kagan, J. Akhurst, J. Alfaro, R. Lawthom, M. Richards, & A. Zambrano (Eds.), *The Routledge international handbook of community psychology* (pp. 229–245). Routledge. https://doi.org/10.4324/9780429325663-19

Vestergren, S., Bamberg, S., & Louis, W. (2024). Responding to the socio-ecological crisis: Activism and collective action. *Global Environmental Psychology, 2*, 1–13. https://doi.org/10.5964/gep.13075

Walker, S. E., Smith, E. A., Bennett, N., Bannister, E., Narayana, A., Nuckols, T., … & Bailey, K. M. (2024). Defining and conceptualizing equity and justice in climate adaptation. *Global Environmental Change, 87*, 102885. https://doi.org/10.1016/j.gloenvcha.2024.102885

Whyte, K. (2017). The recognition paradigm of environmental injustice. In R. Holifield, J. Chakraborty, & G. Walker (Eds.), *The Routledge handbook of environmental justice* (pp. 113–123). Routledge.

Whyte, K. P. (2011). The recognition dimensions of environmental justice in Indian country. *Environmental Justice*, *4*(4), 199–205. https://doi.org/10.2139/ssrn.1855591

Williams, J. (2012). The impact of climate change on indigenous people–the implications for the cultural, spiritual, economic and legal rights of indigenous people. *The International Journal of Human Rights*, *16*(4), 648–688. https://doi.org/10.1080/13642987.2011.632135

Wretched of the Earth. (2019). An open letter to Extinction Rebellion. *Journal of Global Faultlines, 6*(1), 109–112. https://doi.org/10.13169/jglobfaul.6.1.0109

Yarde, E. (2021, January 13). Inaction on global warming amounts to racism – let me tell you why. *The Guardian*. https://www.theguardian.com/commentisfree/2022/jan/13/inaction-global-warming-racism-climate-breakdown-people-of-colour

Index

Note: **Bold** page numbers refer to tables; *italic* page numbers refer to figures and page numbers followed by "n" denote endnotes.

Made in the USA
Monee, IL
14 September 2026

62978589R00157